Emerging Issues in Public Policy:

RESEARCH REPORTS AND ESSAYS, 1973-1976

INSTITUTE OF GOVERNMENTAL STUDIES

Todd R. La Porte, *Acting Director*

The Institute of Governmental Studies was established in 1919 as the Bureau of Public Administration, and given its present name in 1962. One of the oldest organized research units in the University of California, the Institute conducts extensive and varied research and service programs in such fields as public policy, politics, urban-metropolitan problems, and public administration. The Institute focusses on problems and issues confronting the government and citizens of the San Francisco Bay Area, of California, and of the nation.

The professional staff comprises faculty members holding joint Institute and departmental appointments, research specialists, librarians and graduate students. In addition the Institute encourages policy oriented research and writing efforts by a variety of faculty members and researchers not formally affiliated with the staff. The Institute is also host to visiting scholars from other parts of the United States and many foreign nations.

A prime resource in its endeavors is the Institute Library, with more than 350,000 documents, pamphlets and periodicals relating primarily to government and public affairs. The Library serves faculty and staff members, students, public officials and interested citizens.

The Institute publishes books, monographs, bibliographies, periodicals, working papers and reprints for a national audience, as well as the Institute bulletin, the *Public Affairs Report,* which is issued six times a year. In addition, Institute-sponsored lectures, conferences, workshops and seminars bring together faculty members, public officials and citizens. These publications and programs are intended to stimulate thought, research, and action by scholars, citizens and public officials on significant governmental policies and social issues.

Emerging Issues in Public Policy:

RESEARCH REPORTS AND ESSAYS

1973-1976

A collection of four years of

Public Affairs Report

Bulletin of the
INSTITUTE OF GOVERNMENTAL STUDIES

HARRIET NATHAN and STANLEY SCOTT
Editors

INSTITUTE OF GOVERNMENTAL STUDIES
University of California, Berkeley
1977

Library of Congress Cataloging in Publication Data

Nathan, Harriet, comp.
    Emerging issues in public policy.

    Includes bibliographical references and index.
    1. California—Politics and government—1951—
Addresses, essays, lectures. 2. California—Economic
policy—Addresses, essays, lectures. 3. California—
Social policy—Addresses, essays, lectures. I. Scott,
Stanley, 1921-   joint comp. II. Public Affairs
report. III. California. University. Institute of
Governmental Studies. IV. Title.
JK8719.N38   1977   309.1'794'05   77-6469
ISBN 0-87772-227-7

$11.00

Contents

Foreword xvii

Comprehensive Planning for Higher Education:
Focus on New Priorities 1
    Lyman A. Glenny (February 1973)
        Introduction 1
        The Future: State-Level Planning and Coordination. 1
        A Radical Transformation. 2
        New Technologies and Different Requirements. 2
        Faculty Trends: Collective Bargaining and Tenure 2
        Tenure and Rigidity 2
        Autonomy and Prestige. 3
        The End of Expansionism 3
        Tight State Budgets for Higher Education 3
        Private Institutions and Public Funds 4
        Federal Funding: An Uncertain Promise 4
        The Student Pays—and Chooses 4
        A Shift to Proprietary and Industrial Schools 5
        Conclusion 5

Drinking Practices and Problems: Research Perspectives
on Remedial Measures. 6
    Don Cahalan (April 1973)
        Health and Economic Costs of Alcohol's Misuse 6
        Research Efforts 6
        Findings on Drinking Practices 6
        Drinking Problems: An Overview 7
        Drinking Problems Among Younger Men 8
        The Importance of Changes in Drinking Patterns 8
        "Maturing Out" of Problem Drinking 9
        The San Francisco Surveys 9
        Summary of Findings and Implications. .9
        Emphasis on the Need for Prevention 10
        Why Prevention is Slighted 10
        Can an Informational Campaign Succeed?. 10

Needed: Demonstration Projects 10
Tailor-Made Programs 10
Reducing Problem Drinking: Difficult But Feasible 11

The Politics of Technological Choice: Some Lessons from
the San Francisco Bay Area Rapid Transit District (BART) 12
    Stephen Zwerling (June 1973)
        Political Decisions and Expertise........................... 12
        Technology: Choices and Consequences..................... 12
        Early Planning Efforts..................................... 13
        The Goal: To Preserve San Francisco's Preeminence 13
        1951: A Study Commission is Formed.................... 13
        The Issue Posed: Automobile Congestion vs.
        Regional Rapid Transit 14
        The Preferred Pattern: Centralization and Nucleation 14
        1957: BART—To Build an Interurban Railroad 15
        "The Politics of Professionalism" 15
        Some Lessons from BART 16
        Impact Statements: Toward an Exploration and
        Clarification of Consequences 17

The Utility of Public Utilities: Desalination and Local Government
in Coastal California 18
    K. N. Lee (August 1973)
        The Diablo Canyon Case 18
        The Need for Water....................................... 18
        Proposal for a Desalting Plant 19
        Environmental Opposition 19
        The Growth Issue 19
        "Outside" Benefits 20
        1972 Campaigns 20
        Impounding the Opportunity 20
        What Does It Mean? 20
        "Capacity" and "Implementation" 21
        Possible Effects of the Desalting Plant...................... 21
        The Goleta Story... 21
        Water and Politics 22
        Diablo Canyon: An Opportunity Missed?................... 22
        Advantages of a Smaller Plant 23
        A Different Style... 23
        Some Lessons: The Intelligent Use of Technology 23
        Technology as Legislation: Default and Muddling Through 23

Public Expenditure Analysis: Some Current Issues................... 25
    Leonard Merewitz and Stephen H. Sosnick (October 1973)
        Introduction 25
        Planning-Programming-Budgeting 25

Program Accounting 25
Multi-Year Costing 26
Detailed Description 26
Zero-Base Budgeting 26
Benefit-Cost Analysis 27
Technical Considerations. 27
Project Benefit Forecasts. 27
The Environmental Issue. 28
Program Budgeting in Practice. 29
Benefit-Cost Analysis in Practice. 29
The Use of Alternatives. 30
Limitations of the Benefit-Cost Approach. 30
A Concluding Comment: Formulating Alternative Choices 30

Women and Academia at Berkeley: CCEW—Women's Center. 32
Beatrice Bain (December 1973)
Introduction: "What Does Woman Want?" 32
Continuing Education 33
Focus on Berkeley. 33
A Berkeley Women's Center is Proposed 34
The Center Opens Its Doors 34
Academic and Educational Advising: Recognizing and
Circumventing Barriers 34
Offering Alternatives and Coordinating Information. 35
Facts and Practical Details. 35
Career and Job Opportunities 36
The Center as Symbol. 36
Fringe Benefits and Affirmative Action. 36
Women's Studies. 36
Quantitative Skills. 36
The Women's Center: Growth and New Directions 37
Conclusion 37

Comprehensive Health Planning in the San Francisco Bay Area:
Problems and Prospects for the "Federation Experiment" 38
Donald B. Ardell and Richard P. Hafner, Jr. (February 1974)
Introduction 38
Comprehensive Health Planning in the Bay Area:
A New Organization 38
Problems, Goals and Policies. 38
The Milieu. 39
Structure: The Federation Experiment 39
How It Operates: Responsibilities for Planning and Review 40
Special Studies and Public Issues. 40
Financing 40
Communications. 41

Relationships with Other Regional Agencies 41
Some Strengths and Weaknesses 41
The Federation's Accomplishments. 42
Conclusion: Changes in the Wind 42

Changing Regulations: Campaign Finance in the Golden State. 44
   James Fay (April 1974)
Background. 44
Reasoning Behind Campaign Laws 44
Legislative Attitudes Toward Campaign Finance Reform 44
Categories of Proposals 46
The New Law 46
Restrictions on Campaign Contributions and Expenditures. 46
Reporting, Public Disclosure and the Consequences 47
Punishment. 47
Loopholes. 47
Pressures for Further Change 47
Possible Impact of Reforms. 48
Persistent Problems. 49

Public Control of Public Schools: Can We Get It Back? 53
   James W. Guthrie (June 1974)
Introduction 53
The Magnitude of Public Schooling. 53
Expenditure 53
Erosion of Citizen Control 53
Population Growth 54
Proliferation of Districts 54
"Cleansing" and Consolidation 54
Depoliticization, Bureaucratization, and Unionization 54
The Business Model. 54
Expansion of Staff 55
Alienation of Teachers 55
Unions and Teacher Power 55
Public's Dwindling Voice. 55
Schools as Monopolies. 55
Uniformity and Standardization 55
What Can Be Done?. 56
Vouchers. 56
School Site Governance. 56
Conclusion 57

Suicide: Preventable Death. 58
   Richard H. Seiden (August 1974)
What Is the Problem? 58
The Case for Prevention 58

A Historical Perspective. 59
Ambivalence of the Suicidal Person. 59
The Brevity of the Crisis 59
Economic Considerations 59
Survivors. 59
Who Are the High-Risk Special Populations?. 60
College Students 60
Alcoholics. 60
Mental Patients 60
The Aged. 60
Youth 60
Homicide and Accidents. 60
The Vulnerability of Non-White Youth. .61
What Can Be Done Through Public Policy Measures? 61
The Suicide Prevention Movement 61
The Golden Gate Bridge: Need for a Physical Barrier. 61
Proposed Suicide Prevention Act: Senate Bill 1814 62
Conclusion and Summary 62

Fluoridation in California: A New Look at a Persistent Issue. 63
    Harriet Nathan and Stanley Scott (October 1974)
        Introduction 63
        Learning About the Role of Fluorides. 63
        A Recent Research Controversy 64
        California's Relative Standing in Fluoridation. 65
        A Life-Long Advantage. 65
        Economic and Fiscal Aspects: Dental Benefits Far
        Outrank Costs. 65
        Health Measures and Individual Rights 65
        Some Environmental Questions. 66
        Safety Considerations 66
        How Fluorides Reach and Affect Teeth 67
        Dietary Sources of Fluorides. 67
        Topical Applications. 68
        Fluoridated Water: The Prime Protector of Teeth 68
        Considerations in Setting Optimum Fluoride Concentrations 69
        Further Research on Dental Health. 69
        The Importance of Who Decides. 70
        Summary and Conclusion 70

Developing the Ombudsman's Role in Health Care Services 72
    Stanley V. Anderson (December 1974)
        Introduction and Background. 72
        Ombudsmen and Health Care in Prisons 72
        Ombudsmen and Mental Patients 72
        A Limited Role, So Far. 72

Three Models for Further Study 73
Group Conflict, Professional Structures and
Grievance Machinery. 73
When a Patient Complains: The Due Process Approach 73
Medical Association Grievance Committees. 74
General Practitioner as "Ombudsman" 74
The Ombudsman Between Doctor and Patient 74
Organizational Problems: The Ombudsman's Areas
of Concern 74
Location and Designation of a Health Care Ombudsman. 74
Justification for the Ombudsman's Services in
Nursing Homes 75
What the Ombudsman Should and Should Not Do in
Nursing Homes 75
Primary Remedies for Complaints and Exhaustion of
Alternatives. 75
Summary. 76
Conclusion 76

Public Funding of Political Campaigns: Attitudes and Issues
in California 77
    James Fay and Thomas Leatherwood (February 1975)
Introduction 77
Nationwide Polls 77
Some Indications of Californians' Views .77
Citizen Action Groups and a Division of Opinion 78
Supporters' Views: Reducing the Influence of Large
Contributors and Other Goals 78
Encouraging a Variety of Individuals and Groups to
Participate. 79
Stimulating Competition and Attention to Issues 79
Benefiting the Political System 79
Some Principal Arguments Against Public Funding. 79
Cost. 79
The Question of Free Speech 80
The Problem of Visibility and Information About
Candidates. 80
Effects on Parties and Reverse Effects. 80
Dangers of Self-Interest and Concentration of Power 80
Need for Experimentation. 80
A Comprehensive Law: Elements and Problems. 80
An Overview 82
Some Suggested Criteria 82
Options 82
Conclusion 82

Corrections: A Critical Analysis Of The Prison System
in California 84
    Patricia A. Sherman (April 1975)
        Introduction 84
        The Rehabilitative, Medical Model in Penology 84
        Treatment Programs: Plans and Actuality 84
        Educational, Vocational and Industrial Programs 85
        Conflict Between Demands of Treatment and of Custody 85
        Length of Incarceration: The Indeterminate Sentence 85
        Sentencing in the California System 85
        Costs of Incarceration 86
        Equity and Public Safety. 87
        Imprisonment as a General Deterrent .87
        Prison Time, Rehabilitation and Recidivism 87
        Legal Status of California's Convicts 88
        Some Conclusions 88
        Increased Use of Community Treatment Programs 88
        In Custody, But Learning Lawful Behavior 88
        Specific Institutional Reforms. 89
        Some Unanswered Questions. 89

Information, Research and Counseling: The Women's Center
at Berkeley 90
    Margaret B. Wilkerson (June 1975)
        Introduction 90
        Who Uses the Center? 90
        Counseling, Role Models, and Institutional Change 91
        Staff Organization and Principles 91
        Beginning with Counseling 92
        Peer Counseling. 92
        Professional Counseling. 92
        Bulletin Boards and Library 93
        Personal Referral Service. 93
        Working for Institutional Change 93
        Developing the Talent Bank 94
        Research Projects 94
        Programs for the Public. 94
        Plans for the Future 95

Reviving the Inner City: The Lessons of Oakland's Chinatown 96
    Willard T. Chow (August 1975)
        Introduction 96
        Ethnic Neighborhoods: Ambiguities and Choices. 96
        Chinese Settlement in the Bay Area: Some Comparisons 97
        Oakland: The Reemergence of an Inner City 98
        The Challenge of Inner City Development. 98

Pressures on Oakland's Chinatown 99
How Much Community Control? 99
Chinatown Housing and Neighborhood Preservation. 99
A Reappraisal of Costs and Benefits 100
Making Oakland More Attractive. 100
Conclusion 101

Hospitals: From Physician Dominance to Public Control. 103
   David B. Starkweather (October 1975)
      Introduction: Moving Toward Public Control 103
      Ownership and Governance. 103
      Internal Power Structure. 104
      Staff as Private Practitioners 104
      "Interference" in Medical Practice 104
      Peer Review. 104
      Shifting Power from Physicians. 104
      Community Participation 105
      Public v. Consumer Control. 105
      The Hospital as a Public Utility. 105
      Licensing and Accreditation, Including Safety 105
      Franchising: Entry to the Market. 106
      Problems in Franchising 106
      Operational Control: Some Impediments. 106
      Review of Rates by State Commissions. 106
      Role of the Federal Government. 107
      Price-Based Controls 107
      Some Pitfalls. 107
      The Focus of Regulation. 107
      Summary. 108

Juvenile Delinquency: Seeking Effective Prevention 109
   Tom Higgins (December 1975)
      Delinquency Prevention: Introduction. 109
      Does Prevention Work?. 109
      Is Prevention Needed?. 110
      Costs for California 110
      The Causes of Delinquency 111
      Delinquency Prevention Programs: Some Results. 112
      Lessons from Orange County and Richmond, California. 112
      Weighing Other Sociogenic Approaches. 113
      Conclusions and Recommendations .113

A Prescription for Student Aid: Better Information on
Post-Secondary Education. 115
   Wellford W. Wilms (February 1976)
      Introduction 115

The Seminar and Its Sponsors............................115
Equality or Inequality?.................................115
Vocational Education: The Lowest Rung 116
Access to What . . . and With What Results? 116
Consumerism..116
Economic Downturn.....................................116
Underemployment 117
A Caveat on Educational Data..........................117
Nonquantifiable Aspects and Student Decisions 117
Needs for Information.................................117
An Information System in California 118
Cost...118
Existing Federal Legislation 118
Need for State Legislation..............................118
Unintended Consequences..............................119
Recommendations for California........................119
Summary and Conclusion 119

Prepaid Health Plans: California's Experiment in Changing
the Medical Care System 122
    Margaret Greenfield and Alfred W. Childs, M.D. (April 1976)
        Introduction 122
        Federal HMO Act of 1973............................122
        Medi-Cal, The California Medicaid Program..........123
        Persons Eligible for Medi-Cal.......................123
        Medi-Cal Benefits 123
        Medi-Cal Reform Act of 1971........................123
        Anatomy of the PHPs: The Race for Prepayment 124
        The Scramble for Contracts..........................124
        The Showdown: Widespread Criticism 124
        Further Criticism: Inferior Patient Care..............126
        Legislative Action 127
        Persisting Problems 127
        New Effort at Reform................................127
        Alternatives...127
        Direct Health Services by County Hospitals 128

Using Reclaimed Water: Public Attitudes and Governmental
Policy 130
    William H. Bruvold (June 1976)
        Introduction 130
        Background and Aim of the Study 130
        Twenty-five Possible Uses 131
        Consistency of Findings 131
        Water Consumption and Public Health: Traditional
        Criteria 132

Some "Newer" Issues: Viruses, Trace Chemicals and
Possible Long-Term Effects.............................132
What Do Consumers Think About Reclaimed Water?..........132
Policy References......................................132
How Reliable is the Technology?........................133
Some Conclusions and Recommendations...................133
Summary..134

New Issues for California, the World's Most Advanced
Industrial Society...136
    Ted K. Bradshaw (August 1976)
        Introduction...................................136
        California as an Advanced Industrial Society...136
        General Policy Considerations..................138
        Rising Expectations for Increased Productivity.139
        New Opportunities for Maximizing the Use of Scarce
        Resources......................................139
        The End of the Growth Mentality................140
        Conclusion.....................................140

Learning to Live With Earthquakes: Research and Policy for
Seismic Safety in California...............................142
    Stanley Scott (October 1976)
        Major Earthquakes: Low Frequency but Disastrous
        Consequences...................................142
        A Good Beginning...............................142
        Geologic Knowledge . . . and Earthquake Prediction.........142
        Exploring Emergency Measures...................143
        A Safety Rule of Thumb—What Should be Done.....143
        The Basic Objective: An Earthquake-Resistant
        Physical Plant.................................144
        Policy: A Steadying Influence . . . An Improved Capability.....144
        Research Needs for Policy Development..........144
        Understanding Geologic Hazards.................144
        Investigating and Mitigating Structural Hazards.144
        Learning How to Save Lives and Minimize Injuries.........145
        Determining Social, Economic and Fiscal Effects: Costs
        of Earthquakes and Seismic Safety..............145
        Responding to Earthquake Predictions: First Steps.........146
        Putting the Pieces Together: The Role of Strategic Planning....146
        A Future Goal..................................146

Furthering the Mathematical Competence of Women...............147
    Nancy Kreinberg (December 1976)
        Introduction...................................147
        The Pattern of Math Avoidance..................147

How Expectations Are Shaped: The Causes of Math
Avoidance...147
Female Patterns of Education and Employment..............148
Breaking the Pattern.....................................148
Action Programs..149
Math for Girls...149
Conferences for 7th-12th Grade Women.....................149
What's Ahead: A Network of Women, and Role Models........150
Conclusions..151
Recommendations..151

Update From Capitol Hill: Power and Seniority in the
House of Representatives 154
   Hon. Norman Y. Mineta (December 1976) Special Issue
Introduction...154
Shifts of Party Strength in the Congress 154
Trends in Percentages of New Members.....................155
Who is Being Displaced? 155
Effects on Seniority 156
The Shift of Power 156
Reviving the Majority Caucus: Some Consequences..........156
The Caucus and the Chairs 157
Committee Assignments and Subcommittee Chairs............157
Changing the Way Congress Spends Money...................157
Scrutinizing Agencies and Programs 157
Emphasis on Legislative Oversight........................158
Issues and Generations 158
Tilt to the New Generation 158
Changes at the Top.......................................159
Conclusion 159

Author Index 161

Subject Index 163

Foreword

With the third volume of the collected *Public Affairs Reports*—the bimonthly bulletin of the Institute of Governmental Studies—we again make this resource available to readers for long-term use. The *Reports* thus can fulfill a dual role. When they initially appear, they provide "relevant, accurate background information" on current and topical issues, designed to "contribute to informed discussion of public affairs." Then, when compiled, they provide a permanent reference source of policy materials for a reflective readership.

The Institute publishes six individual *Reports* each year as brief, self-contained papers. Each represents recent research findings of the author or authors, or views on policy issues based on long-term specialization.

University faculty and staff researchers are encouraged to submit manuscripts exploring the public policy implications of their research, and by means of the *Report* to communicate in non-technical language with an interested but basically non-expert audience that includes citizens, legislators and policy makers, as well as students, faculty and others. Editorial procedures include review by reading committees of experts—faculty members and others—rewriting as needed, and editing for clarity and style.

For several years, the *Reports* have increasingly focussed on challenging issues confronting California, including many discussions that carry nationwide implications. Major subject groupings in this collection include: educational planning and policy, health and hospitals, politics, campaign finance and congressional power, public finance, science and technology, social problems and remedial policies, urban communities and women's opportunities. Specific examples of topics include the Ombudsman's role in health care, prepaid health plans, campaign finance in California, Bay Area Rapid Transit, use of reclaimed water, California as the world's most advanced industrial society, learning to live with earthquakes, drinking practices and problems, suicide, corrections, juvenile delinquency, the inner city and Oakland's Chinatown, and the mathematical competence of women.

The response to the two earlier volumes, as well as to the individual bulletins, indicates that both the single *Reports* and the collections provide valuable resources of information and views. In short these publications help forge a vital link between academic research and the short-term and long-term policy decisions that face California.

Harriet Nathan and Stanley Scott
Editors

Educational Planning and Policy

Vol. 14   No. 1   February 1973

Comprehensive Planning for Higher Education: Focus on New Priorities

by

Lyman A. Glenny
Professor of Education and
Director, Center for Research and Development
in Higher Education

Introduction

Which way are we heading in postsecondary education? The most realistic answer points toward increased centralization of planning at the state level. This new direction seems both logical and necessary if we are to respond effectively to expressions of current preferences and indications of future demands by college students and society.

After examining the probable new direction of higher education, and the new federal law that gives it impetus, the *Report* will look at trends and conditions that are forcing institutions and faculties to consider novel and sometimes uncongenial adjustments. These influences include: new technologies, pressures on faculty tenure and collective bargaining, attacks on institutional autonomy and jostling for prestige, changes in public priorities and the size of the student pool, student choices related to the dwindling of college expansionism, and students' increased need to qualify for jobs. Clearly, some of these trends appear mutually antagonistic, but the need for a sharper sense of direction seems unmistakable.

The Future: State-Level Planning and Coordination

The major chore for centralized planning will rest squarely on state-level policy planners. It seems clear that each public, private and proprietary (profit-making) institution must be considered as one component in a web of many postsecondary education agencies.

The challenge of planning and coordination in the states encompasses all new postsecondary educational forms, delivery systems, and types of programs—while promoting innovation, flexibility, adaptability and opportunity. These imperatives are now recognized by the federal government with a new law that should stimulate better and more comprehensive state planning.

The Higher Education Amendments of 1972 require improved coordination of postsecondary education in each state. The exact wording is as follows:

State Postsecondary Education Commissions
Sec. 1202. (a) Any state which desires to receive assistance under section 1203 of title X shall establish a state commission or agency which is broadly and equitably representative of the general public, public and private nonprofit and proprietary institutions of postsecondary education in the State including community colleges (as defined in title X), junior colleges, postsecondary vocational schools, area vocational schools, technical institutes, four-year institutions of higher education and branches thereof.

The implications of this provision for state master planning and its consequences for the several types of educational and training institutions, are greater than those of any other single act previously passed by the federal government. The requirement is for a central planning agency, which is to have control of the development of comprehensive planning for all postsecondary education in the state. It may delegate to other boards and commissions some of the planning function, but in the end it must approve all state plans forwarded to Washington for funding under the act. The possibilities for obtaining a single plan with coordinated administration at the state level is greatly enhanced by this legislation.

It is no coincidence that the federal demand for more comprehensive state planning for postsecondary education comes at the same time that federal funds are authorized to finance students in the proprietary institutions.

The Higher Education Amendments of 1972 will encourage acceleration of trends toward the proprietary and private schools. The federal aid programs for students permit them to receive financial aid even if they attend a proprietary trade or technical school. This is a radical departure for federal policy. It has great potential for future state policy on student grants, and on the further redistribution of students away from college-type institutions.

Neither is it a coincidence that the Education Commission of the States, which grew out of the National

Governors Conference, has just authorized a new task force: Coordination, Governance, and Structure of Postsecondary Education. The task force is directed to study and to provide guidelines and models for more effective planning and coordination of *all* institutions, schools, institutes, and agencies engaged in education or training at the postsecondary level.

A Radical Transformation

The cumulative impact of the trends to be discussed below, the new state planning commissions, and the task force of the Education Commission cannot be fully anticipated. The experience of the past decade with the increasingly sophisticated staffs of the state planning and coordinating boards in 27 states, suggests that education beyond high school will undergo radical transformation. No major institutionalized segment will be left out of the planning as it was in the past (e.g., private colleges and proprietary schools). New delivery systems and technologies with potential for extending education to the home, the office and other places, as easily as in an educational setting, will increasingly become a matter of major attention by planners and coordinators. Fortunately for students of all ages, parochial interests of single segments of education are giving way to a more inclusive view concerning the institutions that should be legitimized as educational performers, as well as the very character of the educational content and the processes necessary for both education and training in the challenging era ahead.

New Technologies and Different Requirements

New technologies and a host of other nontraditional means of offering a college education will have profound influence on what is and is not done within the higher institutions. These include: the external degree, the university-without-walls, the work-study program, the new emphasis on part-time enrollment, and videotape cassette and closed-circuit TV. For many years we have discussed the merit of in-and-out education and of continuing adult education for millions of people whose education is incomplete or whose avocational or career interests have changed. Many young people are not waiting for an institutional, a state, or a national plan to provide the continuing opportunity. They make it for themselves. The new technologies for delivery of education are being grasped quickly by these young adults as well as by older persons. Some members of the current legislative master plan committee in California are planning on the assumption that by 1985 the majority of all collegiate instruction will take place off the campus through external means.[1]

Increasingly, too, we will consider the college degree less and less important as certification for particular competencies. External agencies may do much more certifying in the future, giving a variety of certificates, diplomas and awards. In addition to degrees or even without them, the postsecondary institutions may be certifying particular skills or knowledge packages. The degree itself may come to mean little, as a person acquires a series of lesser certificates that indicate his specific capability to conduct certain kinds of occupational tasks.

Faculty Trends: Collective Bargaining and Tenure

Collective bargaining by faculty and changes related to tenure may prove to be significant for higher institutions. These trends can have substantial influence on the autonomy of the institution, and on the rational development of postsecondary education.

Some governing boards are now reasserting powers only recently delegated to administrators and faculties. Moreover, professors continue to demand further control over policy and, as we all know, students also want a "piece of the action." One can hardly keep track of the changing power relationships. Yet the future is likely to make the sharing of power, and the roles of each group, much clearer, primarily because of unionism and collective bargaining. Contracts will not only reassure a threatened faculty fearing possible loss of tenure, but will cover working conditions, teaching loads, advising, independent study, and even the curriculum and hours of teaching. The trade unions have shown time and again that once bargaining starts, regardless of rules and laws to the contrary, anything and everything becomes negotiable.[2]

Since the public institutional leaders and their governing boards cannot bind the state to the financial conditions contained in the bargain, the negotiations and agreements will tend to engage the unions and the experts at the state level. Powers eventually left for the president and his staff could be almost purely ministerial—to carry out the contract provisions. Unionism will result in "conserving" trends. Faculty will protect themselves, more rigidities will confront both administrators and faculty members, and due process provisions of many kinds will be carefully followed. Opportunities for change and adaptability will be greatly reduced, while all of the trends previously mentioned will demand flexibility if collegiate institutions are to respond successfully to the imperative demands of the 1970s and 1980s.

Tenure and Rigidity

Similar rigidities and conserving influences will characterize many institutions whose faculties have a low average age and a high percentage on tenure. Tenure caused few if any problems of institutional inflexibility or inadaptability during the years of doubling and redoubling of enrollments: 1950 to the present. Because of new enrollments, the number of new faculty members required each year provided a margin of error that easily allowed for the shifts in program required in those two decades. This will not be the case in the future for most institutions. An institution or a department with a high percentage of its faculty members already tenured could not have responded to the many changes of the past ten years, much less to the many changes already on the horizon for the 1970s and 1980s.

In a book just published, Robert Blackburn has shown from an exhaustive analysis of available research studies that faculty members on the average seem to be better teachers, better producers of knowledge, and of more value to their institutions, as they gain in academic rank and in age.[3] He also presents evidence that they—as individuals—are adaptable (innovative) to new changes in courses and programs.

But the research studies on which he bases these conclusions were not directed to faculties or institutions in a steady state of enrollment and of financial resources. Nor did the studies address themselves to the problems encountered in great shifts of students from one discipline to another, or to the adaptiveness of faculty members when modern language or history or some other required courses they teach are dropped from the compulsory curriculum.

With few exceptions, faculty members are educated and trained in a single disciplinary area. No matter how adaptable they are to innovative changes in their own disciplinary offerings, they cannot switch from history or education to the teaching of chemistry or biology. But such shifts in student demand have already beset higher institutions, and will intensify in the future.

Clearly an institution with a tenured faculty exceeding 60 percent is courting trouble in its ability to react responsibly to the society that supports it. If the tenured group constitutes 70 percent or more, the institution may find that student numbers drop rapidly when programs no longer respond to new and changing needs. Faculties should be cognizant of the fact that high rates of tenure and concurrent loss of enrollments may easily force the closing off of many tenured positions. A substantial margin of untenured positions provides a flexible reserve for anticipating and responding to changing program and institutional needs. An untenured reserve also assures tenured faculty members that their positions will not be in great jeopardy as curriculum and disciplinary priorities make substantial shifts.

Autonomy and Prestige

In the face of these trends, including several radical departures from the recent past, how do institutions of higher education and their faculties respond? For the most part faculties still believe we are in a *temporary* setback, and that a change in political parties at the state or national level will return things to the *normal* of the 1960s. Most administrators are more fully aware of the new reality than are faculty members.

Both groups have strong desires for status and prestige. Hence we find the junior college trying to become a four-year college, the four-year college a university, and the university a comprehensive graduate-research center. Each tries to obtain as many students as possible, since size is also a measure of "success." Almost invariably institutional projections of enrollment, if aggregated for the whole state, show future enrollments greater than the total number of college-age youth.

I have recently discussed some of the trends mentioned in this paper with the college and university leaders in several states. The response by state college and emerging-university presidents often has been one of outright antagonism. They respond this way not because they believe the trends to be wrongly interpreted but because, if public policymakers accept the trends as reality, the institutional goal of becoming an advanced graduate center is almost certain to be thwarted. Both faculties and institutions must re-evaluate roles. Faculty-oriented wishes and preferences may have to defer to the needs of students and society.

The End of Expansionism

We know that for all save a few exceptional institutions, the great age of expansion is almost over. The private colleges reached this point several years ago and the large universities will shortly do the same. For some of the most distinguished universities, graduate enrollments have passed optimum size and undergraduate enrollments have already become static. The state college-emerging university-type institutions may have another year or so of increase, and the community colleges will be the last to stop growing. A survey by the American Council on Education's "Higher Education Panel" (April 7, 1972) states that:

. . . although first-time, full-time freshmen enrollments increased by an estimated 12 percent between 1970 and 1971, nearly 85 percent of this total increase was accounted for by public two-year colleges. Increases at other types of institutions were well below 10 percent, and public four-year colleges showed a slight decrease.[4]

Moreover, the Census Bureau reports that the number of children under five years of age decreased 15 per cent from 1960 to 1970.[5] Thus the goal will be a slow growth or no growth at all. We will no longer need to worry about setting maximums on college size *or* worry about whether the universities will or will not accept junior college transfer students. For example, The Oakland *Tribune* reported that:

. . . The University of California's Academic Assembly, representing faculty members from all nine campuses, . . . voted to lower admission standards for transfer students during a four-year test period.[6]

With the shortage of students, the institutions' competition for enrollments will increase to unprecedented levels, especially as operating funds are granted public colleges and universities on the basis of the number of FTE (full-time equivalent) students, in most states.

Tight State Budgets for Higher Education

With the exception of a few states, most have reached a funding plateau, and others will quickly do so. Any increase of funds will result from a larger state income generally, not from a larger percentage of the state revenue. In the 1960s, enrollment doubled and budgets for higher education tripled, while the proportion of the GNP (gross national product) allocated to higher education increased from one to two percent. The proportion of the GNP for higher education could not keep that pace, and currently it is not doing so.

For example, in Connecticut from 1962 to 1972, institutions of higher education received varying proportions of the state's general revenue as indicated below:

Year	Proportion of State General Revenue
1962	5.5%
1967	12.0%
1972	10.5%

This decreasing proportion of state revenue occurred in 1972 at the same time that a new medical school enjoyed a $16 million budget, new community colleges were developing, and aid to nonpublic institutions was increasing.

Other states are in a similar situation. A study being conducted by the Center for Research and Development in Higher Education, Berkeley, from which the above figures were drawn, found that twice as many states had reduced the proportion of the state budget for higher education as had increased the proportion. Nationally such support has dropped about one-half of one percentage point.

Moreover, the Census Bureau recently reported that the states were spending more dollars than they were gaining in revenue. During 1971, the states' revenue rose by 9.3 percent, but expenditures rose even more—by 16.2 percent—leaving a deficit of $1.6 billion for all states. It should be noted that normally states have an excess of revenue over expenditures.[7] So the budgetary pressures have increased. And if these factors are not sufficiently convincing, one has only to think of the possibility that the *Serrano* decision in California may lead to much more money being spent on public education and community colleges.[8] Thus, even a slow growth prediction in state general revenue funding for higher education over the long haul would be optimistic.

In addition to money shortages, the establishment of a new set of social priorities will force a slowdown in funding growth for higher education. Thus higher education drops from the top of the "top ten" to a much lower position.[9] Health care, the common schools, the environment and recreation, among others, are surfacing as high priority concerns in the legislature of nearly every state. Unless there is some national catastrophe for which higher education is believed to be the major remedy, the colleges and universities will probably not regain their favored position within the next 20 years. The exceptional states are likely to be those with college-going rates well below the national average and/or states that have an extraordinary pattern of economic growth.

Private Institutions and Public Funds

The so-called "plight of the private colleges" is indeed very real for most of the denominational institutions; even though the problem of some appears to be overexpenditure rather than lack of income.[10] States are beginning to give financial aid including state scholarships, grant and loan programs, and direct grants to private institutions. All, however, will be funded from that same single total amount for higher education in the state budget. No matter who or what is included, the proportion of the state budget for higher education will remain about the same.

A corollary to this trend converts some private universities into public institutions taken over fully by the state systems. As financial conditions deteriorate, additional colleges will sacrifice private status for complete public control and funding. But short of this, private institutions that receive any substantial part of their funds from the state will be increasingly subjected to the master planning, program control, and management constraints of the state to the same extent as the public institutions. Indeed, as the President of the Sloan Foundation has indicated, by definition, if they accept public funds they become public institutions.

Federal Funding: An Uncertain Promise

The promise of substantial amounts of federal aid to promote higher education (rather than research) has been advanced for 15 or 20 years. Such funds, in anything like the sums desired or anticipated, will probably not materialize—not in time to save all the private colleges nor in amounts sufficient to continue the "add-on" method of conducting public college business. New social problems also turn federal priorities away from higher education. At the moment, there is only a remote possibility of large amounts of federal institutional aid. A 1972 Brookings Institution report prepared by Charles L. Schultze, et al., reveals that in past peacetime years, economic growth always has generated sufficient increase in tax revenues to cover increasing government costs, but that is not the case now.[11]

The report also predicts a national debt increase from $15 billion to $20 billion per year until 1975—even if the country achieves full-employment prosperity. Revenues, the report says, will catch up in 1977 *if no new spending programs are started*. To rely on federal aid is to lean on a frail reed. According to Schultze, savings from ending the war in Vietnam are already discounted, and defense costs will rise $11 billion in the next four years. Further, inflation is not under control, and other priorities assert themselves.

The Student Pays—and Chooses

Because of financial conditions, there is an almost inevitable trend to force the student to pay more and more of the total costs of his education. In many states tuitions are already high and some politicians would like to see them even higher. The plan of Ohio's governor seems in abeyance for the moment, but the Governor of Georgia was promoting a similar, more attractive plan at the annual meeting of the Education Commission of the States in Los Angeles, with many legislators and governors in attendance. (The Ohio plan would have required students to repay all educational costs from future income. The plan failed primarily because details were not fully developed prior to the legislative sessions.)

There seems to be growing acceptance for requiring a student either to pay full cost as he attends or to pay back the full cost out of future income. He may receive a government voucher to defray part of these costs, but with increased onus on the student to pay, there will be a free-market situation in postsecondary education.

The student is already examining his personal costs of direct payments and foregone income, and in the future the scrutiny will be intensified.

A Shift to Proprietary and Industrial Schools

The next trend tells us something about how the student is thinking these days. Perhaps the most important of the unexamined trends is the increasing tendency for those who want training in a great variety of skills to attend the proprietary and industrial schools rather than the traditional college and university, including the community college. The Educational Policy Research Center of Syracuse reports that the rate of increase in enrollment in these so-called "peripheral" institutions has been greater than that in higher institutions, and in the future it will be larger still.[12] A recent (unpublished) report prepared for the National Center for Educational Statistics indicates enrollment in proprietary schools at the postsecondary level is over one million. Industrial and military schools enroll many more than that. Thus we see a trend for the older student to pay for exactly the type of training he wants in specialized schools regardless of the fact that similar work is offered by more traditional colleges and universities.

But why should a student from a modest- or low-income family pay the high tuition costs of a proprietary institution when he can attend a community college for much less? A study at our Center is proceeding on the hypothesis that the proprietary school depends on the employment and success of its graduates for income and long-term survival, while the public community college depends on the political process (which may have no relationship to the effectiveness of the training being offered) for financial support. Indeed, students seem to find that it is cheaper to attend a proprietary institution on an intensive basis for a year or less than it is to go to the community college for two years and end up with lesser skills directly applicable to job entry. Further, it is increasingly clear that not all students want or believe that they need liberal arts and bachelors degrees, nor do they wish to be treated as second-class citizens because they reject the academic and intellectual life.

As Amitai Etzioni, Director of the Center for Policy Research at Columbia, wrote recently:

> . . . to solve social problems by changing people is more expensive and usually less productive than approaches that accept people as they are and seek to mend not them but the circumstances around them.[13]

Conclusion

The pressures of these social trends clearly support the state and federal governments' concern with better and more comprehensive planning than we now have. The spectrum of opportunity in postsecondary education is broadening very rapidly, competition for student enrollments increases daily, and the articulation among the many institutions and programs suffers correspondingly. Planning will focus on the creation of many options for all citizens—not just the young—to engage in liberal and humanizing courses and experiences, and to develop capabilities in many career fields.

NOTES

[1] Revealed in personal conversation with the author.

[2] Felix Nigro, "The Implications for Public Administration," *Public Administration Review*, 32 (2): 120–126.

[3] *Tenure, Aspects of Job Security on the Changing Campus* (Atlanta: Southern Regional Education Board, Research Monograph No. 19, September 1972).

[4] As reported in, American Council on Education, *Higher Education and National Affairs*, 21 (15): 3.

[5] U. S. Department of Commerce, Bureau of the Census, *Current Population Reports, Population Estimates, and Projections*, Series P–25, No. 476, p. 5 (February 1972).

[6] Editorial, Oakland *Tribune*, June 12, 1972.

[7] *The Star and News*, Washington, D.C., July 17, 1972, A–15.

[8] Education Commission of the States, *Compact*, April 1972, p. 4.

[9] Jerome Evans, "View from a State Capitol," *Change*, 3 (5): 40 ff.

[10] Columbia Research Associates, *The Cost of College*. As reported in a summary distributed by the USOE, fall 1971, n.d., mimeographed.

[11] *Setting National Priorities: The 1973 Budget* (Washington, D.C.: Brookings Institution, 1972), p. 7.

[12] Stanley Moses, "Notes on the Learning Force," *Notes on the Future of Education*, 1 (2): 7 (Syracuse University).

[13] *Saturday Review*, June 3, 1972, 45–46.

Social Problems and Remedial Policies

Vol. 14   No. 2   April 1973

Drinking Practices and Problems:
Research Perspectives on Remedial Measures

by

Don Cahalan
Adjunct Professor of Behavioral Sciences,
School of Public Health

Drinking alcoholic beverages has been an avocation, occupation, or preoccupation for many Americans ever since the founding of the republic. But no full-scale scientific surveys of drinking behavior in the United States were conducted until the 1960's. This *Public Affairs Report* summarizes some findings and implications of a drinking behavior research program supported by the National Institute on Alcohol Abuse and Alcoholism of the National Institute of Mental Health. The studies were begun in the Bay Area in 1960, and are scheduled to continue into the mid-1970's.[1]

Briefly, one of the most unexpected findings was that men in the youngest age group surveyed (21–24) experience the greatest prevalence of all types of drinking problems. Moreover, such problems decline rapidly after age 25. Nevertheless, long-term serious problems appear to have their origin in drinking habits acquired in an individual's twenties. This emphasizes the potential of *preventive* programs of an essentially educational nature, aimed especially at youthful populations. Further, observed changes in many individuals' drinking patterns over the span of a few years also suggest important opportunities for both *preventive* and *remedial* programs. These and other research findings, as well as their public policy implications, are discussed more fully below.

Health and Economic Costs of Alcohol's Misuse

Alcoholism and other adverse effects of alcohol's misuse constitute a major public health and economic problem in America. Alcohol plays a major role in half of all highway fatalities. Moreover, excessive use of alcohol carries an estimated national price tag of $15 billion a year in accidents, crime and delinquency, and health and welfare cost.

Within California alone, alcoholism is the fourth leading cause of death during the economically productive years of 35–64. Public drunkenness accounts for about half of all California's misdemeanor arrests, and more than 26,000 individuals or families in this state are dependent upon public welfare as the direct result of alcoholism.[2]

Research Efforts

Despite the high cost of misusing alcohol, there has been a dearth of objective research on drinking practices and problems. Recognition of this lack motivated several research efforts: Three national surveys have been completed and the fourth is in progress, and four large-scale surveys have been made in San Francisco. The findings are summarized here, beginning with the national surveys.

Findings on Drinking Practices

The first national survey (1964–65) showed that 68 percent of the adult population drink some alcoholic beverage at least once a year (77 percent of the men and 60 percent of the women).[3] Twelve percent of this national sample were (rather arbitrarily) defined as "heavy drinkers" (persons who drink every day, with five or more drinks per occasion at least once in a while; or about once weekly, usually with five or more at a time). Twenty-one percent of the men and 5 percent of the women were thus characterized as "heavy drinkers." It should not be concluded, however, that most American are regular drinkers, since 47 percent of the adult population were found to drink less than once a month, or not at all.

Drinking and heavy drinking vary considerable according to social and occupational status, education, and ethnic background, with a larger proportion of the more well-to-do drinking at least occasionally. A larger proportion *of those who drank* among the less well advantaged were found to drink heavily. The largest cities had the highest proportion of heavy drinkers, particularly in the Middle Atlantic area, New England, and our own Pacific Coast. For example, drinkers comprised 87 percent of the sample in cities of 50,000 to one million population, compared with only 43 percent among farm residents. The lowest rates of heavy drinking were in the East South Central region, followed by other southern and central areas, and the mountain states. These areas' high proportions of abstainers and low proportions of heavy drinkers appear to depend on their less urban character, and the prevalence of Protestant denominations that traditionally frown upon the use of alcohol.

This national survey also demonstrated that there is no necessary connection between the proportion who drink and the proportion who drink heavily. For example, respondents born outside the U. S. have an above-average proportion of drinkers, but their rate of heavy drinking is somewhat lower than that of the native born.

Drinking Problems: An Overview

After completing a number of Bay Area and national surveys of drinking practices, the second phase of the research program has concentrated upon drinking *problems*. These studies use the concept of *problems associated with use of alcohol*, rather than the relatively ambiguous concept of "alcoholism," following the precepts set down by Thomas Plaut and Genevieve Knupfer.[4]

The classification of problems takes into account severity, reliability of measurement, and time of onset. The surveys cover potential problems (such as a high level of alcohol intake) as well as actual problems as perceived by the respondent. They include frequent intoxication or high alcohol intake (such as drinking five or more drinks-per-occasion at least once a week); binge drinking (staying drunk for two or more days in a row); psychological dependence (drinking for symptom relief or escape); interpersonal problems related to one's drinking; problems with spouse or relatives, friends or neighbors, people at work, or the police; problems with health or with accidents related to drinking; financial troubles; and belligerence associated with drinking.

Table I summarizes the findings for men and women interviewed in the 1967 national survey. Combining the "moderate" and "high" categories (in the High Current Problems Score) shows that a substantial proportion (43 percent of all the men and 21 percent of all the women) experienced a drinking-connected problem or potential problem within three years prior to 1967. The chief specific problems of men were frequent intoxication, symptomatic drinking, psychological dependence, and problems with spouse or relatives. There was no "high" or relatively severe score for women in excess of the 4 percent reporting health problems related to drinking.

TABLE I

PREVALENCE OF DRINKING-RELATED PROBLEMS WITHIN A
THREE-YEAR PERIOD, BY SEX (1967 SURVEY)

Type of Problem	MEN (N = 751)			WOMEN (N = 608)		
	None	Moderate	High	None	Moderate	High
Index of Frequent Intoxication[a]	83%	3%	14%	97%	1%	2%
Binge drinking	97	–	3	100	–	*
Symptomatic drinking[b]	84	8	8	93	4	3
Psychological dependence	61	31	8	85	12	3
Problems with current spouse or relatives	84	8	8	96	3	1
Problems with friends or neighbors	93	5	2	97	3	*
Problems on job	94	3	3	98	2	1
Problems with police or accidents	99	–	1	99	–	1
Health[c]	88	6	6	93	4	4
Financial problems	91	6	3	98	2	1
Belligerence	88	8	4	93	5	3
High Current Problems Score[d]	57	28	15	79	17	4
		(43)			(21)	

[a] Components: frequency and amount-per-occasion, and frequency of getting high or tight.

[b] Difficulty in stopping drinking, blackouts, sneaking drinks.

[c] Told by physician to cut down drinking.

[d] A High Score was determined by the number and severity of problems, ranging from two or more types of problems with at least one being in severe form, to having any degree of problem (from slight to severe) in seven or more areas.

* Less than one-half of one percent.

SOURCE. 1967 national probability sample of adults. Adapted from Table 1 in *Problem Drinkers*, cited in note 1.

Many respondents had more than one drinking problem. For example, frequent intoxication was most often associated with symptomatic drinking and psychological dependence. And binge drinking was most often associated with symptomatic drinking and problems with spouse or relatives, while problems with friends and neighbors were usually accompanied by frequent intoxication, symptomatic drinking, problems with spouse, and health problems. This may be another way of saying that by the time friends and neighbors get around to remonstrating with an individual about his drinking, he will usually have accumulated a host of drinking problems in other areas of his life.

Drinking Problems Among Younger Men

Fully half of the men reported at least a minimal drinking problem, and one-third had had one or more fairly severe problems within three years. Almost three-fourths reported having one or more problems with drinking at some time in their lives. These findings showed up when results for the high-risk group of men aged 21–59 in the 1967 national survey were combined with results from a new national survey of men interviewed in 1969.[5]

Perhaps the most unexpected finding is that all types of drinking problems are most prevalent among men in the youngest age group (21–24). The percentage of men with a High Current Problems Score is almost twice as large (40 percent) as for any of the older groups. These findings are shown in Table II.

TABLE II

SEVERITY LEVELS OF SPECIFIC CURRENT PROBLEMS OF MEN AGED 21–59,
BY AGE GROUP[a] (SURVEYS, 1967 AND 1969)

	21–24 (147)	25–29 (204)	30–34 (186)	35–39 (216)	40–44 (226)	45–49 (201)	50–54 (199)	55–59 (182)	Total (1561)
(n)									
Heavy intake	7%	7%	5%	7%	6%	3%	5%	6%	6%
Binge drinking	10	3	3	3	1	2	4	2	3
Psychological dependence	5	4	4	4	4	5	4	3	4
Loss of control	12	5	4	5	7	5	4	4	6
Symptomatic drinking	26	11	8	7	6	10	9	3	9
Belligerence	15	12	10	8	7	8	6	2	8
Problems with wife	19	17	15	10	9	9	11	6	12
Problems with friends or neighbors	15	5	7	5	4	4	6	4	6
Problems on job	10	4	3	5	5	5	6	2	5
Police problems	10	4	2	2	2	2	4	1	3
Health problems or injuries from drinking	8	4	5	6	4	6	8	6	6
Finances	11	4	6	4	3	2	4	3	4
High Current Problems Score	40	22	20	21	17	17	17	11	20

[a] Adapted from Table 8 in Cahalan and Room, cited in note 1. Definitions of problems are similar to those for Table I, with the addition of "Loss of Control" (inability to stop drinking) and slight modifications in combinations of items.

The high rate of problem drinking among very young men is also revealed in Pelz's and Schuman's survey of youth aged 16–24.[6] Apparently there is a rapid decline in drinking problems after the age of 25. Nevertheless, the longer term serious problems appear to be initiated by drinking habits begun in one's early twenties, rather than by later patterns acquired after the age of 40. Thus the pattern of high levels of youthful heavy drinking runs counter to the stereotype of the "alcoholic" as a skid-row type in his mid-forties or fifties.

Drinking problems were also found to be more prevalent among the following groups: men who were poor; Catholics (especially Irish Catholics) as compared to Protestant denominations advocating teetotalism; residents of big cities, particularly in the coastal areas; and those of Latin-American ancestry. While drinking problems appear to taper off markedly among upper-status men as they move into their forties, there is actually an apparent rise in drinking problems among men of lower socio-economic status in the 45–49 bracket. (This compares with the average age of approximately 40–45 among institutionalized alcoholics.)[7]

The Importance of Changes in Drinking Patterns

The marked changes in individuals' drinking behavior over a span of a few years suggest the highly significant potential of preventive and remedial programs. Of those interviewed in the 1964–65 national survey, half reported changing their drinking habits, either by quitting altogether, or by drinking either more or less. Even among abstainers, one-third said they formerly drank.

These retrospective data on changes in drinking behavior are verified by separate measurements on the same individuals in the 1964–65 and 1967 surveys:

During that three-year period, 15 percent had either moved into or out of the group reporting drinking "five or more drinks-per-occasion some of the time." Moreover, among men 21–59, roughly twice as many reported having had a drinking problem at some time in their lives, as compared with those reporting a drinking problem within the last three years. This implies a substantial rate of remission or improvement of drinking problems that is far greater than can be credited to any formal agencies of intervention. These findings also raise doubts that heavy drinking almost inevitably grows worse in a progressive, irreversible "snowball effect."

"Maturing Out" of Problem Drinking

The evidence that even those with severe drinking problems can change drinking habits implies that the average problem drinker has periods when it is easier to bring his drinking under control. As noted earlier, upper status men in their forties and fifties appear to be more successful at "maturing out" of problem drinking. The maturing out process is also observed among men in smaller towns and rural areas.

Men who matured out of problem drinking more quickly were also more secure in their jobs, were less impulsive, and lived in environments that were less permissive of heavy drinking, as contrasted with those who remained problem drinkers. These national findings are consistent with those of the 1964 San Francisco survey, which found the inveterate problem drinkers to show more signs of childhood stress, to have witnessed drinking problems in the home while growing up, and to manifest anxiety, depression, maladjustment, guilt, and need for approval.[8]

The San Francisco Surveys

As mentioned earlier, there have been four large-scale surveys of the household population of the City and County of San Francisco since 1960. San Francisco findings of special interest include the following:

Those with high problem drinking scores in the 1964 survey had a death rate four years later that was twice as high as the rate of those with low problem drinking scores.[9] This finding demonstrates the life-and-death potential of remedial efforts with problem drinking.

In interviews four years later, a relatively high proportion (about 30 percent) of San Franciscans who had had a high problem score on an initial survey were no longer in the high-problem-drinking class. As mentioned above, those who apparently moved out of the problem-drinking group were primarily motivated to function better socially, or were concerned about preserving their health.

On the basis of high cirrhosis rates and per-capita sales of alcohol, San Francisco has achieved a reputation as a city of hard drinkers. However, analysis of San Francisco surveys and data for comparable American central-city areas indicates that these high rates are particularly explainable by a number of extraneous factors. These include San Francisco's restricted geographic boundaries—it is primarily a core city, virtually without a semi-suburban fringe area.

Other factors are San Francisco's status as a tourist center and international port, and the efficiency of San Francisco's coroner's office in detecting cirrhosis through autopsies.[10] San Francisco men were found to be no more likely than those in other big cities to be binge drinkers, or to have adverse social consequences from drinking. (San Franciscans differed from residents of other big cities primarily in their relatively higher wine consumption, and in slightly heavier drinking on the part of women.)

The highest rates of problem drinking were found in San Francisco census tracts having the highest proportions of low-income families combined with high proportions of single individuals. These appear to be the areas where higher rates of general delinquency are found, jointly with environmental situations conducive to heavy drinking, such as depressing living conditions and a high concentration of lower-class bars.

The San Francisco surveys also found that the ethnic origins of one's friends are about as important as one's own ethnic origins in determining drinking behavior, particularly if the friends are members of groups with higher rates of problem drinking, such as those of Irish or Scandinavian background.

Summary of Findings and Implications

The results of this program of national and Bay Area studies conducted during the last dozen years can be summarized as follows:

1. Drinking is typical behavior in most areas of the United States. Both abstinence and heavy problem drinking are atypical, and most people who drink do not become problem drinkers.

2. The proportion of drinkers is highest among upper status people. But those of lowest status have the highest proportions of heavy and problem drinkers, if one sets aside those who do not drink at all.

3. Heavy drinking and all types of drinking problems are at their height among men in their early twenties. Individuals' drinking habits and attitudes that presage drinking problems in later life probably become established at a relatively early age.

4. Whether one drinks at all appears to be related primarily to such socio-cultural variables as sex, age, social status, region, degree of urbanization, religion, and ethnic origin. However, certain personality characteristics—such as alienation, neurotic tendencies, and impulsiveness—also have a bearing on heavy drinking and problem drinking.

5. All surveys consistently underscored the high importance of early environment and family stability in the individual's susceptibility to drinking problems.

6. The problem-drinking status of many individuals changes over time. There is a general tendency for

individuals—particularly those of upper socioeconomic status—to move out of the drinking and problem-drinking categories as they approach their thirties.

Emphasis on the Need for Prevention

The final phase of this program of longitudinal studies of drinking practices is yet to be completed. But the first dozen years have yielded many findings having highly significant implications for policymakers. Some findings appeared in the recent U. S. Department of Health, Education, and Welfare (HEW) task force report to Congress on alcohol and health.[11] This report placed special emphasis upon the need to work on *preventing* alcohol problems, rather than concentrating primarily on efforts to rehabilitate alcoholics whose habits have become relatively intractable through years of neglect.

Preventive efforts are needed on three levels: primary, secondary, and tertiary. (Primary prevention consists of education and social influences designed to help young people avoid falling into the habit of non-moderate drinking; secondary prevention seeks to modify the behavior of drinkers whose problems are not as yet deep-seated; and tertiary prevention is directed at the rehabilitation of those who have lost control over their drinking to the extent that their health or social functioning has been seriously impaired.)

Why Prevention is Slighted

Prevention of alcohol problems is much like Mark Twain's weather: everybody talks about it, but nobody does much about it. One of the reasons why prevention has been slighted is that it is so very hard to prove the effectiveness of prevention programs because carefully controlled demonstration projects extending over a considerable period of time are necessary in order to show results. On the other hand, intensive efforts to rehabilitate derelicts can show tangible results in a relatively short time.

Another reason why prevention has been slighted is that drinking—and even rather heavy drinking—is so widely accepted that the general public tends to be rather apathetic or antagonistic toward preventive efforts. National prohibition indeed did reduce liver cirrhosis materially, but at a heavy price in loss of respect for the law. A return to prohibition is hardly feasible. While it is possible that more stringent controls over the sale or advertising of alcoholic beverages might reduce problem drinking, such controls need to be applied with great care in order not to discriminate unduly against the majority of moderate drinkers.

Can an Informational Campaign Succeed?

Public informational and educational campaigns have the advantage of not being coercive or punitive, but they are often lacking in effectiveness—as witness the limited impact of the massive anti-tobacco campaigns during the last generation.

Perhaps there is some prospect of success in informational campaigns that involve the whole community in awareness that problem drinking is a serious public health issue, if the aim is public commitment and consensus on realistic goals (such as moderate drinking) rather than the enforcement of complete abstention. Successful information campaigns on how to avoid alcohol problems should take into account the fact that the advertising tactics (such as repetitive sloganeering) that are successful in switching customers from one brand of soap to another are not likely to be effective in getting people to give up heavy drinking unless alternatives are provided that are at least equally attractive. Thus campaigns for moderation that are based on the model of the television commercial are unlikely to succeed, whereas person-to-person appeals from one's associates are more likely to be effective. Since the current research program has shown that personal influences are paramount in drinking behavior, it would seem that setting a good example is more effective than preachments in bringing about moderation.

Needed: Demonstration Projects

It appears that sufficient descriptive research has now been completed to warrant planning controlled field experiments combining action and research, and setting up demonstration projects to establish the relative merits of alternative models of alcohol education and rehabilitation. California now has excellent opportunities to make rapid progress with both prevention and rehabilitation programs, and the outlook recently improved materially when an Office of Alcohol Program Management was established in the state's Health and Welfare Agency. That office's function is to consolidate various fragmented programs into an integrated delivery system for the prevention of alcoholism and for the treatment and rehabilitation of problem drinkers.

As one illustration, a controlled demonstration project is planned for public school education, combining the efforts of the Office of Alcohol Program Management and one or more city and county school systems. The Social Research Group of the University's School of Public Health will serve as the primary research arm. Federal funds are being sought to augment state and county resources for this project. A "values-clarification" approach will be applied throughout selected school systems.[12] The goal will be to develop realistic alternatives to alcohol and other drugs as a means of finding pleasure and a sense of self-worth, and to cope with anxiety and stress.

Tailor-Made Programs

The research findings should contribute to the planning of both national and local programs of preventive or remedial measures to cope with problem drinking. For example, the observed regional, urban, social class, and ethnic differences in drinking behavior argue that preventive or remedial measures should be tailored to specific groups, rather than imposed as a uniform, standardized program.

Our findings suggest that in the larger cities relatively more attention should be paid to reducing the health consequences (such as cirrhosis) of inveterate heavy drinking while in the more rural areas emphasis should be placed upon mitigating the social disruptions and accidental injuries associated with weekend drinking bouts. Further, special research-based programs will need to be designed to reach and to influence people in high-risk subcultures such as the young, the poor, Latin-Americans, and Indian groups. It is exactly these types of groups—including the poor, the isolated, and the uninformed—that stand most in need of effective outreach programs to reduce problems related to heavy drinking, and these are also the groups that tend to be neglected currently in the provision of medical and social resources to cope with chronic disease conditions.[13]

Reducing Problem Drinking: Difficult But Feasible

The 12-year research effort underscores the difficulty of achieving a rapid reduction in problem drinking until prevailing attitudes and values are modified. Habits associated with heavy drinking are hard to change, and are reinforced by a general social climate of dependence upon chemicals to allay anxieties and life stresses. Nevertheless, attitudes and behavior *can* be modified. Our research findings lend confidence that effective preventive and remedial programs can be devised to mobilize the recuperative resources of the individual and his environment. Intelligently guided efforts can succeed in redirecting problem drinking into more rewarding channels of behavior.

NOTES

[1] Two series of studies grew out of the program begun in 1959 by John Philp and A. C. Hollister of the then Division of Alcoholic Rehabilitation in the California State Department of Public Health. One was the series of nine surveys conducted in the San Francisco Bay Area, first headed by Wendell R. Lipscomb and Ira H. Cisin, and later by Genevieve Knupfer. A parallel series of four national surveys was begun by Cisin at The George Washington University in 1962. The two series of studies were rejoined under the direction of the writer in 1968, and became affiliated with the Behavioral Sciences program within the U.C. School of Public Health at the beginning of 1971. Approximately 50 books, monographs and articles have presented the results of these studies; a detailed bibliography is available from the writer upon request. Representative writings concerning the Bay Area studies are Walter B. Clark, "Operational Definitions of

Drinking Problems and Associated Prevalence Rates," *Quarterly Journal of Studies on Alcohol,* 27: 648–688 (1966); and Genevieve Knupfer, "The Epidemiology of Problem Drinking," *American Journal of Public Health,* 57: 973–986 (1967). Most of the national findings are reported in three books: Don Cahalan, Ira H. Cisin, and Helen M. Crossley, *American Drinking Practices* (New Brunswick, N.J.: Rutgers Center of Alcohol Studies, 1969); Don Cahalan, *Problem Drinkers* (San Francisco: Jossey-Bass, 1970); and Don Cahalan and Robin Room, "Problem Drinking among American Men," Rutgers Center of Alcohol Studies, 1973 (forthcoming).

All of the studies in these series involved personal-interview surveys conforming to strict standards for scientific probability sampling of the adult household population.

[2] Recent national data on the social and economic costs of misuse of alcohol are summarized in *Alcohol and Health,* First Special Report to the U. S. Congress, HEW Publication No. (HSM) 72-9099. California statistics on alcohol misuse are from the *Alcohol Strike Force Plan,* prepared by the Office of Alcohol Program Management, California Human Relations Agency, January 1973.

[3] These national findings on drinking practices are from *American Drinking Practices,* note 1 above.

[4] Our "drinking problems" concepts employ two definitions. Plaut's definition: "Problem drinking is a repetitive use of beverage alcohol causing physical, psychological, or social harm to the drinker or to others." See *Alcohol Problems: A Report to the Nation* (New York: Oxford University Press, 1967), pp. 37–38. Knupfer's more general definition: "a problem—any problem—connected fairly closely with drinking constitutes a drinking problem." See Knupfer, note 1 above, p. 974.

[5] See Cahalan and Room, note 1 above.

[6] Donald C. Pelz and Stanley H. Schuman, "Motivational Factors in Crashes and Violations of Young Drivers," paper presented at the annual meeting of the American Public Health Association, Minneapolis, October 13, 1971.

[7] Don Cahalan and Robin Room, "Problem Drinking Among American Men Aged 21–59," *American Journal of Public Health,* 62:1473–1482 (Nov. 1972).

[8] Genevieve Knupfer, "Ex-Problem Drinkers," in: Merrill Roff, Lee Robins, and Max Pollack, eds., *Life History Research in Psychopathology,* Vol. II (Minneapolis: University of Minnesota Press, 1972), pp. 257–279.

[9] Genevieve Knupfer and Mary Milos, "Mortality of Problem Drinkers," unpublished paper dated August 11, 1971.

[10] See Robin Room, "Drinking Patterns in Large U. S. Cities," *Quarterly Journal of Studies on Alcohol,* Suppl. No. 6, 28–57 (May 1972). The extraneous reasons for San Francisco's high cirrhosis rates are also discussed by Wendell R. Lipscomb and Elaine Sulka, "Some Factors Affecting the Geographic Comparison of Alcoholism Prevalence Rates . . . ," *Quarterly Journal of Studies on Alcohol,* 22: 588–596 (December 1961).

[11] *Alcohol and Health,* note 2 above.

[12] Lee R. Slimmon, "Values Clarification and Affective Education (A Drug and Alcohol Prevention Approach)," unpublished mimeo, undated [1973]; and *Fifth Report: Risk Taking and Drug Abuse,* evaluation of the 1970–71 Coronado drug abuse prevention program (Coronado [Calif.] Board of Education, June 30, 1971).

[13] William H. Glazier, "The Task of Medicine," *Scientific American,* 228 (4): 13–17 (April 1973).

Science, Technology and Policy

Vol. 14   No. 3   June 1973

The Politics of Technological Choice: Some Lessons from the San Francisco Bay Area Rapid Transit District (BART)*

by

Stephen Zwerling

Political Decisions and Expertise

In folklore if not in fact, a democracy's political arena begins with citizens coming together to exercise their power to make choices about public issues. At one time, voters actually could be assembled to discuss and make decisions about their lives, but now communities number millions of persons. Even if it were possible to convene citizens today, it is doubtful whether they can still make informed choices in a new and highly complex technological society. If they are to make decisions, new forms of information must be forthcoming. These forms must comprise not just statistics, but analyses of the consequences of technological change as well.

Under conditions of social complexity, experts, i.e., individuals possessing "knowledge" and "information" assume a relatively greater importance in decision-situations because they are considered capable of understanding complicated technical problems. We have thus been led to believe that technical questions should be answered by technical experts, who are regarded as "neutral" and "objective," and who render judgments (not opinions) on the basis of facts (not feelings).

The character of the political arena has changed. Citizens no longer come together to discuss and make choices about their lives in common but, instead, ratify or reject proposals advanced in the name of "the public interest" and propounded by technical experts rather than by political officials.

* Much of the material in this article is based on a more comprehensive analysis by Stephen Zwerling in "The Political Consequences of Technological Choice: Public Transit in the San Francisco Metropolitan Area" (Ph.D. thesis, University of California, Berkeley, 1972) and will be contained in a forthcoming book to be published by Praeger in late 1973 or early 1974. Zwerling is presently serving as associate coordinator of the Experimental Program in Health Sciences and Medical Education on the Berkeley campus.

But political choices are still, as always, far too important to be left to the experts, on whose proposals the electorate can only vote "yes" or "no." We do need expert advice, but should use it where it is appropriate, i.e., in situations requiring substantial assembly of "facts" and objective data. Most essential decisions, however, are based more on subjective attitudes and preferences ("values") than on facts as such. And where personal feelings are concerned, the expert's opinion carries no more weight than the layman's. In short, experts should help provide background on political decisions, but not formulate them.

Technology: Choices and Consequences

When a choice is made from among a set of alternative technologies, it is thought to be the result of thorough and objective analysis by technically qualified experts. But the very *choice of technology* is itself often value laden and determined in large part by perceptions of the problem-to-be-solved and how best to solve it. Furthermore, the initial selection of a particular technology means that subsequent social and political consequences for the citizens affected by that decision follow predictable paths of development.

The decision to build a rapid transit system in the San Francisco Bay Area is a case in point. The 1962 BART (Bay Area Rapid Transit District) bond election is the largest local bond issue so far approved in the United States, and it provides an excellent example for analyzing the role of experts vis-à-vis the electorate. Americans often assume that decisions on matters such as the establishment of transportation systems are made on technical grounds, not influenced by political considerations. Like experts, technologies (or physical "hardware" systems) are generally regarded as neutral and apolitical.

I contend that BART is an example of technology used to "legislate" the future. Whereas the Bay Area's rapid transit planners may have imagined themselves to be predicting the development of a regional community that would be served by BART, BART appears likely to be a major force in creating the urban patterns the planners of 20 years ago thought they were predicting. Because this means forcing the future to fit a particular pattern of development, the decision to build BART represents a pre-emption of the public interest. In order to see how this came to be, let us examine the conditions under which a Bay Area rapid transit system was proposed, voted on, and built.

Early Planning Efforts

Various proposals for rapid transit planning in the Bay Area have been aired since the turn of the century. But most of the planning activity prior to World War II focused primarily on subway systems for San Franciso's downtown business district. However, the voters of San Francisco evidently did not share the enthusiasm of the City's civic leaders for they voted down a subway proposal in November 1939.

During World War II, San Francisco Congressman Richard J. Welch voiced his concern about the strategic importance of traffic movement to national security, and this prompted the federal government to create an Army-Navy Board in 1946 to study the need for additional Bay crossings. Although the Board did not agree with Welch on the immediate requirement for new facilities, it did recommend a completely integrated rapid transit system with an underwater tube between San Francisco and Oakland. While the implications of that study were not immediately obvious, the context of the discussion on Bay Area rapid transit had undergone a shift of major importance: a *local concern* voiced by local elites had become a *regional concern* supported by national authorities.

The Goal: To Preserve San Francisco's Preeminence

San Francisco's civic leaders were convinced that if nothing were done to prevent it, their city would decay for many of the same reasons that other major American cities were decaying. Expanding networks of high-speed public roadways enabled people to move out of central cities into suburban areas. Furthermore, as low-density suburbs began to emerge, retail business and light industry began to leave the urban core to take advantage of new markets and lower costs. Unless these apparent shifts were arrested, prominent San Franciscans foresaw a decline in the City's status as the cultural and economic "capital" of the West.

These civic leaders were convinced that the basic problem was the inadequate transportation facilities. During peak commute hours, for example, there was growing traffic congestion at the six principal gateways to San Francisco.[1] If the problem of traffic congestion could be solved, one of San Francisco's major problems —the shift of consumer buying patterns away from the

central city and toward the suburbs— would be solved as well.

Given (1) the objective of preserving the status of San Francisco within the region, (2) the understanding that one way to do this was by improving access to the City, and (3) the limitation by topographic constraints to six surface points of entry, the answer seemed obvious to the experts: rail transit. Since these points of entry were subject to periodic blockage, the accepted solution was a high-speed, high-capacity transportation system that could operate on its own exclusive right-of-way. But the impetus for rapid transit seemed to arise not primarily from a concern for better transportation to serve the region but rather from a desire to rejuvenate the downtown retail business and financial districts of San Francisco.

1951: A Study Commission is Formed

In 1949 the California Legislature authorized the various local governments in the San Francisco Bay Area to form a rapid transit district (*Statutes* 1949, Chapter 1239). Although many civic leaders were convinced that rapid transit was necessary, the large number of local jurisdictions to be considered as well as the lack of public consensus on the need for rapid transit made the immediate formation of a rapid transit district impractical.

When it became apparent that such a district would not be created without further study, the legislation was amended, and the San Francisco Bay Area Rapid Transit Commission was established (*Statutes* 1951, Chapter 1760). The 26-member commission was charged with the investigation and study of rapid transit problems in the nine Bay Area counties and with the development of a master, coordinated rapid transit plan.[2]

The commission retained the firm of Parsons, Brinckerhoff, Hall and Macdonald (PBHM) in November 1953. PBHM was a New York-based firm of engineering consultants whose founder was chiefly responsible for the development and construction of New York City's subway system. A broad range of studies was conducted under the aegis of the prime contractor, culminating in a coordinated rapid transit plan submitted to the commission and, in turn, transmitted to the Legislature in early 1956: *Regional Rapid Transit* (*RRT*).[3] That report is the basic source document for rapid transit planning in the Bay Area and merits our close scrutiny. What questions were asked? How were the answers formulated?

---

[1] The aforementioned six major traffic corridors are as follows: trans-Bay, Berkeley hills, Cerrito Creek, San Leandro, Peninsula and Golden Gate.

[2] Alameda, Contra Costa, Marin, Napa, San Francisco, San Mateo, Santa Clara, Solano and Sonoma counties.

[3] *Regional Rapid Transit: A Report to the San Francisco Bay Area Rapid Transit Commission, 1953–55* by Parsons, Brinckerhoff, Hall and Macdonald (Engineers), New York, 1956. Hereinafter this document will be referred to as *RRT*.

14

The Issue Posed: Automobile Congestion vs. Regional Rapid Transit

The commission posed four basic questions for the consultants:

1. Is an interurban rapid transit system needed for the Bay Area?
2. If so, what areas should rapid transit serve and along what routes should it be constructed?
3. What type of rapid transit facility would best meet the Bay Area's needs?
4. Is the cost justified?

The problem was defined by the consultants as automobile congestion. Stating the need for both local and interurban express transportation, the consultants noted that although the Bay Area depended upon mass transit, transit patronage was declining. The basic alternatives facing Bay Area citizens were starkly stated:

> ... whether to accept the stagnation and decline of interurban transit and to prepare for drastic decentralization and repatterning of its urban centers to meet the avalanche of automobiles that will result— or whether to reinvigorate interurban transit so as to sustain the daily flow of workers, shoppers, and visitors on which the vitality of these urban centers depends.
>
> (*RRT*, p. 1)

The conclusion reached by the consultants was that transit must be reinvigorated.

> We on our part are convinced that the prosperity of the entire Bay Area will depend upon the preservation and enhancement of its urban centers and subcenters. Sustaining these as concentrations of employment, commerce, and culture will depend on the reinvigoration of interurban transit.
>
> (*RRT*, p.1)

The consultants then proceeded to develop a comprehensive plan for regional rapid transit, a plan "... fundamentally directed at curing traffic congestion" (*RRT*, p. 1). After describing briefly some of the highlights of the comprehensive plan, the consultants observed that

> ... the ultimate decision on whether or not to provide rapid transit will be a matter of policy; it should rest upon the basic decision of the Bay Area citizens as to the type of region they wish it to be.
>
> (*RRT*, p. 2)

The Bay Area is still young enough for its over-all urban development to be purposefully molded into a desired pattern, according to the long-range needs and aspirations of its people. The decisions made daily by individuals, business firms, and legislative bodies will largely determine what form the urban expansion will take; and among the most critical of these decisions are those concerned with transportion services....

> *It is imperative, therefore, that the design of the rapid transit portion of the transportation system be based upon a recognition of its effects on future urbanization. The plan for future regional development forms the foundation for the design of the rapid transit system.* [emphasis supplied]
>
> (*RRT*, p. 18)

The Preferred Pattern: Centralization and Nucleation

The consultants then addressed alternative patterns of future urban organization, which—tersely stated— were centralization or decentralization of commercial activities.

> An effort can be made to encourage the development of large nucleated, high-intensity business districts in appropriate locations. Or an alternative effort can be made to encourage the dispersion of new business establishments in much smaller districts or in scattered, isolated locations entirely outside business districts. *To a great degree, this choice is a matter of public policy....* The development of nucleated centers and subcenters is possible only if these are served by a high-capacity transportation system integrating freeways and rapid transit. To depend on highways alone is inevitably to choose the alternative of dispersion. [emphasis supplied]
>
> (*RRT*, p. 18)

Because the preferred choice between these two alternative futures was clear to the consultants—nucleated (high density, high-intensity) centers versus dispersion—they did not address other alternatives

The consultants recognized that transit planning should follow rather than precede choices on alternative regional futures. Nevertheless, they did not fully discuss various possible conceptions of regional development. In fact, they took the desired pattern of future development as a given:

> The general concept of the region's future organization is that of a system of centers of varying levels of activity, market size, and specialization.... By providing high speed transit service between residential communities and the concentrated business centers, the maximum degree of choice of living place and working place is opened to the population. Only in this way can the desires of the people to live in low-density, suburban residences be economically accommodated.
>
> (*RRT*, p. 20)

Finally, although the total cost of implementing the comprehensive regional rapid transit plan was to be high ($1.545 billion), the consultants endorsed it without qualification.

The essence of the story is that without rapid transit the region will ultimately pay many times its cost in additional hours of travel time, in the additional cost of trucking goods over highways congested by automobiles, in diminished revenues from property depreciated by congestion or swallowed by automobile facilities, and in the premium costs of urban freeways and parking garages. *We do not doubt that the Bay Area Citizens can afford rapid transit; we question seriously whether they can afford NOT to have it.* [emphasis in original]

(*RRT*, p. 3)

1957: BART—To Build an Interurban Railroad

The task of the commission ended with the submission of its report to the Legislature. In early 1957, Senator John F. McCarthy of Marin County, whose previous efforts on behalf of rapid transit brought forth the commission, sponsored a commission-drafted version of a bill to create a rapid transit district. And, in June 1957, the Legislature created BART.

Regional Rapid Transit (1956) provided the groundwork for the *Composite Report* (CR 1962), the second major document guiding the development of rail rapid transit in the Bay Area.[4] Since Parsons, Brinckerhoff, Hall and Macdonald were involved significantly in both studies, it is not surprising that the studies were based upon the same assumptions. Thus, the 1962 planning report, like the 1956 feasibility study, defined the problem as existing and future automobile congestion.

The continuing increase of highway traffic congestion threatens the future growth and well-being of the San Francisco Bay Area. The central cities of San Francisco and Oakland particularly are vulnerable.

. . . . .

The crux of the Bay Area's congestion problem is the growing use of automobiles and the declining use of public transit, especially during the peak travel hours.

(*CR*, p. 76)

Despite the emphasis on congestion in central cities, however, BART was not intended to be an *urban* transit system but, rather, a *regional* and interurban railroad. As its routes and the wide-apart spacing of its stations demonstrated, "The regional rapid transit system transports people between outlying suburban areas and the central core areas" (*CR*, p. 16). In other words, BART was primarily intended for people who had a choice between the private automobile and public transit.

Although rapid transit was justified in terms of its ability to relieve traffic congestion, the specific benefits of BART—listed in the order they appear in the *Composite Report*—were only secondarily concerned with transportation:

1. preserve and enhance urban centers and subcenters;
2. increase property values;
3. help to prevent disorganized urban sprawl;
4. improve employment conditions because transit will attract industry;
5. improve access to social, cultural, and recreational opportunities;
6. increase efficiency of transportation expenditures because transit will reduce the requirements for additional automobile-related facilities; and
7. provide low-cost transportation.

(*CR*, pp. 82–83)

This list of benefits suggests that BART was to be a tool for shaping the future growth of the region instead of a way of relieving urban traffic congestion.

"The Politics of Professionalism"

Because the proponents of regional rapid transit had spoken mainly in terms of a fixed-rail system, it seemed only natural to retain as consultants a firm with an established reputation in that field. Thus, it is not surprising that these consultants recommended a rail system. Furthermore, no alternative type of transportation system was evaluated. Accordingly, it appears that the consulting engineers were selected more to design, merchandise, and implement a particular type of transit system than to discover what future pattern of development was desired by the citizens of the region and then to design a transit system best suited to meet those expressed desires.

The consulting engineers explicitly recognized that the selection of a particular type of transportation system was contingent upon regional objectives. Therefore, their role in promoting BART raises some interesting questions about the "politics of professionalism," or what it means to be an expert. By rendering a technical judgment about a transportation system designed to facilitate what *they* understood to be the most desirable pattern of regional development and growth, the technical experts acted politically to predetermine what was "in the public interest." Not only were they fully aware that the selection of a transportation system was not the primary question, but—*as transportation engineers*—they made a judgment about land-use objectives, a field in which they had little or no claim to knowledge.

Unquestionably, BART was presented to the voters as a remedy for transportation ills, and it seems reasonable to assume that the voters and taxpayers understood BART in terms of alleged transportation benefits.

---

[4] *The Composite Report: Bay Area Rapid Transit, May 1962,* by Parsons Brinckerhoff-Tudor-Bechtel et al. (San Francisco: 1962). Hereinafter this document will be referred to as *CR*.

But the studies themselves, as well as other evidence, suggest that transportation benefits (e.g., relief of congestion) were of secondary importance. Instead the promoters and planners of BART understood their mission mainly in terms of economic benefits; revitalizing the downtown business districts.

If relief of congestion had been a primary concern, the transportation planners would have given careful attention to the needs for first-rate feeder bus service so that transit riders could reach their destinations without resort to automobiles. Yet the feeder-service issue was not regarded as a problem, and was thus virtually ignored. Furthermore, the pro-high-rise implications of BART's construction were never made explicit in the public discussion, although this consideration was uppermost in the minds of many proponents.[5]

While calling attention to the "hidden agenda" of the Bay Area's rapid transit enthusiasts, I do not mean to suggest that this phenomenon is unique to BART. Indeed, America's transportation history is replete with such examples. California's freeway system, for example, was also sold on a partial basis. Moreover, the U.S. Interstate Highway System, the largest public works project in American history, was publicly advocated for defense purposes while actually being intended to stabilize the postwar economy, to give jobs to contractors, and to help truckers profit from long freight hauls. Thus, BART followed a long-established tradition.

Some Lessons from BART

The BART experience is therefore generally instructive about the relationships among planning, tech-

nology, and politics. With respect to planning, I contend that the studies upon which the BART system was founded lacked substance and penetration. The consultants accepted their clients' definition and diagnosis of "the problem." Thereupon, the consultants created a huge analytic apparatus to justify the conclusions that both they and their clients had already reached, i.e., that an interurban rail system should be built. Accordingly, no other alternatives were explored.

Admittedly, *within the boundaries of the task as defined,* the work done was creditable; it is rather that the boundaries were not valid. The major effects of the BART system will be external: shaping the future of the region. Yet there was little analysis of these consequences. Moreover, the citizens were sold on BART for one purpose (congestion relief) while the principal instigators had another purpose in mind (shaping the development of the region for the economic gain of the downtown areas).[6]

Social planners bear a heavy burden of responsibility to ensure that affected citizens are well informed about the broader social, political, and economic ramifications of plans put forth for public ratification. The promoters of rapid transit presented their proposal to the public in such a circumscribed manner as to suggest that there were no such ramifications. The voting public was persuaded that it was being given the opportunity to improve public transit in the Bay Area, but it was not also educated to the fact that, in addition, it was being asked to approve a particular pattern of development for the region. These narrowly technical factors appropriate to engineering decisions were not sufficient for the consideration of BART, a decision with significant political components.

Furthermore, with respect to providing transportation facilities, the dynamic complexity of large metropolitan centers suggests that demand for services changes continually. Thus, in a very real sense, the transportation "problem" cannot be resolved; for no matter how much *know-how* we may acquire in providing transit systems, we lack the *know-what* regarding future transportation requirements. Accordingly the "problem" is not a question to be answered in any final way but, rather, a continuing, evolving situation to be dealt with—democratically, if possible, given our political norms and heritage.

Viewed in this perspective, a transportation system that cannot adapt itself to the changing demands for service would seem singularly inappropriate. Indeed, insofar as it cannot accommodate shifting requirements

[5] Some revealing comments to this effect appear in an article by Burton H. Wolfe (San Francisco *Bay Guardian*, 2, 11 [June 18, 1968]). Roger Lapham, Jr., son of a former Mayor of San Francisco, president of an insurance brokerage firm and early member of the BARTD Board of Directors was quite frank in admitting to Wolfe that "The end result of BARTD is that San Francisco will be just like Manhattan." When Wolfe asked former BARTD President Adrien Falk whether he thought it desirable for San Francisco to become like Manhattan, Falk replied, "It's not a question of whether it's desirable. It's the only practical way. Certain finance, banking industries want to be centralized, want to have everyone near each other. They don't want to have to go one day to Oakland, the next day to San Jose, the next day to San Francisco." It appeared to Wolfe that Falk was speaking in terms of the needs of the business community rather than the citizens. Was it desirable to create a city of huge skyscrapers with a subway system to serve them, like Manhattan? Lapham answered that "It's not a question of whether it's desirable, but what's the practical matter. As a practical matter, you can't have 18 different banking and insurance centers. You have to concentrate them with all the various services around them. The people who run these centers want all their services, the people they work with—advertisers, attorneys, accountants—around them. It's a complete part of the way we do business in this country." But, asked Wolfe, what if some San Franciscans don't want their city converted into a Manhattan? "Then let 'em go someplace else," Lapham replied. "But don't keep complaining about it, because that's what is *going* to happen, and nobody can stop it."

[6] In a recent public address, L. A. Kimball, Assistant General Manager—Administration for BART, stated that the primary purpose to be served by rapid transit was shaping the future growth and development of the Bay Area. During the subsequent question period, Kimball affirmed that conclusion. (Meeting of the Bay Area Chapter, American Society for Public Administration, March 8, 1973.)

for travel, BART's fixed rail technology would seem to be an attempt to *create*, rather than to serve, the future. Because of its enormous capital requirements in the development of a rigid and inflexible system, BART stands as an example of legislating the future through technology; of constraining, if not enforcing, social choices; of pre-empting the public interest.

The development of technologies is a legitimate enterprise in our culture. Technocracy—or rule by technology—is not a legitimate enterprise in our culture, since it tends to corrode the democratic process. BART is a product of both technology and technocracy. *The issue is not whether the job of building BART was done in a technically competent manner; only time will tell. The issue is whether the prior job, deciding to build BART, was done in a politically responsible manner.* I believe it was not.

The BART experience also raises some important questions about politics and the public interest. Obviously, the general public rarely, if ever, possesses the information required to render an informed judgment on proposed technological investments. Voters are frequently asked to rely on the opinions of experts who are alleged to have made a thorough and impartial analysis. But as the BART experience has shown, in the absence of such an analysis and reporting, public interest issues such as the future of the Bay Area are in grave danger of being determined on the basis of what is technically feasible rather than on what may be politically desirable.

Impact Statements: Toward an Exploration and Clarification of Consequences

If democratic values are worth preserving—and I think they are—what is required to safeguard political liberty is a process of technology assessment in the public interest. This could be a functional equivalent of the environmental impact statements required by the National Environmental Policy Act of 1969. The public should receive similar protection—a socio-political impact analysis—with respect to any proposal for investing in large-scale, complex technologies.

The purpose of a socio-political impact statement would be to explore and report the probable consequences of the proposed investment. It would help voters to understand the social and political values that would be served by the proposed investment, and those that would not be served. It would not be a statement for or against any particular technology. Instead it would be a report to the public about important indirect consequences of proposed investments in a technology.

The proposed socio-political impact analysis is neither a panacea nor a substitute for involved citizen participation in public affairs.[7] But, as the BART experience has shown, technology can be used to legislate the future without full public consideration and/or disclosure of the consequences of that "legislative" act. If we regard this as undesirable, and if we wish to guard against this eventuality, careful analysis and public review of probable effects of proposed actions are essential.

I conclude by pointing to the emphasis on *process* that is so persistent in our political heritage. From the founding fathers onward, the thrust of American democracy has been to allow for changing conceptions of what is in the public interest. Thus, while we may not be able to know precisely what our *substantive* preferences for the future are, we should be careful to insure ourselves *the opportunity* of making such choices. We presently lack adequate processes for exploring the policy implications of technology and technological change. The concept of socio-political impact studies, prepared in the public interest, may be a step in the right direction.

---

[7] A recent article suggests that simply requiring an assessment of consequences is not enough, at least not where the Federal Highway Administration is concerned. In an effort to learn more about the implementation of the National Environmental Policy Act (NEPA), James B. Sullivan and Paul A. Montgomery analyzed 76 final-draft impact statements required for proposed urban highway projects ("Surveying Highway Impact," *Environment*, 14 (9):12–20 [November 1972]). Their carefully documented findings are not encouraging: "The impact statements surveyed contain arguments rather than findings, opinions rather than studies, and generalities rather than facts."

Science, Technology and Policy

Vol. 14   No. 4   August 1973

The Utility of Public Utilities:
Desalination and Local Government in
Coastal California*

K. N. Lee

Assistant Research Social Scientist,
Institute of Governmental Studies and
Institute of International Studies

There are some goods and services we call "public utilities." We use them routinely, we pay for them willingly, but by and large we are hardly aware of them. Electricity, gas, and water come readily to mind as examples. Recently, however, we have been threatened with an "energy crisis," caught up in "runaway growth," asked to consider the "quality of life." What have such words to do with everyday life? They signal the emergence of public utilities as major problems of public policy.

As the names of these issues suggest, many have gained prominence in the so-called "environmental crisis." The fight against pollution has altered the rules of governmental choice. New criteria have been added to the existing emphasis on low cost, service (widely or fairly distributed), and efficiency. But the issues range beyond ecology and the need to repair a damaged environment. These concerns are part of a growing public awareness that adopting technological innovations—even in something as mundane as a water purification plant—can have surprising and sometimes unpleasant social consequences. Public utilities are

major technological investments. Can we develop an alertness to their social implications? That is the question to be explored here.

The Diablo Canyon Case

A recent case provides a concrete setting for discussion. In 1971 officials of the federal and state governments announced a proposal to build the world's largest desalting facility on the central California coast, at Diablo Canyon. Residents of San Luis Obispo and Santa Barbara counties who would have received—and partly paid for—the fresh water produced by the plant, debated its merits during the electoral campaigns of 1972. As that discussion moved toward a conclusion, federal officials shelved the proposal, in part because of local opposition. But even though the Diablo Canyon desalting facility will not be built, the story of its emergence as a public issue sheds valuable light on how technology can become a political problem.

The response to the desalting plant was not only political, it was institutional as well. The plight of the town of Goleta, a suburb of the city of Santa Barbara, and site of a University of California campus, exemplified this aspect of the problem. The analysis of Goleta and its water problems, in turn, will lead to some observations on the hazards and opportunities presented by technologies licensed or operated by public bodies, and to some suggestions for coping with those hazards and capitalizing on those opportunities.

The Need for Water

On the average, Americans consume about 100 gallons of fresh water per person each day. A small fraction is used directly for drinking and cooking, but most goes for bathing, laundry, and sanitary uses. In addition, industrial processes require large quantities of water, though not all of it needs to be pure enough to drink. Resource engineers who design reservoirs and aqueducts usually describe water supplies in terms of "acre-feet." An acre-foot is the amount of water needed to cover an acre of land to a depth of one foot. An average family of four consumes about one

* This *Report* is based on a study for which Professor Todd R. La Porte was Principal Investigator and Kai Lee was Co-Principal Investigator; Lee's co-authors were U. C. students Diane L. Fernandez, Leland D. Hodges, and Charles Slayman. The study is *Water, Growth and Politics in Central California: The Diablo Canyon Desalting Facility*, Working Paper #5 (Berkeley: Institute of Governmental Studies, University of California, 1972). During the period of research, Lee was a research training fellow of the Social Science Research Council, 1971–1972. Additional support for the study was provided by the Water Resources Center of the University of California.

The full report is scheduled for publication by Praeger under the title, "Public Participation in the Use of Technology—The Diablo Canyon Desalting Facility in California."

acre-foot a year. A population of 10,000 persons—the central coast of California has *grown* this much *each year* in the last decade—consumes annually a "body" of water 10 feet deep and three-quarters of a mile in diameter. Because reservoirs do not fill up in a year, the actual size of a reservoir must be 10 to 20 times its annual yield. Water resource management is big business.

Santa Barbara County is already short of water. The shortage has reached crisis proportions in suburban Goleta, which has tripled in population in the last ten years. Water shortages mean the end of the meteoric growth of the 1960's. Without more water there can be no net increase in homes, or in businesses that provide jobs.

The shortfall in San Luis Obispo and Santa Barbara counties is projected to be 36,000 acre-feet per year by 1990. Acting to prevent a growth-choking shortage, the governments of the two counties arranged during the 1960's to buy water from the State Water Project, the massive aqueduct bringing water from Northern California to the arid Los Angeles basin. State Project water would be pumped through the coastal mountains in expensive new tunnels. Engineering studies indicate that this supplemental water would cost twice as much as the existing supplies.

Proposal for a Desalting Plant

It was against this backdrop that federal and state officials proposed in 1971 to build a desalting plant at Diablo Canyon. The Pacific Gas and Electric Company is currently building a pair of nuclear reactors in the canyon to generate electricity by the late 1970's. Nuclear reactors produce a great deal of waste heat as a by-product, hence the power plant's location near the cold waters of the Pacific Ocean. The desalting proposal, authored by the U.S. Office of Saline Water and the California Department of Water Resources, envisaged a large-scale plant using part of the nuclear power station's waste heat to purify seawater.

Although the idea of obtaining fresh water from the ocean is an old one, the technological problems have been hard to overcome. One of the main difficulties is corrosion of the desalting equipment. Sea salt is a powerful oxidant, a fact graphically demonstrated by the rapid rusting of cars in seaside towns. Nonetheless, in recent years substantial progress has been made. In the judgment of federal engineers, the time had come to try out in a new full-scale facility designs already tested in pilot plants. Such a demonstration plant would provide a valuable learning opportunity for water-resource engineers. In addition, its successful operation would be an eye-catching sign of progress to agencies all over the world that spend public money on water supply problems.

With a peak capacity of 40 million gallons per day of fresh water, the Diablo Canyon plant would have had an average output of 36,000 acre-feet per year, just matching the projected needs of the two-county service area. Federal and state agencies promised to put up $136 million in direct subsidies to pay for the plant, for part of the piping needed to distribute the water, and for part of the plant's operating costs as well. The operating subsidy was set with an eye on the counties' plans for eventual connection to the State Water Project. Thus for the first ten years of Diablo Canyon's operation, the price support would make desalted water equal in price to State Project water. By the end of that period, presumably, the link to the State Project aqueduct would be in place. Santa Barbara County would pay for part of the water pumping network: a $27 million segment that would also be needed if the county is to draw water from the State Water Project. Since this part of the system would have lasted far longer than the remainder of the desalting experiment, it seemed fair to ask county residents to pay. All in all, the proposal looked good. The counties would pay no more than they would have had to pay anyway, and the engineers stood to gain useful experience in learning how to run a full-scale desalting plant.

Environmental Opposition

From the first, however, not everyone considered the plant a good idea, and the opposition included many who could not be dismissed as mere soreheads. Interestingly, most critics did not attack the desalting proposal itself, but concentrated instead on its social implications and hidden meanings. Apparently, the designers fell short in not seeing the full social context of the plant.

The most vociferous opposition came from an environmental group called the Scenic Shoreline Preservation Conference, Inc. SSPC fought the nuclear power plant in Diablo Canyon through a protracted series of court suits. Noting that the electricity from the power station was destined for users in the Central Valley 100 miles to the east, SSPC charged that the desalting plant was a sop, a device to make it appear that the nuclear plant was actually contributing to the welfare of its immediate neighbors. Although SSPC lost the battle over the power plant, it won the war: in November 1972 the voters of Santa Barbara and San Luis Obispo counties both gave resounding support to California Proposition 20, a citizen-originated intiative requiring close scrutiny of future coastline development plans. The initiative passed handily.

The Growth Issue

The plant's large size and high cost would also be a strong incentive for substantial population growth.

The design of the desalting plant was based upon analyses used in State Project water negotiations that were conducted when growth seemed desirable. In recent years, however, with the coming of smog and sprawl, continued expansion has seemed less and less appealing to Santa Barbara's upper and middle class residents. They already enjoy a blend of artistic, business, and cultural advantages characteristic of the urban environment, with few of the problems of megalopolis. Still, with civic leaders to whom growth has traditionally meant prosperity and an expanded tax base, change has been slow. But the anti-growth forces appear to be gaining around.

"Outside" Benefits

To engineers in state and federal agencies, however, Diablo Canyon would obviously have been a good thing. The benefits to be gained outside the local area were of overriding importance to them. Several factors were involved. First, desalination will open up a source that someday may provide much of the world's fresh water. Given the political and economic importance of many of the desert nations of the world, including the oil-rich Arab states, American successes in developing desalting technology would give the United States a valuable advantage in international technical assistance. Second, the term "desalting" actually describes a whole family of methods for decontaminating water. This is clearly a task that will have to be performed on a large scale if the nation's polluted rivers and streams are to be made clean again. Third, the Diablo Canyon plant would have given engineers in the state Department of Water Resources time for further planning to prepare for the extension of the State Water Project into the two-county area. Finally, state and federal engineers who have devoted so much effort to supplying water to the dry Southwest have an understandable enthusiasm for desalting research in general.

1972 Campaigns

These divergent views landed squarely in the laps of local government officials and office holders. Throughout most of the controversy, public officials held to their original stands favoring the plant. To most officials, future water shortages are virtually inevitable unless supplemental water is provided. Their principal worry was that, at the end of the ten-year subsidy, the need for water might be so great that the desalting plant would have to be kept in operation, even though water prices would then sky-rocket.

But if the incumbents continued to be stolidly pragmatic, those campaigning to unseat them had more vivid visions to dangle before the electorate. The issue of galloping growth had surfaced. Candidates in both counties ran on promises to tame the rapid suburbanization of the landscape, and they did surprisingly well.

Of the six county supervisorial seats being contested, two were won by incumbent supervisors who favored continued development, though cautiously. The other four races were swept by the anti-growth forces. Moreover, notwithstanding the Nixon landslide, both counties helped to pass a number of environmental initiatives, including the statewide coastline measure mentioned earlier. The desalting plant began to look less like a winner, though definitive county action on the project lay some time in the future.

Impounding the Opportunity

Then, late in 1972, the federal Office of Saline Water reported to Congress that a desalting plant should not now be built at Diablo Canyon. The recommendation seemed to have been based on a number of recent developments. First, a plant quite similar to the Diablo Canyon facility has been proposed for a site in Hong Kong. It is expected to yield equivalent learning benefits to the world engineering community. Second, the plant may have been a victim of the administration's efforts to hold the line on federal spending. Even though the plant was not canceled outright by budget-cutters, the rapidly changing priorities for large federal projects suggested caution. Third, the political payoff of a major desalting experiment would be much greater if the plant were sited elsewhere. The most attractive alternative is the lower Colorado River, near the Mexican border. There, the purified water could be pumped across the border to be used by Mexican farmers. For years the diversion of Colorado River water westward to Southern California has deprived local Mexican agriculture of badly needed irrigation supplies. Even worse, the diminished flow of fresh water in the river has permitted salt water to back up into the river valley, poisoning some of the fields. With a large desalting plant this long-standing injustice could be remedied, at least in part. In addition, there would be none of the opposition that has been mobilized in California.

What Does It Mean?

Was this, then, a victory for the environmentalists? If so, who won and what did they win? The water shortage is still present, and the State Water Project is now the only water source that is taken seriously as a policy alternative. Others, such as increased recycling of waste water or more efficient use of the existing supplies, are either insignificant in quantity or else too difficult to implement at the county level. The growth issue, too, remains unresolved, though public discussion of how to enforce and clarify zoning regulations proceeds apace.

The social meaning of the Diablo Canyon proposal remains unclear. The federal decision to shelve the project ended the possibility of the plant's construction.

But it did not tell us what opportunity was thereby missed, or what liability avoided. It is to this interpretation that we turn next.

"Capacity" and "Implementation"

Before beginning that interpretation, however, it will be helpful to explore briefly what we mean by the word "technology." Often we take the word to mean machines of some kind, but there is more to it than that. A technology is also a way of doing something—and often doing *more* than we are initially aware of. Thus, a car serves to move people from place to place, but it also emits air pollutants. Automobile technology, we may say, is made up of a number of *technical capacities;* the *primary* capacity is transportation of people and goods; one of several *secondary* capacities is air pollution. Thinking about a technology as a bundle of capacities enables us to talk about what people mainly use it for (moving around), and what they do unintentionally when employing the technology (pollute the air).

There is more to technology than capacities, however. In order to cut down air pollution, the federal government now requires the installation of emission control devices in new cars. This raises the price of a new auto, so that some people who could afford a new car last year can no longer afford one now. That is, the federal regulations serve to *distribute* the capacities of automobiles differently. We may say: the *implementation* of the technology—the way the capacities are distributed spatially, economically, and socially—has been altered. Such changes, as the example shows, can have unanticipated social effects.

Possible Effects of the Desalting Plant

The primary capacity of the Diablo Canyon plant would, of course, have been the production of fresh water. One of its secondary capacities would have been to use some of the waste heat from the neighboring nuclear power plant. Less desirably, the desalting plant would have altered the pattern of land use on its small part of the California coast.

Nonetheless, the impact of the Diablo Canyon plant on its natural surroundings would have been relatively slight. Far more consequential, potentially, would have been its effects on the *social* environment. The plant would have become a major source of water in the two-county region. Financing the Santa Barbara portion of the pumping system—part of the implementation—would have significantly increased that county's tax burden. This in itself would have encouraged further growth, in a quest for revenue to pay for the system without raising property tax rates.

More subtly, all the users in the service area would have come to depend on a single large source of water,

and this might eventually have led to some unpleasant surprises. In the past, when the population was smaller and more dispersed, each community's water supply was independent of others in the area. Even though all depended upon adequate rainfall, no one worried about how much water a neighboring town would consume. With a single source supplying a large fraction of the region's needs, towns would start to affect one another in new ways: a sudden population surge in one place, for example, could have led to a water shortage elsewhere.

Thus both in administering the distribution of water and in arranging to pay for it, local government officials would have had their choices altered by the desalting plant. Both the instances cited here would have encouraged important and controversial possibilities: growth would have been made attractive by the economics of the desalting system, and interdependence of communities in the area would have been increased. From the decision-makers' point of view, the flexibility to shape the social evolution of the coastal counties would have been significantly altered.

The Goleta Story

The inflexibilities and possibilities of the desalting plant are also related to the existing structure of water delivery. Water is distributed in California through water districts and related public agencies that purchase fresh water and deliver it to residential and industrial consumers in a geographically defined area. A look at one such agency, the Goleta County Water District, provides a clear case history of how the technology of water acquires social and political meaning.

The Goleta district is governed by a board of five water commissioners elected by district residents. During the past decade of explosive growth the commissioners have been preoccupied with the problem of securing enough water to supply the burgeoning population. Accurate predictions of water shortages are virtually impossible in regions such as Goleta, because the major population changes are caused by migration. As a result, the time available to plan new supplies may be insufficient, and often is.

Some short-term water shortages might be smoothed out by sales of water across district boundaries, and to some extent this does happen. But by and large surpluses that develop tend to go unused while shortages go unfilled. Furthermore water sales are hampered by restricted information flow, the inevitable result of poor coordination among water districts. During the summer of 1972 the Goleta district water engineer ordered water mining. This means that more water was drawn than will be replaced by a normal year's rainfall. Mining thus uses up future resources to meet present demands, a desperate step.

The severe shortage in Goleta was partly the product of an extended drought, but by far the greatest cause was the inadequate organization of water use in Santa Barbara County. In the late 1940's the county built the Cachuma Dam on the Santa Ynez River in the northern part of the region. The water districts in the county signed contracts to take portions of the dam's annual yield. But growth was slower than had been projected in most water districts, and for many years the allotments were not fully utilized.

Goleta boomed, however, and it became the first district to use its allotment to capacity, early in the 1960's. Since then, the Goleta district had purchased parts of the allotments of neighboring districts. By 1970, however, the rest of the county had grown to the point that the surpluses were no longer available. Goleta was suddenly thrown into a crisis, with less water than it had for a number of years. Rapid growth, with its unpredictable demands, had combined with poor information exchange between water districts to produce an emergency. The real difficulty was communication and administration; water shortage was only a symptom.

Water and Politics

Would the Diablo Canyon facility have helped matters? The answer is probably "no," for the desalting plant would have provided water and little else. Although the Goleta district is desperate for water, a permanent, large addition to the county's water supplies would have been at best a mixed blessing. The desalting plant would have permitted the water agencies to delay further a major overhaul of their already antiquated procedures for disbursing water. The next water shortage—which might well have come with the phasing out of the state subsidy for the plant's operation— would have had repercussions felt in most of the county, not just in one district.

Further, once the desalting plant became identified with growth, it was swept up in political debate. The project had acquired a social meaning, and it was no longer just an exotic technical experiment. To be sure, the emergence of political conflict in the normally quiet area of water resources depended in a crucial way on the emergence of an environmental awareness. But once a consciousness of suburban sprawl developed, the role of the water commissioners changed from public officials whose principal concern was efficient public service, to advocates for specific points of view and policies regarding growth.

In November 1971 three new commissioners were elected to the Goleta water board. During the campaign all three had taken firm stands against growth, though none had presented concrete proposals to use water policy to limit development. Before they could

wield their majority power, however, one of the three was transferred to a new job outside California. The new three-out-of-five majority against growth was reduced to a two-all deadlock. Growth had become so controversial politically that the two senior commissioners, who were more inclined toward expansion, formed an effective coalition against the newcomers. (The water district can appoint members to fill vacancies, but since the fifth member would have had the decisive vote on growth, neither side would accept the other's candidates.) Finally, a pro-growth commissioner was appointed by the county board of supervisors, which at that time favored continued development. In the months of conflict and inaction, however, administrative damage had already been done. The district water engineer resigned, and the problems of water shortage are now being handled without a professional hydraulic engineer.

Diablo Canyon: An Opportunity Missed?

The analysis to this point simply confirms a trend observed repeatedly in the environmental struggles of the late sixties and early seventies. A large public investment becomes the occasion for a loud, sometimes bitter political conflict. The project, though planned in good faith to serve the public interest, is suddenly alleged to be a conspiracy against Nature. Alternative courses of action are proposed, often amounting to abandoning the project in question, and on all sides one hears calls for "rational" planning. Such claims, of course, obscure the conflict over the *ends* sought (growth or stabilization) by concentrating on *means* (such as water policy) whose merits are supposedly open to objective evaluation. But if one plan is rational, in the sense of achieving its goals in an efficient or effective manner, that does not imply that other plans are irrational. They may simply serve different goals. Arguing over goals, the process of politics, is thus necessary as an integral part of formulating a workable plan. It makes sense, then, to ask whether the discussion of Diablo Canyon could have been framed to encourage the necessary debate over ends. More concretely, could the threat of unwanted growth have become an opportunity to use the Diablo Canyon plant as a creative element in the evolution of coastal California? The pursuit of such brighter possibilities brings us back to the technical details.

The conceptual design of the Diablo Canyon plant called for twin desalting modules, each producing 20 million gallons of fresh water a day. As noted above, the nuclear power station providing the energy for the desalting facility is built as a pair of reactors. Each desalting module would be powered by one reactor. The important point is that each of the 20 million gallon desalting units would by itself have provided a useful engineering experiment. (Note, by comparison, that the largest single module now in operation produces only 6 million gallons per day.) The twin-module design was chosen primarily to meet the projected water needs of the two-county area, and those needs are now in dispute.

Advantages of a Smaller Plant

Therefore, on both technical and social grounds, a single 20 million gallon module would have been worth thinking about. A single module would have alleviated the existing shortages, and it would have provided a cushion for moderate growth. It would also have cost less than the full 40 million gallon plant. Conceivably, the resources saved by building only "half" the plant could be used to encourage governmental and political work on stabilizing population and economic development. If well spent, such resources could have stimulated an open and reasoned appraisal of the problems of nongrowing societies, an appraisal that could easily be of national importance.

Indeed, some of the money saved on the full-size plant could have been used to pay for design work to make the plant more flexible. The single module, for example, could have been designed to permit the addition of further modules at minimal capital expense. Then, if growth had again become an accepted community goal an inexpensive source of water would be at hand. Contrariwise, the aqueduct carrying the desalted water could have been rerouted to discourage future links to the State Water Project. Such a change would have helped limit future growth. This kind of flexibility, in turn, could make it much easier to adjust to the necessities of an uncertain future.

A Different Style

The possibilities are manifold, for what was plausibly within reach at Diablo Canyon was a rethinking of the style of governmental cooperation. The counties could have helped increase the technical learning opportunities of state and federal engineers in exchange for increased social and political flexibility regarding growth policies.

Such an approach would not have been without its costs, to be sure. In proportion, the smaller plant would be considerably more expensive than the design proposed. A 20-million-gallon-per-day plant would cost well over half the $136 million in federal and state funds originally offered. The size of the state and federal contribution, however, could have been adjusted by changing the price charged for desalted water. A higher price, established by a service contract between county water agencies and state and federal engineers, would help control growth. Further, stabilizing water needs would bring indirect savings, because a smaller

population would require reduced expenditures for welfare, public libraries, swimming pools and other social services and facilities.

It is important to stress, however, that the scenario sketched here is not a recommendation for a smaller desalting plant. At most one might suggest that the plant could have been used as an occasion for flexibility and cooperation, rather than conflict. A workable consensus opposing growth may not even exist, and the economics, the engineering, and the politics of a smaller plant have not been closely studied. Both opponents and proponents of Diablo Canyon tended to assume, however, that the plant represented a stop-or-go decision about growth in the area, and no further possibilities were recognized.

Some Lessons: The Intelligent Use of Technology

The Diablo Canyon experience reminds us of some important lessons:

1) Large-scale technological investment, even in mundane projects, is socially meaningful. Designers of public projects cannot restrict themselves to engineering. *Any* technological implementation has values and policy implications, hidden or otherwise. To ignore them invites political protest.

2) The preservation of social flexibility is essential if meaningful planning is to be possible at the local government level. By encouraging the development of different kinds of social and technical patterns of use and dependence, however, large-scale technologies shape the opportunities for governmental action and regulation. Sometimes options are foreclosed in areas that appear remote indeed from the specific project at hand. Who would have thought a desalting plant would have become involved in a struggle over growth?

3) Sometimes a major technological investment can be an opportunity to control an uncertain future. If the Diablo Canyon plant had been built, further growth would have been strongly encouraged. But uncertainty is an opportunity as well as a threat. It is vital to ask whose flexibility is being diminished and whose options are being foreclosed.

Technology as Legislation: Default and Muddling Through

Finally, there is a conceptual lesson here. In recent years, as technology has become increasingly controversial, a teapot tempest has arisen over whether technologies are inherently good or bad, or whether they are instead ethically neutral. The case of Diablo Canyon shows us that this argument is pointless. For it assumes that the choice of technology relates only to the primary *capacity:* fresh water, in the instance of the desalting plant. While the decision on the plant can be framed in terms of whether to install a new water supply, it can also include questions of how much water should be added to existing supplies and where it should be added. In other words *implementation* is also a crucial dimension in the choice of technology.

But assessment of implementation is a difficult task. One needs data on present patterns of use, and a theory describing the probable consequences of supplying more water in particular places. The data are few and the theory, nonexistent. So designers muddle through, basing decisions on such tenuous principles as subsidizing water to meet the price of the cheapest available alternative, the State Water Project in the present instance.

Muddling through gets the job done, but the process is shot through with value presumptions. The harried administrator decides, half-consciously, what he can safely ignore, what kinds of judgments he will not need to defend; and each time he is presuming, on little or no evidence, that some set of values does not count. In these circumstances, it does not matter whether the technical capacity is "inherently" good or bad. Both the good and the bad have been distributed in specific ways, ways that affect people's lives.

The fact remains that we have few means of comparing, let alone evaluating, alternative implementations of a new technology. Implementation is often seen as a purely technical feature of design, made up of boring details to be handled by engineering firms for pay, not by politicians for power or glory. So no one pays much attention—and the value choices are made by default, a by-product of muddling through.

A conveyance system is built to carry water from the desalting plant, but it also favors later commitment to the State Water Project. Water to relieve a critical shortage is delivered, but at a price that drives out agricultural use and encourages residential development. Thus technology becomes legislation, channeling the activities of the users it was supposed to serve.

The smooth operation of a public utility permits us to forget or to ignore responsibilities that we would otherwise have to attend to. If a public utility is a way of forgetting, however, we also need politics as a way of remembering. Public choices are, in the end, our choices and our responsibilities. Accordingly, the challenge to local governments does not lie in seeking ways to make public services forgettable again, but in finding ways to help the citizenry remember—and learn about—our mutual obligations. Utilities provide more than creature comforts; they can be, and are, instruments of social policy. Conversely, utilities have widespread, often surprising social consequences. We ignore these at our peril. Such realities should be more than sobering: they should also serve to enhance and to reinforce our sense of the *utility* of public utilities.

SELECTED BIBLIOGRAPHY

The issues discussed here are part of a larger set of concerns. A readable introduction to the problem of technological change as a social force may be found in Heilbroner. The theoretical framework I have used here is described more fully in the two essays by La Porte. An informative set of readings about the assessment of technology may be found in Teich, and a contrasting view of the dynamics of government is entertainingly put forth by Wildavsky.

Heilbroner, Robert L. *The Limits of American Capitalism* (New York: Harper Torchbooks, 1965). See esp. Part II.

La Porte, Todd R. (Principal Investigator). *Social Change, Public Response, and Regulation of Large-Scale Technology.* Progress Report (Berkeley: Institute of Governmental Studies, University of California, 1972). See esp. Chapter 1.

_____ . "The Context of Technology Assessment: A Changing Perspective for Public Organizations." *Public Administration Review,* 31:63–73 (1971).

Teich, Albert H., ed. *Technology and Man's Future* (New York: St. Martin's, 1972).

Wildavsky, Aaron B. *The Revolt Against the Masses* (New York: Basic Books, 1971). See esp. "Toward a Radical Incrementalism," and "A Strategy for Political Participation."

Public Finance

Vol. 14   No. 5   October 1973

Public Expenditure Analysis: Some Current Issues

by

Leonard Merewitz
School of Business Administration
University of California, Berkeley

and

Stephen H. Sosnick
Department of Agricultural Economics
University of California, Davis

Introduction

We have all heard recently of the struggle between the President and the Congress over who has the ultimate right to decide whether funds authorized and appropriated by Congress will be spent. In addition, we have come to understand that the aggregate level of federal spending has a major impact on the level of employment and the rate of price inflation. Less well known are the techniques by which either branch of government decides when a particular project should be funded, or whether a combination of programs is working effectively and efficiently. What, besides rhetoric, determines budgetary decisions at the federal and at the state level?

Public administrators now have some techniques other than simple budgets for organizing thinking about public spending. In the past decade the technique of Planning-Programming-Budgeting has become popular for the systematic evaluation of the worth of public expenditures. This paper attempts to explain some basic concepts in nontechnical language. (For a more complete analysis, see Merewitz and Sosnick, *The Budget's New Clothes: A Critique of Planning-Programming-Budgeting and Benefit-cost Analysis* (Chicago: Markham, 1971).)

Planning-Programming-Budgeting

In the 1960's, Planning-Programming-Budgeting (PPB), a way of describing, proposing, and defending expenditures, took the country by storm. The action began in 1961, when Charles J. Hitch became the Assistant Secretary of Defense. In 1965, President Lyndon Johnson ordered all agencies of the federal government to adopt PPB; in 1966 Governor Edmund G. (Pat) Brown did the same for California, and at least 14 other states and uncounted numbers of counties, cities, and school districts have followed. The political party in power seems to have made no difference. Both Johnson and Brown were Democrats, but their Republican successors quickly reaffirmed the commitment to PPB. In 1971, however, President Richard Nixon's Bureau of the Budget, renamed the Office of Management and Budget (OMB), quietly ordered a retreat.[1] Director George Shultz and his staff had decided that PPB was expensive and was not accomplishing its objective, namely, to produce better decisions about the amount and composition of expenditures. Nevertheless, many federal agencies still use PPB for their internal management even though they do not submit the material formally to OMB.

PPB has five distinguishing operational features. They are (1) program accounting, (2) multi-year costing, (3) detailed description of activities, (4) zero-base budgeting, and (5) benefit-cost analysis. We shall describe and evaluate each of the five parts.

Program Accounting

Program accounting consists of grouping together expenditures having the same purpose, regardless of which subagencies spend the money or what types of goods are purchased. It means focussing on outputs rather than inputs.* A program budget shows a hierarchy of totals. It shows the total outlay proposed for each type of output, for various subgroups of outputs, for various groups of these subgroups. The Department of Health, Education and Welfare, for example, showed total expenditures for work on Heart Disease, for Increasing Knowledge, for Development of Health Resources, and for Health, the last being one of the department's four broad "program categories."

Program budgets are intended to supplement conventional government budgets, but not supplant them. Conventional budgets classify proposed expenditures by type of input and by administrative unit. They show, for example, total expenditures for each type of input, such as personnel or travel acquired by each

---

* Input: goods or services used in a production process.
Output: that which is produced, as in this case, a government service.

subagency, total expenditures for various groups of inputs or groups of subagencies, and total expenditures for various groups of these groups. Because elected officials authorize positions, salaries, capital outlays, and total expenditures separately, conventional budgets are also useful. They tell legislators, administrators, and auditors what expenditures are allowed for each input and each agency. Program accounting thus adds a third type of classification: expenditure by *program*.

It is doubtful that the benefits of program accounting outweigh the costs. Costs arise in delineating and re-delineating programs and in producing an additional set of statements and reconciliations. The benefits of program accounting supposedly are better high-level decisions about spending, based on knowledge of the amount spent for each purpose. However, the additional information has limited value: it reflects discretionary groupings of activities and judgmental allocations of common costs, does not show how much money would be saved by scaling down an activity, and often is ignored by busy bureaucrats.

Multi-Year Costing

Multi-year costing is the second component of PPB. It consists of reporting, along with proposed first-year expenditures, the expenditures predicted for at least one future year. President Johnson's Bureau of the Budget instructed each agency to submit annually a "Program and Financial Plan" that showed outlays for every program element in the "fiscal year just past, the current year, and the budget year, plus at least four future years."[2]

Multi-year costing is useful in two circumstances. One relates to an investment whose payoff requires expenditures in future years. For example, multi-year costing was intended to help Secretary of Defense identify weapons systems whose ultimate cost would be prohibitive and reject them before the services got their foot in the door. The other use relates to a multi-year commitment, as with a new welfare program. In both cases multi-year costing can, by revealing future costs, facilitate rejection of exorbitantly costly activities.

With respect to ongoing activities, however, multi-year costing has little value. That future-year estimates for, say, law enforcement, seem excessive is not a good reason to curtail apparently worthwhile current expenditures. Future expenditures can be scaled down when they are proposed. For established activities, multi-year costing diverts attention, consumes time, paper, and storage space, produces numbers whose meaning is uncertain, and—because officials tend to hold themselves and their subordinates to whatever has been recorded—inhibits adjustment as more information becomes available.

Detailed Description

Detailed description of activities is the third component of PPB. It requires reporting for each program element (1) *objectives* (i.e. intended benefits) of the activity (e.g. the Department of Transportation listed safety and three other objectives); (2) *effectiveness* (i.e. a numerical indicator of actual or expected suc-

cess) for the past year, the current year, the budget year, and at least four future years, (e.g. the number of accidents prevented); (3) *output* (i.e. a numerical indicator of actual or intended results) for the past year, the current year, the budget year, and at least four future years (e.g. lane-miles of interstate highway completed); (4) *choices made* (i.e. courses of action selected) for the budget year (e.g. work on Interstate 80); (5) *alternatives considered* (i.e. courses of action deliberately rejected) for the budget year (e.g. work on Interstate 5), and (6) *reasons for the choices* (e.g. Interstate 80 is busier and cheaper than Interstate 5). Many will recognize this as a "systems approach."

It is important to contrast an activity level with an effect. If the objective is to get people to use libraries, then the number of libraries built or square feet constructed is a measure of activity level. A measure of effectiveness, however, might be the proportion of the population using a library once or more each year.

Detailed description of activities may be helpful to policy-makers. It may clarify what their subordinates are trying to accomplish, what the average cost will be, and where the subordinates exercised discretion. This information may help policy-makers both to compare benefits with costs and to review techniques. If so, the decisions that emerge after review will be more like those that would have been reached if every reviewer could have made his subordinates' decisions as well as his own. High-level officials presumably will view this result as beneficial. So do we—despite some reservations concerning overcentralization. Whether the gain outweighs the costs, however, is not clear.

Zero-Base Budgeting

Zero-base budgeting is the fourth component of PPB. It consists of defending the total expenditure proposed for a program. A program was to be defended by listing its objectives, the choices of subprograms within it, the alternatives considered but not appearing in the proposed program, and the reasons for the choices. The objective was to discourage administrators from taking it for granted that programs should be perpetuated and also to encourage policy-makers to reallocate funds.

While this objective is laudable, zero-base budgeting is not a promising way to accomplish it. Whether a discretionary program should be continued is a matter of judgment, not of demonstration. Furthermore, as the Secretary of Defense and others soon learned, it is hazardous to base this judgment on the reports of interested subordinates: they find something favorable to say about every program. To ignore the change from the previous appropriation, furthermore, simply makes evaluation more difficult.

Knowing what change is proposed enables policy-makers to use their impressions about the current state of the program, to see whether new policy or new commitments are at issue, and to apply whatever imperatives exist concerning total spending. Focusing on changes economizes both review time and political capital.

In 1963, Wildavsky and Hammann studied zero-base budgeting in the U.S. Department of Agriculture. They found that it had little effect on decisions. It did, however, consume over 180,000 administrative man-hours. Of 57 high officials interveiwed, none favored repeating the experience annually.[3]

There are better ways to encourage officials to re-allocate funds. One way is to give each department a devil's advocate, charged with presenting reasons why programs should be contracted or eliminated. The California Legislature has given a valued advisor this function: he is the Legislative Analyst. Another way is to require each administrator to disclose what would be gained or lost if his agency's appropriation were to be (1) the same amount as last time, (2) the amount that would be needed to hold his agency's output constant, and (3) the proposed amount. Given this kind of information about incremental gains and losses for various subagencies, higher officials would be able to redirect funds from seemingly less valuable to seemingly more valuable uses.

Benefit-Cost Analysis

Benefit-cost analysis consists of making a numerical estimate of at least one desired or undesired consequence of at least two alternative courses of action. President Johnson's Bureau of the Budget instructed federal agencies to "maintain a continuing program" of benefit-cost analyses, to start and finish them as seemed appropriate, and to make one "whenever a proposal for major new legislation is involved."

Benefit-cost analysis started in the 1930's with large public investments in water development. Planning and construction costs were heavily subsidized by the federal government.

Technical Considerations

The criterion implicit in benefit-cost analysis calls a change "good" if the sum of the gains (to whomever they accrue) exceeds the sum of the losses, i.e., if the benefits exceed the costs. There is no requirement that gainers compensate losers to make the latter (at a minimum) indifferent to the change. In *The Budget's New Clothes* we proceed from philosophical to analytical criteria of desirability: benefit-cost ratio (gross and net), the internal rate of return, and net benefits. No single criterion is without problems in some imaginable contexts, but the most reliable is to maximize the present value of net benefits (of the set of projects chosen) subject to budget constraints. For example, many analyses imply that the best project is one with the highest benefit-cost ratio. However, the scale of a project that maximizes the benefit-cost ratio is not necessarily the scale that maximizes net benefits. The benefit-cost ratio is misleading when not enough funds are available to do all "feasible" projects, i.e., those with a benefit-cost ratio greater than unity (1.0).

There are two reasons to discount future accruals. First, people are impatient, preferring benefits sooner rather than later. Second, capital can be used in many ways to increase welfare. If one opportunity is exploited, the gains on another must be foregone. Low discount rates favor school buildings over teachers; letter-sorting machines over clerks and mail handlers; dams over flood-plain zoning; and guided missiles, helicopters, and automatic weapons over soldiers.

Water development agencies have used discount rates near and below 3 percent. The President's Water Resources Council, which has been enforcing higher rates, suggested in a recent proposed policy statement that "the full cost . . . of long-term borrowing . . . is at least 7 percent and can be as high as 10 percent." These rates were imposed by President Nixon's OMB. All non-water agencies were directed to use 10 percent, while water agencies were allowed 7 percent—considerably higher than the 4⅞ percent they were using in 1970. The effect of a higher discount rate is to make future net benefits seem smaller, and consequently the project seem less desirable.

Uncertainty is a problem that affects public investments as well as private and indeed affects any planning that is oriented toward the future. The scenario for the St. Lawrence Seaway did not include the existence of "supertankers"—large ships that do not use the Seaway. Although many outsiders criticize them, planning agencies have not always been overly optimistic. In some cases whole classes of benefits that were ignored in planning now yield the bulk of benefits from projects. An example is outdoor recreation, which was not considered until recently in the planning of water resources projects. Now water-based recreation often contributes over half of the benefits at reservoirs. Some suggest that since the government combines so many investments, it need pay less attention to uncertainty than the private sector. The law of large numbers assures that the actual value of the government's entire portfolio will be "very" close to its expectation. This observation leads to the conclusion that the government should employ a riskless discount rate. Others counsel using discount rates that include a risk premium.

Project Benefit Forecasts

Benefits have been attributed for the outputs of water, transportation, urban renewal projects and for "human capital improvements" obtained through health and education. Calculating benefits typically involves estimating the demand for particular public services. Demand estimation is a difficult forecasting problem. Often the demand for public services is more difficult to predict than the demand for private goods or services.

Project benefits have been estimated in four ways: (1) the willingness of beneficiaries to pay in the form of actual or imputed user charges; (2) the increase in capital values, if any; (3) cost savings, whether actual or potential; (4) increase in national income. Examples of these approaches follow. (More are discussed in Chapter 8 of *The Budget's New Clothes*.)

The value of the output of projects may sometimes be determined by a market, but frequently the output is not sold on a well-functioning market: for example, recreational services at federal parks and reservoirs are often underpriced or given away. Sometimes markets can be simulated, as one was for recreation. This method depends on the observation of associated costs, particularly the cost of traveling to a recreational site. Observing the response of quantity demanded to changes in the cost of using a facility is one way to estimate a demand curve when market-clearing prices are absent.

Transportation projects involve benefits to (a) traffic diverted to a particular means of transportation as well as (b) traffic generated by a new highway, rapid transit system, or airport. A new transportation facility often diverts users from an existing one, and thus reduces congestion. Foster and Beesley found that the major beneficiaries of the Victoria Line addition to the London Underground were nonusers: motorists, bus riders, and other Underground line users.[4] This realization is behind the increasing tendency to require motorists to subsidize mass transit. Their *quid pro quo* is reduced congestion on the roads. A key element in transportation benefit analysis is the value imputed to travel time, a subject of continuing controversy.

The general approach to measuring the benefits of education has been to estimate the present value of increased lifetime income due to education. Before-tax income is what counts. For present purposes, taxation can be viewed as simply a transfer from the earner to the government. One researcher found the rate of return to society from college education not materially different from the rate on business capital. However, because of subsidies to education, the *private* rate of return on college education has been higher than on physical capital. Any non-economic returns to education are above and beyond this.

Like expenditures for education, those for health have been regarded as preventive or remedial maintenance expenditures for human capital. But we do not undertake health expenditures solely to prevent depletion of our human capital. We wish to reduce suffering and save lives for their own sakes, not only for the sake of the net income contributed by healthy taxpayers.

Benefits of new airports or better facilities at existing airports have been measured as the reduction of "airport ineffectiveness": delays, diversions, cancellations, or accidents. The same concept of *cost savings* has been employed to estimate the benefits of syphilis treatment, and reducing mental illness.

Transportation projects such as roads in underdeveloped countries have been analyzed using input-output analysis to predict the *change in national income* due to the project.

Priorities for attacking particular diseases were determined by a combination of cost data (deaths averted vs. dollars expended) and "benefit" data (the value of curing or preventing various diseases in terms of present expected value of future earnings). The result was the following priority of attack: motor vehicle accidents (seat belts, head restraints, prevention of pedestrian injury), arthritis, driving while intoxicated, syphilis, cervical cancer, lung cancer, breast cancer, tuberculosis, the licensing of drivers, head and neck cancer, colon-rectum cancer.

One problem with forecasts of benefits is that other aspects of the environment may change as the project is being built. The demand for shipping at one port is heavily dependent on what is done simultaneously at other ports. Similarly the number of visitor-days at a recreational site is heavily dependent on access roads or other complementary transportation facilities. Price charged affects quantities demanded, yet many economists ignored this relationship when it was fashionable to say that design of public investments was independent of repayment policy.

Measurable benefits, even if relatively minor, tend to dominate an analysis of benefits and costs, and immeasurable or intangible benefits are usually ignored. If air pollution were ameliorated, certain producers—perhaps farmers and people with respiratory diseases—would benefit discernibly, but the largest benefit might be the increased psychic income to the whole society from the amenity of clean air. Usually there is no satisfactory way to measure such intangible gains, so measurable benefits dominate the analysis.

The Environmental Issue

Public investments have natural enemies. Frequently, residents oppose the taking of land through eminent domain either because they lose their land or because they are opposed to the proposed use. Lately, a new issue—concern for the natural environment—has gained legitimacy as a vehicle for their opposition.

Several recent court cases have stopped public and private developments. In July, 1971, a U.S. Court of Appeals found that the rules adopted by the AEC were inadequate and that continued construction of an atomic power plant approved under the lax rules should be stopped. A proper "balancing" between economic factors and environmental considerations was lacking. Independent evaluation and balancing of certain environmental factors such as thermal effects were considered necessary:

> The Environmental Impact Statement required shall include a cost-benefit analysis which considers and balances the environmental effects of the facility and the alternatives available for reducing or avoiding adverse environmental effects, as well as the environmental, economic, technical and other benefits of the facility. . . . [T]he cost-benefit analysis shall . . . for the purposes of the National Environmental Policy Act consider the radiological effects together with the thermal effects and the other environmental effects of the facility.[5]

This decision resulted in the mitigation of the environmental effects of many riparian nuclear reactors by provision of cooling towers so that less heat was transmitted to the river water.

Other projects—including a reservoir project in Arkansas, the Cross-Florida Barge Canal, and a real estate development in Mono County, California—were at least temporarily delayed because of environmental considerations. The Arkansas reservoir project created flat-water recreational lakes at the expense of one of the last undammed rivers (the Cossatot), in the area.[6] The court, by inference, found that, if the wild river were adjudged to be worth $5.5 million, the benefit-cost ratio of the proposed project would be less than unity—1.0.[7] The Florida Canal project represents a rare case of a public works project stopped after it was almost a third complete.

Giving attention to projects' effects on the natural environment implies exploration and explicit statement of effects on people other than the intended beneficiaries of the project. It does not mean that no additional effects will be tolerated. Another salubrious effect is that alternatives are required to be examined explicitly, a step that might not have been considered otherwise. For example, attention must be given to the possibility of leaving a river alone or of adding cooling towers to a nuclear electric plant.

Income distribution effects of projects have been discussed for twenty years, but the environmental quality objective has gained wide attention only recently. In fact, environmental aspects of projects are much more closely scrutinized now than the project's effects on the distribution of income. Perhaps it is harder to get consensus on the latter.

The Water Resources Council has suggested that each project's benefits and costs be analyzed under four rubrics: National Economic Development, Environmental Quality, Regional Development, and Social Well-Being. Both beneficial and adverse effects would be listed under each rubric.[8] No one, however, has suggested a systematic way to make the net figures in these four accounts commensurable.

Program Budgeting in Practice

In observing the application of PPB in the military services, observers have noted that colonels learned the system and that some, knowing the basis on which decisions would be made, began to select and even falsify data so that budgetary decisions would be made in their favor. In effect, the operating bureaucrats who create information can refuse to collect data that show a program to be ineffective.

California school districts resisted the state's efforts to impose PPB on them. A public accounting firm handling the effort for the state tried to convince selected school districts that participation in the pilot program was to their advantage and that no straight-jacket categories were to be imposed from above. The districts would have the opportunity to formulate their objectives, to organize their teaching effort to serve these objectives, and to compose their own program structure. Despite there reassurances, many teachers were convinced that Sacramento intended to eliminate art, music, or programs considered potentially subversive, such as social studies.

New York was both the first state to adopt PPB and the first to discard it. Pennsylvania made the greatest effort to make it effective. Everywhere it has met resistance from people opposed to change.

Benefit-Cost Analysis in Practice

The present institutional context of benefit-cost analysis biases its results. Thus, the agency that will later oversee the engineering and construction of a candidate project often has done the analysis that is intended to decide which project—if any—to do. Given common organizational objectives of continued existence and growth, the agencies have an interest in a favorable prospectus. The problem is not solved when an outside consultant is engaged to make a feasibility study. Typically the consultant learns explicitly or implicitly which result will favor his client's goals. It is a rare consultant who is willing to give the client bad news.

Two projects to which benefit-cost analysis was applied offer insights into its long-run impact. One, the California Water Project (CWP) went ahead despite several negative recommendations. Another, the Supersonic Transport (SST) prototype development, was finally cancelled perhaps in part because of the adverse findings. However, the SST project went on for eight years despite negative analyses by reputable firms and individuals. Both projects received favorable and unfavorable reviews in the course of many studies. Some studies are tactics for delay, or deflections of criticism, undertaken while the project quietly marches down its critical path.

The State of California, instead of the federal government, built the CWP in part to avoid the provision of the federal Reclamation Act of 1902 that forbids delivery of federally subsidized irrigation water to holdings in excess of 160 acres per owner. When "feasibility reports" were released before the bond election the following headlines appeared in two newspapers:

"FEATHER RIVER PROJECT GETS SOUND RATING IN TWO REPORTS"
—Los Angeles *Times*

"STATE WATER PLAN CALLED IMPOSSIBLE"
—San Francisco *Chronicle*

Clearly, it was possible for both papers to read what they wanted into the reports. The Feather River Project survived. The Oroville Reservoir and the California Aqueduct are completed. (As this is being written, however, a Peripheral Canal to take surplus Sacramento River water south is still under debate.) One element, the Dos Rios Reservoir, was eliminated despite a claimed benefit-cost ratio of 1.9. Thus it seems that *who* gets the benefits is more important to decision-makers than how the benefits compare numerically with the costs. Sometimes wealthy landowners are favored. Other times (if rarely) the poor are favored, but economic efficiency is rarely persuasive.

President John F. Kennedy committed the country to the development of a Supersonic Transport (SST) in 1963 despite a Stanford Research Institute report that advised against federal subsidy. Later, an Institute for Defense Analyses report was pessimistic on demand for SST's. Despite these negative (and courageous) conclusions, the Federal Aviation Administration continued to advocate the program, commissioning other consultants to counter the views of its negative consultants.

When President Nixon took office, he appointed an *ad hoc* committee to advise him on the subject. Several members of that committee later testified that their views were misrepresented by an Undersecretary of Transportation, who championed the project. Subcommittees on economics, balance of payments, and environmental and sociological effects all reported negatively. A subcommittee on technological spillovers reported them to be minor. In 1971 the federal government ended its subsidy of prototype development.

Rhetoric was dominated by allegations of impact on the environment. Senator William Proxmire had waged a vigorous campaign showing that most states would pay more in taxes for the SST development than they would benefit by it. Previous studies of the SST were certainly extant, however, having been brought together by the FAA in an *Economic Feasibility Report* (1967).

In the planning of both the CWP and the SST project, it appears that government officials did not ask, "Should the government spend money on this type of project?" They asked instead, "Do the benefits exceed the costs?" By analogy, if someone were to show that the benefits exceed the costs in producing and selling Bobby Fischer chess sets, this would indicate that government also should undertake that enterprise.

The Use of Alternatives

Typically, in public investment, one alternative is tentatively chosen and an effort is made to show that it is "feasible." Somewhere in the background there almost certainly has been consideration of other alternatives, but only the preferred one is analyzed in detail and considered publicly. But the essence of that much-overused term "systems analysis" is the use of *alternatives*. If we have several alternatives thoroughly analyzed, then we can compare them and recognize rates of exchange of economic benefits for environmental degradation; for example, all man-made structures have some environmental impacts, usually negative. We are not, of course, ready to stop building more structures, but we do wish to anticipate what each intrusion is likely to cost us, in order to help judge alternative ways of accomplishing a purpose or alternative uses of public funds. Models of good systems analyses of real alternatives are presented in works by Meyer, Kain and Wohl,[9] the U. S. Department of Transportation,[10] and Robert N. Grosse.[11] We do not necessarily agree with their conclusions, but they exemplify admirable method in seriously considering alternatives.

Benefit estimates are frequently inflated to serve the purpose of the agency doing the analysis. Cost estimates are usually at the lower limit of actual costs.[12] There is much discouraging indication that Congress cares little for economic efficiency. The Flood Control Act of 1936 required that "benefits to whomsoever they may accrue [should] exceed the costs,"

but not that a chosen project have the greatest net benefits among all admissible projects.[13] Perhaps the only thing Congress intended was that benefit-cost screening be adequate to exclude grossly uneconomic projects. Legislators seem to prefer to have civil servants prescreen certain types of projects so that the burden of a negative decision can be shifted from themselves.

Congress is reluctant to refuse to spend, but if it wishes to regain lost control over public expenditures it must equip itself to evaluate and cut where necessary. An analytical arm responsible only to Congress might be some improvement. It would give Congress the expertise that operating agencies now have. But there is no assurance congressmen would heed its advice. It seems that congressmen still are preoccupied with the regional distribution of federal spending. Having an analytic agency responsible to the Legislature has worked well in California. The Legislative Analyst is respected and is non-partisan. His advice is frequently sought on implications of legislation.

Limitations of the Benefit-Cost Approach

Benefit-cost analysis is more effective in *comparing* projects than in deciding whether or not to pursue a single project. Analysis has not been an effective sieve, but it has served the purposes of the agency doing the analysis. Only recently, with the advent of environmental issues, have some proposed projects been pared.

Decision-making strictly according to the results of benefit-cost analysis is better adapted to those functions of government that are most similar to business, especially public utilities such as water, waste disposal, power production, and transportation projects. But in human resource fields, analysis can only be a partial aid to decision-making. Further, quantitative evaluation is more useful for intraprogram choices (for example, choosing which of several harbor-deepening projects to pursue) than for interprogram choices (for example, choosing harbor-deepening at the expense of medical research).

A Concluding Comment: Formulating Alternative Choices

One function of administrators can be called intelligence: gathering information for problem solving. A second function is design: the formulation or invention of alternative courses of action among which choices can then be made. Executives spend the least amount of time on the third step, the actual choice, and most of their time on design.[14]

The function of design and formulation of alternatives is crucially important. Further, it is far more fruitful to spend time exploring, developing and formulating alternative uses of resources than it is to investigate a single use exhaustively. Accordingly, benefit-cost analysis should be much more heavily employed in the design function, and less in the final choice among alternatives. Choosing among alternatives is relatively easy. The generation of imaginative choices should come first, and ranks first in importance.

FOOTNOTES

[1] U. S. Office of Management and Budget, *Circular No. A-11, Revised, Transmittal Memorandum No. 38* (Washington, D.C.: June 21, 1971).

[2] U. S. Bureau of the Budget, *Bulletin No. 68-2* (Washington, D.C.: July 18, 1967).

[3] Aaron Wildavsky and Arthur Hammann, "Comprehensive Versus Incremental Budgeting in the Department of Agriculture," in Fremont J. Lyden and Ernest G. Miller, eds., *Planning Programming Budgeting: a systems approach to management* (Chicago: Markham, 1967), p. 161.

[4] C. D. Foster and M. E. Beesley, "Estimating the Social Benefit of Constructing an Underground Railway in London," *Journal of the Royal Statistical Society* vol. 126, (1963) pp. 46–58.

[5] *Federal Register* XXXVI: 175, 9 Sept. 1971, p. 10872.

[6] *Environmental Defense Fund, et al.* v. *Corps of Engineers of U. S. Army, et al.*, 325 *Fed. Supplement* 728 (1971). The injunction was dissolved after a new impact statement was filed, 4 *Environmental Reporter Cases*, December 8, 1972.

[7] 325 *Fed. Supplement* 757 (1971). A benefit-cost ratio of unity or above does not necessarily imply that a project should be undertaken.

[8] *Federal Register* XXXVI: 245, 21 Dec. 1971, p. 24144.

[9] *The Urban Transportation Problem* (Cambridge: Harvard University Press, 1965).

[10] "Urban Commutation Alternatives Special Analytic Study" reprinted in Joint Economic Committee, *The Analysis and Evaluation of Public Expenditures* vol. 2, pp. 698–733 (Washington, D.C.: 1969).

[11] R. H. Haveman and Julius Margolis, *Public Expenditures and Policy Analysis* (Chicago: Markham, 1970) pp. 518–48.

[12] See Leonard Merewitz, "Cost Overruns in Public Works," in *Benefit-Cost and Policy Analysis Annual* (Chicago: Aldine, 1973).

[13] Congress' wording seems to suggest satisficing or choosing a "good enough" alternative rather than maximizing.

[14] John Dewey, *How We Think,* Chapter 8 (New York: Heath, 1910).

Women's Opportunities in Education

Vol. 14   No. 6   December 1973

Women and Academia at Berkeley:
CCEW—Women's Center

Beatrice Bain
Associate Director
Women's Center

Introduction: "What Does Woman Want?"

During the past decade, many women in the United States have discovered that they need and deserve access to higher education and its consequent benefits. In increasing numbers, American women have come to recognize academic education as vital to their future: it is a principal access route to development of the individual's potential, to expanded career opportunities, and to recognized achievement. While there is much talk about abstractions such as changing women's image, a concrete long-range goal for women—regardless of age or ethnic origin—is a fair share in the advantages that higher education offers.

Two developments have been occurring simultaneously: (1) the women's movement is highlighting educational needs and uncovering academic discrimination, and (2) a loose coalition of students, educators, legislators and citizens are challenging educational policy for its failure to respond to the needs of society as a whole. Such criticism reinforces doubts about both the equity of women's treatment in the educational structure and the rigidities of higher education, with its inflexible time-tables, exclusionary procedures and high costs.

Women have participated in University life both as students and faculty members since the mid-nineteenth century, but their numbers in higher education have been small. Educators have often treated this situation as a fault of women rather than of the system. Others, while admitting that discrimination exists, find it difficult to understand that such inequity is a problem demanding serious attention. Meanwhile, through neglect more than by intent, a valuable human resource is being lost: the capabilities and the potential of educated women.[1]

The most recent Carnegie Commission report (*Opportunities for Women in Higher Education*) documents the drop-off in women's participation as one moves up through the system. About half the nation's high school graduates are women, but this proportion declines at each successive level of educational advancement. Thus, women hold 43.1 percent of the bachelor's degree and 36.5 percent of master's and doctor's degrees.

Basic academic capabilities are not determined by sex. Nevertheless, society has held differing expectations for men and women students. Until recently, this differential view was shared by women themselves. A man's path was seen to be directed toward a career; a woman's life was not similarly career-oriented. Thus barriers to women persist both in society and within the educational structure. The *Report on Higher Education* of the President's Task Force, chaired by Frank Newman of the Stanford faculty (March 1971), sums it up succinctly. The lead paragraph of the chapter on women reads:

> ... three major types of barriers ... block full participation by women in higher education: first, overt discrimination by faculties, deans, and others acting in official capacities; second, practical institutional barriers, such as rigid admission and residence requirements, and a lack of campus facilities and services, which makes participation in higher education incompatible with many women's other interests and activities; and third, the ingrained assumptions and inhibitions on the part of both men and women which deny the talents and aspirations of the latter. ...

> Higher education exerts another kind of leverage as well. Colleges and universities take upon themselves the task of forming and sanctioning the attitudes and practices which educated people will thereafter consider reasonable. If it is fairness which they sanction, all women are helped; but if it is discrimination they sanction, all women are hurt, educated or not.[2]

In clarifying women's role in higher education in the United States three important questions have been asked.

First: Are women as "qualified" (i.e., as capable) as men? The answer is "yes."

Second: When women gain higher education, do they use it? Again, the answer is "yes," even if "use" is narrowly defined. Traditionally, higher education is seen as an investment by both society and the individual in the person's future worth, which is often measured solely in monetary terms. Moreover, the measure is usually applied only to women's work outside the home. Consequently, for working women—as for men—there is a strong correlation between educational level and salary level,[3] even though women's goal of "equal pay for equal work" is still more of a promise than a reality. Further, the majority of women now working in the United States are employed not primarily for personal fulfillment, but rather because they need the money. Participation in higher education can thus be seen as playing an essential social and economic role in bettering the status of women; it is crucially significant for minority women.

Third: If many women have demonstrable educational needs today, how can these needs be met?

The answer may lie in changes in the educational structure itself, as suggested by a new look at higher education, new definitions of the roles and responsibilities of women, and new directives provided by federal legislation. Earlier directives in the mid-'60s termed "affirmative action," applied special opportunity principles by indirection to academic institutions; the Higher Education Act of June 1972[4] now requires equal treatment of men and women in college admissions, access to scholarships and fellowships and to a variety of other educational facilities and programs. Realization of equal access may imply modifying requirements for full-time study, provision of child-care facilities, and lifting of sex-based barriers to financial aid.

As a corollary, further questions arise: Now that discrimination has been identified as both inequitable and illegal, will visible changes in educational structure follow? And if so, when?

The Carnegie Commission study suggests a slow pace predicting that not until 2000 will new policies add sizable numbers of women to faculties (the final step in educational attainment for women). But the report urges the early removal of "all improper barriers to the advancement of women," active search for talented women as candidates for appointment at every level, and formulation of policies that allow more part-time appointments, child-bearing and child-rearing leaves, and a reduction in the severity of the anti-nepotism rules.*

The Commission recommendations thus address two related but distinct goals. As indicated earlier, higher education for women is linked both to the number of job opportunities for women and their upward mobility in business, industry and the professions. Emphasis on increasing the numbers of women in senior faculty positions is related partly to increasing job opportunities. But perhaps more significant would be the symbolic and actual recognition of women's scholarly capacities, and even more important the consequent increase in their ability to influence high-level academic decisions.

Continuing Education

What happens during the transitional period, while women's needs are being identified, academic responsibility defined, and institutional changes evolved? One institutional response has been identified as Continuing Education of Women.

Several such centers were established during the '60s to deal with problems of women's re-entry to college. In large part, they adapted the "veteran's" pattern of re-entry. Some centers received budgetary allocations, but most were voluntary. Some were attached to large state universities, such as Michigan and Minnesota; others were peripheral to a complex of small colleges, such as the Claremont Colleges. Some offered special brush-up courses for rusty skills; some raised scholarship funds and offered financial assistance. An unique development was the Radcliffe Institute, which made small grants to help talented women continue their own projects, but did not necessarily re-introduce them into the formal academic setting. The Institute also supplemented the established seminars that, like extension courses elsewhere, were open to the community on payment of a fee.

By the late 1960s continuing education programs for women were widespread; most served an advisory function or were related to an extension system. In California, the junior colleges—later officially designated community colleges—were regarded as both the primary re-entry avenue into higher education and the principal vehicle for high school graduates to obtain two more years of public education. At the University of California, extension courses were offered in response to the expressed needs of women students, whatever their interests might be. The drawback is that although community colleges and University Extension perform certain functions very well, both offer only limited academic credentials and at restricted levels.

Focus on Berkeley

For over a decade, ad hoc groups formed by women associated in some way with the Berkeley campus, plied the University administration with proposals that would help women resume and renew their educations. In 1970, a subcommittee of the Berkeley Academic Senate added impetus to these proposals by publishing the *Report on the Status of Women of the Berkeley Faculty*. The report dealt only indirectly with mature women students, but did focus attention on (1) the admission and completion problems of women graduate students, and (2) the sparsity of women members of the Academic Senate (that is, the scarcity of women holding regular faculty appointments above the lowest grades). In 1970, women comprised only 2.3 percent of all full professors at Berkeley. The ratio has not improved subsequently. Larger proportions of women held lower positions lacking both tenure and status.

One year earlier, an Association of Academic Women had been formed on the Berkeley campus, including

* The dictionary defines "nepotism" as "favoritism shown to a relative." Colleges and universities have used anti-nepotism rules to prevent the employment of fully qualified women if their husbands were working in the same departments or institutions in which the wives would be employed.

women faculty members as well as nonsenate academic research and professional employees of the University. The association issued reports and met with University administrators to clarify and emphasize the needs of women. As noted earlier, when "affirmative action" legislation was applied to universities holding federal grants, the law also called for re-examination of the position of women and minorities. The Berkeley campus was one of those affected. Court actions also directed special attention to the treatment of academic women. Moreover, both academic and staff "status of women" committees, and the continuing unofficial ad hoc women's committees, added to the pressure and continued to urge University action.

A Berkeley Women's Center Is Proposed

In 1971, Chancellor Roger Heyns appointed a Chancellor's Advisory Committee chaired by Dean Frances Le Pron Davis to survey and report on the establishment of a Center for Continuing Education of Women.[5] Early in 1972, the committee reported to Chancellor Albert H. Bowker, and called for the establishment of such a Center.[6]

As the *University Bulletin* noted:

> The Advisory Committee pointed out that women seeking higher education often face uncertainties about career objectives, rules and regulations that discourage study on a part-time basis, and financial problems—particularly child care expenses.

> [It] contradicted the frequently-held view that women are poor risks in college. Women who complete their training, the report said, are likely to use it.

The Committee went on to suggest the basic functions for such a Center:

> ... the expansion of educational opportunities for women, with emphasis on the needs of mature women and women from minority groups.

> The Center will facilitate educational opportunities by working to make University regulations more amenable to women's needs. It will also undertake academic planning and referral, serving the Berkeley campus and possibly other Bay Area colleges and universities.

> Other functions of the Center will be to encourage research on the role of women, seek financial support for its clientele, and provide visible evidence of the University's concern for the education of women.

The Chancellor accepted the report's recommendations. Professor Hanna Pitkin, Political Science, and chairperson of the Academic Senate Committee on the Status of Women, was named to head the search committee to find a Director for the new Center. In July, 1972, Professor May N. Diaz of Anthropology was appointed Director. The Chancellor's office made funds available, supplemented by a special gift from the alumnae of the Prytanean Association (a campus women's honor society) for the Center's initial year.

The Center Opens Its Doors

In October, 1972, the Center for Continuing Education of Women, U.C., Berkeley, opened its doors in the Women's Faculty Club building. The name was immediately shortened to *CCEW-Women's Center* and the prospectus stated:

> The Center is designed to serve women on the campus and off-campus. We will provide activities related to general areas of interest and concern to women:
>> Academic counseling and advising for women planning to enter college or resume their education.
>> Coordination of information about educational opportunities in the Bay Area.
>> Exploration of career and job opportunities for women, particularly in areas traditionally closed to them.
>> Discussion groups concerned with problems of special interest to women.
>> Compilation of data on women's studies courses on the Berkeley Campus and research on the status of women.

During the first months of operation, May Diaz described one of the Center's aims: "Generally, we'll be a visible welcome sign to women who wish to return to higher education but who are wary of the problems and difficulties they might encounter." The Center staff began with basic functions and explored possibilities for expansion. Noting the initial directives of the Chancellor's Advisory Committee, the Center gave prime attention to academic and educational advising. The staff recognized the points of greatest difficulty, and began to work on the most urgent problems.

Academic and Educational Advising: Recognizing and Circumventing Barriers

In general, it became clear that women wishing to enroll on the Berkeley campus were fully aware that the requirements include evidence of highest aptitude and achievement, dedication to scholarship, and knowledge of regulations. Nevertheless, for many women students whose education has been interrupted, the real barriers appeared in the rigidity of certain additional requirements.

To begin with, the return of the mature woman as an undergraduate has never been made easy, although it is sometimes possible. But difficulties arise immediately, because it is only as an exception and in response to a specific plea that a working woman or mother of young children is permitted to carry a class load of less than full time. Such barrier requirements are primarily the outgrowth of a period of overcrowding on the Berkeley campus, and fortunately are expected to change. Meanwhile, the Women's Center assists students in formulating requests for exemptions, and otherwise advises and counsels on procedures.

On the Berkeley campus, however, the largest group needing help consists of women seeking admission at the graduate level. This is particularly true of disciplines that traditionally have not welcomed women at higher levels. Teaching, social welfare, library science and some of the humanities are examples of fields regarded as being related to service and thus much more available to women. Some women do indeed prefer these fields. Many more, however, who are excluded from their first choice, settle on the "women's fields" as their only accessible alternative, and by the weight of numbers tend to crowd out male applicants. Equitable admissions policies, it is suggested, might relieve such artificial pressures to enter the "women's fields" and permit a more natural balance of women and men in all areas.

Giving women equal access to academic disciplines does not mean that University departments must accept less-qualified candidates for graduate programs, just because they are women. Instead, it means that departments are requested to refrain from the pre-judgments that prevent the entry of well-qualified candidates who happen to be women, or who are no longer youthful. Departments are encouraged to take a positive rather than a negative approach to the experience that comes with age. Further, departmental advisors are asked to devise more flexible concurrent or interim patterns of courses for graduate students in technical or professional fields, particularly in scientific areas where technological change is rapid. (This need for flexibility holds true for returning men as well as returning women.)

The Women's Center at Berkeley does not now offer such innovative courses itself. But other centers on other campuses do so, as well as other branches of the University of California (mostly Extension programs).

More women wish to come to the University of California at Berkeley than facilities and current admission requirements permit, and these women require a wide range of help. On one hand, the qualified candidate with a sense of direction and purpose, intentions to complete work in an accepted field, and no financial problems, requires only minimal assistance. From the Center, she can gain information on new and expanding programs in the area and how to use them.

But for most women students who have interrupted their education and are seeking admission to Berkeley the Women's Center can play a much larger role including informational assistance, letters of recommendation, individual help, knowledge of the Berkeley academic pattern, and assistance in arguing a case before the academic hierarchy. For those who are innovatively seeking new career lines, the Center can serve a supportive function. "What are the requirements? How can I use the background I already have? What is the real possibility of acceptance as a student in genetic counseling as compared to acceptance at the U.C. School of Nursing?" The Women's Center can help raise and discuss such questions. As one woman commented in an unsolicited letter:

Your office . . . gave me much information about financial assistance in the form of grants, loans, and scholarships and helped me make an appointment with a representative in the Financial Aid office. Members of your staff also suggested professors who might help me initiate an independent major program. I not only received the most comprehensive information that I have obtained in any one office

since approaching the University two years ago, I was treated with heart-warming courtesy and interest by your staff.

Offering Alternatives and Coordinating Information

For many women wishing to return to academic work, the University of California at Berkeley is only one alternative among the colleges and universities in the San Francisco Bay Area. The educational advising service presents specifics about programs at community colleges and the special advantages of "returning" to study in an atmosphere with less pressure. In fact, the undergraduate candidate is often advised to consider the Berkeley campus only after transfer from a local community college.

Special colleges have certain technical advantages and offer individualized programs. The State University system, with master's programs in many fields—and with at least three campuses within commuting distance of Berkeley—offers a more realistic alternative for many women who do not contemplate a Ph.D. Other information provided by the Center includes University and college extension offerings, new Extended University possibilities, and other "individual" approaches to higher education, as in the Open University pattern. Another important alternative is the redirection of many women students who do not have a realistic picture of the demands and practical problems of present-day graduate education. The Center staff feels that such a function is significant, whether or not the woman student ever attends the University of California. As a knowledgeable participant in that University's future—certainly as a citizen taxpayer, possibly as the parent of a student, probably as a consumer of University research—any woman assisted by the Women's Center will gain increased understanding of the University as a whole.

The Center has on hand educational material, program brochures, data on times and places for application to all Bay Area colleges and universities, and a network of names of specific individuals who can be consulted directly. The staff assists in their use, as well as providing information on all departments and procedures on the Berkeley campus, and collects catalogues covering other U.C. campuses and universities not in the immediate vicinity.

The advising and coordinating function of the Center has been handled in various ways. Material is always available for perusal, supplemented by questions, and upon request, individual appointments may be made with any member of the staff. In addition, informal discussion meetings are held with community women in special fields. For example, groups of women graduate students have met, by department. Also, a general group has viewed the life style of the woman graduate student and its special demands. The group process has seemed particularly effective in "What now?" discussions, and may also be used in the coming year as vocational and career counseling expands at the Women's Center.

Facts and Practical Details

Both present and prospective women students also need information on other women's organizations and specialized material on women's health and legal problems—what the Women's Center calls "practical details." The Center coordinates such information and acts as a referral center to other Women's Centers, and to various special interest and community groups. A representative evaluation of this type of activity was expressed by one visitor: "Thanks again for your concern and for your much needed efforts on behalf of women such as myself. At least, you're *doing* something and not just talking about it, and for that, you deserve considerable praise and support."

Career and Job Opportunities

The most important added function for the Women's Center in its first year has been exploration of career and job opportunities for women.

Women seeking employment with their newly won degrees find the traditionally oriented employment and placement agencies, both academic and professional, still asking "but can she type?" In answer, the Women's Center offers a nontraditional approach, in that job advising relates to development rather than placement. It is realistic, yet tends to emphasize expansion of horizons even in a period of economic difficulty and retrenchment.

Counseling is also offered for women who are reexamining their skills before re-entering the job market—assessing their supplemental needs, both educational and technical. The Center also emphasizes opportunities for minority women, as exemplified by several one-day conferences of Black women sponsored by and held at the Center.

The coordination of information about, and cooperation with newly organized women's professional organizations (usually caucuses of existing professional organizations) marks the beginning of an information network that will aid development of job opportunities, particularly those in the academic world.

Initial efforts in this direction have won praise. A woman Ph.D. visitor wrote, "As you may recall, I was in the Bay Area for interviews for an administrative position, and quite frankly, I got more solid information and advice from you than from all my other contacts combined."

The Center as Symbol

As indicated earlier, the Center's functions can be classified as providing information, advice and service. Further, the Center's structure offers the University demonstration of several principles associated with women and their needs. For example, part-time flexible scheduling, and less-than-full-time employment are recognized as important for women's effective participation. Accordingly, part-time employment is encouraged at the Center. In addition to the director, who continues her academic departmental teaching at the University, there are two associate directors and an academic counselor, each half time. The administrative assistant is a full-time office manager, but two women share the general assistance position, and six to eight work-study student advisors are all part-time. Part-time interns from other graduate programs supplement the staff.

As another example for the University, the Center responds to women's requests for broader participation in decisionmaking. At the Center, decisions and coordination are achieved collegially and by consensus, rather than hierarchically. Information and advice are gathered and shared. Although there is some division of responsibility, cooperative functioning is stressed. Initial screening, advising, assistance with educational materials, answering vocational questions, may be done by work-study students trained by the academic counselor, or by interns who are graduate students in counseling at various universities. In addition, the directors and counselors have their own areas of specialization, but are available for consultation and advising in all phases of the Center's activities.

Fringe Benefits and Affirmative Action

Within the University system, the Women's Center has focused on several areas, including fringe benefits and affirmative action. For example, nonacademic employees, who are mostly women, need assistance in using a significant fringe benefit that comes with working for the University. Under certain circumstances the employee may take course work leading to better job performance and advancement, as well as eventual degree attainment. The Women's Center has already moved to suggest additional implementation and simplification of this University process. Further, the Center and segments of the University administration are exploring the upward mobility of women, the personnel practices under which they are hired and advanced, and the levels to which they may aspire.

In addition, in cooperation with the various Status of Women committees on campus, the Center continues with its basic task of implementing affirmative action in its best sense, i.e., recognition of the talents of able academic women.

Women's Studies

The Women's Center maintains a special interest in courses currently designated as "women's studies." Although very few such courses are now offered on the Berkeley campus, the Women's Center plans to assist students interested in this focus. Preliminary talks have concerned the possible establishment of a women's studies group major as well as individual majors. The Center itself will offer some lectures and discussion series in areas of women's concerns. Two directions have been chosen for development. The first, a series called "Women in . . ." will explore the realities of nontraditional occupations for women. The second, a series devoted to "Practical Details for the New Woman," discusses areas in which women need specific knowledge in order to maintain their independence. The Center will present research of special interest to women as well as work by women researchers.

Quantitative Skills

A pilot class is contemplated to explore women's confidence in their ability to absorb mathematical training at various levels. This is important because women have been counseled to bypass or avoid mathematical fields, on the assumption that they lack the necessary aptitudes for quantitative studies. The Women's Center is prepared to examine this entire matter fully.

The Women's Center: Growth and New Directions

The Women's Center now has a new location in the heart of the University campus[7] and a slightly expanded budget implying some confidence on the part of the academic community. Accordingly the Center plans to continue pilot projects, form additional groups, expand discussion series, regularize outreach to minority communities, cooperate with community college programs, and increase publicity for the Center and its purposes.

Moreover several new areas of concern will be added, as suggested earlier.

1) The Women's Center will direct increased attention to women students currently on the campus. University practices and procedures will be re-examined in the light of women students' needs. Attention will be focused on barriers to achievement, which are so traditional as to go almost unnoticed. Career counseling in nontraditional fields will be expanded, and encouragement offered to creative approaches for women's future use of present education. Special attention to the problems of women graduate students will be extended in many ways—to women undergraduates and (in concert with the University Director of Relations with Schools) to prospective undergraduates from high schools and community colleges. Attention will also extend to a distinctive clientele, the wives of faculty members and students.

2) Vocational and career counseling will be expanded by the addition of one new half-time counselor who will develop more contacts in the community, seek to extend and expand women's opportunities, and educate other groups on the possibilities of flexible scheduling. She will also be especially concerned with needs of minority women.

3) The Women's Center will establish a talent bank with particular attention to the West Coast. It will list women with capabilities and interest in academic administration. Women are under-represented in this area, and few "role models" exist. Recruiters still say, "We wanted to hire a woman, but we couldn't find one."

4) The Center will also initiate other research on women and women's needs. For the present, women practitioners and professionals will be encouraged to present their findings for discussion and possible publication. Publication of research materials dealing with feminine perspectives can demonstrate the validity of new educational directions, and provide the University of California's Berkeley campus with the leadership position in education for women that it already holds in many other fields of endeavor.

Conclusion

Visitors to the year-old Center have commented on the enthusiasm of the staff and the atmosphere of optimism. Both staff and clients recognize, however, that effecting changes in institutional attitudes requires consistent effort over time. An educational institution is no exception to this rule. Accordingly, the Center's staff, clients and friends see sustained effort of the kind they have embarked on as essential to winning fair access for women. With hard work, they see the goal being achieved, and the entire University community benefitting. They see the Women's Center, the first on the Berkeley campus, as tangible evidence that a century-old University can still change for the better.

NOTES

[1] See K. Patricia Cross, "The Undergraduate Woman," Research Report 5, American Association for Higher Education (1971) and "The Woman Student," in *Women in Higher Education*, background papers for participants in the 55th Annual Meeting of the American Council on Education (1972). See also an Educational Testing Service Survey on the graduate, based on 1971 data.

[2] President's Task Force on Higher Education, *Report on Higher Education* (U.S. Office of Education, Washington, D.C., 1971).

[3] See various recent studies (1971 & 1973), U.S. Dept. of Labor, Wages and Standards Division, Women's Bureau, particularly *Educational Attainment of U.S. Women; Why Women Work;* and *Women and Work.*

[4] See the work of Dr. Bernice Sandler, Project on the Status of Women, American Association of Colleges (various publications), outlining and interpreting bills and executive orders that are generally understood to deal with "affirmative action."

[5] Chairman Frances Davis was also Assistant Dean of the California College of Trial Judges. Five faculty members served on the Committee: Elizabeth Colson (anthropology), Paul Heist (education), Dean George Maslach (engineering), Roberta Park (physical education), and Margaret Gordon (industrial relations). Also on the Committee were community leader Erma Rice, faculty wife Frances (Mrs. Charles) Townes, law student Joan Hanrahan, and Marion Sproul Goodin, who has long been active in University affairs.

[6] For the Announcement see *University Bulletin*, June 19, 1972.

[7] The Berkeley campus Women's Center is located in T-9, north of the main library.

Health and Hospitals:
Planning, Governance and Finance

Vol. 15   No. 1   February 1974

Comprehensive Health Planning in the San Francisco Bay Area: Problems and Prospects for the "Federation Experiment"

Donald B. Ardell and Richard P. Hafner, Jr.
Executive Director,   President, BACHPC, and
Bay Area Comprehensive   Public Affairs Officer,
Health Planning Council   U.C. Berkeley

"The fact is that despite dramatic technical gains, medicine is a sick industry. Its organizational structure is obsolete and its practitioners show little willingness to aid in the rational reorganization of the health care delivery system. Shortages and maldistribution of health manpower and facilities continue, and charges keep soaring . . . double that of the general advance in the consumer price level. . . . Opinion is spreading . . . that high costs could be reduced considerably were the industry run more efficiently.'"

Introduction

Pressures to contain increasing health costs, reduce program fragmentation and improve the availability of health care motivated the 89th Congress to enact the "Partnership for Health" in 1966. This act (P.L. 89–749) authorized the formation of state and area-wide planning councils to be controlled by consumers of health services. The councils' function was to plan "comprehensively" for health manpower, facilities and services, and for environmental health. By the beginning of 1974, comprehensive health planning (CHP) had been established and was operating in all 50 states and in 218 regions. Its level of effectiveness is a matter of some controversy, first in terms of return on investment of volunteer labor and dollar expenditure, and second with respect to its impact on the health problems that led to the creation of CHP.

This paper will review the nature of the present CHP program in the San Francisco Bay Area, and focus on the results of and prospects for effective Bay Area health planning in the years to come. Particular attention will be given to the unique aspects of the "Federation Experiment"; to the kinds of health problems identified in the Bay Area and what might be done about these problems; and to relationships between the health planning council and other regional planning mechanisms.

Comprehensive Health Planning in the Bay Area: A New Organization

Following the enactment of P. L. 89–749, much activity, concern and political intrigue were devoted to the establishment of *the* official areawide comprehensive health planning (CHP) agency for the San Francisco Bay Area. Existing organizations now termed the "associated" organizations (including the Northern California Hospital Planning Council, Bay Area Social Planning Council, Association of Bay Area Governments, and the Bay Area Health Association) competed for the coveted designation, with its responsibilities and federal funding. After almost two years of attempts to obtain consensus, the major organizations agreed to create a new body that would represent certain elements they all wanted. In 1970 the federal Department of Health, Education, and Welfare (HEW) provided financing to organize and develop the Bay Area Comprehensive Health Planning Council (BACHPC).

Problems, Goals and Policies

Health problems in the San Francisco Bay Area are not markedly different—except in scale—from those throughout the United States. Skyrocketing costs for hospital and medical care, inadequate distribution of health services, insufficient supply of health resources, waste and duplication, poor coordination—the list of problems is familiar. One of the federation's first challenges was to identify the nature of these problems within the Bay Area, and to define a limited number of issues on which the modest resources and mandate of the CHP program could be focused. The issues were formulated into a set of long-range goals and policies that won federation-wide approval. The nine major goals are as follows:

(1) Comprehensive health services to be equally available, acceptable and accessible to all Bay Area residents.

(2) Medically underserved groups to be provided with equal access to comprehensive health services.

(3) Consumers to have a major voice in all health planning and policy decisions.

(4) Social problems that cause or compound health problems to be recognized and reduced.

(5) A health delivery system to be provided for the Bay Area; one that makes health services readily available, utilizes health resources efficiently, and that is strongly linked to provide continuous and comprehensive care services.

(6) Health care services and facilities to be adequately distributed in balance with community needs.

(7) Health care costs to be maintained at a level the community and individual consumers can afford and one that supports an adequate program of health services for all.

(8) High quality health care services to be provided for all.

(9) A Bay Area health system to be adequately supplied with the needed numbers and types of health manpower, appropriately trained and distributed.

Each of these broad goals was followed by a series of specific policy statements expressing ways health policy could be made effective. The statement of goals and policies was approved by the BACHPC in January 1973, and made possible the next stages of plan development and implementation.

The Milieu

BACHPC is currently one of the largest and most highly developed of the nation's areawide comprehensive health planning organizations. It encompasses the 9 Bay Area counties: over 7,000 square miles in area and 4.7 million people. Included are 105 hospitals, 306 nursing homes, 35 home health agencies, 44 clinics, 31 mental retardation centers, 2 alcoholism hospitals, 12 long-term (nursing home) facilities, and 15 establishments for handicapped persons. The California State Department of Health has divided the Bay region into 18 "health facility planning areas" based on population size and travel time to health facilities. The recognized planning area districts are the official boundaries for calculating need requirements at the county level; these districts constitute the basic parameter for much of the BACHPC's review work.

Structure: The Federation Experiment

The structure for comprehensive health planning in the Bay Area is unique. In most areas, planning and decision making are organized at a single location, often in concert with and subordinated to an overall regional planning agency with responsibilities much wider than health (e.g., COGs like the Association of Bay Area Governments). In contrast, the Bay Area's CHP is decentralized among 9 county CHP councils *and* linked in San Francisco by a regional or "headquarters" office, henceforth simply referred to as BACHPC.

The term "federation" best describes the Bay Area plan; the "Statement of Agreement" signed by all 9 county councils defines the federation as

a structure uniting the Bay Area Comprehensive Health Planning Council (the official entity responsible for the regional program) and the 9 county councils for the purpose of comprehensive health planning in the San Francisco Bay Area . . .

This "federation" is an attempt to realize the best of both worlds: i.e., maximum local citizen involvement and determination of community health policy, combined with areawide specialized technical excellence on complex issues that transcend county lines. Put another way, the federation facilitates maximum local responsiveness balanced by the wider regional view. The federation model for CHP has attracted national attention in the past year; for this reason and because of its importance to the shaping of Bay Area CHP issues and relationships, a fuller explanation of the federation mechanism is in order.

The BACHPC governing board now consists of 47 members, of whom a majority are (and by law, must be) consumers of health services.[2] There are three categories of board members: (1) 3 county council-member delegates from each of the 9 constitutent county CHP councils; (2) 4 associate delegates, one each from the 4 "associated" organizations having related areawide health interests; and (3) 16 at-large members chosen from throughout the Bay Area to insure wider representation of concerned and affected interests. Of the three delegates appointed by each of the 9 county councils, one must be a consumer, one a provider, and one representative of the "medically underserved." Many "associate" and "at-large" delegates are also county council members. Elections are held annually with members holding three-year staggered terms. (See end notes for glossary and background details; and chart of organizational structure.) In addition, all BACHPC committees, including the policy-guiding Executive Committee, include at least one representative from each county council. (BACHPC committees are jointly staffed by one regional and one county director, although one or the other has primary responsibility.)

Councils have developed differently in each county. Some have been based on pre-existing health councils; others grew in response to federal legislation and were originally convened by representatives of the state and federal governments. Some council members were self-nominated and came forward in response to notices in the media; in other cases the county health officer, after consultation with the board of supervisors, named members from a list compiled from suggestions by interested individuals and organizations. In all cases, councils are required to meet specific federal guidelines that include principles of representation and accountability. Each of the county CHP councils is a legally incorporated, nonprofit, private organization with a lay membership of interested volunteers. Each council hires its own staff, maintains local offices, and in all respects except size meets federal and state guideline criteria for CHP eligibility (e.g., consumer majority, broad representation). To avoid having 10 separate CHP programs in the one Bay Area region, the board leadership of all 9 county councils and the BACHPC in 1972 devised the "Statement of Agreement" (noted above) that defines the respective prerogatives, powers, and responsibilities of the county units and the parent BACHPC organization, and serves as the federation's constitution.

How It Operates: Responsibilities for Planning and Review

Plan and Work Program. The core of the Bay Area's CHP program is the Comprehensive Health Plan. Its purpose is to provide for the most effective and equitable organization of health care services, facilities, and manpower from the standpoint of the public interest. The plan document specifies ways that community health can be enhanced through systems of illness prevention and health care delivery that provide services at reasonable cost. The plan is the foundation for all other functions of the organization and has critical importance as the framework for all BACHPC review activities (discussed below).

The federation headquarters staff and volunteers formulate the general sections of the plan: background on the service and how it is currently provided; summary of trends; identification of geographic service areas for planning; guidelines to shape policy choices; inventory of resources; and estimates of need. The county staffs and volunteers provide the all-important action recommendations and implementation. Again, interaction continues between the headquarters and county units through the work of the management team, committee deliberations, and other mechanisms.

A "management team" of county and BACHPC staff meets every Friday to review the business of the organization, including follow-through reporting on work assignments, problem analysis and delegation of assignments. The "management team" facilitates the high level of staff interaction and coordination needed for the widely dispersed staff and council operations.

The federation model is further characterized by the development, conduct, periodic revision and expansion of the Bay Area CHP work program. The management team prepares the initial statement of work possibilities and the statement is then circulated for comment to the county councils and BACHPC. It then goes back to the BACHPC Executive Committee prior to full BACHPC deliberation and adoption. The process is repeated every six months.

Review and Comment/Approval. The BACHPC also has responsibilties for reviewing 17 federal and/or state programs. In addition, private sources (lending institutions, foundations, UBAC) frequently ask the organization to review health-related applications for funds. Of all the review tasks, the most significant is related to the "certificate of need" mandated by the California Legislature in 1970 (Chapter 1451, *1969 Revised Statutes*). This law requires any hospital or nursing home proposing to increase its bed complement or change a licensure category to first obtain the approval of the designated areawide CHP agency. This must be based in large part on the proponent's showing of community need for the project.

In conducting these and other review functions, BACHPC delegates initial review tasks to the relevant county council. In the case of legally mandated certificate-of-need reviews, BACHPC retains authority for the final decision but acts on recommendations from the county council, which conducts the required public hearing and supervises preparation of the staff report.

BACHPC headquarters, which is best equipped with technical staff, assigns experienced health planners to help county directors in the initial analysis of applications. In the case of applications having primary impact only on a single county, BACHPC delegates authority for the final decision to that county. (These procedures are detailed in a review manual approved by the county councils and BACHPC.)

Special Studies and Public Issues

Most of what is being done about health problems under the federation CHP program falls within four basic functions: (1) plan development and implementation, (2) special studies, (3) public issue involvement, (4) and project review. Plan development (1), and project review (4) have already been noted. A brief summary of (2) special studies and (3) public issue involvement may be helpful here. Note that some of the functions overlap, and each supports the others.

The special studies function requires that the agency investigate and analyze components of the health delivery system and needs of special population groups in order to (1) promote certain actions, e.g., to control and prevent construction of skilled nursing home beds when a need cannot be shown; and (2) to expand the breadth and detail of the Comprehensive Health Plan.

Public issue involvement requires the agency to take positions on current issues, controversies, and other public concerns about local, state, or national health matters. As of the new year (1974), all areawide CHP agencies must also demonstrate their contribution toward three priority areas, as required by the Secretary of HEW: (1) cost control; (2) prevention of uneconomic duplication; and (3) fostering of competition.

Financing

BACHPC is presently (1974) funded at approximately $1 million per year. Sources are as follows:

Source	Percentage of Total Receipts
HEW	41
County govts.	32
Private funds	13
State govt.	9
UBAC (United Bay Area Crusade)	5
Total	100%

BACHPC is the official grantee for all federal and state funds in support of the 9-county program. The county councils bear the major share of the program load and employ 16 of the 24 professionals on the federation staff. Of the total 1974 budget from all sources ($1,001,072), the county councils utilize $602,696 or 60 percent.

Federation resources also help attract important financial support from county boards of supervisors, which provide BACHPC with most of the local dollars to match available federal funds. It is unlikely that BACHPC could obtain these scarce allocations from local governments, unless it had the local staff, volunteers, and other on-the-scene resources of the county councils. Annual fund raising solicitations—consisting of a limited mailing of request-for-support letters to major Bay Area institutions—and an aggressive search for supplemental grants for special studies, provide additional staff manpower at the federation headquarters.

Communications

Maintaining communications with a membership of more than 350 volunteer directors, plus another thousand or more committee and task force members, is a continuing and complex task. There are monthly meetings, with a heavy flow of reading material from both the county and BACHPC offices in advance of the meetings. Moreover, the headquarters staff distributes weekly, monthly, quarterly, and annual reports on CHP activities and progress throughout the Bay Area. Further, seminars on CHP are held annually throughout the area, on special topics and complex issues, e.g., the special training provided by county councils for persons who will serve on hearing panels. Most of the training sessions are held under county auspices.

Relationships with Other Regional Agencies

Many planning functions performed by BACHPC and the constituent county councils, however, require more than the mandate and resources assigned to the CHP program or the effective workings of the federation itself. Accordingly, good working relationships with other regional planning agencies are of great consequence to the Bay Area CHP program, and, in fact, one of the required functions for all CHP organizations is to establish relationships with other regional planning bodies. The Association of Bay Area Governments (ABAG) heads the list of agencies with which planning coordination and collaboration is most essential. ABAG is the area's COG, and its multifunctional planning organization. BACHPC and ABAG have enjoyed a close association on common tasks relating to health for more than two years: a formal "Statement of Agreement" defines the expectations and commitments that each pledges to the other. The agreement makes such provisions as sharing of data and other information, assistance in review and comment and in plan development and analysis of the other's special reports. In addition, ABAG and BACHPC have contracted for joint support of staff on projects of mutual interest. As noted earlier, ABAG is one of the four Bay Area agencies that send a delegate to the BACHPC board of directors. Finally, it should be noted that the two agencies are presently (January 1974) awaiting word on HEW funding for a joint demonstration project grant ($200,000) to finance expanded common efforts on key regional issues of mutual interest.

BACHPC also has established linkages with the United Bay Area Crusade, Mental Retardation and Developmental Disability Area Boards, Hospital Council of Northern California, county health departments and the Bay Area Health Association, Bay Area Social Planning Council, health training programs at universities in the Bay Area, Metropolitan Transit Commission, California state and local medical societies,

California Hospital Association, voluntary health agencies and, last but certainly not least in terms of either significance or time expended, the new State Department of Health. In most of these relationships, the focus is on a two-way exchange of information, participation in meetings and program assignments of mutual interest, receipt of regular activity reports, and varied additional efforts at mutual support and collaboration. In addition to these BACHPC relationships, each of the 9 county CHP councils seeks to create close ties with local organizations that can be helpful in federation planning or that might benefit from awareness of CHP activities.

Some Strengths and Weaknesses

The strengths of the federation model have been suggested or are evident in the foregoing commentary. Potential hazards of the federation approach, that can be viewed as possible weaknesses, relate to the same elements that can be considered as strengths. Another clarifying look at a few of the basic aspects of the federation help to illustrate this:

(1) It takes effort to frame the issues, orient the membership, and make decisions commensurate with the large number of county and BACHPC committees and councils that must participate in health policy-making. A smaller structure would be easier to operate.

(2) Managing a federation of 10 corporations with independently employed, locally accountable executives takes more time and presents greater administrative challenges than would be expected in the customary regional agency where operations are centralized. The management function in the Bay Area CHP federation consumes 15 percent of the program resources.

(3) The work program in a decentralized organization reflects a different set of priorities from those a regionally focused operation would address. Tasks that might receive less attention under an alternate central planning framework include neighborhood local services, health care needs in selected communities within a county, and issues of primarily one-county interest.

(4) Under a strongly centralized regional pattern, there would probably be more plan preparation and development and less plan implementation. Specifically, the designated CHP body would use available resources to employ a diverse range of technical expertise to *produce* plan sections on a broad range of issues (e.g., health financing, environmental planning). Community organization and other action-oriented mobilizations now highlighted in the federation pattern would receive less attention, and one result might be less follow-through on plan recommendations.

On these and other counts—such as the fact that any staff director is not accountable for overall program performance because he cannot hire/fire and otherwise direct all federation staff—the federation format both confers benefits and carries shortcomings. One's final evaluation depends on his point of view, location within the organization, philosophy of administration, and other factors. But at this time all parties seem to agree that federation strengths far outweigh potential weaknesses. Accordingly, they would create a federation along the above lines if one did not exist.

The Federation's Accomplishments

BACHPC and its constituent county councils, acting as a united federation for over three years, have scored a number of accomplishments.[3] None of the modest "success stories" has either changed the system or dramatically reduced costs. But the overall results clearly demonstrate that planning efforts have nevertheless proven sound investments. Among the federation's principal recent accomplishments are:

(1) Savings to the general public of $14,728,600 in construction costs that would have resulted from unnecessary hospital construction, and another $1,159,640 in unnecessary nursing home construction. Their avoidance was made possible by the federation's exercise of its veto power, under certification-of-need authority.

(2) Completion and state approval of the hospital and nursing home sections of the Comprehensive Health Plan, which contain specific recommendations for development of county health programs and detailed guidance for the review of project applications.

(3) Passage of moratoria in two counties temporarily prohibiting further increases of acute hospital beds (those vacated after 10 days) and skilled nursing home beds.

(4) Publication of the long-range goals and policies document that provides guiding principles for health service development and project reviews.

(5) Investigation and subsequent publication of an extensive report on the State Medi-Cal "Reform" Program, which documented the many deleterious effects of the program on poorly served populations, and contained a series of recommendations for improvements and follow-up analyses.

(6) Preparation and utilization of county plans for mental health, emergency medical services, hemodialysis (kidney machine) services, hospital mergers, joint services and sharing, home health services, and the revision of outmoded hospital districts (to make them consistent with planning areas that conform to changes in population trends).

BACHPC staff has also identified and substantiated the high cost paid by the public for an excess of hospital beds. Such under-utilization is caused by unnecessary and/or inappropriate expansions and institutional competition. The available Bay Area supply of 17,258 beds (medical/surgical, obstetric, and pediatric services), presently occupied at an average 60 percent rate, suggests that approximately 6,885 beds are empty in the Bay Area. At an estimated (conservative) bed cost of $26.00 daily, these empty beds cost the citizens of the area $65,407,500 per year. Put another way, there are presently enough beds in the San Francisco Bay Area to meet state need projections as far ahead as 1990. These illustrative accomplishments suggest that

—while major changes in the system, and impacts on health levels of the population are not yet readily discernible as a consequence of Bay Area CHP endeavors —other less dramatic but nevertheless useful results have been produced.

Conclusion: Changes in the Wind

The "Partnership for Health" legislation that underlies all of this activity and the federation's existence will expire in June 1974. The scope of new proposals being placed before the U. S. Congress is another story in itself.[4] A strong movement from several quarters is underway to change the constituency of the planning councils to insure greater local governmental control, to increase the emphasis on regulatory controls, to provide greater power and resources for the planning function, and to call for a more demanding performance accounting from the designated organizations. Many other changes have been advocated by legislators, special study commissions, and administration officials in HEW, and it is not clear at this point what might result. Continuation of the status quo for another year is also a rumored possibility.

Whatever the outcome of efforts to alter the planning function as currently practiced by areawide CHP agencies, BACHPC, and its constituent county CHP councils, the Bay Area's federation experiment is not likely to go unnoticed. It could very well be a national forerunner or model for the next stage in the evolution of more effective planning mechanisms. This nation's health system is still "unwell," as dramatically stated in the Institute's report quoted at the beginning of this article. But, at least one condition is different today, in part due to CHP and related programs, and in part due to worsening health system problems. This crucial new factor is public recognition of and determination to do something about the major health care delivery system. Health has become a preeminent social issue. Major proposals to restructure the health care system are before the Congress. A heightened consciousness of the importance of preventive health maintenance has taken hold. We can also expect other major and welcome changes. Areawide Comprehensive Health Planning is a useful mechanism for citizen participation in determining the direction and speed of such needed change.

NOTES

1. Margaret Greenfield, *Meeting the Costs of Health Care: The Bay Area Experience and the National Issues* (Berkeley: Institute of Governmental Studies, University of California, 1972), p. 124.

2. The definition of "consumer" as opposed to "provider" has never been rendered exact, but it is generally interpreted by federal program officials to mean an individual not employed by or trained in a health related occupation—or married to someone who is.

3. Recommended readings for persons interested in learning more about the CHP program in general or the Bay Area Federation in particular include the following articles and special reports: (1) "Limitations and Priorities in CHP," *Inquiry*, 10:49–56 (September 1973); (2) Block, McGibony and Associates (8777 First Avenue, Silver Springs, Md.) reports on *Plan Development; Selection and Management of Committees; Review and Comment; Orientation and Continuing Education*

of Boards and Staff; Relationships in CHP; and Fund-Raising in CHP; and (3) Annual Report for 1972–73 and Areawide Health Facilities and Services Plan published by BACHPC (16 California St., Room 302, San Francisco, Calif., 94111).

4. The "National Health Policy and Health Development Act of 1974" (HR12053) would succeed CHP legislation. Introduced by Congressmen Roy, Rodgers, and Hastings, HR12053 would establish a network of areawide Health Services Agencies (HSA's) to combine the functions of existing areawide CHP and Regional Medical Programs.

Glossary and Some Background Details

County Councils:

Size: 30 to 45 members; lay persons who are volunteers.

Each council is a legally incorporated nonprofit organization that adopts its own by-laws and procedures. These must be approved by the Bay Area Comprehensive Health Planning Council and the funding sources, according to governmental guidelines.

Each hires staff and an executive director, although Napa, Solano and Sonoma councils presently share one executive.

Each county council sends 3 delegates designated by the council president to the regional council: one provider, one consumer, and one person who represents the concerns of the medically underserved.

Examples: *Providers* include hospital administrators, physicians of various kinds including those in group and private practice, nursing home representatives, community clinic operators (free clinics), social workers and other mental health workers.

Consumers include representatives of labor, business, local government (mostly county), and consumer action groups, minority organizations, professional and academic groups.

Medically underserved include those eligible for categorical federal assistance such as Medicaid and Welfare, those who feel disadvantaged and/or subject to racial discrimination, and rural residents who must travel long distances for primary care.

Bay Area Comprehensive Health Planning Council (BACHPC):

Associate delegates: Each of the four influential associated organizations, Bay Area Social Planning Council, ABAG, Northern California Hospital Planning Council and Bay Area Health Association sends a board member to sit on BACHPC. Each sits as an associate member with full voting powers.

At-large delegates: Designated by BACHPC as needed to balance federation structure so that it will be representative of the community as required.

Executive Committee: Consists of 4 elected officers, plus presidents or their designates from other counties not represented by the elected officers.

Management Team: Consists of staff members of county councils and of the BACHPC.

Bay Area Comprehensive Health Planning Council: Organization Table

Federated Agency Structure: Volunteer Board Members

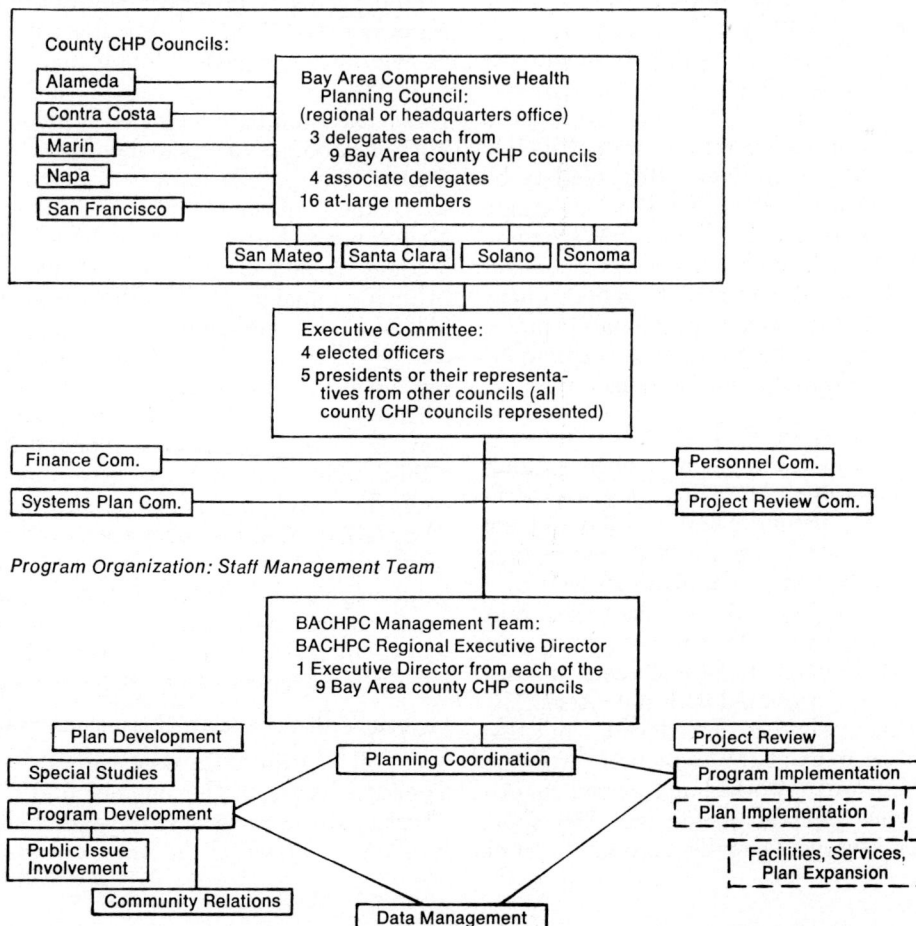

Program Organization: Staff Management Team

Politics: Campaign Finance; Congressional Power

Vol. 15   No. 2   April 1974

Changing Regulations:
Campaign Finance in the Golden State

by James Fay

Department of Political Science
California State University, Hayward

The Watergate scandal sparked a widespread resurgence of interest in and a lively debate concerning the financing of political campaigns; it also triggered some important consequences in California. In 1973, California passed a new statewide campaign finance law (AB 703), which tightened some of the regulations on registration, reporting, contributions and expenditures. In addition, a coalition of citizens' groups succeeded in placing on the June 1974 ballot a statewide initiative that would institute reforms in campaign finance more stringent than those provided by AB 703.

Despite substantive action by both activist citizens and lawmakers, and media attention devoted to misuse of campaign money, the specifics of campaign finance abuses and the possibilities for reform are not widely understood. Among the many issues that need to be clarified are the following: What kinds of campaign finance laws has California had in the past? Were these laws adequately enforced? What were and are some of the major loopholes? What recent actions have tightened laws in this area? What are the public policy objectives underlying campaign finance legislation? And what pressures add to the reform momentum?[1]

Background

Until 1973 California's campaign finance statutes were weak, loophole-ridden laws that gave a superficial appearance of regulation. These statutes did not require much more control over election finance than candidate reports of the names of individuals who gave $500 or more to a campaign. As we shall see, some loopholes still remain. In an effort to strengthen controls, the California leadership of the citizens' interest group, Common Cause, consulted with state Assemblyman Henry Waxman, who had introduced a bill that tightened several sections of the campaign disclosure laws. Waxman's bill was reworked and passed the Assembly. A somewhat different version (SB 509), sponsored by Senator Mervyn Dymally, passed the state

Senate about the same time. Representatives of Assemblyman Waxman, Senator Dymally, Secretary of State Edmund G. Brown, Jr. and Common Cause worked out the compromise, AB 703, that Governor Ronald Reagan signed into law.

Reasoning Behind Campaign Laws

Before examining the strengths and weaknesses of AB 703 and the subsequent initiative (Political Reform Act of 1974), it may be useful to consider briefly a basic assumption of reformist philosophy and some legislators' attitudes toward reform. Historically, campaign finance statutes have been geared to the concept that public disclosure of the source and use of campaign contributions would cause an alert electorate to punish candidates who (1) accept contributions that are excessive or come from questionable sources, or (2) make expenditures beyond acceptable limits.

At the very least, the voter could discern those to whom the candidate might be beholden. The underlying policy objective was to increase citizen control over the electoral process. It was assumed that if the voter was denied information about the critical issue of campaign finance he was thereby denied the possibility of holding elected officials accountable for the conduct of their campaigns and for the action they took on behalf of their contributors. The public was cast in the role of Adam Smith's invisible hand, delicately balancing the electoral process in accord with the dictates of existing political norms. It was thought that in this way, state restrictions on campaign finance could be safely minimized and the government bureaucracy could be freed to attend to more pressing concerns. The realities of election finance were found to be somewhat more perverse, however, and the invisible public hand appeared to exercise only minimal and inadequate control. Whether voter information and choice will be increased with more comprehensive campaign finance laws remains to be demonstrated.

Legislative Attitudes Toward Campaign Finance Reform

A poll of California state legislators, conducted by Common Cause in the summer of 1973, revealed the officials' attitudes toward the tightening of campaign laws. Fifty percent of the state senators and 60 percent of the assemblymen responded to the questionnaire on a non-confidential basis. (Tables 1 and 2 summarize their responses.) They disclosed an apparently substantial bipartisan base of support for more comprehensive campaign disclosure laws. Further, a heavy majority in both houses favored audits by the state Franchise Tax Board for all campaign finance statements. Sizable majorities in the Senate and Assembly also supported limits on contributions by individuals and on expenditures by groups not under the control of a candidate.

There was bipartisan agreement in the Assembly on the desirability of placing a ceiling on campaign spending; in the Senate, the GOP was evenly divided, while the Democrats heavily favored a limitation.[2] The only item that generated major partisan conflict was the issue of public financing of campaigns. Democrats, whose party has had severe financial problems in recent years, strongly favored public financing, and Republicans, whose financial base has been more secure, strongly opposed it.

TABLE 1
Common Cause Campaign Finance Poll of California Senate (40 members)
(related to SB 509)

| | Number Responding | | | | | | | | |
| | Total | | | Democrats | | | Republicans | | |
	Yes	No	Other	Yes	No	Other	Yes	No	Other
Disclose all contributions and expenditures over $100	18	1	–	9	1	–	9	–	–
Disclose home address, occupation, employer & business address of all contributors over $100	15	3	2	8	1	1	7	2	1
Audit all campaign finance statements by Franchise Tax Board	14	3	2	6	1	2	8	2	–
Require reporting of off year contributions & expenditures	20	–	–	10	–	–	10	–	–
Require public financing for most campaign costs	9	10	1	7	2	1	2	8	–
Limit individual contributions	15	3	1	8	–	1	7	3	–
Limit campaign spending by groups not under candidate's control	17	1	1	8	–	1	9	1	–
Limit total campaign spending	14	5	–	9	–	–	5	5	–

TABLE 2
Common Cause Campaign Finance Poll of California Assembly (80 members)
(related to SB 509)

| | Number Responding | | | | | | | | |
| | Total | | | Democrats | | | Republicans | | |
	Yes	No	Other	Yes	No	Other	Yes	No	Other
Disclose all contributions and expenditures over $100	45	1	–	31	–	–	14	1	–
Disclose home address, occupation, employer & business address of all contributors over $100	36	4	4	25	3	1	11	1	3
Audit all campaign finance statements by Franchise Tax Board	35	5	1	24	3	–	11	2	1
Require reporting of off year contributions & expenditures	42	1	–	29	–	–	13	1	–
Require public financing for most campaign costs	26	10	2	24	2	1	2	8	1
Limit individual contributions	28	11	1	18	7	1	10	4	–
Limit campaign spending by groups not under candidate's control	32	5	–	20	2	–	12	3	–
Limit total campaign spending	34	5	1	24	1	1	10	4	–

The legislature may have been stimulated to act with unusual vigor through the efforts of Assembly Speaker Robert Moretti and Senate Majority Leader George Moscone, then both seeking the Democratic nomination for governor in 1974. Moretti and Moscone may have sought to remove or mute discussion of campaign finance in the 1974 campaign, and thus remove a prime issue for Brown, who was the early front runner in the public opinion polls. The announced intention of Common Cause, the People's Lobby, Brown and other proponents to put a comprehensive political reform initiative before the electorate in June 1974 may also have goaded the Legislature to act on the bill.

Categories of Proposals

Advocates of campaign finance reform had made many suggestions during the past few years. Their ideas were reflected in a potpourri of 1973 bills that in turn served as material for shaping AB 703. Such reform concepts fall into nine basic categories:

1. Prohibiting or limiting campaign contributions by candidates, individuals or groups (AB 590 and SB 234).
2. Limiting campaign expenditures (AB 121 and SB 63).
3. Relating to campaign finance disclosure (AB 316, AB 703, SB 312, and SB 509).
4. Providing for public financing of campaigns through state treasury funds (AB 363 and SB 234).
5. Establishing a Fair Campaign Practices Code and a Fair Campaign Practices Commission (AB 145 and SB 352).
6. Providing public campaign funds through forgiveness provisions on the state income tax (SB 487).
7. Requiring thorough auditing of campaign finance reports (AB 316 and SB 234).
8. Providing for state publication of a comprehensive report on the financial transactions of all campaign committees (AB 316 and SB 234).
9. Enforcing the various reform suggestions by giving appropriate investigative agencies subpoena power (SB 509) and allowing the public to sue to enforce compliance with the law (SB 487).

In addition to the above approaches, there were also proposals to upgrade enforcement by encouraging citizen oversight of the campaign finance process. Public plaintiffs thus could recover 50 percent of civil action judgments against individuals who violate provisions of campaign finance laws.

The New Law

Rarely if ever does the final version of a law incorporate all of the components reformers would like, and the Waxman-Dymally Campaign Disclosure Act (AB 703) was no exception. The major reforms included:

1. Listing by name, city, occupation, and employer or principal place of business the contributors who give $100 or more.
2. Listing by name and city those to whom expenditures over $100 are made.
3. Registering with the Secretary of State all campaign committees that collect or expect to collect $500 or more in a calendar year.
4. Identifying the individual who files the campaign statement by name, residential and business address, and phone number.
5. Filing campaign statements as of 10 and 28 days before and 31 days after the election.
6. Reporting political contributions or expenditures in non-election years.
7. Requiring that virtually all candidates for office file statements even if they spend under $200 for their campaigns.
8. Prohibiting anonymous contributions and those made in the name of another.
9. Prohibiting cash contributions of $500 or more.
10. Easing provisions for public inspection and copying of campaign finance records.
11. Providing for stricter enforcement by specifically directing the Secretary of State and county clerks to report violations to law enforcement authorities, and by directing the Attorney General and district attorneys to enforce the campaign finance statutes.
12. Authorizing plaintiffs in a civil action against violators of the campaign laws to receive 50 percent of any campaign money unreported or improperly reported.
13. Providing for the State Board of Equalization to audit all campaign finance statements of individuals who receive 15 percent or more of the vote in special or general elections, and of all candidates who have spent $25,000 or more in any election.

Thus the major impact of AB 703 will be to disclose a larger percentage of campaign contributions, to disclose more contributions before the election, and to eliminate the legal laundering of funds.

Restrictions on Campaign Contributions and Expenditures

California currently provides four major restrictions on campaign contributions. The first two restrictions antedated and were not changed by AB 703: (1) Any individual who holds a state license is prohibited from making a contribution to the official who awards such licenses, and the official is similarly forbidden to accept any such contributions (Cal. *Elections Code* 12042, 12043). (2) Candidates are not permitted to solicit contributions from state employees (Cal. *Gov't Code* 19730). AB 703 added the following provisions: (3) Anonymous contributions of more than $100 are prohibited, as are all contributions made in the name of someone other than the contributor (Cal. *Elections Code* 11561, 11563). (4) Cash contributions of over $500 are forbidden (Cal. *Elections Code* 11565).

California's only substantial restriction of campaign *expenditures* (eliminated by AB 703) listed items for which money might legally be spent by a candidate or his supporters.[*]

The only incentive to encourage campaign contributions was a pre-AB 703 provision for individual tax deductions up to $100 for political gifts (Cal. *Revenue and Taxation Code* 17234).[*] Presumably, this was in-

---

[*] Note: In addition to code sections cited in the text, see also code references in "Summary of Comparative Provisions" at the end of this report.

tended to encourage a large number of modest contributions and to help reduce candidate dependence on relatively few large contributors.

Reporting, Public Disclosure and the Consequences

Record-keeping and reporting by an impartial official agency are essential if control is to be effective and restriction meaningful.

Under AB 703, all candidates and the treasurers of their campaign committees must prepare and file with the Secretary of State (or with the county or city clerk) a list of receipts and expenditures for which the candidate or committee was responsible (for primary and general elections). The statements are submitted on standard forms (Cal. *Elections Code* 11584) and must be filed as of the 28th and 10th days prior to, and the 31st day after, the election. They list cumulatively all contributions and expenditures.

Reporting campaign finances is intended to force disclosure of contributions and expenditures, so that the public presumably will take into account this information on voting day. But the realities of the reporting process frustrate this goal, since some of the information is made public only after the election, when it is too late for the voters to react. AB 703, for example, does not require the listing of contributors' addresses, so that identification of the contributor is all but impossible for the voter.[4] Further, the candidate and committee reports flow into the Secretary of State's or the county clerk's office, where they remain until four years after the winner finishes his term of office. No summaries are prepared.

Oregon, more solicitous of public need for such data, does prepare summaries, and sends them to all newspapers, radio and TV stations in the state.[5]

As might be expected, the law provides for automatic reporting of missing statements to an appropriate legal authority for prosecution (Cal. *Elections Code* 11585). But this is a recent reform. Prior to AB 703, if a candidate or a campaign committee failed to file a report of campaign contributions and expenditures, or reported illegal expenditures, there was no automatic alert, and no code provision requiring any official to audit the statements for completeness or accuracy.[6]

As a consequence, before 1970 many candidates failed to file campaign finance statements, and prosecution of violations was rare. From 1966–1971 the Secretary of State recommended prosecution of only one individual, who was acquitted. Since 1971, the filing provision of the law has been strictly enforced and nearly complete compliance has resulted. In four instances, the office recommended that county district attorneys prosecute campaign finance law violators, but no one has actually been prosecuted.[7]

Punishment

If someone were knowingly and willfully to violate a campaign finance statute and be prosecuted under AB 703, he could be found guilty only of a misdemeanor, whereas under the pre-1973 law some such violations would have been felonies. Moreover, under the old law, a candidate could also be disqualified from office. Not so under the new law. The net result is thus a weakening of the penalty provision.

Loopholes

As we have seen, AB 703 leaves several loopholes, including the following:

1. No name requirement for contributions under $100.
2. No prohibitions against contributions by foreigners or by minors.
3. No prohibitions against cash contributions under $500.
4. No restriction on contributions by corporations and unions. A candidate or his family can contribute as much as they wish to his campaign or to others.
5. No restriction on the use of non-descriptive front names, such as the Association for Better Citizenship.
6. No subpoena power for the Secretary of State and county clerks to obtain documentary evidence for investigating campaign finance fraud, although under AB 703 the State Board of Equalization can obtain a subpoena as part of its audit of campaign statements. (Cal. *Elections Code* 11614)
7. No convenient, easily referenced official summaries of campaign contributions and expenditures. Thousands of pages of reports must be examined for a comprehensive picture of campaign finance for statewide elections.
8. Finally, the Secretary of State and most county clerks do not have sufficient staff to determine completeness and accuracy of finance statements. Whether the Legislature will provide the Board of Equalization with adequate staff to audit election returns properly remains to be seen.

Pressures for Further Change

Regardless of the short term impact of reforms or the fate of future proposals, there are two major reasons why it is unlikely that the issue of campaign finance will quickly fade away. First, the statewide initiative, the 1974 Political Reform Act, will be voted on by the electorate in June 1974 and the interest it has generated is likely to last.

Second, a small but powerful group of political activists, those who provide many of the large contributions in California, appear to be interested in changing the current ground rules of campaign finance. During the summer of 1973, the writer sent questionnaires to 264 individuals (and interest groups) who contributed $250 or more to the 1972 presidential campaign, the 1968, 1970 and 1972 congressional campaigns, and the 1972 state Senate races (See Table 3). Ninety-seven questionnaires (37 percent) were returned. Interestingly, 94 percent of the Democrats and 80 percent of the Republicans who responded supported restrictive laws limiting the amounts of money that could be contributed, collected and expended in political campaigns. Most would set campaign spending limits well below the usual levels for legislative and statewide office in hotly contested races (See Table 4).

TABLE 3
Categories of Contributors Queried

Level of respondent's contribution	Democrats			Republicans		
	Queries #	Replies #	%	Queries #	Replies #	%
$1000 or more to the 1972 presidential campaign	39	18	46	39	8	21
$250 or more to the 1972 presidential campaign	39	22	56	39	13	33
$250 or more to 1968, 1970 & 1972 congressional campaigns	38	13	34	36	14	39
Interest groups who contributed $250 or more to 1972 state Senate campaigns	13	4	31	21	5	24
OVERALL	129	57	44%	135	40	30%

Since there are no composite lists of contributors with addresses for all the campaigns covered, it was not possible to take a random sample of contributors in all categories. In many cases, most of the names on the available lists were included.

TABLE 4
Contributors Preferring Laws to Limit Campaign Expenditures

Campaign limits favored	All respondents		Democrats	Republicans
$40,000 or less for state legislators	Number	51	32	19
	Percent*	61	62	59
$60,000 or less for U. S. representatives	Number	49	31	18
	Percent*	58	61	56
$500,000 or less for U. S. senators or state governors	Number	54	31	23
	Percent*	64	60	72

* Percent of those who responded on each question.

TABLE 5
Contributors Preferring a Law to Provide for Government Subsidy of Campaigns so as to Eliminate Private Contributions

	All respondents			Democrats			Republicans		
	Yes	No	Total	Yes	No	Total	Yes	No	Total
Number ...	48	45	93	39	17	56	9	28	37
Percent ...	52	48	100	70	30	100	24	76	100

The contributors, both Republicans and Democrats, favored limits on amounts an individual or family can give or lend to any candidate as well as limits on funds made available to any family member who is a candidate. Over 80 percent of the Democrats and over 70 percent of the Republicans favored a limit of $5000 or less for contributions or loans to any candidate; and similar percentages favored limits ranging between $500 and $10,000 for individual and family contributions to a candidate's own campaign. In every case Republican contributors favored slightly higher contribution and expenditure limits than did their Democratic counterparts.

A sizable majority of contributors (roughly 80 percent of the Democrats and 70 percent of the Republicans) also favored total prohibition of contributions or loans both by business organizations and by unions. The only area with a major difference of opinion concerned public subsidies to fund political campaigns. Views on this issue split along party lines, with Democrats heavily in favor and Republicans even more heavily opposed (Table 5). In staking out such opposite opinions the California respondents reflect accurately the views of their respective state party chairmen.[8]

Despite this one major point of difference among the large contributors, a sizable majority of these individuals apparently support code revisions that go well beyond the present disclosure laws. Since these contributors comprise an influential constituency, they are in a position to press lawmakers to alter the structure of campaign finance.

Possible Impact of Reforms

The initial impact of California's 1973 disclosure law will probably not be great, although it may cause some candidate reluctance to accept contributions from lobbyists, whose contributions will now more easily be identified and publicized. The value of such publicity was recently illustrated in Ruben Ayala's victory in a special state Senate election in the 20th District. A key element of Ayala's election strategy was to publicize, with a massive advertising campaign, the financial contributions given to his Republican opponent, Assemblyman Jerry Lewis. Of course, disclosure laws might also pressure both contributors and candidates to avoid reporting contributions that might embarrass either the donor or the recipient.[9]

The 1974 Political Reform Act (Proposition 9) on the June ballot would tighten disclosure laws and establish a state Fair Political Practices Commission. More significantly, it would impose expenditure ceilings on candidates for statewide office, on party committees, and on independent committees. Expenditure ceilings are mixed blessings, however, since there is evidence that by themselves, in the absence of other campaign finance reforms, they work toward the advantage of incumbents.[10] To offset the incumbents' natural advantages in obtaining publicity and raising campaign funds, some public financing of elections might help. Neither AB 703 nor Proposition 9 provides for public financing.

If partial or complete public subsidy of political campaigns develops, over time it might be expected that candidates would be recruited from a slightly broader spectrum of society than they are now, since criteria other than wealth or access to wealth would become more important. Competition for political office might also become more widespread, since political resources other than money might be mobilized to challenge incumbents. Elected officials would probably become more responsive to other elements in their constituencies in addition to those able to provide sizable campaign contributions. This in turn could lead to substantially different policy outcomes, as lawmakers perceive that their political careers are determined more by their responsiveness to broader interests in their constituencies than had formerly been the case.

Persistent Problems

Before substantive reform in financing campaigns becomes a reality, however, a number of serious problems must be overcome. One of the most critical is finding a device for reducing the number of candidates, a traditional function of the high cost of campaigning. With public financing, the cost barrier would no longer be a critical screen. It might be that the only candidates who could obtain public financing for their campaigns would be those who could collect the signatures of several hundred or several thousand registered voters, or who could obtain endorsement from relevant political party organizations.

If party endorsements become crucial to obtaining public financing, official party organizations might experience a renaissance of prestige and influence. On the other hand, the impact of strong party organizations on the selection of candidates might also widen the policy gap between the two major parties, since candidates might be chosen by amateur party activists who tend to take more ideological policy positions than the electorate at large.

Public financing must be applied to primaries, as well as to general elections. Because primaries are expensive, great wealth becomes a dominant factor in the nominating process, and effectively undercuts the substance of reform.

Individual and group interests in the United States who have influence, and benefit from the current rules of financing campaigns, cannot be expected to give up their advantages easily, as attested by the defeat of a strong lobbyist-regulation bill in the California State Senate in the closing hours of the 1973 session.[11] If a tough public campaign finance bill becomes law, passes the constitutional test and is enforced, groups with current influence in Sacramento can be expected to find alternative ways to use their political resources. Political reformers will need to monitor constantly and analyze the uses of political resources and, within constitutional limits, regulate them so as to minimize the impact of wealth on political decisions.

Comprehensive campaign finance reform cannot and will not usher in the political millenium. It must be seen as part of a process, and not the ultimate goal. If enacted, reforms will perhaps effect a moderate redistribution of political resources and a moderate alteration in the political equilibrium of our society.

The reformers' hypothesis remains untested. It assumes that campaign finance reform will promote democratic values by exercising a leveling effect on one campaign resource: money; and that it will thereby make elected officials more accountable to a broader-based constituency. Since our national experience with strict campaign finance laws is so limited and our experience with public financing nonexistent, it is impossible to construct a reform agenda with great confidence. Thus, we need to experiment.

The wisest course may be to test a variety of public financing plans at the state and local levels, and to determine which works most equitably and efficiently. The sooner experiments begin, the sooner we can start to accumulate a body of experience. With such experience as a basis, we may be able to develop the kind of consensus that will make reform of political financing a reality.

NOTES

[1] The most convenient summary of California campaign finance laws is a booklet, *California Election Laws, 1972* (San Francisco: Carlisle Graphics, 1972). See also their *Supplement to California Election Laws, 1972.*

[2] When the compromise version of the campaign finance bill came to a final vote, the Senate passed the amended bill 35–1, and the Assembly approved 77–0. Hence, the Common Cause poll appears to have reflected legislative opinion accurately.

[3] Citizens' Research Foundation, *A Survey of State Statutes Regulating Political Finance* (Princeton: Citizens' Research Foundation, 1971).

[4] Before AB 703, laws governing campaign financing of ballot measures were somewhat tighter than those governing candidates. See California *Elections Code,* Secs. 11800–11835. AB 703 has blurred these differences.

[5] Oregon, Secretary of State, Elections Division, *Summary Report of Campaign Contributions and Expenditures, 1972 General Election* (Salem, Oregon: 1973).

[6] Statements are now checked for completeness and correctness of arithmetic, although as Common Cause researchers have discovered, the Secretary of State's small staff has not checked with complete accuracy. Under AB 703 (California *Elections Code* Secs. 11610–11614), statements of almost all major candidates will be audited.

[7] Telephone conversation with Daniel Lowenstein, special consultant to the Secretary of State, February 1, 1974. Apparently, the district attorneys did not prosecute because the candidates finally agreed to file proper campaign finance statements.

[8] Interviews with a number of state party chairmen around the country revealed that 20 Democratic state chairmen including California's, but no Republican state chairmen, favored federal subsidies for campaigns. Twenty-two Republicans including the California chairman, and only six Democratic chairmen, opposed such subsidies. See "Should Tax Dollars Pay for Politics?" *U.S. News and World Report,* 75 (8) August 20, 1973.

[9] Kenneth Reich, "Republican Aides Fault Nixon for Defeat in State Senate Race," Los Angeles *Times,* January 17, 1974, pp. 1 and 28.

[10] U.S., Congress, House, 93d Cong., 1st Sess., *Congressional Record,* 117: 33137–33140 (September 23, 1971). Representative Frenzel inserted into the *Record* an article documenting the advantages of incumbency in elections, and warning that imposing equal campaign expenditure limits on both incumbents and challengers would make the congressional election process even less competitive than it is now.

[11] Bruce Keppel, "Open-government initiative," *California Journal,* 4: 373–374 (November 1973).

50

SUMMARY OF COMPARATIVE PROVISIONS

(Asterisk* indicates sections referring to the California *Government Code: Government of the State*.
All other citations refer to the California *Elections Code* or proposed amendments.)

Pre-AB 703	AB 703	Proposed Political Reform Act of 1974 (Prop. 9)
I Fair Political Practices Commission 1) None.	1) Same as Pre-AB 703.	1) Establishes a Fair Political Practices Commission. Chap. 3

II Registration of Political Committees and Filing of Reports

Pre-AB 703	AB 703	Proposed Political Reform Act of 1974 (Prop. 9)
1) Committees not required to register.	1) All committees which receive contributions of $500 or more for political purposes in a calendar year shall register and report to the Secretary of State. 11531	1) Same as AB 703. 82013
2) Each candidate and each committee which conducts a campaign for a candidate, a group of candidates, or a political party must file a campaign statement after the election detailing the receipts and expenditures of the candidate or committee. Candidates for local office who collect and spend under $200 are excempt. 11560–11563 Committees which support or oppose ballot measures by collecting or spending $1,000 or more must file three reports before and one after the election detailing the receipts and expenditures of the committee. 11801, 11829, 11830, 11833, 11834	2) Each candidate and each committee supporting or opposing candidates or ballot measures must file two reports before and one after the election detailing the receipts and expenditures of the candidate or committee. 11550	2) Same as AB 703. 84200
3) No specific requirements covering candidates for federal office. Such candidates are treated the same as those running for state or local office.	3) All candidates for federal elective office shall file copies of their campaign statements required by the Federal Election Campaign Act of 1971 with the Secretary of State and with the appropriate county clerk. 11570	3) Same as AB 703. 84208

III Reporting

Pre-AB 703	AB 703	Proposed Political Reform Act of 1974 (Prop. 9)
1) Candidates and committee statements must be filed 20 days before the election and 35 days after the election. 11563, 3750–3751*	1) Candidate and committee statements must be filed as of 28 and 10 days before the election and 31 days after the election. 11550	1) Candidate and committee statements must be filed not later than 40 and 12 days before the election and 65 days after the election. 84200 If an election is held less than 60 days following a primary campaign, statements must be filed not later than 33 and 7 days before the primary, not later than 7 days before the election and 65 days after the election. 84201
2) Ballot measure campaign statements must be filed not later than 35 days after a measure does or does not qualify for the ballot; between 40–45 days and 7–12 days before and within 30 days after an election. 11829–11830, 11833–11835	2) Ballot measure campaign statements must be filed as of 28 days after a measure does or does not qualify; as of 35 and 14 days before the election and 38 days after the election. 11552–11553	2) Ballot measure campaign statements must be filed within 65 days after a measure does or does not qualify; and not later than 35 and 7 days before the election and 70 days after the election. 84202–84204
3) No requirement for filing statements between elections.	3) Candidates and committees that receive contributions or make expenditures and all elected officials must file annual campaign statements. This section does not apply to elected officials wi h salaries below $100 or to judges unless the elected officials or judges are candidates or receive contributions or make expenditures during the year. 11553.5	3) Requires campaign statements to be made semi-annually (instead of annually). Otherwise, same as AB 703. 84206

Pre-AB 703	AB 703	Proposed Political Reform Act of 1974 (Prop. 9)
IV Contributions		
1) Contributions by lobbyists permitted.	1) Same as Pre-AB 703.	1) Contributions by lobbyists prohibited. 86202
2) Anonymous cash contributions permitted.	2) Anonymous contributions prohibited. 11563	2) Same as AB 703. 84304
3) Cash contributions over $500 permitted.	3) Cash contributions of $500 or more prohibited. 11565	3) Cash contributions of $50 or more prohibited. 84300
4) Contributions made in the name of another (second party contributions) not specifically prohibited.	4) Contributions made on behalf of a second party must identify that party. 11562	4) Same as AB 703. 84302
5) No specific requirement for contributors to use their correct legal names.	5) Contributors must identify themselves using correct legal names. 11561	5) Same as AB 703 84301
6) Contributors who give $500 or more to a candidate must be identified by name. 3750*	6) Contributors who give $100 or more to a candidate or a committee must be identified by full name, city, state, occupation, and employer. 11518	6) Contributors who give $50 or more to a candidate or a committee must be identified by full name, street address, occupation and employer. 84210
7) Contributors who loan $500 or more to a candidate must be identified by name. 3750*	7) Contributors who loan $100 or more to a candidate or a committee must be identified by full name, city, county, and state. 11518	7) Contributors who loan any money to a candidate or a committee must be identified by full name, street address, and occupation. 84210
V Expenditures		
1) Each person to whom an expenditure is made must be identified by name only. 11503 Each person to whom an expenditure of $10 or more was made in a ballot measure campaign must be identified by name and address. 11831	1) Each person to whom an expenditure of $100 or more is made must be identified by full name, city and state in the campaign reports to the Secretary of State. 11518	1) Each person to whom an expenditure of $50 or more is made must be identified by full name and street address in campaign reports to the Secretary of State. 84210
2) No limit.	2) Same as Pre-AB 703.	2) Limits expenditure on races for statewide office, on qualifying statewide ballot measures, on statewide ballot campaigns, and on independent political committees. Incumbents' maximum expenditure limits are ten percent less than non-incumbents' limits. Chap. 5
VI Administration and Enforcement		
1) No provision for making an official report on the filing of campaign statements. No provision for automatically notifying law enforcement officials of violations of campaign finance laws.	1) The Board of Equalization shall send a report of its investigations to the Secretary of State and to the Attorney General. 11613	1) The Franchise Tax Board shall report to the Fair Political Practices Commission and to the Attorney General if there is probable cause to believe that the campaign finance laws have been violated. 90002
2) Persons who violate the campaign finance laws can be held guilty of a misdemeanor. Persons who knowingly and willfully violate the Conflict of Interest sections of the law can be held guilty of a felony. 3754*	2) Persons who knowingly and willfully violate the campaign finance laws can be held guilty of a misdemeanor. 11601	2) Same as AB 703. 91000
3) No provision for specific penalties.	3) Same as Pre-AB 703.	3) A fine of $10,000 or three times the amount the person failed to report properly, or unlawfully contributed or spent may be imposed for each violation. 91000

52

Pre-AB 703	AB 703	Proposed Political Reform Act of 1974 (Prop. 9)
4) No provision to disqualify those convicted of violating the law from running for office or acting as a lobbyist. A candidate convicted of violation of the *Elections Code* in a primary election is disqualified from holding the office for which he was a candidate. 12054	4) No provision to disqualify those convicted of violating the law from running for office or acting as a lobbyist.	4) A person convicted of a misdemeanor under this law may not run for elective office or act as a lobbyist for four years after the date of conviction. 91002
5) No provision for citizen suits for injunctive relief to compel compliance with the law except in the case of payment of campaign debts. 11628	5) Provision for citizen suits for injunctive relief to compel compliance with the law. 11605	5) Same as AB 703. 91003
6) Civil suits may be brought against violators of ballot financing statutes. The defendant is liable to a penalty up to $1,000. 11890	6) Civil suits may be brought against violators of the act for the amount of money not properly reported. Plaintiffs shall receive 50 percent of the amount improperly reported. 11603	6) Plaintiffs shall receive 100 percent (instead of 50 percent) of the amount improperly reported. Otherwise, same as AB 703. 91004
7) No provision to subpoena records or witnesses.	7) Board of Equalization may subpoena documents and records. 11614	7) Fair Political Practices Commission may subpoena records and witnesses. 83118
8) Campaign finance records for ballot measures must be open to public inspection. 11862 No provision for candidate campaign statements to be made available to the public. No provision to ensure that documents may be copied at a reasonable price.	8) Provision for public inspection and copying of campaign statements. 11581–11582	8) Same as AB 703. 81008

VII Auditing Statements

1) None.	1) The Board of Equalization shall investigate and audit the campaign statements of each candidate who receives 15% of the vote cast for the office for which he was running, or who spent $25,000 or more in a campaign and of each committee which supported such candidates. A similar investigation and audit shall be conducted on any political committee which spends $10,000 or more in a calendar year. The Board may investigate any other candidate who is required to file periodic reports with the Secretary of State. 11610–11613	1) The Franchise Tax Board is to investigate and audit. Otherwise, same as AB 703. 90000–90006

52

Educational Planning and Policy

Vol. 15   No. 3   June 1974

Public Control of Public Schools: Can We Get It Back?

by James W. Guthrie

Associate Professor, School of Education, and
a Principal of the Childhood and Government Project

Introduction

Who governs America's public schools? Conventional wisdom and democratic ideology hold that the social services crucial to the public's welfare and survival should be subject to the public's will. Schooling is no exception. The United States has a long history of citizen control over public education, but since World War II the balance has shifted markedly. Changes such as population growth, urbanism, school district consolidation, and the unionization of teachers have combined subtly, but steadily, to erode the public's control over its schools. The erosion seems general, although it varies among states and among local school districts.

It has become apparent recently that the public's consciousness has been raised. Numerous citizen groups have been formed expressly to regain a measure of power and influence over the schools. Through what reforms can these citizens restore control? What are the conditions that led to loss of public power in the first place?

These are the major questions to be treated, after a brief description of the magnitude of the public school enterprise; they are intended to demonstrate that the issue at hand is control of a major portion of the nation's entire public sector. Few outside the education profession realize the awesome extent and range of American education.

The Magnitude of Public Schooling[1]

Once only the children of an elite few were educated, but now elementary and secondary schooling is practically universal in this country. In the 1972–73 school year, there were 51.1 million enrolled children between the ages of five and seventeen. Of this number, 50.8 million were enrolled in grades kindergarten through twelve. More than 90 percent of these were in *public* schools. To serve this school population, almost 3 million classroom teachers and other educational professionals are on the public's payroll. Thus educators and their families now account for a larger segment of our population than the historically powerful farm bloc. Moreover, they are becoming as well organized as agriculture, with all the implications that such capability portends in political influence.

Expenditure

It takes a lot of money to support such an operation. Total 1973 school expenditures were almost $52 billion exclusive of construction costs.[2] This is approximately one half of all local government expenditures. Accordingly Americans spend almost as much local money for schools as they do for *all* other local services combined: e.g., fire, police, safety. In addition, the price of education has been increasing rapidly. In 1940 the national average expenditure per pupil in grades kindergarten through twelve was $100. The equivalent figure today is $1,000 per pupil. Even discounting for raging rates of inflation, real dollar increases in school expenditures have escalated fivefold in three decades. These increases outstrip growth in our Gross National Product. Moreover, even though the rate of increase is likely to slow in the next several years, the U. S. Office of Education predicts that public elementary and secondary expenditures will exceed $70 billion by 1982–83. No other major industrialized nation has seen fit to invest so heavily in the public schooling of its youth. Thus, it is somewhat ironic that, in the face of such faith and commitment, the public should increasingly be denied a say in how schools are run.

Erosion of Citizen Control

Our thesis is simple. The public no longer completely controls one of its major institutions, the schools. This loss of power has not been the result of any simple process, or set of recently evolved conspiracies. Moreover, not all parts of this power shift are unique to public education. In some ways, bureaucratization and the blighting concept that "bigger is better" have drained citizen control from many branches of government. But few endeavors are as crucial as schools to the maintenance and cohesion of society. Consequently it is essential to understand the forces eroding the public's ability to shape public education.

54

Population Growth

Early development of America was dominated by small towns and face-to-face communication; close personal contacts were the rule. The school was frequently the focal point for town activity: meetings, government functions, and social events. Each town was legally constituted as a school district with a board of school trustees having widespread responsibilities. They were expected to hire and fire the teachers, maintain the school physical facilities and equipment, order supplies, and keep accounts. Then, there were no professional school administrators to whom such duties could be delegated.

Proliferation of Districts

As our population grew and moved westward, the number of school districts proliferated. At the peak of their expansion, in the late 1800's, there were more than 100,000 operating school districts throughout the nation. These were by far the most numerous units of government. Initially, school boards tended to be comprised of three members. In time, the modal number grew to five. By 1900, the ratio of trustees to citizens was one to 200. It was quite possible for a district's trustees to outnumber its teachers or perhaps even its pupils.

"Cleansing" and Consolidation

The transition to the twentieth century was marked by a great cleansing of local government, including education.[3] The "muckrakers" found that schools came in for their share of poor management and corruption. This was particularly true in our largest cities, where schools frequently were under the control of ward-based political machines. Teaching jobs and school construction contracts were a regular part of the widely accepted spoils system.

Reformers had a dramatic impact upon schools then, and their influence is still felt. In order to insulate schools from the "evils" of partisan politics and to gain greater efficiency, a move was begun to consolidate schools into larger districts, to have citywide central school boards, and to rely more heavily on professional school administrators.

The school district consolidation movement has been remarkably effective. By the Fall of 1962, the number of districts had been reduced threefold to only slightly more than 33,000. In the following decade, the number shrunk even further to its present 16,000 (approximate). Thus, one of the largest and perhaps most important local governmental changes in our nation's history—a five or sixfold reduction in public school districts—has gone virtually unnoticed.

Consolidation of school districts, and the consequent reduction in numbers of school boards and school trustees, occurred during a vast population increase, especially of urban population. While large numbers of school districts were being consolidated out of existence, the citizenry grew by approximately 70 million people.

Consequently, where a school board member once represented about 200 people, today each board member must speak for approximately 3,000 constituents.

The variation around this mean is wide, and in cities such as New York and Los Angeles, each trustee must translate the will of literally millions of his fellow laymen. In general, school board members are now but a minuscule group relative to the size of their constituency, students, and staff. Their ability to sense and articulate the values and desires of their constituents, and translate them into policy, has correspondingly dwindled.

Depoliticization, Bureaucratization, and Unionization

Turn-of-the-century governmental reformers believed strongly that political machines, bossism, and local corruption were caused by an excess of democracy. By permitting cities to be organized on the basis of subunits and wards, unscrupulous politicians had too many opportunities to rise to power. The answer was to centralize many governmental functions into citywide systems. Thus the reformers hoped to attract higher caliber public servants by increasing the visibility, responsibility, and honor attached to public service. In large measure, for municipal services, these reform efforts were successful.

Education in particular was to be insulated from partisan politics. Ward school districts gave way to centralized city school boards that were held separate from city councils, the mayor's office, or other bodies of general government. Schools were to have their own special government outside the sphere of politics.

Further, separate election procedures and qualifications were established for school board members. In many places, school trustee candidates were prohibited from running as members of a political party. Furthermore, school board elections were moved to "off years" and "off months" so as not to coincide with other elections. In addition, school boards were given their own taxing power, presumably free from even the slightest taint of partisanship.

The Business Model

To ensure further that schools were not tied to petty political wheeling and dealing, reformers advocated the appointment of "professional" school managers, trained experts in the operation of schools. Schools were to model themselves after businesses. All decisions were to be based on expert managerial judgment, and managers were to meet criteria of efficiency and productivity. Once they had evolved broad "corporate strategy," school board members were not supposed to interfere in the running of schools any more than a group of stockholders or business board members would think of telling a plant foreman or manager how to fix a broken machine. The new ideology drew a line between policy setting and administration, and laymen were not to cross over into the sacred, politically sanitized realm of professional school administration.

As enrollment increased, the idea of a cadre of trained professional school administrators was attractive for several reasons. The growth of cities combined with the elimination of many small, ward-based city districts, meant that school board members could no longer act as executive officers. Control problems had simply begun to exceed their managerial grasp, and it made good sense for professionals to run the school in accord with board-established policies.

Expansion of Staff

As numbers of students increased, numbers of teachers, counselors, and other employees increased as well. Such expanded staffs demanded, in turn, more school administrators. Thus, there began to evolve a bureaucracy of school professionals whose ostensible function was to translate board-determined policy into the details of educational practice. One outcome was the interposition of several layers between school board members and the classroom teacher. Such bureaucratic entities include, for example, the superintendent of schools, his immediate staff, and assorted other "central office" personnel concerned with accounting, supplies, curriculum coordination and personnel matters. On individual school sites, the administrative hierarchy may consist of a principal and several intermediaries above the level of teachers and students.

Alienation of Teachers

Bureaucracy and bigness have not only reduced the potency of public policy makers, but also severely curtailed teachers' feelings of efficacy. As school systems grew and came under the dominance of expert managers, teachers lost their ability to communicate freely with their employers, school trustees or even with the superintendent and his staff. In most schools, the principal was still available to teachers, but his power had become so severely eroded that he was seldom able to comply with a teacher's request or resolve grievances. The frustration was heightened as city schools became more populated by children from low income households and minority groups whose backgrounds and values were frequently at odds with those of middle-class teachers. Under such circumstances, teacher alienation became more real and more intense. Who would hear the teacher's voice? How could teachers begin to participate in the decisions that affected them so immediately?

Unions and Teacher Power

The answer was "unions," or unions under a different name. By banding together, threatening to withhold their services and to engage in collective bargaining, teachers became a potent force. Public sector bargaining is frequently illegal, and almost nowhere are teachers granted the statutory authority to strike. Nevertheless, teachers do bargain and, on occasion, strike. The outcome has frequently been complicated by sets of contracts that specify working conditions, transfer procedures, pay, hours of work and classroom duties. Whereas they were once relatively voiceless vassals, teachers' organizational spokesmen frequently are as powerful now as a district's professional administrators. A big city board could not conceivably enact and implement a new policy without the consent of teacher spokesmen. In effect, teachers have been accorded veto power over school board policy making.

The rise in "teacher power" occurred after World War II, when many middle class citizens were moving from cities to suburbs, and minorities in the cities had not yet achieved a high degree of political awareness. Consequently, a political power vacuum was created into which teachers moved. Their ascendancy was aided by the very reforms that in an earlier era had been designed to limit citizen participation and to improve the schools.

Public's Dwindling Voice

By the beginning of the 1960's, with the efforts at depoliticization, the growth of administrative bureaucracies, and the escalation of teacher power, the public's ability to express its will regarding school policy had become badly diminished.

What difference has it made that lay decision makers now have substantially less authority than they once had? Answers are difficult. There are so few indicators of how schools are performing that it is hard to know if they are doing a better or worse job today than previously. The absence of base-line indicators and a commonly accepted measure is itself symptomatic of the problem. Professional educators have steadfastly resisted means by which school productivity could be measured. Teachers and administrators have rightly recognized that the measurement of school outputs would be a strong lever by which lay policy makers could recapture control of school operation.[4]

Schools as Monopolies

School costs provide one of the few available measures of citizen impotence in policy setting. In private sector bargaining, both sides realize that if a wage settlement is so high as to render a manufactured product uncompetitive, it will cost management profits and labor jobs. No such market pressures exist in public sector bargaining. Schools are in effect monopolies whose customers are guaranteed by compulsory attendance laws. Consequently, educational personnel costs have increased faster than over-all economic growth and faster than comparable occupations. Moreover, as suggested earlier, few if any gains in productivity have accompanied such salary increases.

Uniformity and Standardization

An additional price of depoliticization appears to have been uniformity. Under the aegis of professionals, teachers and administrators, schools have become standardized to a remarkable, some say oppressive, degree. Seldom do schools admit to the real diversity of tastes and values among their clients. If a large body of technical knowledge existed to support the rigid prescription of professional behavior, then the exclusion of lay voices regarding the nature of schooling might be better justified. However, in the absence of such scientific underpinnings for schooling, it would seem more reasonable, and ultimately more productive, to permit wider choice in the styles, modes of operation, and instructional strategies of schools.

The promotion of conflict appears to be another consequence of the erosion of lay control. Parents' and other citizens' inability to make their wishes heard provides an incentive to aggregate demands until complaints are sufficiently loud and pressing to be heard.

Moreover, because *individual* teachers and administrators frequently have no power to alter the situation, it may be necessary to escalate the demand all the way to the school board in order to have it acted upon. Small wonder that the media increasingly portray parents petitioning and picketing board members. Citizens fear that they will go unnoticed otherwise.

What Can Be Done?

Though by no means a revolution, there is a substantial hint of reform in the air. Many of these change efforts show promise of taking root and appear worthy of careful scrutiny by policy makers. These changes are characterized by two basic features. First, an effort has been made to reduce the size or redefine the basic management unit of schooling so as to restore personal contact and clarify who is responsible for what. Second, lay participation has been increased either by injecting an element of the market place into school decisions or by enlarging the number of citizens who determine how schools should be operated.

Examples of such reforms are to be found in every region of the United States. Because space does not permit a detailed description of each, we will concentrate on two of the more interesting illustrations: a "Voucher" experiment in Alum Rock, California and School Site Governance in Florida.

Vouchers

The voucher experiment to assess the consequences of consumer choice in education, is taking place in the Alum Rock school district near San Jose, California. Financial support is provided in part by the federal Office of Economic Opportunity (OEO). The Rand Corporation and other agencies are seeking to determine the degree to which the experiment increases parent satisfaction, diversity of school offerings, teacher morale, and student performance.

In brief, the voucher plan operates as follows. For each child they intend to enroll in public schools, parents are accorded a "coupon" equal to the price of schooling.[5] This chit is then redeemable at the school selected from about two dozen choices. The problem of proximity to a child's home is in part solved by dividing each school building into several subunits (mini schools), each with a different instructional style, tone, or theme. For example, some schools emphasize the 3 R's and basic school offerings. Others have "open classrooms" in which instruction is substantially more informal. Yet other schools may emphasize the dramatic arts, science, or cultural pluralism.

The budget for a particular school (or mini school) is a function of the number of students who choose to attend. Revenues from vouchers purchase the services of teachers, counselors and other staff. (Parent choices are made sufficiently early in the preceding school year to permit orderly staff planning to take place.) If a school's enrollment decreases, it loses revenues and must decrease its staff. Conversely if enrollments increase as a consequence of parent choice, the school obtains added resources. The funds purchase either goods or services; students can be taken for field trips,

guest artists and lecturers can be brought to the school, teacher aides and teachers can be hired.

The Alum Rock experiment is only now concluding its second year and it is too early to assess its overall success or failure. However, it is already clear that, when given a choice, parents will choose schools other than those assigned to them. Moreover, if dissatisfied, they will move their children. Consequently, some schools are oversubscribed and others are short of students (and funds), thus providing clear signals as to which schools are judged "good" and those that are in some fashion found wanting. Under these conditions, professional educators appear to intensify their sensitivity to the lay public by whom they are employed.

School Site Governance (Governance of Individual School Plants)

In 1973 the Florida State Legislature adopted a far reaching, but not quite radical, set of reforms intended to reinforce the responsiveness of schools to the public. The Florida Plan in the ideal has several crucial components. First, it declares the individual school site to be the basic unit for educational management, in recognition of the fact that school districts typically are such large units as to mask in their averages the performance of any individual school. Conversely, individual classrooms and teachers are too small as units for evaluation of performance. Today students have more than one teacher during the course of a day or week.

Second, each school site is provided with an elected Parent Advisory Council (PAC), with numbers proportional to the school's enrollment. Among the council's duties are the selection, in cooperation with the school district board of trustees, of the school's principal. Principals are then placed on contract, with renewal substantially influenced by the PAC.

The principal is clearly designated as the manager of the school, and selects the school staff. The principal may take the advice of the PAC regarding kinds and characteristics of teachers, but the actual selection is exclusively the principal's function. Similarly, the PAC can advise with regard to such concerns as curriculum and school discipline.

Each school district is responsible for keeping its fiscal accounts on a school-by-school basis. This permits parents, school personnel, and policy makers to assess the way resources are allocated. (Previously, Florida, and most other states, have had difficulty with funds "leaking" away from uses intended by the legislators or school board.) Under ideal circumstances, money due a school site arrives in a lump sum, with its allocation determined by a principal, school staff, and PAC.

Each school publishes an annual Report of School Progress. This document includes measures of the school's and pupils' performance during the year; it is published in local newspapers, sent home with each student, and prominently displayed in the school building. Under ideal conditions, this Report gathers basic data for districtwide and state needs.

The ultimate objective of the Florida Plan is to permit citizens to have a greater role in policy setting, to provide them with the data necessary for wise judgments, and to make it clear which professionals are responsible for implementing their decisions. As with Alum Rock, it is too soon to determine the degree to which the reforms will make a difference. However, there are hopeful signs. The Legislature permitted a generous phase-in period. In order to comply, each district needed to adopt the slate of reforms for only *one* of its schools during the initial year of implementation. However, somewhat surprisingly, given the intensity of some of the changes, a number of school district boards mandated that every school within their jurisdiction adopt all the reforms in the first year. Apparently, when provided with the opportunity, such districtwide lay school board members recognized the wisdom of expanding public participation in the control of public schools.

Conclusion

In schools as in other forms of governance, each generation must recognize that reform is needed. As we have seen, governmental corruption and population growth led to earlier moves for increasing professionalism, centralization and bureaucracy in the schools.

These developments spawned alienation on the part of teachers and loss of responsiveness of schools to the electorate. Now reform efforts are moving toward specification of responsibility, increases in diversity, and expansion of choices for parents and students. Although the outcome is still unclear, the new wave of school reform may demolish at least some of the current roadblocks to improved public education.

NOTES

1. The following figures are from *Statistics of Trends in Education 1962–63 to 1982–83* (U. S. Government Printing Office, January 1974).
2. When non-public schooling and higher education are added, the dollar total is a staggering $89 billion.
3. The history of this transition is described well by Joseph M. Cronin in *The Control of Urban Schools* (New York: The Free Press, 1973).
4. The article by Leonard Merewitz and Stephen H. Sosnick, "Public Expenditure Analysis: Some Current Issues," *Public Affairs Report,* 14(5) (Berkeley: Institute of Governmental Studies, University of California, 1973) contains an excellent explanation of the utility of quantitative measures in the assessment of public sector activities.
5. The experiment was deliberately limited to choices of public schools so as not to risk violation of the First Amendment prohibitions regarding separation of church and state.

Social Problems and Remedial Policies

Vol. 15   No. 4   August 1974

Suicide: Preventable Death

by Richard H. Seiden
Associate Professor in Residence
School of Public Health

What Is the Problem?

Suicide, the voluntary and intentional taking of one's own life, has consistently ranked among the dozen leading causes of death for the United States. In the Pacific Coast states the suicide rate is even higher than the national average, and for California, suicide is about the 6th or 7th leading cause of death. These comparatively high figures are all the more remarkable since it is well known that because of social, economic and religious stigma, the true suicide picture is under-reported. The real incidence of suicide is at least from one-third to one-half again as large as the official figures reveal.

Accordingly there are probably more than 30,000 suicide deaths each year in this country. This figure approaches the order of magnitude of automobile-related fatalities, which ran about 50,000 annually before lowered speed limits went into effect. But suicide-caused deaths are only the tip of the iceberg. Thus it is conservatively estimated that for every suicide death there are approximately eight to ten times as many suicide attempts. This means a quarter of a million U.S. citizens try to take their lives each year. Add to this number the family and friends who are directly affected by the personal and economic losses caused by suicides, as well as the guilt and stigma attached to such actions, and we are talking about behavior that touches millions of lives each year. Further, as will be discussed later, we are experiencing a substantial increase of suicides among young people in general, and among non-white youth in particular.

In summary, because of its heavy incidence and widespread distribution, suicidal behavior poses a major public health problem. Yet ironically only limited and inadequate preventive measures are taken, although suicide can often be prevented. Furthermore the long-term prognosis for recovered well-being is generally favorable, even among high-risk "susceptible" individuals, if suicide attempts can be successfully forestalled.

The Case for Prevention

Does a person have the right to take his own life? This question is frequently asked of those of us in suicide prevention work. Surprisingly, the answer most suicide prevention workers would give is "Yes, in a democratic society a person should have the right to live his life any way he sees fit, even if this means ending it." But the question as posed over-simplifies the issue considerably.

Proceeding further, we can ask whether a person has a right to take his life if it also involves taking the lives of several other unwilling persons. Consider, for example, a suicidal airline pilot who fantasies crash-diving his airliner into the ground. Most of us would agree that he does not have this right, and that individual rights are to some degree conditional upon the rights of others.

None of us lives in a social vacuum, and all are dependent on others to some degree. Nevertheless if for the sake of argument we assume that nobody else would be adversely affected by a specific suicidal person's death, that still does not mean that suicide prevention efforts are unwarranted or ineffective. Such an assumption usually presumes that the person in question is elderly, in his 70's or 80's, perhaps is also afflicted with a terminal illness, and that his future probably holds nothing but pain and suffering. Certainly, many observers would agree that anyone in this condition should be allowed to end his own hopeless existence with some dignity. But are scenarios like this typical of the actual daily cases of suicide? The answer is "no," such a scenario is extremely rare.

Much more frequently we are faced with persons overwhelmed by acute crises, who feel they have no acceptable options, and who, as if they were wearing blinders, see suicide as the only way out of what looks like a hopeless situation. Frequently they are young people on the threshold of life, or perhaps economically successful heads of households, or maybe persons impulsively reacting to acute life crises that may be of short duration. They all see suicide as a means of solving their problems. And it does solve problems, but at an awful cost: providing a permanent, irreversible and socially damaging solution to what is frequently a temporary and manageable problem.

A Historical Perspective

The modern-day rationale for preventing suicide rests upon an understanding of psychodynamics gained from clinical and epidemiological studies of the suicidal process. However, from an historical perspective, the early opposition to self-destruction was based upon moral and religious grounds. Although the Bible records several suicides—notably Samson and Judas—it neither sanctions nor condemns such acts. Early Biblical scholars such as St. Augustine argued that suicide was a violation of the commandment, "Thou shalt not kill," but theirs was a practical argument intended to forestall the numerous suicides of early Christians. It implied no moral judgment. Apparently early Christian believers would confess their sins, and then, absolved, kill themselves, reasoning that in their state of pristine piety they would be transported directly to heaven.

During the hundreds of years that followed the early Christian era, public attitudes toward suicide exemplified man's wretched treatment of his fellows. Those dead by suicide were often considered to be pariahs. Their burial in consecrated ground was often not permitted. Their families were deprived of their goods and property. In extreme instances, as a final indignity a stake was driven through the heart of the suicide, the last recorded example of such treatment taking place in England in 1823.

Some early attitudes and practices have found their way into the common law, such as the idea that suicide was a crime, a *felo de se*. In England, as recently as 1961, completed suicide was considered a felony and attempted suicide a misdemeanor. The United States has no federal law against suicide, despite Judge J. Skelly Wright's declaration in the Georgetown Case that "there is a public policy against suicide." Legal prohibitions against suicide vary from state to state. California has no law that prohibits suicide or attempted suicide. (It is, however, a crime to aid or abet a suicide.) States having laws against suicide rarely enforce them, except to facilitate mandatory hospitalization to protect the person from harming himself. Perhaps there is an appreciation that illegality per se is not much of a deterrent to anyone intent on suicide.

Religious and legal arguments aside, the more cogent psycho-social issues that motivate current programs of suicide prevention can be sumarized as follows:

Ambivalence of the Suicidal Person

To a suicidologist, the suicidal person does not have a unitary and single-minded death wish. Instead he is considered to be in the midst of an acute crisis, wracked by indecision, and highly ambivalent—he wants to die and to live; to kill himself and to be saved; he may cut his throat but cry for help with his next breath. The ambivalence of the suicidal person betrays his on-going struggle between wanting to live and wanting to die. On behalf of his client the suicidologist opts for living by aiding the forces that favor life over those that favor death. He transposes the question, "Does a person have a right to die?" into "Does a person have a right to live?" The suicide prevention movement is guided by the words of Justice Benjamin N. Cardozo, "A cry for help is a summons to rescue."

The Brevity of the Crisis

Suicidal crisis is not a lifetime characteristic of most suicide attempters. It is rather an acute situation, often a matter of only minutes or of hours at the most. The most dangerously suicidal person is at great risk of self-destruction for only a few days out of his entire lifetime. During this acute phase the Suicide Prevention Center (discussed below in the section titled "The Suicide Prevention Movement") operates in a crisis intervention role, not to effect a permanent solution to the caller's problem, but rather to provide immediate relief and hope. Since the self-destructive mood is usually so temporary, the center focuses on dealing with and averting the immediate crisis, thus buying time to seek long-term solutions.

The episodic nature of suicidal behavior is also evident in follow-up studies of those who attempt suicide. Contrary to popular opinion, few—only about 10 percent—of those who attempt suicide and fail, actually do kill themselves at some later date. My current research on suicide attempts from the Golden Gate and San-Francisco-Oakland bridges indicates that only 4 percent of those successfully restrained from suicide on either of the bridges have later killed themselves.

Economic Considerations

A number of economic considerations attach to a death by suicide: the public cost of police investigation and of the required coroner's report, which may include autopsy, laboratory tests, and inquest. There is the public or private cost of emergency room and hospital care. And, where the deceased has been the breadwinner, there is often the public cost of long-term welfare support of the survivors and the absence of taxes that mean an economic deficit to the community of many tens of thousands of dollars.

Survivors

Despite a trend toward more humane legal and medical treatment, death by suicide still frequently leaves a stigma upon the survivors that is not associated with any other mode of death. It has been stated that the suicide leaves a psychological skeleton in the closet of his survivors. His family and friends are often plagued with guilt, wondering what real or imagined acts of theirs caused the victim to kill himself, or what they could have done to prevent his death. This conflict becomes especially critical where the survivors are children or adolescents, who tend to be most deeply affected by the suicidal loss of family members, especially the loss of parents. Research indicates that these children frequently suffer from depression and suicidal preoccupations that may require hospitalization and psychiatric care to head off severe emotional disorders and suicidal orientations in later life.

The suicidology profession is not composed of modern-day Canutes attempting desperately to hold back inevitable death. Indeed the American Association of Suicidology (AAS) has taken a strong interest in the kindred subject of euthanasia and, as a group, favor euthanasia, literally, "easy death." They oppose needless "heroic measures" that artificially prolong existence beyond any realistic hope for recovery. Consequently it is not death per se that the suicidologist strives to prevent, but the premature, stigmatizing and unnecessary death that characterizes so many cases of suicide.

Who Are the High-Risk Special Populations?

Although suicide behavior is democratically distributed, affecting all class levels among all types of people, the risk of suicide seems unusually high for certain groups. These include college students, alcoholics, mental patients, the aged, and (to a greater degree than previously thought) the young, especially young non-whites.

College Students

Early studies have indicated that the suicide problems on campuses were substantial, and that the risk of suicide was greater for students than for their nonacademic age peers. These early studies were almost entirely descriptive, and while they did offer informative insights, they did not provide for control groups against which their findings could be compared. About five years ago, jointly with Dr. Henry Bruyn, the then Director of Cowell Student Hospital on the University of California Berkeley (UCB) campus, the writer helped design a study to determine whether students were in reality at greater risk of suicide than non-students. We first studied the incidence of suicide among the University's Berkeley campus students over ten years, 1952 through 1961, and compared these figures with California's suicide rates standardized by chronological age. Students were indeed found to be at greater risk of suicide, although their general mortality was considerably lower than that of their age peers. During those ten years there were 23 student suicides, compared to the 13 that would be expected if the general statewide rates held for students.

We compared the students who committed suicide with their non-suicidal university classmates: The suicidal group was older, included greater proportions of graduates, language majors and foreign students, and gave more indications of emotional disturbance. In addition, the suicidal students who were undergraduates fared much better than their fellow students in academic achievement. This is part of a pattern that has been reliably reported throughout this country as well as in England: The suicidal college student tends to be brighter, more intellectually distinguished, and enrolled in a highly rated prestigious university. Thus a selective factor operates: from an intellectual point of view, we are losing the cream of our college students to suicide, the second leading cause of death among this age group.

Alcoholics

Of all the drugs related to the commission of suicide, ethyl alcohol has the strongest relationship to self-destruction. It is no coincidence that San Francisco and Sacramento, with the state's highest suicidal rates, also have the highest rates of alcoholism. The relationship can work in a number of ways, but usually alcohol lowers inhibitions and allows impulsive behavior that can be either suicidal or homicidal in nature. Additionally, the drug alcohol is used as a suicidal agent, usually in conjunction with barbiturates, since the combination of the two drugs may work synergistically in causing serious adverse reaction. Moreover demographic studies

have also revealed a very high risk of suicide among chronic alcoholics. During the ten-year interval 1958 to 1967, there were 122 official documented suicides in San Francisco's skid row. This represents a mean yearly rate of 64.4 per 100,000, three to four times the rate for California's general population.

Mental Patients

Individuals with a history of psychiatric disturbances, particularly those with prior psychiatric hospitalization for suicide attempts, form a high-risk group with respect to future suicidal behavior. According to research done at Napa State Hospital in the 1960's, therapeutic approaches must be revised to help this population deal with practical, down-to-earth problems reported by patients. Problem areas included social skills and socializing, work adjustment, loneliness and drinking.

The Aged

Little work has been done with the most vulnerable group in the entire population—the older male—whose suicide rate is strikingly higher than for any other category. For example, at ages 65 to 69, the white male suicide rate is about three and a half times that of the entire population, and at age 85 and over, it is five times that of the total population. Also, the aged person who contemplates suicide is less ambivalent and more likely to use methods that do not permit intervention and rescue.

In particular, we know that widows and widowers are more prone to suicide than any other segment in the community, and that severely depressed persons are more likely to be suicidal than those who are not. These features are found more often among the aged, and serve as a predictive indicator of their suicidal risk.

Youth

One of the more distressing aspects of the suicide problem is the fact that deaths by suicide have increased in the youthful years 15–24. As Table 1 indicates, the overall national suicide rate has varied little, but in 1970–72 the rates for the 15–24 year age group were almost doubled, as compared with the average for the prior 25 years, 1945–69.

TABLE 1

TRENDS IN YOUTHFUL SUICIDE RATES, U.S.
(Suicides per 100,000 per year)

		Age Range		
	All ages	15–24 yrs	25–34 yrs	35–44 yrs
1945–69	10.9	4.8	9.9	14.5
1970–72*	11.6	9.2	14.1	16.7
Change in rate per 100,000	+.7	+4.4	+4.2	+2.2
Percentage Change .	+7%	+92%	+43%	+15%

* Rates for 1971 and 1972 are provisional estimates based upon a systematic 10% sample of deaths.

Homicide and Accidents

Coincidentally, the rates for homicide and accidental death (primarily automobile accidents) have increased even more dramatically in this age group. We are currently facing a substantial increase of violent deaths in our youthful population. Drugs such as alcohol and heroin play a significant part in this increase; however, this investigator feels that such factors as excessive violence in films and television may inure young people to the effects of violence in their daily lives and should not be casually dismissed.

The Vulnerability of Non-White Youth

For several years we have been aware that non-white youth have been particularly vulnerable to suicide; the research based upon Black, Chicano, and American Indian populations has demonstrated a different age patterning for suicide when compared to the nation at large. The high-risk period for non-white youth and younger adults occurs from 15–44 and then trails off, whereas for the majority Anglo population the risk of suicide rises with increasing age on almost a one-to-one basis.

It is a provocative question why non-white males should experience their highest suicide rates at much earlier ages than whites, whose rate keeps rising steeply until about age 60 and then remains relatively high. The consensus is that a white person does not realize until middle age that he may not reach goals he has set for himself, and that he must then accept his limitations, or resign himself to a life of quiet desperation. These depressing feelings occur at a much earlier age among young non-whites, when they see doors that will be permanently closed to them. At any event, we have a national increase of suicides among young people in general, most pronounced among non-white youth. It could even be called an epidemic because it exceeds normal expectations based upon past experience.

What Can Be Done Through Public Policy Measures?

The study of suicide is but one facet of, and cannot truly be separated from, the broader study of mental health. In turn, the study of mental health leads to questions regarding the types of communities and societies we have created. Therefore on the broadest level, programs that attempt to correct imperfections in our society or try to insure social justice for all citizens will have a beneficial effect on the suicide rate. For example, the question of gun control interests suicidologists, since the easy availability of lethal weapons has been shown to correlate highly with impulsive suicidal or homicidal activity. Another example is the campaign for tighter controls on barbiturate prescriptions. The use of barbiturates as a suicidal agent is so widespread that it is now the number one method in California. Accordingly, any programs that could control the availability of barbiturates would help to lower the suicide rate.

The Suicide Prevention Movement

During the past fifteen years there has been a renewed awareness that suicide can be scientifically studied, frequently predicted, and, in numerous cases prevented. This scientific and humane approach to the study of suicide and suicide prevention has led to the development of the interdisciplinary field of suicidology. An impressive feature of this new discipline is the establishment of more than 200 community-based Suicide Prevention Centers (SPCs) throughout the United States, with 29 in California alone. These centers are basically telephone emergency services that treat suicidal crises while they are in progress and, in many ways, are models of ideal community mental health centers.

A more descriptive term might be "crisis centers," for although only a fraction (one-quarter to one-third) of the callers are strongly suicidal in nature, almost all calls are from persons undergoing some sort of acute crisis. Center telephones are manned by professional and non-professional volunteers trained to find out what is troubling the caller, to provide reassurance and help, and to refer him to appropriate community agencies or services where necessary. The centers are open around the clock, and their services are available without charge.

Beyond their immediate life-saving activities, the suicide prevention centers represent the altruistic impulse of a community in its finest sense. Unpaid volunteers give their time and energies to help troubled fellow beings, and incidentally derive constructive personal gratification in the process. Certainly the picture of grass-roots person-to-person involvement is in sharp and welcome contrast to the cynicism and impersonality that seem to abound in many aspects of the urbanized way of life.

The existence of a Suicide Prevention Center is an indication to the would-be suicide that there are people who wish to help and will work with him during the time of his crisis. This attitude is conspicuously absent in other areas, as in the case of the Golden Gate Bridge.

The Golden Gate Bridge: Need for a Physical Barrier

The Golden Gate Bridge is well known as one of the world's most beautiful bridges but it also has the unhappy reputation of being an enticing suicide landmark of epidemic proportions. In fact, outside of Japan, it is the world's single most frequently used location for suicide. Just how many have died there will probably never be known. But one thing is certain: the reported number of suicide deaths (now more than 500) is overly conservative.

While one often hears the common-sense argument, "If you stop somebody from jumping off the Bridge he will just go someplace else," this contention is disproved both by objective examination of the experience at other suicide landmarks, and clinical experience in dealing with suicidal patients.

For example, the suicide rate in England has dropped more than one-third, largely because of a seemingly unrelated change in policy. For years, coke gas had been a popular method of self-destruction. But when the English switched to less lethal natural gas, the suicide rate dropped and it has remained at the reduced rate for the ensuing three years rather than regaining its previous level. Quite clearly the "unrelated" change to less lethal fuel has brought about a permanent reduction in the suicide rate, just as the recent reduction in the speed limit has also significantly reduced auto-accident fatalities.

Previous studies of suicide landmarks indicate that physical barriers can drastically reduce suicide deaths at particular locations. Moreover, as suggested earlier, overwhelming evidence supports a favorable prognosis for persons who are prevented from completing their suicides. There is little or no evidence to suggest that they will invariably go someplace else to kill themselves. Rather, the nature of suicidal fantasies seems highly specific and focused on a particular method.

fresh and sea water, in vegetables, in blood and milk, and thus to be ubiquitously distributed." (p. 88)[6]

But only much more recently was it clearly established that fluorine, in the form of ionic fluorides, plays what appears to be a crucial role in the development of teeth that are resistant to decay. Moreover there is also some evidence suggesting that it may be an essential trace element needed for growth, bone development and other purposes. For example, a number of studies of mice and rats reported in 1972 suggest that fluoride is an essential nutrient and is required for normal haemopoiesis [formation of blood cells], fertility and growth. The full story of fluoride's possible further effects, however, lies in the future and will depend on additional research. Its importance to dental health is now recognized, but its other possible roles are not yet fully understood or explored.

Knowledge of fluorides' special ability to help produce decay-resistant teeth, however, is well established, and has been rather thoroughly studied. It involves strengthening the tooth's enamel crystal against acid attack, "inhibiting the biochemical cycle involved in the bacterial production of the attacking acid," and "promoting remineralisation" of teeth so as to retard decay. (p. 236)[7]

The investigation of fluoridated water and good teeth began more than 50 years ago, when attention was drawn to the fact that many people in some areas—such as portions of Colorado—had brown markings, or "Colorado stain" on their teeth. Further investigation revealed that an unusually large number of people in these areas also had good teeth. The next step was identifying trace elements in the water, which was found to be naturally high in fluorides. When research began to focus on fluorides, they were found to have a key role in causing both tooth mottling and resistance to decay.

The research history of controlled fluoridation as a caries preventive began about 30 years ago. In 1944 and 1945, basic and significant studies were undertaken in the paired New York cities of Newburgh (fluoridated) and Kingston (non-fluoridated). Experiments were extended to cities with various levels of natural fluoridation, and also some with controlled (artificial) fluoridation. These included: Aurora, Muskegon and Grand Rapids (Michigan), Brantford, Sarnia and Stratford (Ontario), Evanston (Illinois) and Athens (Georgia). Numerous additional studies were reported from other cities in the U.S. and Canada, as well as around the world. [2,7,9] Fluorides were credited with reducing the number of carious lesions (points of decay) from slightly under to well above 50% in children in various age groups.

Both the early studies and later confirming research have documented the benefits of fluoridation, including the increased retention and good occlusion of teeth, i.e., good contact between upper and lower teeth. P. Adler referred to the well-known comparative studies of Kingston and Newburgh, noting that in non-fluoridated Kingston 35.2% of children had lost a first molar, whereas in fluoridated Newburgh only 8.1% had done so. He observed further that malocclusion, caused by migrating and tilting of teeth, was found more often in Kingston than in Newburgh, because the continued presence of first permanent molars helps keep other teeth in place. (p. 351)[8] Y. Ericsson also has called attention to the "advantageous" effect of fluorides "on the frequency and severity of periodontal disease" as well. (p. 13)[8] (Periodontal disease affects the gums and bone and connective tissue near the teeth.)

A Recent Research Controversy

A controversy posing different views of research methodology and findings surfaced recently (July 18, 1974) in Jack Anderson's "Merry-Go-Round" column. He quoted Dr. Edward Groth III (Research Fellow, Cal Tech Population Program, California Institute of Technology) who both in his doctoral dissertation and in a letter to an official in the federal Food and Drug Administration questioned the accuracy and methodology of some of the early fluoridation research. Groth was quoted as saying that key studies that seemed to support the effectiveness and safety of fluoridation were in fact lacking "the most basic elements of 'blind design' which insure total objectivity." Further, he stated that "factors such as the subjects' dental care, diet and fluoride intake were never even cranked into the studies." (Groth does not maintain that fluoridated water fails to reduce tooth decay. As he said in a phone conversation on September 27, 1974, "The evidence is very convincing that there is substantial benefit from drinking fluoridated water.")

On July 26, 1974, Dr. Ernest Newbrun (Professor of Oral Biology and Chairman, Section of Biological Sciences, School of Dentistry, U.C. San Francisco) addressed an 8-page letter to Jack Anderson, questioning the views mentioned in the Anderson column and some of the others stated in Groth's thesis. Before commenting on several fluoridation experiments Newbrun said, "One need not be a scientist to evaluate the simple yet elegant experiments which substantiate the effectiveness of water fluoridation."

He pointed out that "blind design" means that "the person who evaluated the results is not informed of the treatment." The dental x-ray films (such as those in the Aurora and Rockford, Illinois studies) were evaluated by an examiner who did not know of their source. "These conditions clearly fulfill the requirement of 'blind design.'" In the Newburgh-Kingston study, "The films, after being developed, were sent to the central office in Albany where statisticians randomized the film series so that the interpreters did not know whether they were reading Newburgh or Kingston films." Newbrun added, "As far as other variables are concerned, both cities are situated on the Hudson River about 30 miles apart.... Both cities bore a close resemblance to each other in respect to size and socio-economic conditions."

The conclusion in his final summary stated:

... the effectiveness of water fluoridation in reduction of dental decay is well substantiated by meaningfully conducted and scientifically well-designed experiments.

California's Relative Standing in Fluoridation

The proportion of California's population using fluoridated public water supplies is low, but has slowly been increasing. Total percentages rose from 12.8% in 1966 to 15.9% in 1969, to 19.6% in 1972. The largest increase in fluoridation in California was provided for recently with the adoption of an ordinance by the Los Angeles City Council in September 1974. As reported in the Los Angeles *Times*, the first reading passed by a 10 to 4 vote. Final reading and passage of the Los Angeles ordinance came on September 11, and it was signed by the acting Mayor shortly thereafter.

Los Angeles, one of the six U.S. cities with populations of one million or over, will be the last of these major cities to get fluoridation. (Houston's water is partly fluoridated naturally.) Philadelphia (1954) was the first of the others to fluoridate, followed by Chicago in 1956, New York City in 1965 and Detroit in 1967.

When Los Angeles City water is fluoridated, roughly 35% of the state's population will be receiving the benefit of optimally fluoridated water. Even so, California will not have appreciably bettered its rank among the states in fluoridation coverage, because the other states appear to be moving ahead more rapidly. In 1966, with 12.8% fluoridation, California ranked 42d. Using 1972 figures (from the *U.S. Statistical Abstract 1973*) for the other states, at least 39 had more than 35% of their public waters fluoridated. Thus even after the Los Angeles fluoridation, California's 1974 rank would still be about 40th, and possibly lower.

Although there was some interest in statewide action in the mid-50s and 60s, the State of California has not yet passed a fluoridation law. A number of legislative proposals were shelved or failed while Governor Ronald Reagan expressed the view that the issue should be resolved by action at the local level. Meanwhile ten states have acted in two different ways to encourage or require fluoridation for their residents. As reported by the American Dental Association, the State of Kentucky "has a public health regulation in effect requiring fluoridation for approval of water supplies." Nine other states have passed laws requiring fluoridation: Connecticut in 1965, Minnesota and Illinois in 1967, Delaware and Michigan in 1968, South Dakota and Ohio in 1969, and Georgia and Nebraska in 1973. And of course large numbers of cities have chosen fluoridation by referendum or council action.

Drinking water is being fluoridated in many jurisdictions in many countries, totalling thirty-three including the United States, according to available figures. Many of these are comparatively small countries, like Australia, Canada, Chile, Colombia, Czechoslovakia, Ireland, New Zealand, and Panama, which, despite their substantial rates of fluoridation, constitute only a relatively small proportion of the world's population. The United States is the only large nation to have such a high proportion of its population drinking fluoridated water: nearly 60% of those who use public water supplies in this country were reported as drinking fluoridated water in 1972. On a worldwide scale, incomplete figures as of 1973 indicate that at least 148,049,000 persons were served by fluoride-supplemented water. Of these, more than 86 million were in the United States.

A Life-Long Advantage

The desirability of exposing children to fluorides while their teeth are in the process of formation has been widely documented. But as Hodge and Smith stated, "... a common misconception holds that the benefits of drinking fluoridated water are confined to the younger age groups, in fact to children. All available evidence indicates that *the benefit continues into adult life*." (emphasis supplied) Further, they noted that early studies by Forrest, et al., in three high fluoride areas in England also revealed that fewer of the teeth with some evidence of decay were missing, and that "caries attack was less severe in the teeth which were present." (p. 477)[2] The fluoride helped to preserve teeth that would otherwise have been lost, and also helped teeth resist decay, even where complete caries prevention could not be achieved.

Economic and Fiscal Aspects:
Dental Benefits Far Outrank Costs

Dr. Roger O. Egeberg, then Assistant Secretary for Health and Scientific Affairs, HEW, in 1970 commented (in "Fluoridation for All: A National Priority") on the monetary savings that fluoridation had provided for public care programs in Head Start projects:

> The average [dental] treatment costs per child in fluoridated San Francisco and Vallejo were $26.35 and $27.77 compared to $70.01 and $85.58 in ... nonfluoridated ... Berkeley and the San Joaquin Valley.

Thus dental costs in fluoridated San Francisco were only 37% of those in Berkeley, whose presently unfluoridated water is provided by the East Bay Municipal Utility District. Similarly, costs in fluoridated Vallejo were only 32% of those in the unfluoridated Valley. If the San Francisco and Vallejo children can continue to drink fluoridated water to age 18, they can anticipate continued lower dental costs—and fewer tooth-related miseries—in later life as well.

Arguing successfully for the fluoridation of Los Angeles City water, proponents estimated savings in medical and dental bills for children alone at close to $6 million annually (L.A. *Times*, Sept. 5, p. 26). For that large city, total estimated annual costs for fluoridating the water, including amortized capital outlay, ranged from $380,000 to $585,000 depending on the form of fluoride used. Estimated costs per person annually were only 13¢ to 20¢. (L.A. departmental worksheet, no. 7)

Health Measures and Individual Rights

The early legal challenges to controlled fluoridation have been settled. Sixteen state supreme courts have held that water fluoridation does not infringe upon the constitutional rights of individuals, and the U.S. Supreme Court, by denying certiorari, has permitted those rulings to stand. Briefly, the courts have consistently held that the state's sovereignty embraces power to provide for the health, safety and general welfare of the community, and further that the problem of dental caries is a public health problem. Although dental decay is neither infectious nor contagious, it is held to be a serious chronic disease of major importance.

We know that when optimum concentrations of fluoride are present in drinking water, the result is major reduction in tooth decay. Fluoride added to water can be called either a nutritional supplement, or preventive medication, or both. But in any event, controlled fluoridation of drinking water is clearly considered a legitimate exercise of governments' public health powers and responsibilities.

Moreover, since there are no known religious objections to the fluoride found in varying natural concentrations in water, milk, eggs and tea, for example, it seems hard to understand objections to consumption of the same substance when present in fluoridated drinking water. But for those who, for whatever reason, do not wish to drink fluoridated water, low-fluoride bottled water is readily available at modest cost. It has also been suggested that a fluoridation policy could provide at public expense for supplies of low-fluoride bottled water for those who prefer to drink it (letter from Edward Groth, September 19, 1974). In terms of public dollar cost, such a measure would probably be no great expense, as it is unlikely that more than a tiny fraction of the population would make use of the bottled water.

Some Environmental Questions

Possible effects of fluoride on the environment have been questioned, since much of the domestic water used eventually finds its way into rivers, streams, or the sea. With respect to fresh-water streams and aquatic life, no substantial or widespread effects have been identified, even in areas using fluoridated water for as long as a quarter-century. Nevertheless we do not know for sure that long-term or cumulative effects may not occur, so prudent monitoring of the future contribution of water fluoridation would be in order.

But on balance it should also be noted that in many areas the big problem is water contamination by sewage and various industrial emissions, not fluoridation. Certainly stream and river contamination by domestic and industrial wastes are damaging both aquatic life and water quality in clear and direct ways. Unlike fluoridated water, these wastes are doing demonstrable harm now. This unfortunate situation exists principally because controls on the industrial release of toxic substances are not yet fully adequate, nor is the treatment of sewage.

If the environmental protection movement proceeds, our rivers and streams will be cleaned up, and these conditions alleviated. In this connection, it is suggested that secondary treatment of sewage may reduce its fluoride content by 70% (letter from Groth, September 19, 1974). Accordingly these measures are available if they should prove necessary in the future. Presumably they will be employed anyway in the course of cleaning up the wastes and contaminants that now enter streams and rivers.

So much for fresh water. With respect to the ocean and fluoridation, there is no problem of any conse-

quence. Seawater already contains about 1.4 ppm of fluoride. Accordingly, adding runoff water with approximately 1.0 ppm of fluoride would not raise the fluoride concentration of seawater, even in the immediate vicinity of the outflow. And in worldwide terms, the contribution to seawater made by domestic water runoff and sewage would be exceedingly small compared with the flows of the earth's rivers, and the huge amounts of precipitation directly into the ocean.

Another environmental question relates to the atmosphere and fluorides carried in the air. But air-borne fluorides are exceedingly minimal, except near certain industrial plants, and then only where "scrubbers" and other devices for controlling air pollution are not used. In addition, in a few areas like Tennessee, fluoride dusts occur in the soil. Atmospheric pollution is discussed further in the "monitoring" section, below. In the San Francisco Bay Area, such air pollution is under the observation and regulation of the Air Pollution Control District.

Safety Considerations

Weighed against the demonstrable dental-health benefits of fluoridated water, what is the genuine risk of fluoridation to people who have individual susceptibilities such as allergies? First, as E. R. Schlesinger reported in the article "Health Studies in Areas of the USA with Controlled Water Fluoridation," "In summary, there have been no adequately documented reports of any adverse systemic effects from fluoride ingestion even at levels several times greater than those used in water supplies for the prevention of dental caries." (p. 310)[8]

It may be useful to allude briefly to a group of medically related objections raised by some opponents of fluoridation, and to see how they were analyzed by the Justice of the Australian Supreme Court in an exhaustive report published in 1968. Following Justice Crisp's statement, the determination of optimum methods for conveying fluorides and optimum concentrations will be discussed.

The Honourable Malcolm Peter Crisp, Justice of the Supreme Court of Tasmania (Australia) in his 1968 *Report . . . into the Fluoridation of Public Water Supplies* commented on "responsible opponents of fluoridation and . . . serious matters to be discussed." But he also noted "Some Absurdities" in arguments and allegations. As an example, he quoted the charge that fluoridation resembles "a chemical lobotomy" producing "a lackadaisical attitude with over-indulgence in SEX, ALCOHOL, sleep, food and spending money." (emphasis in the original) He also alluded to charges "expressed in pseudo scientific jargon and with specious semanticism [that] would hardly call for comment were it not for [their] . . . prevalence and . . . obvious intention of appalling the ignorant." (p. 135)[7]

But Crisp also recognized the question of the "abnormal individual," one who has a particular infirmity or susceptibility of which he may or may not be aware —as a matter deserving careful investigation. The question is: Would drinking water with approximately 1.0 part per million of fluorides be likely to cause harm to specific "abnormal individuals"? After examining claims, records and investigations concerning the abnormal individual, Crisp concluded:

> ... I would agree that it is a hallmark of a civilized society that the rights of minorities ... of individuals, are of importance.
>
> [After referring to safety of fluoridation and its proven advantages to normal individuals, he continued:] But the case of the abnormal individual has seemed to me to be of importance. If there are such individuals, and if the possibility of harm is substantial and substantiated this must obviously be a consideration that would give pause. But, if the community advantages be undoubted ... such a risk to be countervailing must be more than theoretical and the existence of the individual who would be affected must be more than a speculation. ... I have sought to examine the cases of the so-called allergic or abnormally intolerant individuals. I am by no means sure that they do exist, although I admit the possibility. If they do exist, the statistical significance of such individuals is so small, the consequent harm so slight, and once recognized so easily prevented, that in relation to the expected benefits of fluoride I can see no real balance being achieved [by withholding fluoridation]. (pp. 132–133)[7]

Thus he clearly came down on the side of fluoridation, seeing no merit or "real balance" in withholding fluoridation from the general public on such tenuous and limited grounds as his investigation revealed. In summary, the certainty of benefit was found to be of far greater weight than the comparatively small, unproven, and perhaps even non-existent hazard.

While not expressly disagreeing with the Crisp thesis, Groth, in his extensive survey of the fluoridation literature stated:

> No large-scale studies have been conducted to attempt to determine whether such reactions have been encountered in fluoridated communities, and if so, with what frequency. The number of cases reported in the literature is very small; if physicians in most fluoridated communities have observed similar effects, none has attempted to alert his colleagues by publishing his observations, aside from those reports already cited. (p. 308)[10]

Finally, the executive committee of the American Academy of Allergy stated in 1971, "There is no evidence of allergy or intolerance to fluorides as used in the fluoridation of community water supplies."

Evidence with respect to other possible adverse effects is similar. Suggestions of cancer relationships go back more than 20 years to the work of one researcher, whose work is questionable. Moreover as Groth commented, "Vital statistics show no increase in deaths due to cancer in fluoridated communities." (p. 283)[10] Likewise the suggestion of a relationship to mongolism goes back to the work of one single researcher, whose work is clearly flawed. While there is limited evidence that some individuals with kidney disease may not eliminate fluorides as effectively as normal individuals, adequate monitoring of bodily responses should enable their physicians to take appropriate measures. Persons who must use kidney machines (hemodialysis) may encounter problems, but the remedy is simple, i.e. avoiding the use of fluoridated water in the machines.

How Fluorides Reach and Affect Teeth

Before considering various methods of providing fluorides for teeth, it may be useful to note the effects of fluorides on teeth. Such statements concerning fluorides and teeth are numerous in the scientific literature. (Myers pp. 74–87)[6] A clear, nontechnical statement was provided by Justice Crisp:

> The effect of the fluoride ion when incorporated into the teeth is to enhance calcification [one of the first steps in the formation of bone], to provide stronger and more resistant enamel and favourably to influence the shape, structure and appearance of the teeth. (p. 236)[7]

In order for these benefits to occur, bone-seeking fluorides must reach the teeth. They do so in two ways: (1) through the body by ingestion and inhalation, (2) and topically through direct external contact "by ion exchange at the crystal surface" of the teeth. Fluorides also reach the teeth by being "incorporated into the physical structure by cellular activity during [tooth] formation in which case it is said to be taken up systemically or by accretion. ... In the case of teeth, uptake by accretion is not significant after childhood and further augmentation of the fluoride content of the teeth, and the enamel in particular, is dependent on topical uptake." (p. 236)[7] This last comment suggests the continuing benefits of fluoridation to adults as well as children.

Dietary Sources of Fluorides

A number of fluoride-enriched edibles have been suggested as supplements or alternatives to fluoridated water to help make sure that adequate amounts of fluorides are obtained, especially while teeth are being formed. These edible substances include salt, milk, flour, fluoride tablets, vitamin-fluoride tablets and even types of candy that do not cause tooth decay. All are swallowed, so that in varying degrees the fluoride supplied is incorporated systemically.

Fluoridated salt or flour. Adler noted that "For districts without a piped water supply system, the best alternative at present appears to be enriched cooking salt." (p. 351)[8] Because of lack of central water supplies in some areas, Austria (260-13-9B)[9] and Switzerland have found fluoridated salt useful (288-13-9B).[9] More positively, Adler noted that fluoridated cooking salt, like flour, requires "much less of the chemical and much simpler control measures than fluoridation of piped waters." (p. 343)[8] Crisp reported that the salt provided some caries reduction (8 to 28% in various age groups of children examined, compared to the 50% or higher reduction accomplished through use of fluoridated water). (p. 218)[7] Fluoridated salt is cheap, and permits the individual to accept or reject its use.

Major disadvantages include the fact that salt consumption is lowest "... when the need for maximum uptake would be at its highest . . . in the first decade of life." (p. 218)[7] Further, the average intake of salt does not provide sufficient caries protection, and if taken with meals, fluoride absorption may be reduced appreciably if the food is rich in calcium. Thus Adler warned,

> before fluoride enrichment of flour or any other staple food can be recommended on a large scale a number of investigations have to be performed: mapping of the consumption variations in different countries and areas, testing of the systemic and dental absorption of fluoride from the respective vehicles, and clinical testing of the caries-preventive effects. (p. 343)[8]

Milk. Fluoridating milk has been suggested as an alternative to water. To fluoridate milk would be far more costly than fluoridating water, because milk is not usually handled through a central source. It is produced by a series of private entrepreneurs, rather than a public agency. Also, even very young children vary in their capacity and willingness to consume milk or sometimes to tolerate it.

Fluoride tablets. Ingesting such tablets has been reported to give good results in reduction of tooth decay. (201-12-9)[9] Further, Newbrun has cited "clear evidence of a posteruptive effect, suggesting that fluoride tablets should be kept in the mouth as long as possible." Tablets have been variously described as an acceptable alternative to fluoridated water (especially where fluoridated water supplies are not available), and as one of several useful supplements to water that is inadequately fluoridated. (269-13-9B and 292-10-9A)[9] Drawbacks to this method of providing fluorides or even obtaining reliable research results include the fact that teachers and parents change their minds about continuing the long-term commitment, children "cheat" and fail to take their tablets, or refuse to cooperate, and families move and drop out of programs, especially those related to schools. Unfortunately, to be effective as a basic supply or as a supplement, tablets must be taken regularly over a long period of time.

Vitamin-fluoride tablets. At least two major studies have reported benefits of this combination (p. 47 re: Stookey 1966 and Arnold et al., 1960)[8] partly because people remember to take them with greater regularity than fluoride tablets alone. Speculation suggests that while fluoride tablets appear to be forgettable and boring, the vitamin-fluoride combination may be more interesting. Whatever the reason, such combinations are recommended medically only when they enhance the effectiveness of the element in question. In the case of vitamins and fluorides, the combination is not recommended: it fails to meet qualifications of efficacy and safety. The combination provides no greater caries prevention than fluoride alone; makes fluoride more costly than it would be alone; and blurs controls on the precise quantities of fluoride being taken. Since many people tend to overdose with vitamins, use of such combinations could mean that an individual would get more fluoride than necessary.

Accurate measurement is a problem common to all such foods as fluoride supplements, since the population varies in age, activity, appetite and eating habits.

Topical Applications

While fluorides ingested during tooth formation provide the greatest benefits in caries prevention, measurable improvements have also been noted with topical (tooth-surface) applications after teeth have emerged. Thus ingesting fluoride tablets daily, after keeping them in the mouth as long as possible (p. 19),[9] would combine internal and topical administration. Fluorides may also be applied externally to the teeth by having a dentist or technician "paint" them with a chemical solution such as sodium fluoride, or by do-it-yourself administration of fluoridated toothpaste, gels and mouthwashes, repeated regularly for many years in order to provide more lasting protection. Newbrun believes that of this group, fluoride mouth washes used under school supervision offer the most practical route of *topical* fluoride application as a public health measure, provided washes are used regularly (daily or weekly). Evaluations of other self-administered techniques have been mixed: J. C. Muhler reported in 1968 that six studies found such techniques "effective in reducing incidence of dental caries on a mass basis," (282-13-9B)[9] while school "brush-in" programs, and programs of self-applied stannous fluoride zircate treatment paste have appeared to produce inconclusive data.

Thus, topical self-administration was found to require persistence and years-long supervision and attention for even partial effectiveness. Topical application by professionals presents difficulties arising from cost in time and money and a shortage of available personnel.

Fluoridated Water: The Prime Protector of Teeth

This review of alternatives and supplements makes it clear that water fluoridation is the best and most consistently effective means of providing optimum dental benefits for people of all ages. As Adler indicated,

> The best way to ensure adequate fluoride consumption is by fluoridation of drinking water, which is a collective measure of benefit to all those drawing water for drinking and cooking purposes from a central supply system. When nutrition is adequate . . . 1.0–1.2 ppm is advisable in temperate zones. In warmer regions, the content should be smaller.

> Experience to date indicates fluoridated drinking water to be superior to all other vehicles, since these [others] do not ensure permanent and optimal ingestion of fluoride. (p. 351)[8]

The one recognized hazard in fluoridating water seems to be the possibility that it might convey a false sense of security—that one who drinks fluoridated water all his life might think he need pay no attention to his diet or to mouth care. Such an assumption would be far from true. In reality fluoridated water is but one of four elements needed for healthy teeth: it is a *necessary but not wholly sufficient component*. For best results, teeth require (1) fluorides (most effectively contributed by public water supplies), (2) a good diet with a minimum of sugar, (3) consistent personal mouth and gum care, including brushing, and (4) regular attention by competent professionals.

But fluoridation is crucial. It is by far the single most significant factor that has been found in producing caries-resistant teeth. As Crisp summarized, "Dietary discipline may contribute significantly to caries freedom in individuals by removing the carbohydrate ... base for caries attack. It does little or nothing to promote host resistance [to caries]. In relation to the latter, nothing has proved as effective as fluoride." (p. 236)[7]

Further, as a practical matter, the general public has been and still is unable to maintain anything like an acceptable level of caries resistance by good eating habits, regular brushing and dental hygiene. The general public needs the help of a years-long, consistent, continuous, and safe supply of fluorides like that provided by controlled fluoridation of public drinking water if tooth decay is to be controlled.

Considerations in Setting Optimum Fluoride Concentrations

Public water supplies are fluoridated with the underlying assumption that fluoride concentrations will be maintained at optimum levels. "Optimum" means levels that provide maximum benefits and avoid possible adverse effects. Components of the optimum include items such as fluoride intake from food, drink, and the atmosphere; the air temperature; and long-term observation and continuing research on individuals using fluoridated water.

Engineering controls that can ensure delivery of precisely measured amounts of fluorides are of course a pre-requisite in a fluoridation program. These are well established and readily available (see note 4). Of course, employment of these engineering procedures needs to be monitored on a regular basis to ensure maintenance of high standards of actual performance.

Levels of fluorides in food, drink and in the air can be monitored. The fluoride content in foods that appear in the markets and on the table in an area can be determined by "market basket" studies and analyses. "Comprehensive investigation of the fluoride content of specific items of food in various countries have been made" at least since 1939, and studies appropriate to specific areas have continued. (p. 32)[8] Eating habits and local preferences are also included in such market basket studies, although interpretation can vary concerning food quantities actually consumed. Atmospheric fluorides, even though present at very low levels, can be and are monitored by air pollution agencies.

For example, a spokesman of the San Francisco Bay Area Air Pollution Control District indicated that fluoride monitoring on a continuing basis is conducted at nearly 100 sites, and field observations of sensitive indicator plants are routinely made in potential trouble areas. Any indication of excessive fluoride levels is followed up promptly. The district in the past has successfully required one industry to stop localized releases of fluorides.

Air temperature is a major long-term phenomenon with important implications for setting fluoridation levels. Such temperatures can be determined with precision, and the mean temperatures vary only slightly from year to year. Thus fluoride concentrations in water can be adjusted according to the mean maximum temperature of each area.

Locally, in 1967, the California State Department of Public Health, Division of Dental Health, reported on a 5-year study headed by Dr. Lloyd F. Richards. Among other findings, the study produced "Recommended annual average fluoride ion concentration for domestic water supply" at three ranges of mean maximum [daytime] temperatures: at 65°F or lower, the recommended minimum-maximum range was 1.1 to 1.3 ppm. At 66 to 79°F the recommended range was 0.8 to 1.0 ppm; at 80°F or higher, the range was 0.5 to 0.7 ppm.[5]

As an indication of where local areas would fit on the chart, the Richards study identified coastal Berkeley with a 65°F mean maximum temperature. 1974 data from the East Bay Municipal Utility District showed that Lafayette, on the valley side of the hills, had a mean maximum of 69.1°F.

Individual bodily responses to fluoridation can be monitored both to ensure safety and to provide a continuous flow of information on nutritional uses of fluorides. As Hodge has stated, "It is not only possible, it is mandatory to search vigorously and without letup for *any evidence* of ill effect. . . . [however] *No injury* from fluoridated water has been proven to date." (emphasis added) (p. 131)[6]

Monitoring in all its aspects can be seen to play a double role: (1) it is essential for maintaining reliability and safety of fluoride intake, and (2) it provides important information for further research. As Groth stated (in a letter September 19, 1974) "monitoring ... is essential if we are to have adequate information on who is getting how much fluoride, and from what sources. . . . Saying it needs to be done doesn't make it happen; it takes money, and staff and facilities to analyse samples and to process data, and a lot more. It takes positive governmental (or bureaucratic) action to make it happen." As indicated earlier, some monitoring is now being done regularly, but many interested individuals and groups will feel that more is needed in the future.

Further Research on Dental Health

In addition to further study of fluoridation questions research on all aspects of dental health should be pursued vigorously. As things stand now, fluoridation of drinking water is clearly by far the best and most effective single measure that can be taken against tooth decay. But it is not the entire answer, nor, fortunately, the final answer. Promising leads suggest that further research along several avenues could, if successful and when the findings are put to work, almost eliminate tooth decay as a public health problem:

It seems unlikely that any single measure will be found sufficient to control this multifactorial disease. Consequently, we must continue the search for new means to increase the caries resistance of teeth, to reduce the cariogenicity of foodstuffs, and to check the deleterious activities of cariogenic bacteria. Anticaries food additives and antibacterial agents ... seem to be approaching practicability. Past performance warrants expectation that ongoing fundamental investigations will produce leads for future development and application. (p. 1204)[11]

The Importance of Who Decides

More than 65% of California's population now lives in areas that do not have fluoridated water. Continued efforts at fluoridation by local option will no doubt make progress toward extending fluoridation, but the process will be slow. Substantial advances like the one begun by the recent favorable action of the Los Angeles City Council will be rare, because Los Angeles is by far the largest city in the state. Of course, there are also a few large districts that supply water to sizable populations, like the East Bay Municipal Utility District, which serves approximately 1,086,000 people.

But for the most part, achieving fluoridation by local option and especially by referendum will be slow. It will involve contentious struggles, requiring campaigns in the individual communities concerned. Meanwhile much of the population now growing up with unfluoridated water—two youthful Californians out of three—will continue throughout their lives to have dental problems that could largely have been avoided. The cost of caring for bad teeth and gums, as well as the almost legendary traumas of the dentist's chair, plus the pain and discomfort caused by troublesome teeth, argue strongly that the problem is a substantial one. Furthermore, bad teeth often have an adverse effect on other aspects of one's health and well-being.

Allowing an avoidable problem of such dimensions to continue affecting such a large proportion of the population seems to merit intense statewide attention. Accordingly it appears that a good way to study and perhaps resolve a policy issue of this magnitude is thoughtful and careful consideration at the state level, by the Department of Health, the Legislature and Governor.

In the absence of state action, of course, the only other ways of obtaining water fluoridation will be either a national decision at the federal level, or local option exercised by local councils or through referenda. This emphasizes the current importance of questions such as the one posed on the November 1974 ballot of the East Bay Municipal Utility District. The question is formulated as follows:

"Shall the East Bay Municipal Utility District add fluoride compounds to the public water supply of said district subject to the regulations of the California State Department of Health?"

Summary and Conclusion

Persons who grow up in communities with fluoridated water have far less tooth decay than those reared in areas without fluoridation. Decay and caries reductions as high as 50% and more are noted. Economic savings from lower dental care costs are quite substan-

tial. No definite evidence of adverse effects have turned up, despite thirty years of controlled fluoridation in the United States, and similar although somewhat more limited experience in about thirty-two other nations. Much longer experience—a century or more—with naturally fluoridated water in many U.S. communities has shown no adverse effects except tooth mottling where the fluoride content is high enough to cause it. Controlled fluoridation deliberately sets the fluoride level low enough to avoid any noticeable mottling.

The courts have ruled that water fluoridation is a legitimate exercise of governments' public health power, and does not infringe the constitutional rights of individuals. Moreover fluorides in many forms are already consumed in water, beverages, and food. This suggests that there should be minimum personal objection to consuming a substance in fluoridated water that is already being consumed in smaller quantities anyway, as long as the total is beneficial. Continued research and monitoring are in order. But thirty years of experience shows that under present conditions fluoridation of drinking water in temperate zones at 1.0 ppm is the best way to obtain maximum dental benefits. These levels can of course be adjusted in the future if need be.

Fluoridated water has not presented any demonstrable environmental hazards. At present, the real environmental hazard to water supplies is caused by sewage and industrial wastes. As these are cleaned up by sophisticated treatment, the latter may also remove most of the fluorides from the effluent. But in any event, prudent future policies must include continued monitoring of the effects of fluorides and *all the other substances* that man adds to the environment.

At present about 20% of California's population is drinking fluoridated water. In September 1974 the Los Angeles City Council voted to fluoridate the city's water supply. When that decision is implemented, California's percentage will go to about 35%. The East Bay Municipal Utility District ballot of November 1974 carries a fluoridation referendum for its population of nearly 1,100,000. But beyond the few large jurisdictions like those, further fluoridation will require either (1) the slow and time-consuming process of local option, (2) action at the state level—as ten other states have done—or (3) action at the federal level. The last has not been seriously discussed recently.

Thus it appears that there is one good way remaining to try to resolve the public policy issue of water fluoridation both expeditiously and with thoughtful evaluation of the principal considerations. This is by action at the state level by the Department of Health, the Legislature and the Governor, which seems both appropriate and timely. Meanwhile approximately two-thirds of the children of this state will continue to grow up without the life-long dental benefits of fluoridated water.

Notes

[1] Information gathered eight years ago was presented in the Institute's *Public Affairs Report,* October 1966, Nathan and Scott, "Fluoridation in California: An Unresolved Public Policy Issue." For the present paper, the writers acknowledge the con-

tribution of Institute staff members: Linda Harris who surveyed the literature and prepared the material on legal questions and of Peter N. Sinegal who prepared material on fluorides in the atmosphere and pollution control.

[2] *Fluorine Chemistry*, ed. J. H. Simons. Vol. IV, by Harold C. Hodge and Frank A. Smith (New York: Academic Press, 1965).

[3] U.S. Department of Health, Education and Welfare, *Natural Fluoride Content of Community Water Supplies* (Bethesda, 1969). See p. 12.

[4] *Fluoridation Engineering Manual*, by Ervin Bellack (Environmental Protection Agency, Office of Water Programs, Water Supply Programs Division, 1972).

[5] Lloyd F. Richards, et al., "Determining optimum fluoride levels for community water supplies in relation to temperature," *Journal of the American Dental Association,* 74: 389-397 (1967).

[6] *Fluorides and Dental Caries*, ed. Ernest Newbrun (Springfield: Charles C. Thomas, 1972.) Articles by seven contributors.

[7] *Report of the Royal Commissioner* (The Honourable Malcolm Peter Crisp, a Justice of the Supreme Court of Tasmania) into *The Fluoridation of Public Water Supplies* (Hobart: 1968).

[8] *Fluorides and Human Health* (Geneva: World Health Organization, 1970). Articles by twenty-nine contributors, "Prepared in consultation with ninety-three dental and medical specialists in various countries."

[9] Additional study locales involved in various kinds of fluoridation experiments included Darmstadt, Wroclaw, Hamburg, Karl-Marx-Stadt, Hartlepool and York, Denver, Southampton, Carnarvon, Hastings, Cork, Porter County, Frankfort (Ky.), Fayette, Silver Bay, Tiel and Culemborg, Mallnitz, Selz-Umhausen, Seefeld, Easton and Bethlehem, Bartlett and Cameron, Montreal and Toronto. Further fluoride experiments have also been reported in numerous other countries including Austria, Brazil, Colombia, Czechoslovakia, Hungary and eastern European countries, Paraguay, Sweden, Serbia, South Australia. See *Fluoride Abstracts:* 1969–1971, No. 10, May 1972; 1969–1971, No. 11, September 1972; 1969–1971, No. 12, March 1973; 1966–1968, No. 13, March 1973. Supplement to: *Annotated Bibliography: the Occurrence and Biological Effects of Fluorine Compounds. Vol. I, The Inorganic Compounds.* (Department of Environmental Health, Kettering Laboratory College of Medicine, University of Cincinnati).

[10] Edward Groth III, "Two Issues of Science and Public Policy: Air Pollution Control in the San Francisco Bay Area and Fluoridation of Community Water Supplies," Stanford University, Ph.D. dissertation, biological sciences, 1973.

[11] Henry W. Scherp, "Dental Caries: Prospects for Prevention," *Science,* 173 (4003): 1199–1205 (Sept 24, 1971).

Health and Hospitals:
Planning, Governance and Finance

Vol. 15   No. 6   December 1974

Developing the Ombudsman's Role
In Health Care Services

By Stanley V. Anderson[1]
Department of Political Science
University of California, Santa Barbara

Introduction and Background

Favorable experiences with the score of general Ombudsman offices established during the past twenty years suggest that it may be timely to try variations on the office that would bring the Ombudsman into fields previously neglected, or explored only in a restricted fashion. Health care is such a field. This paper will examine some of the characteristics and experiences of the Ombudsman that would support broad experimentation in the health care field, as well as some of the cautions and limitations implied in such a venture.

The Ombudsman is an independent and impartial expert who investigates complaints from citizens, and helps solve their problems with government. His only power to command the government is to elicit information. Beyond that, he can recommend remedial action in specific grievance cases, and can also urge more general administrative reform, where he sees the necessity. His regular reports to the Legislature with respect to administration help the Legislature in its oversight role, and occasionally lead it to enact minor reforms. Most often, the Ombudsman's investigations help clarify and explain government action, and contribute to improvement of public understanding of government.

Although it has antecedents in Sweden and analogues elsewhere, the modern office of Ombudsman dates from the Swedish Instrument of Government in 1809. Subsequently, Ombudsmen were established in Finland, Denmark, Norway, New Zealand and in various Canadian provinces and Australian states. In the United States, Herman Doi took office as the first state Ombudsman in Hawaii in 1969. Iowa and Nebraska have named Ombudsmen, and at the city level, so have Dayton and Seattle.

Ombudsmen and Health Care in Prisons

The general similarities of these offices around the globe has been striking. In fact, the only radical innovation is the development in the United States of an Ombudsman whose jurisdiction is limited solely to prisons and prisoners. Along with patients in mental hospitals, prisoners constitute the limited populations whose health care has so far been monitored by Ombudsmen. Minnesota was the first state to name a prison Ombudsman in 1972, followed by Connecticut, Michigan and Kansas. At the instruction of the state Legislature, the Iowa Ombudsman office has added a special deputy for prisons.

The prison setting, of course, has unique characteristics.[2] The state pays for medical treatment, and inmates are placed in custody involuntarily. Services are centralized, there is a chain of command, and the staff are government employees. The provision of services is circumscribed by regulations that the Ombudsman, over time, can help to refine. In such a setting, Ombudsmen have demonstrated an ability to investigate and pass independent expert judgment on the medical services provided to prisoners.

Ombudsmen and Mental Patients

Ombudsmen have also been effective in a more limited fashion in dealing with patients committed involuntarily to long-term care facilities such as mental hospitals. The Ombudsman is often initially concerned with the propriety of commitment, but does not usually challenge professional judgment on this question. Once having received a complaint, the Ombudsman may consider the quality of care, particularly when the patient is physically restrained, drugged or isolated. More often than not, the Ombudsman offers reassurance to family, friends and the public that the treatment is necessary, humane and defensible.

Others, of course, also perform such services—medical personnel, ministers, lawyers, judges, legislators and governors. But it is also valuable to have an Ombudsman perform such a role as well, and on a consistent, methodical basis, because involuntary hospitalization and physical restraint are drastic measures that call for safeguards against improper use.

A Limited Role, So Far

Over all, the most striking element in the health-care-related activities of Ombudsmen so far is how restricted they have been in scope. Ombudsmen have not monitored the grievance machinery of health care services with respect to individuals (doctors, nurses, pharmacists, technicians) or institutions (hospitals, nursing homes, medical insurance companies). This conclusion is based primarily upon interviews and review of cases and annual reports of Ombudsman offices both in this country and overseas.[3]

The question remains how an expanded and effective role could be developed for the Ombudsman in the area of health care services; and further, what model and structure would be most appropriate; what problems would be encountered; and under what conditions would success be most likely?

Three Models for Further Study

There are three majors ways of handling complaints: the professional, bargaining, and due process models.[4] Where *professional* personnel are relied on, the British bureaucracy provides the classic prototype. The civil servant is a highly educated career official working in anonymity and virtual secrecy, who sees himself as not an adversary but a "servant" of the public. It is generally assumed that he is dedicated to the general weal, knows his job, and will work best if he is left alone because other inputs might distract, confuse and possibly corrupt him. Carried to an extreme, this model provides for no grievance machinery.

As used in the medical world, the professional model relies on self-discipline, acquisition of skills, and adherence to rigorous standards (e.g., the Oath of Hippocrates). In order to maintain these skills and standards, non-coercive peer review is sometimes used.

In a system of individual or group *bargaining*, an individual patient may "bargain" with his doctor on the treatment to be undertaken. After being informed of the alternatives—which may require "second opinions" —the patient may give informed consent to the treatment. The group bargaining model is identified with consumerism, and implies a kind of adversary relationship between providers and consumers of health care, wherein the public shares in deciding on the kinds of medical services to be provided. At present, the group bargaining effort appears to be combative, with recognition and legitimacy as important as any other specific goals.

Due process also contrasts with the professional approach (which resolves complaints unilaterally by the professional or his peers), and with the bargaining approach (which resolves issues by agreement). The due process approach instead requires the exercise of third party judgment to resolve conflict. Normally, the third party does not establish his own criteria. He is guided by rules, and the permissible form and content of alternative decisions. Malpractice proceedings (as discussed later) could be considered as one example, using a panel or arbitration board as an alternative to legal proceedings; another is full-scale litigation.

In sum, the Ombudsman concept of complaint handling has elements of the *due process* approach, although unlike the rulings of a court of law, for example, the Ombudsman's decisions are not binding. The Ombudsman also uses a kind of peer review (as in the *professional* model, and may also attempt to mediate (as in the *bargaining* approach).

Group Conflict, Professional Structures and Grievance Machinery

As we have seen, while peer review and non-binding due process adjudication are normal functions of an Ombudsman, mediation of group conflicts is not. Ombudsmen who enter the medical field will face two major obstacles: the organizational anarchy of the medical profession, and the relative absence of adequate grievance procedures. If he should venture into mediating between the public and the medical profession, however, the Ombudsman would probably try to encourage the rationalization of medical service organization, and to foster the creation of efficient and fair grievance machinery. He would then help to create an atmosphere in which he could function normally to receive, investigate and judge the merits of individual complaints as well.

As an Ombudsman attempts to investigate complaints, he can also evaluate existing avenues for conflict resolution. Consequently, once an Ombudsman has presented his findings, most agencies will improve internal procedures for handling complaints if they are shown to be inadequate.[5]

Restructuring grievance machinery in the medical industry is a particularly formidable task, in which the Ombudsman concept has not yet been notably successful. The task is complex for a number of reasons. Complaints can cover a wide range of topics. Further, organizational lines of authority and responsibility are not clear to patients except possibly those in highly structured health care systems like the Veterans Administration, the armed forces, state mental hospitals, and local public hospitals. Despite these difficulties, the Ombudsmen could help focus attention on the need for reform, even if they have only limited ability to draft or implement reforms themselves.

When a Patient Complains: The Due Process Approach

What happens if a patient is still dissatisfied after having used existing complaint machinery (if any) in the hospital's hierarchy, or in any identifiable professional group? The latter might include a medical association, a state regulatory agency such as the Department of Health, or in some cases, the Board of Medical Examiners. All such agencies are headed by doctors, and the disgruntled patient may see the discussants as professionals primarily interested in protecting fellow professionals.

The patient may then determine to sue, but malpractice litigation, the primary avenue for due-process grievance resolution in the medical field, is judged a failure if not an outright catastrophe on a number of counts. It is cumbersome and costly for the patient. Moreover it is undesirable for doctors because malpractice insurance premiums are exceedingly high and will see additional sharp rises in 1975.

Further, malpractice charges can escalate a dispute from (non-coercive) peer review through panels and arbitration boards to costly and unsatisfactory litigation. In addition, both patients and doctors suffer from the exercise of "defensive medicine," whereby decisions about diagnosis and treatment are based on the doctor's wish to avoid being sued, rather than on the needs of the patient.

Because malpractice procedures are so unsatisfactory, most such claims are in fact resolved by bargaining rather than through the full due process system. The amount of settlement is usually based on guesses as to what a judge and jury would award.

Medical Association Grievance Committees

Many medical associations now have grievance committees.[6] When a doctor is sued or threatened with suit, the appropriate grievance committee investigates. Based upon the information made available to it, and turned up by its own investigation, the grievance committee will recommend denial or settlement. Usually, the insurance company accepts the recommendation.

Such arbitration committees play an Ombudsmanlike role. They are independent of the interested parties; they are expert; they get the facts. Further, their final decision is not binding. It is only in their lack of accessibility that they still fail to meet the standard definition of an Ombudsman. Their existence is not advertised, however, and the general public cannot normally turn to them. Consequently, the committees hear only those disputes that have reached the level of threatened litigation. In sum, this system still falls substantially short of the role of the Ombudsman.

General Practitioner as "Ombudsman"

We conclude that a well-publicized Ombudsman, available to consider all complaints, would represent a further substantial and constructive extension of peer review in the medical field. In order to be a "peer," of course, the Ombudsman would have to command general medical expertise. In fact, David Mechanic characterizes the general practioner, in the regular conduct of his practice, as a kind of medical Ombudsman, expected

> to make assessments of the quality of specialized services available, to channel his patients into those routes most likely to offer a high quality of care, and to survey and, if necessary, intervene in the medical care provided to his patients so that their interests are best served.[7]

Such a practitioner is actually playing an Ombudsman role, but his impartiality is undercut by his own pecuniary involvement, present and prospective. Moreover, he is accessible only to his own patients. Finally, a practitioner would obviously be unable to play an Ombudsman role with a distrustful patient, perhaps on the verge of suspecting his doctor of malpractice.

Mechanic later alludes to a medical Ombudsman who would avoid these shortcomings. He would have to have

> sufficient technical training to know his way around medical settings and the variety of medical specialties, but also would be sufficiently trained to be sensitive to the social and behavioral aspects of care, the coordination of services, and the need for and availability of social services in general.[8]

The Ombudsman Between Doctor and Patient

The medical care Ombudsman's function would bring together the professional and the due process concepts. Because he must rely on reasoned persuasion, his mode would expand to include an element of bargaining. If he aids communication between doctor and patient, or between health-providers and health-consumers, he may play both a bargaining and an educational role by clarifying the facts and reducing conflict. In short, the Ombudsman may provide an avenue to "informed consent." Mechanic describes the educational role of his medical Ombudsman as possibly serving to

> improve communication and coordination among the various persons involved in providing health care, contribute to educating the patient about the nature of his care and health status generally, and . . . [serving] as the point of unification of all medical, rehabilitative, and social services provided for the patient within the context.[9]

Organizational Problems: The Ombudsman's Areas of Concern

Ombudsmen whose spheres of responsibility take in many institutions and cross political boundaries will face severe organizational problems. It is difficult to impose an orderly procedure for complaint handling upon a system in chaos, like the present condition of organization for health care. Consequently, in order to function in the health care field, the medical Ombudsman will have to join others in advocating governmental reorganization as it might improve health services and their regulation. By seeking reform of governmental functions, the Ombudsman would avoid attempting directly to regulate the private sphere. Instead, he can monitor the manner in which government inspectors enforce prevailing standards.

Accordingly an Ombudsman can appropriately address himself to three major areas of organizational and procedural reform: establishment of (1) standards of performance, (2) requirements for licensing, and (3) primary control through inspection. He should also work toward a range of sanctions short of license revocation. Drastic punishments lack credibility, because they are only used in flagrant cases.

Ombudsmen interviewed by the writer accepted the suggestion that the existence of standards, licensing and and inspection at the primary level of regulation was essential for the normal functionings of a medical Ombudsman. Further, as former Seattle Ombudsman Leland Walton states, Ombudsmen should not wait for these conditions to be established, but should work to stimulate their development.

Where standards are relatively high, inspections frequent and probing, and reasonable penalties exacted, an Ombudsman could readily handle complaints against marginal defects. If the converse is true,[10] the Ombudsman would have to begin his work by lobbying for statutory or regulatory standards, licensing, inspections and proportionate sanctions, as well as for adequate primary appeal mechanisms.

Location and Designation of a Health Care Ombudsman

Health care could be placed under the jurisdiction of a general Ombudsman, or an Ombudsman office could be established specifically for health care. There is little effective difference between a separate medical Ombudsman office, and a medical section within a general Ombudsman office. Either way, it is essential to require medical expertise, i.e., the medical Ombudsman or deputy should be equipped with extensive previous training and experience in both medicine and administration.

Should health care Ombudsmen have general medical jurisdiction, or should there be specialized Ombudsmen in particular areas, such as long-term care? The Governor's Task Force on Aging, in the State of Washington, made the second choice, urging the Governor

> to establish, in the Health Division of the Department of Social and Health Services, and throughout the state, a system of Ombudsman on behalf of nursing home patients.[11]

For optimum effectiveness, a nursing home responsibility could be included in the purview of a broadly based medical care Ombudsman who would monitor the regulation of a number of long-term care facilities. An Ombudsman concerned with regulation of nursing homes would, of course, need to have expert knowledge of their operation.

Ombudsmen could function effectively both in nursing homes and other long-term care units. Several characteristics especially recommend them for ombudsmanic supervision. Doctors, who are relatively free of any form of control including peer review, are also in the strongest position to resist such innovation, but they are few in number and spend relatively little time in nursing homes. Nurses, orderlies and administrators, however, are far more numerous in such settings, and are relatively more accustomed to working within a chain of command. The latter group might welcome an Ombudsman as a buffer within the chain.

With respect to long-term care generally, people in this situation comprise a special population subject to intensified risks. Their risks are not necessarily dissimilar in kind, but are greater in degree than those of other hospitalized persons, or even outpatients. Of course, questions of treatment quality and communication between medical staff and patient arise in a variety of health care settings. High-risk and vulnerable individuals in long-term care thus serve as heightened examples that help emphasize the relevance and need for health care Ombudsmen.

Justification for the Ombudsman's Services in Nursing Homes

Many long-term care facilities are populated by the aged, who are in a strong moral position to demand the extra protection of an Ombudsman. Although they have not been committed—like prisoners and some mental patients—many residents must in effect remain in nursing homes for the rest of their lives. Accordingly, society has a special obligation to insure that the quality of their care is satisfactory and their treatment humane.

The elementary preconditions for the functioning of an Ombudsman in nursing homes seem to be present: Standards are set by state statute or regulation, usually conforming to federal grant-in-aid requirements. Licensing and inspection requirements vary among states, and in accordance with the level of care. Governmental regulation is highly significant, particularly since many nursing homes are owned and operated privately, and since public funds also support many nursing home residents.

What the Ombudsman Should and Should Not Do in Nursing Homes

In long-term total-care institutions, the Ombudsman monitors an important part of the life of the residents, but by no means all of it. His attention is directed to such matters as quality of food, cleanliness of beds and clothing, spaciousness of rooms, promptness of attendance, and questions of quality of health care in general and as raised by complaints.

But the whole field of interpersonal relationships is essentially outside the Ombudsman's purview: relationships with fellow residents, friends outside the home, family, businesses, and governmental agencies not related to the provision of medical care. To the resident, these matters will often appear even more important than those for which an Ombudsman is primarily responsible. Other aspects of nursing home life that are largely beyond the Ombudsman's direct responsibility are the boredom, loneliness and despondency that often afflict patients of total-care institutions, conditions that are caused in part by the absence of interpersonal relations.

In this group of problem areas, the need may be for simple information or service that may not relate directly to government regulation. Here the Ombudsman can try to play a dual role: First, in an information and service vacuum, an Ombudsman would probably stimulate the provision or improvement of services, possibly with the help of volunteers. In this way, he would respond to needs and still avoid being swamped with service requests and informational inquiries.[12]

In addition to channeling queries to such services, an Ombudsman in a nursing home would have to develop outreach for his government-related responsibilities. Residents in long-term care facilities are often unable to visit government offices, and may have difficulty in writing. Accordingly like most other American Ombudsmen, he should accept complaints by telephone. Further, the general reluctance to accept third-party complaints should be overcome in favor of complaints brought by family, friends and volunteers. (A similar exception is already made for patients in mental hospitals.)

Primary Remedies for Complaints and Exhaustion of Alternatives

In dealing with complaints, the Ombudsman should first be sure the other remedies have been exhausted. This is efficient procedurally, and in this way the Ombudsman could perform an educational function by encouraging people to try first to solve their own problems. Also, when the Ombudsman receives a complaint that should be handled by an agency of government or by a private agency, he should help the complainant find the appropriate channels. Perhaps the Ombudsman should set up an appointment or interview, and follow up to ensure that the agency in question responds to the complainant.

The Ombudsman should see to the designation of a proxy to act on behalf of complainants who do not seem to be capable of pursuing remedies, or should himself communicate with the agency concerned. But if the agency in question has previously been unresponsive, the Ombudsman should not require the complainant to repeat the process.

While the interests of the complainants are being defended, careful precautions should also be taken to maintain the purity of the Ombudsman concept. This care is not an idle formalism, but a necessity to protect the peculiar combination of characteristics that permit an Ombudsman to perform his special function of using feedback from complaints in order to correct deficiencies in government's other control mechanisms.

Summary

To summarize some recommendations growing out of this discussion:

(1) Health care Ombudsmen should possess a high degree of expertise. The performance of the first health care Ombudsmen in any jurisdiction would be crucial to the encouragement of further extensions of the concept;

(2) Health care Ombudsmen should be set up either as separate offices or as part of a general Ombudsman office;

(3) The jurisdiction of the health care Ombudsman should encompass all health care services, including nursing homes and other services and facilities related to long-term care. The fragmentation that already plagues health care organizations should not be repeated and extended by the Ombudsman function and its organization;

(4) In responding to complaints and on his own motion, the health care Ombudsman should direct his attention particularly to (a) the adequacy of standards, licensing, inspection, and use of appropriate sanctions; and (b) the adequacy of primary grievance mechanisms within nursing homes, hospitals and medical insurance agencies, both from the point of view of the consumer of medical services and of the practitioner; and

(5) With regard to long-term care, the health care Ombudsman should avoid being deluged by informational and service requests. Thus he should encourage the creation of other mechanisms for dealing with such queries.

Conclusion

The Ombudsman represents a professionalization of complaint-handling, through centralization and specialization. His expertise and access to information enable him to use reasoned persuasion to promote procedural and structural reform.

For many reasons—including increased sensitivity to patients' needs and disenchantment with malpractice systems—the time seems ripe for experimentation with medical Ombudsmen. But the inherent limitations of the institution must also be kept in mind:

An Ombudsman cannot supply services where none exist, supplement their quantity when in short supply, coordinate the services of others, or administer a program of care. These responsibilities rest in the hands of the health service agencies themselves. They should not be the main task of the Ombudsman, whose role and functions are, instead, to resolve grievances, improve administration, and aid its oversight.[13]

Notes

[1] Professor Anderson is Principal Investigator of the Institute's Ombudsman Activities Project. This paper is based upon a report prepared for the Bureau of Health Service Research and Evaluation, Health Services Administration, Department of Health, Education, and Welfare (Contract No. HSM 110-73-461).

[2] See Susan Alexander, "The Captive Patient: The Treatment of Health Problems in American Prisons," *Clearinghouse Review* (May 1972), reprinted by the American Bar Association Commission on Correctional Facilities and Services. See also generally, Timothy L. Fitzharris, *The Desirability of a Correctional Ombudsman* (Berkeley: Institute of Governmental Studies, University of California, 1973), and Lance Tibbles, "Ombudsmen for American Prisons," 48 *North Dakota Law Review* 383–441 (1972) (reprinted by the Institute of Governmental Studies).

[3] See Stanley V. Anderson, "Assessment of General Ombudsman Activities in Response to Complaints Regarding Long-Term Care," a report prepared for the Department of Health, Education, and Welfare (Contract No. HSM 110-73-461), typescript (1974). For a similarly pessimistic evaluation of grievance machinery in a sister profession, see F. Marks and D. Cathcart, "Discipline Within the Legal Profession: Is It Self-Regulation?" 1974 *Illinois Law Forum* 2: 193–236, reprinted by the American Bar Foundation.

[4] Adapted from the models used by David Kirp of the Graduate School of Public Policy, University of California, Berkeley, to analyze the way in which school children are classified for admission to special programs. See Kirp, W. Buss and P. Kuriloff, "Legal Reform of Special Education: Empirical Studies and Procedural Proposals," 62 *California Law Review* 1:40–155 (January 1974).

[5] See Stanley V. Anderson and John E. Moore, eds., *Establishing Ombudsman Offices* (Berkeley: Institute of Governmental Studies, University of California, 1972), p. 59. See also Walter Gellhorn, *Ombudsmen and Others,* and *When Americans Complain,* both from Harvard University Press, 1966.

[6] R. Winikoff, "Medical-Legal Screening Panels as an Alternative Approach to Medical Malpractice Claims," 13 *William and Mary Law Review,* 693–723 (1972) concludes that "while they have been successful in some areas, medical-legal screening panels are not, as presently constituted, an acceptable alternative solution to this urgent problem of national concern."

[7] *Public Expectations and Health Care* (New York: Wiley, 1972), p. 58.

[8] Ibid., p. 77. See also R. Conant, A. DeLuca and L. Levin, "Health Education—A Bridge to the Community," *American Journal of Public Health,* 62: 1239–1244 (September 1972).

[9] Mechanic, p. 77. See also N. Hansell, M. Wodarczyk and H. Visatsky, "The Mental Health Expediter," *Archives of General Psychiatry,* 18: 392–399 (April 1968).

[10] An article entitled "Sharp Blast At Nursing Homes" appeared in the San Francisco *Chronicle* November 20, 1974, p. 12. The opening paragraph stated: "Nursing home safety inspections are 'a national farce' despite constant government rhetoric heralding crackdowns and fund cutoffs, a Senate report said yesterday."

[11] ...*None Would Be Old* (n.d. [1972]), p. 81. See also House Bill No. 954, State of Washington, 43rd Regular Session (Read first time February 12, 1973).

[12] See Alan J. Wyner, ed., *Executive Ombudsmen in the United States* (Berkeley: Institute of Governmental Studies, University of California, 1973). See also G. Wolkon and S. Moriwaki, "The Ombudsman Programme: Primary Prevention of Psychological Disorders," *The International Journal of Social Psychiatry,* 19:220–225 (Autumn/Winter 1973).

[13] Paraphrased from Matthew Huxley, ed., *Ombudsmen for Nursing Homes,* a report prepared for the President's Nursing Home Program, Department of Health, Education, and Welfare (mimeo., January 28, 1972), p. 1.

Politics: Campaign Finance; Congressional Power

Vol. 16   No. 1   February 1975

Public Funding of Political Campaigns: Attitudes and Issues in California

By
James Fay
Department of Political Science
California State University, Hayward
and
Thomas Leatherwood
Department of Political Science
California State University, San Francisco

Introduction

The implementation of recent federal reforms concerning disclosure of campaign contributions, and vigorous enforcement of existing California laws, have begun to reveal in a clearer light than ever before many specific facts of election campaign finance. These facts demonstrate what political critics and observers have long maintained, i.e., that the election process is extremely expensive, and that candidates depend heavily on the donors who make large contributions.

The way campaigns are conducted in the United States, it takes a lot of money to pay expenses and communicate with the voters on a mass basis. As a matter of either habit or conviction, most citizens do not contribute to candidates or political parties. Accordingly, the prospective candidate is forced to draw on personal or family resources, or else to rely on the largess of wealthy individuals or special interests. Existing disclosure laws—which simply remove the secrecy from campaign funding—do not significantly alter the ground rules of campaign finance. Consequently, such laws can reveal the problems but cannot solve either the matter of high costs of campaigning or of candidate dependence on large contributions.

The Watergate morass, which brought current methods of campaign financing into profound discredit, forced policymakers to propose legislation that would go beyond disclosure and provide a further reform: the use of public funds to help finance election campaigns. For example, the national government and the State of New Jersey have broken ground by passing laws providing public money for presidential and gubernatorial campaigns, respectively. In addition, since early 1973 a number of bills have been introduced in the California Legislature proposing some form of public funding for campaigns, plus other major changes in statutes regulating campaign finance.

Along with this developing interest in reform comes the realization that public financing of political campaigns is highly complex and its results are still largely unpredictable. This paper will attempt to assess the degree of public acceptance of the concept, primarily in California; some of the major arguments for and against the reform; the probable elements of and the problems posed by a comprehensive law; some suggested criteria for evaluating proposals; and a few recommendations for procedures in California.

Nationwide Polls

There are indications that a tenuous, evolving, but still unclear consensus may be developing that favors this innovation. Recent national polls, conducted in 1974, have shown opinions supporting publicly financed election campaigns, ranging from a slim plurality to 2-to-1 or even greater majorities. Such trends cannot be considered conclusive, however, because a Harris Poll in 1973, for example, showed a 4-to-1 margin against public subsidies for elections. Differences in the context of events and wording of poll questions also tend to present difficulties in the assessment and comparability of poll results.

Some Indications of Californians' Views

At this writing, no statewide public opinion polls are available on the issue of public financing, and there is no conclusive information on the attitudes of Californians concerning election subsidies. There are, however, some indications of Californians' views. For example, a group of names chosen from a necessarily incomplete list of large campaign contributors in the summer of 1973 showed divergent views on campaign subsidies. Seventy percent of the contributors to Democratic campaigns (in the 1970 and 1972 general elections) *favored* subsidies, while 76 percent of the contributors to Republican campaigns *opposed* them. (See Table 1.)

Similar diversity of opinion appeared in an (unpublished) early 1974 random survey by James Fay of Republican and Democratic political activists (delegates to national conventions, members of state central committees, county chairmen, and members of political

Table 1

CONTRIBUTORS PREFERRING A LAW TO PROVIDE FOR GOVERNMENT SUBSIDY OF CAMPAIGNS
TO ELIMINATE LARGE PRIVATE CONTRIBUTIONS

	All respondents			Democrats			Republicans		
	Yes	No	Total	Yes	No	Total	Yes	No	Total
Number	48	45	93	39	17	56	9	28	37
Percent	52	48	100	70	30	100	24	76	100

Source: Fay survey in 1973 of California contributors who gave $500 or more to campaigns in the 1970 or 1972 general elections in California. Names were chosen from lists available at the time. The lists were not complete.

clubs). Based on an overall response rate of 36 percent, the Democratic activists overwhelmingly *favored* publicly financed elections; with the exception of members of the California Republican League, Republican groups were overwhelmingly *opposed*.

A Common Cause Survey of California state legislators found in late 1974 that of the 80 assemblymen (all recently elected), 49 of the 72 who responded, or 61 percent, said they favored campaign subsidies. In the Senate, 16 of the 20 winners in the 1974 general election replied; 11 (55 percent) favored publicly subsidized election campaigns. (See Table 2.)

Table 2
ATTITUDES OF CURRENT CALIFORNIA LEGISLATORS[a]

	Election for all state offices should be financed by a combination of public funds and small private contributions		Limits should be placed on campaign expenditures by candidates and independent committees		Strict limits should be placed on the size and source of private contributions	
	#	%	#	%	#	%
Assembly: 80 potential respondents (winners)[b]						
Support	49	61	48	60	47	59
Oppose	15	19	10	12	8	10
Unclear response	8	10	14	18	17	21
No response	8	10	8	10	8	10
Senate: 20 potential respondents (winners)[c]						
Support	11	55	11	55	12	60
Oppose	3	15	3	15	2	10
Unclear response	2	10	2	10	2	10
No response	4	20	4	20	4	20

[a]*Source:* Common Cause Poll.

[b]All 80 assemblymen ran for election.

[c]Only those incumbent senators up for reelection were polled.

Of the present political leadership in Sacramento, both Governor Edmund G. Brown, Jr. and Assembly Speaker Leo McCarthy have indicated support of election subsidies. The same is true of the chairmen of the Elections and Reapportionment Committees in both houses as well as the chairman of the Senate Finance Committee. On the other hand, the Assembly Ways and Means Committee does not appear sympathetic to public financing at the present time. Thus, it is by no means certain that a bill agreeable to all parties can be worked out in the legislative committees.

With respect to some of California's more important interest groups, a telephone survey revealed that few had taken a clear stand on either the general concept or specific details of financing campaigns with public funds. Spokesmen for both the Democratic and Republican parties also remain noncommittal, while some of the state's minor parties are clearly uneasy about new campaign finance laws that might be manipulated by the major parties to further complicate their status and the prospects of small or new parties.

Among the state's major newspapers, the Sacramento *Bee*, and the San Jose *Mercury*, and to a limited extent the San Francisco *Examiner*, support campaign subsidies. Other major papers are either noncommittal or oppose such subsidies. The writers have observed that some newspapers based their positions on careful consideration of major issues, while others had not yet evaluated the arguments for or against public financing of campaigns in California. Newspaper spokesmen asserted repeatedly that incumbents should not enjoy undue protection from challengers, and indicated that they would strongly oppose measures that might ensure such protection. (See Table 3.)

Citizen Action Groups and a Division of Opinion

Citizen action groups were primarily responsible for placing Proposition 9 on the June 1974 ballot, and their efforts were in large measure responsible for its success. But these same groups are not likely to present that same united front on the issue of public financing. Common Cause, with 60,000 members in California and apparently possessing substantial public influence, strongly supports the principle. On the other hand, People's Lobby, whose corps of volunteers gathered the majority of the signatures that qualified Proposition 9 for the ballot, have announced opposition to public financing of campaigns on the ground that it provides an unwarranted subsidy to politicians. They have decided instead to support former Governor Ronald Reagan's proposal to eliminate all group-based political contributions, and to continue to focus their energies on closing what they see as loopholes in the Political Reform Act of 1974 (Proposition 9). This division of opinion, combined with current fiscal stringencies, would make it difficult for citizen action groups in California to again use the "threat" of the initiative for introducing legislation if lawmakers do not respond to reformers' wishes.

Supporters' Views: Reducing the Influence of Large Contributors and Other Goals

What do the proponents of public financing hope to accomplish? The broad goals of proposed reforms can be

Table 3   79

PRESS ATTITUDES ON CHANGES IN ELECTION FINANCE LAWS

Newspapers	Support the concept of publicly financed elections	Strict limits should be placed on campaign contributions	Strict limits should be placed on campaign expenditures	Tax check-offs should be used to help support an election subsidy system
L.A. *Times*	No. Wait to see if Proposition 9 works	Yes	Yes	Conditional support. Would prefer to see if Proposition 9 works
L.A. *Herald Examiner*	No	No position	No position	No position
San Diego *Union*	No	No	No	No
Sacramento *Bee*	Yes	Yes. As long as incumbents don't receive a great advantage	Yes. As long as	Yes
Sacramento *Union*	No	No	No	No position
San Francisco *Examiner*	Would support a limited experiment for a statewide office	Yes	Yes	Yes
San Francisco *Chronicle*	No	No	No	Yes
San Francisco *Bay Guardian*	No	No	No	Lean against
Oakland *Tribune*	No position	No position	No position	No position
San Jose *Mercury*	Yes	Yes	Yes	No position

Source: Fay and Leatherwood survey, January 1975.

---

placed in several categories, including reducing the power of big money, increasing access to policymaking, stimulating competition, and rejuvenating the political system, as discussed below.

A principal objective of public funding is, of course, to reduce the influence of wealthy contributors and free-spending special interest groups. As a consequence of removing such pressures, it is believed that elected officials could more readily base their judgments on the merits of issues, and on constituents' interests, rather than on the preferences of a few large campaign contributors.

Encouraging A Variety of Individuals and Groups to Participate

Furthermore, public funding would help qualified candidates who lack access to great wealth, but who have demonstrable public support, to run more effective campaigns. This would help both citizens of modest means and interest groups that have public support but limited funds, to compete in the policymaking process on a more nearly equal basis than is possible now.

Stimulating Competition and Attention to Issues

Thus, public funding is intended to increase competition in the electoral system, by reducing the advantage that incumbents normally have in their easier access to large private contributions. Moreover, it is thought that public funding would encourage candidates to spend more of their campaign time and effort in dealing with the electorate and discussing the issues, rather than working endlessly on fund-raising.

Benefiting the Political System

Public funding could also help reduce an anomaly in the election system, whereby the force of the Supreme Court's one man-one vote dictum is eroded by the ability of large campaign contributors to play a dominant role in elections. Moreover, public funding is seen as a way of helping reduce citizens' cynicism and fear that public decisions are unduly influenced by powerful and selfish economic forces. Funding would thus restore a sense of confidence in the processes and legitimacy of government. Such a change in attitude could lead to increased participation in voting and other more demanding types of campaign activity.

In sum, the principal objective of advocates of public financing is to make major alterations in the processes of campaigning, elections, and governmental decision making, rather than to achieve specific changes in the policy output of government. But most self-identified reformers also assume that these changes will result in more equitable public policy decisions.

Some Principal Arguments Against Public Funding

Some of the principal arguments against reform proposals are reviewed below, including questions relating to cost, free speech and visibility, effects on political parties, realities of self-interest and the concentration of power, and the need for experimentation.

Cost

It is alleged that even if one of the more frugal proposals becomes law, the program will be expensive.

Given the short-term economic pinch, public money for campaigns might appear to be a luxury, a point recently emphasized by the current Assembly leadership.

The Question of Free Speech

An objection based on constitutional guarantees suggests that public financing and limits on campaign contributions and expenditures may also limit what some consider to be a form of free speech and political participation, i.e., making financial contributions to political campaigns. Not every interested individual can contribute the (unregulated) time or skills that are the equivalent of (regulated) money. Further, limits on group contributions can be seen as discrimination against the special interest organizations through which most individuals make themselves heard in a mass society.

The Problem of Visibility and Information About Candidates

Limiting campaign expenditures may prevent relatively unknown challengers from gaining public visibility and provide further benefits for incumbents or celebrities with well-known names. Further, spending limits might reduce availability of voter information about candidates and issues. Finally, with less money to spend on such items as direct mail, candidates might be even more dependent than at present on access to media coverage for essential communication with the electorate.

Effects on Parties and Reverse Effects

It appears that, at least in the short term, public funding would probably provide greater benefits to the Democratic party candidates who often, although not always, have had more difficulties than Republicans in raising funds. There are also risks that rigid formulas for public fund distribution might "artificially" sustain either or both of the major parties while reducing the chances of minor parties or independent candidates. On the other hand, providing public money directly to candidates and not to parties could reduce still further the power of the parties, and in fact push them virtually to the brink of irrelevance.

It is also possible that capable candidates may be discouraged from running for office because limits on contributions may force them to work unduly hard to collect small amounts of money. They would have less opportunity to campaign and presumably to discuss issues and communicate with voters, thus frustrating the goals of the reformers.

Dangers of Self-Interest and Concentration of Power

Some contend that current proposals for election subsidy are inherently unstable because they are subject to appropriations that must be approved by a two-thirds legislative majority each year. Candidates would have to approach campaigns uncertain whether they would receive public money to compensate for restricted campaign contributions. Challengers would also be aware that incumbent legislators could be tempted to refuse to fund upcoming elections adequately and thus minimize newcomers' chances for success.

In addition, some opponents argue that placing centralized control over the sensitive electoral process in the hands of a three-person majority of the Fair Political Practices Commission may be questionable. These critics contend that even with checks on capricious behavior, the situation may require more wisdom, discretion and fairness than should be expected from individuals in positions of great power.

Need for Experimentation

An objection can be based on inexperience. It is not known how these innovative laws will work because there has not yet been time for a complete campaign and election cycle under the new state or federal disclosure laws. Further, since there is no readily available information concerning publicly financed election programs, it could be argued that action should be postponed pending such evaluations.

However, if there is sufficient momentum to pass legislation now, California might experiment with campaign subsidies in a few districts in 1976, and/or a few statewide offices in 1978. Information from such experiments could be used to fashion a workable law for succeeding elections.

In sum, plausible counter-arguments have been made concerning reformers' goals and opponents' objections, but neither proponents nor opponents can foretell the future. The issues cannot be definitely resolved unless and until campaign finance laws are enacted and analyzed.

A Comprehensive Law: Elements and Problems

"Publicly subsidized elections" is a broad generic term embracing several loosely related objectives in the restructuring of campaign finance. A comprehensive campaign finance law would probably embody the broad elements discussed below.

1. Limiting campaign contributions by candidates and their families, as well as by individuals, groups and political parties. The stringency of the suggested limitations varies, and some proposed bills omit such limits. The most difficult problem is to define "group contribution," and to determine whether and how group contributions should be limited.[1] The most recent report available (1971) indicates that 32 states and the federal government prohibit direct campaign contributions by corporations.[2] Four states and the federal government prohibit direct campaign contributions by labor unions.

Drafters of California bills will have to decide whether a corporation should be considered a group or a person. If a corporation is defined as a group, should it be limited to one contribution to each candidate, or should the corporate divisions, affiliates and subsidiaries also each be allowed to contribute?

Labor unions present similar problems. Should a county labor council be enjoined from contributing to a specific campaign if the statewide labor federation also contributes? Similarly, should a union local be preempted from contributing to a candidate if the statewide parent union has previously contributed? Legislative leaders must make difficult choices on this issue. Almost any of the choices may well be offensive to one or more major economic or political forces.

2. Specifying whether a campaign finance law applies to both primary and general elections, or to general elections only. Proponents of change are sharply divided on the question of election coverage. A bill dealing only with the general election would be less costly and easier to administer, because funds would be provided only for certified major and minor party nominees, and perhaps an occasional independent candidate. But if that meant leaving the present system in operation for the primaries, most of the existing problems of campaign finance would be compounded, and most of the "fat-cat" and special interest money would be effectively funneled into primary campaigns. In many districts, of course, registrations heavily favor one party, so that the party primary becomes the only arena where competition has any meaning.

3. Limiting legislative campaign expenditures.[3] In addition to providing public funding, reform meaures would place a ceiling on the aggregate spending by a candidate and all of his subordinate committees. All campaign expenditures (excluding petty cash items) would be made through a centralized account. This requirement would facilitate monitoring the outflow of funds, both by the candidate and by the state agency charged with enforcement. Under most proposals, ceilings would be higher for general elections than for primary elections, but establishing the levels of the ceilings remains an issue of major policy difference.

To plug a potential loophole, supporters of campaign finance laws are concerned with establishing spending limits for individuals, groups and committees that are *independent* of the candidate. Similar limits on political party spending for a specific candidate would also be required. In this connection, legislators must take care not to violate legitimate constitutional rights of free speech. But unless some controls are devised — especially for those election year committees formed solely for the purpose of supporting an individual candidate — any public finance bill would be seriously compromised. Indeed, many observers believe that this issue will cause schemes for public financing to run into major roadblocks.

4. Determining how candidates qualify for public funds. In the primaries, means must be devised to separate frivolous candidates from those with sufficient support to wage a serious campaign. Agreement seems likely on a mix of two criteria: (a) the ability to collect a substantial number of supporting signatures from voters registered in the candidate's own party and district, and/or (b) successful solicitation of a sizable number of contributions in amounts ranging from $25 to $100. Each signature of endorsement could be assigned a dollar equivalent, say $1.00 or more; the qualification "threshold" could be reached at a predetermined level. This threshold sum could be computed on the basis of a percentage of voters registered in the candidate's party in his district. Those winning in the primaries would be eligible for public funds in the general election.

5. Establishing formulas for allocating public funds to candidates. With respect to primaries, there is general agreement that candidates who achieve the threshold would then be eligible for public funding on a matching basis. With this approach, every private contribution up to, say $100, would be matched by state funds on a 1-to-

1, 2-to-1, or 3-to-1 basis. Signatures might also be assigned a dollar value for matching purposes.

For the general election, some bills under consideration provide for a flat grant to those who survive the primary. Alternatives would provide for a substantial initial subsidy; the candidate would then be required to raise some small contributions to be matched by public funds to a specified limit. Supporters of the latter alternative emphasize that solicitation of funds in small amounts would require extensive contact with voters and probably discussion of issues.

Those who argue for the first alternative tend to be skeptical of fund-raising requirements on two grounds: (a) fund-raising might in fact divert the candidate from thoughtful consideration of and discussion of the issues, and (b) incumbents are likely to raise such contributions with greater ease than their challengers. Minor party subsidies would be pro-rated; but to avoid penalizing minor party candidates with some "Catch-22" formula, current party registration might be the basis for funding rather than the number of votes in the previous election.

6. Deciding the levels of public funding for each campaign, as well as the annual aggregate for the state's program of campaign finance. Typical proposals for a State Senate race range from a "bare bones" sum of perhaps $15,000 to more ample figures like $68,000, a closer approximation of the actual cost of recent competitive races. The total state-funding package for legislative and statewide elective offices could run between $10 million and $70 million every four-year electoral period, depending on the proposals adopted.

Because of the difficulty of assuring that a two-thirds majority in each house of the Legislature can be counted on for a yearly affirmative vote, other funding proposals have been offered. One is similar to current federal legislation that would allow each California taxpayer to earmark up to $5 of his or her personal tax liability ($10 on a joint return) to a state campaign financing fund for candidates in the general election. It is uncertain whether such a fund would remove the need for annual legislative approval of this item. It may be that a trust fund established by a statewide initiative would be the best way to ensure stable funding that would remain relatively secure in the face of short-term political pressures.

7. Reducing dollar subsidies to candidates by providing information services about the candidates directly to voters. These services could take the form of subsidized mailings prepared by the candidates, or an enlarged version of the present voter pamphlet featuring expanded profiles of the candidates.

8. Assigning responsibilities for administration and enforcement, and establishing penalties. All the major proposals presume that the public financing system would be administered by the Fair Political Practices Commission established by statewide voter initiative in June 1974 (under the Political Reform Act, Proposition 9). Equitable and effective administration and enforcement are obviously crucial because campaign finance laws in California and elsewhere have in the past foundered on the rocks of partisan administration, or administration by officials appointed by and beholden to those whom they are expected to regulate.

Several bills would give the state Attorney General

82

specific responsibility for enforcement, and provide for citizen suits to compel compliance. Other proposals do not specify which state officer has enforcement power, or whether citizens have the right to sue. Proposals for penalties range from (a) misdemeanors, with prison sentences and heavy fines, plus several years' suspension of the candidate's right to run, to (b) felonies with maximum sentences of seven years in prison and $10,000 fine.

9. Monitoring the results. The campaign finance package favored by some proponents would require the administrative agency in charge to make detailed analyses and to report on the operation of the new system. Such comprehensive reports could include data on the number of candidates who qualified for public funding, the amounts spent for each race, the aggregate expenditure of the entire program, the estimated impact of the program on private contributions, and the level of special interest group as well as individual contributions in each campaign. Further, it could cover the changes, if any, in candidate expenditures of campaign funds; the system's effect on campaign competition; the number of major and minor violations and the disposition of charges against violators; and the administrative problems encountered.

Campaign finance laws in the past have failed to provide for systematic analysis of the way the legislation works, or for an evaluation of its results. Consequently, both administrators and legislators often remained unaware of the merits and deficiencies of the regulation, and thus have been unable to make timely corrections. If such legislation is seen as an on-going process rather than a once-and-for-all enactment, future amendment of the initial legislation should be anticipated, based on continuing analysis and reporting of actual experience.

An Overview

California legislators, while not in full agreement, seem to share a special perspective on election finance. Predictably, they do not want a law that will provide such easy access to public campaign money as to encourage opponents in their own districts. They would, however, welcome ceilings on spending that would prevent candidates with enormous financial resources from conducting massive challenges in their districts. For example, a few candidates each spent in excess of $100,000 in the last elections, far more than the amount assumed to be adequate to mount an effective campaign.

Legislators tend to differ somewhat on one aspect of campaign reform. Some resent the assumptions they see underlying Proposition 9 and current campaign finance bills, finding implications that legislators are corrupt or easily led to corruption. On the other hand, many would welcome laws that would free them from the demeaning and at times compromising task of collecting campaign contributions.

Non-legislative proponents of change have a different outlook and are wary of any bill that, from their perspective, looks like an "incumbent protection act." Such a bill might set an unrealistically low ceiling on contributions or expenditures, or provide such minimal subsidies to challengers as to preclude meaningful opposition for incumbents.

Some Suggested Criteria

If a public election finance program appears likely in the near future, the following questions may serve as criteria for assessing pros and cons of a proposal:

1. Will it unduly protect incumbents from effective electoral competition?
2. Will it cover both primary and general elections, and thereby substantially raise the cost of the program?
3. Will it cover only general elections, thus minimizing costs but ignoring the significance of primaries in many legislative districts?
4. Will minor parties and independent candidates be dealt with fairly?
5. Will group contributions be limited, and if so, how and how effectively?
6. Will there be provisions for monitoring the new program and reporting back to the Legislature and to the public?
7. Will in-kind services, such as state subsidized mailings or an expanded voters pamphlet, be used in lieu of any or all direct subsidies to candidates?
8. Will a tax check-off provision be employed to fund part of the new program?

Options

A final major question is: will the initial proposal enacted make public financing experiments in a smaller number of legislative districts, to allow for collection of more information before enacting major electoral changes? Or will the advocates of public financing, fearing a loss of reformist zeal and momentum generated by Proposition 9, decide to take the risks inherent in pressing for a major public financing bill in this session?

Conclusion

If passage of a campaign finance measure seems probable in the 1975-76 session, the writers would prefer some form of experimentation, carefully monitored and closely evaluated. While there may be some constitutional problems in selecting only non-incumbent races and special elections for public monies, this approach seems most desirable at the outset. Lawmakers might choose to begin with the 1976 general election, or with the statewide campaigns in 1978. Several additional suggestions might be considered.

First, careful analysis of data available from recent elections should help determine what amount of money is required for a challenger to offer serious competition to an incumbent. In the primary, some of these funds could come from private contributions that would be matched with public funds after a reasonable threshold of signatures and total of small contributions is achieved. In the general election, a block grant to all qualified candidates might be combined with some matching formula, after a certain level is reached. When trying to decide on specific dollar amounts and matching formulas, it should be remembered that statistics generated by our present electoral system may be inadequate to predict needs and behavior under a publicly subsidized plan.

Second, we must be wary of adopting severe limitations on individual or group contributions, unless they are combined with adequate provisions for state funding. Otherwise the fund raising potential for challengers might be seriously restricted, while incumbents would probably retain their traditional advantages. Probably even a large number of small contributors would fail to compensate for the losses caused by such restrictions. If the intention is to remove the unwarranted influence of special interest money, and if adequate funds are to be provided to cover the high cost of campaigning, then alternative sources of funding must be found. Under such circumstances, some form of public funding or indirect subsidy would seem to be the only reasonable possibility.

Further, to avoid handicapping challengers, some differential on expenditure ceilings might allow challengers to spend 10 percent to 15 percent more than incumbents.

In sum, Californians have a unique opportunity to discuss seriously and plan carefully what could be a major innovation in electoral politics. The writers have sought to open the door to contingency planning and discussion by politicians, interested citizens, the legal community, civic groups, and the academic community

by presenting the major components of a public financing system, and suggesting some of the benefits and difficulties that it might generate.

Public subsidy for elections will not provide a political utopia. The concept is complex and surrounded by uncertainties. As a proposal, it provides a plausible response to the obvious flaws of an election system that is under sustained attack. Whether the subsidy proposal is the correct response remains to be seen.

NOTES

The writers are staff directors of the Political Reform Evaluation Project, Center for Ethics and Social Policy, Graduate Theological Union, 2465 Le Conte Ave., Berkeley 94709. They are supervising a comprehensive study of contemporary political reform in California.

[1] First Amendment and "equal protection" pitfalls pervade the whole topic of publicly subsidized elections. A public financing bill based on voluntary compliance may solve some constitutional problems raised by compulsory measures.

[2] Citizens Research Foundation, *A Survey of State Statutes Regulating Political Finance* (1971).

[3] State Proposition 9 now places limits on expenditures by candidates for all statewide offices and on expenditures for statewide referenda, but does not apply to races for the state Legislature.

charged with providing "secure detention, humane support and corrective treatment" for those offenders convicted and sentenced to state prison. By the use of "indeterminate sentencing," a concept introduced into the California system in 1917, each offense carries both a minimum and a maximum term fixed by statute; a convicted offender becomes eligible for release at the conclusion of one-third of the minimum term, and is entitled to release at the completion of the maximum term.

Setting specific terms or determining when a prisoner can be released conditionally on parole is the responsibility of the Adult Authority (or, in the case of female felony offenders, The Women's Board of Terms and Parole).[10] The Adult Authority wields considerable discretionary power, therefore, because the time range of imprisonment for a given offense may extend from "one year to life" or from six months to 20 years.

Implementation of the indeterminate sentence has differed from the model. For example, the California Adult Authority (appointed by the governor) originally was intended to function as an independent board of experts with varied backgrounds, who would evaluate the progress of each convict in order to assess his readiness for parole. Thus, the term of imprisonment would be set to correspond to the length of time needed for rehabilitation.

In practice, however, all nine members of the Adult Authority (as of 1974) had strong backgrounds in law enforcement or corrections. They devoted an average of 10 minutes to each "hearing"[11] for granting paroles; hearings were generally conducted by a two-member panel. The Adult Authority had established no criteria for determining the optimum time for release, and had not been provided with statutory guidelines. Until recently, it was not required to provide written reasons for its decisions. In fact, the California Assembly Committee on Criminal Procedure reported in 1968 that the time spent in California prisons depended on three factors: 1) the values and perceptions of the individual members of the parole board, 2) the "perception of the mood of the public," and 3) population pressures within the institution.[12]

Recently, however, a spokesman for the California Adult Authority called attention to new procedures that became effective March 1, 1975. A memo "to all inmates under the jurisdiction of the Adult Authority" from Chairman R.K. Procunier, stated that "the Adult Authority intends to fix parole release dates for as many inmates as possible at the time of their regular parole consideration hearings. The time to be served for each inmate will usually be fixed from within time ranges set by the Adult Authority." These and other proposals deserve detailed analysis, but within the limitations of this *Public Affairs Report* it is possible to give only an indication of topics included in the statement on "Parole Consideration Hearing Procedures" inclosed with the Procunier memo. They include: Establishing Parole and Discharge Dates; Time Credits; "Good Time" Credit; Subsequent Offenses; Parole Violators; Indeterminate Maximums; Review of Difficult Cases; Appeal; and Subsequent Review. A suggested draft of Base Ranges includes 17 major crime categories, typical and aggravated, with adjustment ranges and a format for establishing confinement period.

If a hearing panel sets a sentence outside guideline ranges, "the panel will state the reasons in writing for that action." In addition, the memo stated, "It is our hope that by March 12, 1976, most inmates in the Department will know what date they can expect to go home." (Letter and enclosures from Harold G. Riddell, Assistant to the Chairman, March 27, 1975.)

In addition to departmental actions, groups including prisoner organizations and the California Legislature continue to generate comments, criticisms and new proposals relating to sentencing. Some examples include the following.

The Coordinating Council of Prisoner Organizations issued a *Determined Sentencing Proposal* (January 1975), which defined and divided felony offenses into eight categories with a specific number of years' sentence for each, combined with formulas to help establish degree of seriousness; and with the provision, "There shall be no parole." The Article on Sentencing Philosophy (p. 2) stated in part:

> Sentences should balance societal demand for punishment, the general deterrent effect of sanctions, and the desire to minimize any lasting damage to the offender by the experience of incarceration.
>
> The general deterrent effect of sentences exists in a widespread public understanding of the price to be exacted for the commission of a crime. Therefore, it is desirable to establish a limited number of categories of crime, readily understood by the citizenry, graduated by seriousness of offense type, for which sentences are prescribed.

In response to the proposals and memos of the Adult Authority, more than 400 prisoners at the Sierra Conservation Center in Jamestown signed a four-page letter dated March 6, 1975, in which they claimed that the new system of terms is "even worse" than the old system, and that California prisoners would still do "more time than the national median terms, or the federal system."

Further, several bills have been introduced into the State Legislature proposing changes in sentencing and parole. An example is SB 42 (introduced by Senators John A. Nejedly and Howard Way, with Coauthor Assemblyman Frank Murphy). Briefly, SB 42 would generally substitute for the indeterminate sentence law "a system whereby the judge selects a term of imprisonment from three statutory choices, with a new state agency administering revised provisions relating to sentencing, good time credit and paroles..."

Nationwide, there is evidence that the indeterminate sentence is being reviewed critically. The Task Force on Corrections of the National Advisory Commission has proposed replacing the indeterminate sentences with determinate sentences limited to a maximum of five years for most offenses, and sentences limited to 25 years for persistent or dangerous offenders and professional criminals.

Costs of Incarceration

Commitment to a state correctional facility is only one

of various types of sentences imposed on felony offenders, but it is by far the most costly. The average annual per capita cost of state incarceration in California ($5,934 in 1974-75, and $6,237 estimated for 1975-76) is significantly higher in direct cost alone than probation, parole, or commitment to a county jail or a community correctional facility.

Correctional costs reflected in California's state budget have shown steady increases in net totals for programs:

1973-74	$167.1 million
1974-75	$195.2 million
1975-76	$201.0 million (proposed)[13]

Of these amounts, the bulk goes to maintenance and treatment programs for adult male and female felons in California's 12 major correctional facilities. In addition, there are indirect costs of incarceration, such as increased welfare caseloads that include prisoners' families, and loss of state revenue from taxes normally generated by an individual's residence in the community.

Equity and Public Safety

A discussion of the costs of incarceration also raises questions of overall perspective, including the proportion of felons who actually receive prison sentences, the disposition of various offenders who have committed violent crimes, and problems of equity in imprisonment. Available data are not always ideally comparable, but the following may give at least some indication of the size of the problems involved.

As shown in the table below, adult felons sentenced to California state prisons in 1971 represented only 0.75 percent of all the felony crimes reported; they represented only 2.3 percent of all adult felony arrests; and those imprisoned were only 9.6 percent of all adult felons convicted of crimes. In summary, it appears that very few of those who engage in felonious activity are actually apprehended, arrested, or incarcerated.

Felonies and Prison Sentences in California, 1971

Sentenced to prison

5,386 adult felons or
9.6 % of the	56,018	adult felony convictions
2.3 % of the	229,476	adult felony arrests
0.75% of the	714,688	felony crimes reported

Source: *Report of the Governor's Select Committee on Law Enforcement Problems* (California: August 1973) p. 87.

With respect to the most prevalent type of crime, by far the largest proportion, about 85%, of all felony crimes reported in California in 1973 were property crimes. Conversely, only about 15% were crimes of violence, i.e., those involving bodily injury or threat to human life, such as homicide, aggravated assault or armed robbery. Nevertheless, the latest available figures (for 1974) concerning felons presently in California prisons, indicate that a substantial majority of nearly 60% have committed "crimes against the person." Even so, the number convicted and sent to prison each year reflects only a small proportion of the total number of acts of violence reported annually in the state (e.g., 116,506 in 1973).[14]

In addition, it was estimated that at least half of the men who enter state prisons each year may be offenders whose crimes are no more serious than those of many others who are retained in correctional systems below the state level. This inequitable disposition develops because judges vary widely in their sentencing policies. Thus, among the 13 largest counties in California, rates of prison commitment for convicted felony offenders range from 11 percent to 36 percent.

The present system therefore appears unsatisfactory on two counts: first, it is inequitable in that it treats similar offenses differently; and second, this inequitable treatment provides little assurance to the public that violent offenders will be dealt with logically and systematically.

Imprisonment as a General Deterrent

Traditionally, actual or potential imprisonment was thought to serve both as a general deterrent to discourage members of the public from entering criminal activity, and as a specific deterrent to discourage known offenders from engaging in further criminal acts.

With respect to general deterrence, the facts as known do not appear to support the effectiveness of threatened or actual incarceration. For example, in 1961, the California Legislature increased the penalty for possession of marijuana from an optional maximum of 12 months in the county jail to a mandatory state prison commitment of 1 to 10 years. Between 1961 and 1966, arrests for marijuana offenses jumped from 3,500 to 18,000 annually. By 1968, the yearly arrest rate was 56,800.[15] While the increase in the offense rate may well be attributable to a number of factors, it is clear that one could not find in the increased prison sentence sanction any proof of deterrent effect.

Prison Time, Rehabilitation and Recidivism

A randomized study in 1973 of the relationship between time served in prison and parole outcome found that with comparable groups serving differing lengths of incarceration, there were no significant differences among those randomly assigned shorter or longer periods of incarceration. The study concluded that time served in prison could be reduced without affecting the convicts' subsequent level of recidivism.[16]

The former Chairman of the California Adult Authority has acknowledged that the length of time served by California prisoners bears no relationship to their performance after release.[17] Further, the somber conclusions of the Task Force on Corrections of the National Advisory Commission on Criminal Justice Standards and Goals (1973) stated on page 1:

The failure of major institutions to reduce crime is incontestable. Recidivism rates are notoriously high. Institutions do succeed in punishing, but they do not deter. They protect the community, but that protection is only temporary. They relieve the community of responsibility by removing the offender, they make successful reintegration into the community unlikely. They change the committed offender, but the change is more likely to be negative than positive.

Thus, while prison is largely ineffective in terms of doing prisoners good, it often does them harm. As the Task Force report states (on p. 597), "The prison, the reformatory, and the jail have achieved only a shocking record of failure. There is overwhelming evidence that these institutions create crime rather than prevent it."

Legal Status of California's Convicts

The convict's changing legal status remains at best that of a second-class citizen, although recent legislative acts and judicial rulings have modified procedural guarantees in revocation of parole and disciplinary hearings. Convicts are no longer referred to as "civiliter mortuus" or "slaves of the state," but California still has a Civil Death Statute (Penal Code ¶ 2600), which suspends all of a convict's civil rights.

Even in on-the-job training in prison, California convicts fail to receive job benefits enjoyed by other workers. The convicts' minimal payment (currently the maximum is 35 cents per hour) includes neither accident compensation nor contributions to the Social Security system.

At the federal level, the Thirteenth Amendment to the U.S. Constitution specifically excludes felons from its prohibitions against slavery and involuntary servitude. This attitude has a carryover in the failure to accord convicts basic rights, such as a reasonable right to privacy. The consequences include undermining a major element of the rehabilitative strategy, for example, the lack of privacy in the relationship between prisoner and therapist. The entire confidentiality issue is undergoing spirited debate concerning therapist-patient relationships both within and outside of prisons, but it may be particularly sensitive in a prison setting. The State Attorney General has issued an opinion declaring that treatment personnel are employees of the State Department of Corrections and therefore on request are obligated to turn over all files on their prisoner-patients.

Some Conclusions

This paper has noted some of the major elements in the failure of California's treatment model in corrections. Briefly, studies have shown that prisons do not rehabilitate; treatment programs as such are under-financed and frequently conflict with requirements for custody; the indeterminate sentence often appears capricious and arbitrary partly because it presupposes measurable rehabilitation; incarceration is costly and inequitable, and provides only limited protection to the public; prison penalties do not apparently serve as a deterrent to crime; and many constraints on prisoners tend to interfere with their rights as citizens.

This litany of criticism and delineation of problems evokes some tentative proposals for reform and poses some problems that as yet appear to defy solution.

Increased Use of Community Treatment Programs

For purposes of discussion, however, offenders may be divided into two groups: those who can remain in the community and participate in community treatment programs, and those who must spend some time in custody.

First, with respect to alternatives to incarceration, the National Advisory Commission has recommended diversion from the criminal justice system for certain types of offenders, and the increased use of community treatment programs. To underscore its insistence on the use of alternatives, the commission proposed a 10-year moratorium on the construction of correctional institutions unless no alternative is possible. There are community treatment programs already operating throughout the country, primarily for juvenile offenders. Characteristically, supervision and control are scaled to the individual's requirement, on the theory that "the least is best."

Community treatment seems most appropriate for "middle-risk" offenders whose success is related to the type of supervision they receive. This view has influenced the development and use of offender classification techniques, differential caseload management and "intensive intervention" programs for those seen as most likely to benefit from increased services. Such services include job training, placement, medical care, and financial aid. These specially focused programs may be based in either residential or nonresidential settings. Residential settings include group homes, halfway houses or community correction centers, depending on the extent and type of supervision required. Non-residential programs are preferred by many, however, as having a less disruptive effect on the normal life of the offender and thereby speeding his reintegration into the community.

In Custody, But Learning Lawful Behavior

For those offenders who must spend time in custody, smaller custody centers could emphasize expanded chances for convicts to learn lawful behavior as opposed to the more enforced treatment programs found in prison settings. One such experimental justice model is currently being operated by the Illinois Center for Criminal Justice, where the attempt is made to encourage the offender to participate actively in the correctional process. The center is designed for a maximum of 300 residents, and provides for law libraries, an independent Ombudsman (an official who would deal with complaints by prisoners about the operation of the correctional system), legal assistance, setting wages for prison industry at rates prevailing on the outside, some self-government, removal of mail censorship, an extensive furlough program, conjugal visiting, open access by the press, the use of a contract system for parole (whereby private agencies under contract provide certain services related to parole), and the introduction of compensation and restitution for victims of crime.

Regardless of the way it may work out in practice, such a correctional model offers a dual appeal. First, it helps reaffirm concepts of individual responsibility. Second, it increases cost-effectiveness by reducing capital outlay and increasing revenue available to the system, the offender and his family. The revenue increase develops as offenders participate in work furlough programs and receive pay. A portion is returned directly to the institution.

Specific Institutional Reforms

From a slightly different point of view, the National Advisory Commission Task Force, for example, advocated institutional reform. Specifics included definitions of prisoners' rights, rules of conduct, and development of disciplinary and grievance procedures, and revision of the indeterminate sentence. In addition, the Task Force recommended reforming existing laws that deprive ex-offenders of civil rights and employment opportunities (such as the licensing restrictions found in the California Business and Professions Code). In this connection, the (California) Attorney General's Task Force called attention (p. 32) to changes embodied in SB 1767 (now Ch. 1321 Statutes of 1974) which modified

> the statutory disability relating to certain vocational licensing occurring as a result of a conviction of a felony...The general effect...is to eliminate as a basis for denial of a license evidence of a lack of good moral character or similar grounds relating to an applicant's character and to impose a rational test related to...the licensed business or profession.

The report also urged that "each of the sixty trades or professions requiring licensure status should be studied to assist in determining what, if any, crimes are related directly to the licensed activity." The thrust of the recommendations is to seek ways to open up more licensed trades and professions to former prison inmates.

In addition, reformers have proposed that prisons be considered appropriate only for dangerous offenders who must be confined because their release would endanger public safety. As suggested in the Model Sentencing Act, a dangerous offender would be defined as one who (1) has committed a serious crime against a person and shows a pattern of persistent assaultiveness based on serious mental disturbances, or (2) is deeply involved in organized crime.[18]

Further, although not everyone would agree to some of the specific reform proposals made by the National Commission and other study groups, there is evidence of a growing consensus among correctional experts that the entire criminal justice system needs reevaluation, that realistic goals need to be set for the correctional system, and that corrections, the courts and law enforcement elements need to interact more closely.

Some Unanswered Questions

As the foregoing discussion has indicated, the corrections system can, at best, hope to influence only a small percentage of the total number of criminal offenders, given present knowledge and state of the art. It is therefore essential that California's correctional resources be directed to those who are likely to benefit from the services, treatment or control that the correctional system offers, on one hand, and on the other, to those who pose the greatest danger to society.

For those who can benefit from appropriate settings and treatment, one major question appears to be whether the state's resources can be reorganized and marshalled in a rational manner so that the greatest degree of effectiveness can be achieved; and whether the funds, personnel and public understanding for such changes will be forthcoming.

Still unanswered is the question of how best to deal with those who remain a danger to society and for whom no successful rehabilitative treatment has yet been found. The earnest wish to achieve universal rehabilitation must not be allowed to obscure the fact that California, among other states, does not yet know how to protect society from dangerous offenders, while also dealing with those offenders in a just, humane and constructive way.

Notes

The writer was formerly affiliated with the International Institute of Human Rights.

[1]California, Assembly, Ways and Means Committee, *The California Prison, Parole and Probation System; It's Time To Stop Counting,* James Robison (Sacramento: 1969). Technical Supplement No. 2 to: *Preliminary Report on the Costs and Effects of the California Criminal Justice System and Recommendations for Legislation to Increase Support of Local Police and Corrections Programs* (Sacramento: April 1969). Hereafter, *Costs and Effects.*

[2]Robert Martinson, "What Works? — Questions and Answers About Prison Reform," in *The Public Interest,* 35: 22-54 (1974). See also Walter Bailey, "Correctional Outcome: An Evaluation of 100 Reports," 57 *Journal of Criminal Law, Criminology and Police Science* 2:155-160 (1966).

[3]*Report of the Attorney General's Task Force on Prisoner Rehabilitation,* Evelle J. Younger, Attorney General (Sacramento: January 1975), pp. 3-4.

[4]For Corrections budgets, see *State of California Supplement for Health and Welfare, Education* [Corrections] (Sacramento: 1974-75), vol. II, hereafter *Budget Supplement.* See esp. p. 225; also *Governor's Budget for 1975-76.* See esp. pp. 775-776.

[5]*Budget Supplement,* p. 225.

[6]*Governor's Budget,* pp. 772 and 776.

[7]Noted by Edmund E. White, Deputy Attorney General, California, in a telephone conversation, March 4, 1975.

[8]Henry Boies, *The Science of Penology* (New York: G.P. Putnam's Sons, 1901), p. 90.

[9]Cf. United Nations Department of Social Affairs, *The Indeterminate Sentence* (New York: 1954), p. 90.

[10]Female felony offenders account for less than 5% of the total institutional population. Although the comments herein apply equally to male and female offenders, the statistics cited refer to male felons unless otherwise noted.

[11]Douglas Hitchcock, "The California Adult Authority — Administrative Sentencing and the Parole Decision as a Problem in Administrative Discretion," *University of California at Davis Law Review* 360-384 (1972). See p. 372.

[12]California, Assembly, Committee on Criminal Procedure, *Deterrent Effects of Criminal Sanctions* (Sacramento: 1968), p. 40. For a discussion that rejects the medical model and the use of the indeterminate sentence, see *Struggle for Justice* (New York: Hill and Wang, 1971).

[13]*Governor's Budget,* p. 772.

[14]For 1973 figures, see California, Department of Justice, Bureau of Criminal Statistics, *Crime and Delinquency in California 1973* (Sacramento: 1975), esp. p. 52. For 1974 figures, see *Governor's Budget,* p. 773.

[15]California, Assembly, Office of Research, *Crime and Penalties in California* (Sacramento: March 1968), pp. 10-11; *Costs and Effects* (note 1 above), p. 86.

[16]California, Department of Corrections, Research Division, *Time Served in Prison and Parole Outcome; An Experimental Study,* John E. Berecochea, Dorothy R. Jaman, and Welton A. Jones (October 1973).

[17]Statement of Henry W. Kerr, cited in *Costs and Effects* (note 1 above), p. 107.

[18]National Council on Crime and Delinquency, Council of Judges, *Model Sentencing Act* (2nd edition 1972), Section 5, in *Crime and Delinquency,* 18 (4) (October 1972).

Women's Opportunities in Education

Vol. 16   No. 3   June 1975

Information, Research and Counseling:
The Women's Center at Berkeley

By
Margaret B. Wilkerson
Acting Director

Introduction

A hundred queries a day pour into the Center for the Continuing Education of Women (Women's Center) at the University of California's Berkeley campus. As a staff member said, "If you want to understand the frustrations and problems women face, answer our phones for one hour."

Here are some examples of comments and questions:

"I have been out of school for 10 years, and hadn't worked for some time before that. I think I want to return to school, but I'm not sure what I want to major in — what I'm really aiming for is a good job."

"I'm interested in the health sciences, but I was never very good at math, and nursing doesn't appeal to me. What are the alternatives in medical careers?"

"I've been an elementary teacher for 5 years, and I no longer enjoy it. How can I use my education and training in other ways?"

"I'm trying to return to graduate school after 15 years' absence, and I'm having a hard time finding sources of financial aid. Are there any organizations that subsidize older women returning to school?"

"I've been working in an office long enough to become very tired of clerical work. I think I would like to be trained as a carpenter, but I don't know where to begin."

"Many years ago I flunked out of school, and now that I want to apply to UC Berkeley, my grade point average is too low. What should I do?"

It may seem strange that such questions would be directed at any unit of a major university. Their tone reveals a vulnerability that most persons try to hide in the competitive circles of higher education. But the UC Women's Center has become known for its receptivity to the academic and vocational problems of women, encouraging callers to be candid about their concerns.

The Women's Center opened in October 1972 as a University-funded program of information, research and counseling in areas of interest and concern to women. Established under Chancellor Albert Bowker, the Center and its program are the result of a decade of discussions, proposals and studies by women and men associated with the University.[1]

The proposal for the establishment of the Center[2] presented a general charge to the new unit: to broaden opportunities for women in higher education. Within this context the Center designated specific goals: to provide information and resources that allow women to make realistic decisions regarding career and education; to offer academic and vocational counseling and programs that reflect the changing roles and aspirations of women; to stimulate, encourage and coordinate research by and about women; to energize University resources on their behalf and sensitize the campus to their concerns; and to be a visible "welcome" sign on the Berkeley campus for all women. As a major academic women's center on the west coast, the new unit has begun to define the unique role such organizations can play in the life of a university and the non-campus community as well.

Who Uses the Center?

Who actually uses the Center? The number and variety of women who come to the Center are not easily described in composite terms or pictured accurately as "median women." A composite profile can, however, be roughly sketched on the basis of 309 client questionnaires completed from March through June 1974: The Center user is female; 31-35 years old; Caucasian; married; has children; lives in a nuclear family; resides in Alameda County (where the Berkeley campus of the University is located); has a bachelor's degree; is not a student; is not working; and came to the Center for counseling related to a job or career.

Narrative data gathered from these questionnaires provide additional insights: Many users are frightened of beginning something new. They are not sure whether they wish to go to work, or back to school, or neither, or both. They are also unaware of available opportunities.

Many are accustomed to being directed and motivated by others. Most of their lives have been spent serving other people's needs and adapting to the schedules and requirements of others. Women who have been at home for years often lack confidence in their abilities, and are unsure where they can fit into the outside world.

Some are realistic about what the Center can offer. Some hope it will answer difficult questions about their future that only they themselves can resolve. A number of the younger women are on welfare or receiving unemployment compensation. Many have moved from the east to the west coast. A large number are divorced or getting a divorce, and are learning to depend on themselves. A significant number have small children still at home.

About 60 percent to 75 percent of the women who request job counseling are interested in entering the helping professions, especially counseling. Many library inquiries come from older women who want information on what the job market may have to offer them. The Center also attracts women doing research papers, seeking references to other women's centers, or wondering how to launch a center themselves.

Although the Center is widely known in the larger community as well as on the campus, only a modest number of Third World women use its resources on a regular basis. Ida Dunson, a Black staff member who specializes in vocational counseling, notes that Third World women do attend special workshops such as the vocational programs she has designed especially for them. "But," Ms. Dunson observes, "our women simply are not using the Center on a *regular* basis as they should. Some are unaware of it; others identify the Center as a 'white women's bag.' Those that I personally invite come and rave over the materials we have here. The problem is getting them into the Center." On the other hand, programs featuring outstanding Black women—Dr. Frances Welsing, psychiatrist from Howard University; Gwendolyn Brooks, Pulitzer Prize-winning poet; Shirley Graham Dubois, lecturer, traveler and wife of the late W.E.B. Dubois—have been very well attended. Special workshops, such as "Academic Survival for Black Women," have also attracted large audiences. Currently, Ms. Dunson is coordinating an outreach program designed to attract more Third World women.

An increasing number of men are using the Center and showing interest in women's concerns, although the actual count is small in proportion to women clients. In response to this interest, counseling coordinator Marilyn Jacobson has introduced a pilot workshop on "Change in the Lives of Men and Women." Men are welcome to all programs, but are especially recruited for this workshop, which is led cooperatively by Ms. Jacobson and a male counselor. The workshop focuses on male/female role stereotypes and their impact on careers and life styles.

Counseling, Role Models, and Institutional Change

The Center's present activities are divided into three operational areas: (1) direct services, (2) indirect services, and (3) programs to change institutional attitudes and policies that restrict women's educational opportunities. Counseling is the focal point for direct services, taking the form of peer-group workshops as well as individual conferences. Indirect or self-help services make materials and information accessible to clients, but place reliance largely upon the individual's efforts. The staff uses both

role-model examples and programs to work toward institutional change. Research projects are included in this category because of their practical emphasis and potential effect.

The Center has developed several policies that are integral to the unit's goals and direction. For example, all services are offered free to both the campus and the larger community, in an effort to include a broad range of women and particularly those returning to higher education. This open policy differs from that of most campus counseling units.

Volunteer help is not accepted, though frequently offered. This policy is designed to discourage the use of women's talents without pay, and is made possible by University support for paid staff. The staff's half-time, flexible schedules are designed to demonstrate the feasibility of such arrangements in educational institutions.

While staff members try to help clients, they discourage dependent relationships and urge independent pursuit of contacts and opportunities. On the other hand, they affirm the power of example and attempt to provide role-models for many of the principles they espouse.

In summary, the Center's counseling effort depends substantially on the persuasiveness of role-models, importance and helpfulness of peer support, and relevance of work experience to academic goals.

Staff Organization and Principles

Although the CCEW has a full-time equivalent of only five persons, it has increased effectiveness by maintaining half-time positions that permit a large staff: three administrators, four counselors, four counseling interns, five work-study students, a library assistant, a bibliographer and an administrative assistant. The staff's experience with this arrangement demonstrates that more ideas are generated, more motivation provided, and greater output achieved with a largely part-time staff; twice the number of staff members provide twice as many backgrounds and personal experiences. The number of role-models is likewise increased.

Further, the half-time arrangement allows administrators to hold faculty appointments and conduct research in their specific disciplines. Counselors and other staff are freed for a variety of activities, e.g., to continue their academic training, spend additional time with their families, or work as consultants. One major advantage of part-time employment is that staff members make optimum use of their work hours and are less likely to take time out for other matters, even when allowed to do so.

Administratively, half-time staffing causes no increase in cost, but requires more paper work. "How to keep in touch with the work that colleagues are doing and the information they are collecting, is one of our major challenges," says Diana Gong, administrative assistant and the only full-time staff member. "We have a regular staff meeting every two weeks and maintain a notebook for the unending flow of information that must get to counselors and administrators."

"Judge an idea by its merit, not its source," is the tacit rule in staff meetings. Despite the range of academic levels in the Center's work force—faculty, non-academic personnel and students—all are encouraged to discuss all issues. As one result, innovative ideas relating to the informational services have come from students who handle phone counseling and some of the Center's paper work. Work-study students are sometimes available for only one or two academic quarters, but are nevertheless encouraged to select or develop projects as part of their job commitment. Several excellent articles about the work of CCEW have been written by students on the staff. The non-hierarchical structure has fostered productivity and allowed staff members to develop new skills and, in several cases, to upgrade their job classifications.

Beginning with Counseling

Center resources have become so extensive that persons making their first contact are urged to enroll in "Group Advising," a comprehensive two-hour introduction to the Center's educational and vocational services. Following this orientation, involving group and individual counseling, clients can sign up for more specialized workshops.

Counseling services were the first to be developed because of the numbers of women, over 4100 since the Center's opening, who came for advice and information. Under Professor May Diaz, the first Director, self-direction became the key. Counselors found that women had been taught to avoid "masculine" pursuits (such as mathematics, engineering and the like), and that many lacked access to information needed to help them choose careers. Further, they had become too dependent to make independent decisions, and knew few of the available alternatives.

Consequently, the staff developed programs that would help women to choose career/life styles for themselves and to choose wisely. Counseling workshops are set for four-week periods (two per week) only. Rarely, if ever, is one allowed to repeat enrollment in the same workshop. At present, four counselors handle individual appointments and organize the workshops that include "Planning for the Future," "Career/Lifestyles," "Group Advising," "Employment Development," "The More Mature Woman," "Education and Job Relevance," and "Undergraduate Women."

Peer Counseling

The success of these workshops can be attributed to the counselor's skill as well as to the effectiveness of the peer counseling relationship. Mary Anne Almazol-Schonbrun, graduate student in counseling, who leads "Group Advising," agrees that the workshops provide an opportunity for clients to share opinions and information. "Sometimes a woman will be talking about wanting to leave a particular field and she'll be sitting next to a woman who wants to enter it," she said. "Peer counseling can be very valuable." The technique, developed by the Center, is being observed by and incorporated into other counseling units at UC Berkeley.

The most popular workshop is "Planning for the Future," led by Sarah Fike, who has a master's degree in counseling from California State University at Hayward. During the fall of 1974, 76 women attended four two-hour sessions that began with the questions: "Where are you now in your life cycle? How do you define yourself now? Are you planning for the future?" Through writing autobiographies and taking the Strong Vocational Interest Test, participants assess their goals and synthesize their experience into workable resumes. One woman wrote the following evaluation:

> As a result of the techniques learned from the group I have gotten a job as a simultaneous interpreter, and am now in training at the Monterey Institute of Foreign Studies... Even though I (will) see my husband only three days a week until September 1, I think that my getting out will strengthen our marriage rather than threaten it. Who wants to live with a disintegrating vegetable![3]

Professional Counseling

Marilyn Jacobson, academic counselor and counseling coordinator, has a master's degree in counseling from California State University at San Francisco, and is currently working on her Ph.D. in Education at UC Berkeley. During the fall of 1974, she conducted 80 individual appointments and led a career exploration workshop for undergraduates. During a one-hour session she can give a woman a head start toward independently exploring alternatives on her own. "Most women don't realize that they can make use of skills they already have," she says. "Women with B.A.'s don't have to settle for secretarial positions, and if they're going back to school I urge them to pick a field where there aren't many women already—like business or public administration."

Many of the women attending workshops already have some idea of their future direction, but need extra encouragement to act. A 31-year old woman came to the Center last spring with plans pending for law school, but unsure that she wanted to go. Her oldest child was five years old, her youngest, 2½, and she was certain of only one thing—she didn't want to be a housewife. After four sessions of "Planning for the Future," she decided to go ahead and this year enrolled at Hastings Law School in San Francisco.

Another woman was 43, a reformed alcoholic and in the process of divorcing her husband when she came to the Center last year. A biochemist, she had not been employed for 17 years, and was no longer interested in that field. She signed up for two workshops, "The More Mature Woman" and "Planning for the Future," and now is a student in the psychology department at California State University at Sonoma. She also works as a counselor at ACCEPT, a center for alcoholics in San Francisco.

Some women decide not to return to school or to work. They may make "traditional decisions," to be at home with a family, for example. Counselors emphasize the importance of the individual's making her own decision, based on the best available information, and deciding according to her own insights and desires.

Questionnaires and letters from Center participants reveal the range of decisions made by these clients. One woman admitted, "I realize that it will take time to make the decisions and life changes that I want. I've decided to wait rather than throw myself into something without proper contemplation." Another stated, "My feelings about my goals were... reinforced." A mother of two wrote, "I am more willing to wait to enter the job market and enjoy kids and family now. I realize what a lot of time is ahead of me." Another commented, "I am feeling stronger. I believe now that I can get some kind of work that would support me and have plans to return to school."

Bulletin Boards and Library

Counseling takes other forms as well. For some, simple access to information or a timely referral will suffice. The Center's interior walls have become bulletin boards that display everything from job announcements for academic positions to notices of consciousness-raising groups, scholarship opportunities, and national conferences. The Center has become "the place to go" to find out what is happening in the arena of women's concerns. More than 150 persons drop in to consult the wall bulletins weekly.

During the first year, counselors found that they needed more substantive information, especially to serve the growing interest in feminist issues and research. Library materials were acquired with the help of funds from the Alumnae Association of Prytanean, UC honorary society for women. Although the library began informally as counselors accumulated materials for their workshops, it has rapidly become a more extensive and valuable asset. Open weekdays, it is housed in a comfortable, quiet room; the collection of non-circulating materials includes books in the areas of literature, social sciences, herstory, politics/law, education, biography/autobiography, health and physiology. There are bibliographies on women's studies, women and work, graduate education, non-sexist literature, and a number of other fields. Newsletters from women's centers in other parts of the country, feminist journals and reports line the shelves. Career information includes Catalyst Publications (designed for women who wish to combine career and family responsibilities), materials on the job market, and books on career-planning and job-hunting. Academic catalogs from Bay Area colleges and universities are also available.

One of the most unusual resources in this library is the "binder series." As brochures, print-outs and articles poured into the Center and as counselors collected important news and magazine articles useful to their workshops, Ms. Fike designed a series of loose-leaf notebooks that expand as needed, so that the material can be used by the public. Categories include Education, Careers, Employment, Life Styles and Life Crises, Sex Discrimination, Health and the Feminist Movement. The binder on Financial Aid is the most popular because it contains one-of-a-kind information on scholarship opportunities for special programs in various parts of the United States. Shelley Orren-McNulty, Center librarian, checks magazines, book reviews and other sources for publications that will enrich the Center programs; she regularly clips articles from Bay Area newspapers in order to keep both staff and clients informed of current events and developments. The Center library is unique in the East Bay Area, both with respect to the focus and range of the materials available, and because it is open to users both on campus and in the community.

Personal Referral Service

The Center also provides a more personal, specialized type of information. "Whenever possible, we refer women to a person, not an office," says Helene Wenzel, Associate Director. "Since the Center cannot be all things to all people, we maintain an extensive referral service, which requires us to know what is happening in the area and to identify persons who will be helpful to our clients." The informal network of campus contacts includes faculty members, departmental staff, deans, graduate students and other campus personnel, as well as individuals from the non-campus community. These names are particularly useful in graduate counseling. One woman who applied to a graduate department on the Berkeley campus remarked, "The faculty person you referred me to went out of her way to explain the department's emphasis. She even told me about a new program that I can qualify for." This kind of contact begins to de-mystify the application process and helps potential students to assess their alternatives in a realistic manner.

There is, however, a fine line between support services and dependency-creating services. The informal, comfortable atmosphere and staff attitudes lead most visitors to view the Center as a welcoming place where, as one woman stated, "I am treated as a human being, not a statistic.... There is good feedback, good leadership." Another client commented, "Even though I was a complete stranger with no connection to the University, they were extremely helpful and went out of their way to assist me...."

While the staff intends to create an open, accessible service, it carefully avoids making the Center a refuge or substitute for confronting the outside world. The University has a formidable image in the minds of many individuals, both women and men. The Center helps them past this otherwise intimidating facade.

Working for Institutional Change

Counseling is only one part of the program. The Center also tries to influence institutional attitudes and practices. The campus location permits access to University personnel, while the campus community outreach maintains direct contact with persons trying to cope with obstacles posed by University policies. During the Center's second year, campus departments and individuals have often called to consult on student and staff problems. Inquiries range from procedural questions to grievances, and are handled by Center administrators, whose University experience and academic backgrounds make them the peers of the campus personnel with whom they confer. A file on affirmative action and similar concerns is being compiled so that the directors can continue their efforts to make campus units aware of women's questions and problems. Recently, the directors advised personnel officers about hiring and employment grievances and discussed with senior staff of the University library the impact of affirmative action on management attitudes. Personnel officers from local cities have also consulted with the Center staff on unconscious modes of discrimination caused by sexual perceptions.

Other consultative services include providing letters of support for campus and community projects such as the current proposal for a women's studies major on the Berkeley campus. The staff also studied the proposed guidelines for Title IX of the 1972 U.S. Education Amendment banning sex discrimination in educational institutions. The directors consulted with University officers who were drafting the official response to the guidelines, and later sent an independent, unofficial assessment on specific sections of the regulations.

Developing the Talent Bank

Search committees from departments at Berkeley and other campuses frequently approach the Center seeking qualified individuals for faculty and administrative positions. The staff makes available listings of professional women from its file of national registries in various fields. The Center holds memberships in national organizations, such as the Federation of Professional Organizations for Women, that provide access to other academic listings and personal contact with individuals around the country.

"We cannot find qualified women," is a frequent complaint of academic employers. While various professional associations have developed availability pools of women qualified in specific academic disciplines, few have focused on academic administration, where many important educational policies are determined. Most available resources are located on the east coast. Accordingly, the Center is developing a Talent Bank for Women Academic Administrators, and encourages women to seek jobs in higher administrative ranks by informing them of the existence of such positions. The Berkeley area has attracted a number of women with the qualifications or the potential to become college administrators. More than 200 resumes have been collected through informal solicitation from faculty members, local graduates, visitors to the Bay Area, and others.

As bibliographer Eleanor Robbins explained,

We also plan to assist women in reassessing their experience in terms of administrative skill. This is necessary since many of them have not held positions that normally grant access to administrative jobs. We intend to follow up on these referrals to see if women are hired. Although we do not have enough funds to make the Bank fully operative at this time, we are turning available resources to its immediate development and are seeking additional monies for the project.

The Center has already opened doors for women interested in academic administration. The first Director, May Diaz, became Provost of Kresge College at UC Santa Cruz, and is a top-ranking woman in the University system; Frances Coles, formerly Associate Director, became Assistant Dean of Admissions at Boalt Law School; and Beatrice Bain, also an Associate Director, was appointed Academic Assistant to the University of California Provost for the nine-campus system.

Research Projects

The Center is actively developing a research component. Due to budget limitations, the first phase deals with coordination of materials readily within the Center's grasp. Two graduate students, Kelly Lee and Lindsay Desrochers, hired in the summer of 1974, produced bibliographies on *Financial Aid in Higher Education* and *Getting Into Graduate School*. Copies have been placed in the Center's library, and additional copies are being published. Projects-in-progress include bibliographies on "Women and Employment," "Declared Majors of Berkeley Undergraduate Women During the Past Decade," "Ageism and the Woman Student/Employee," and an "Evaluation of Women's Studies Courses on the Berkeley Campus."

During Spring quarter, 1975, a series of panels presented women and men faculty members discussing research needs in areas related to women. Using these and other sources, the Center will prepare a file on potential study topics, and will identify faculty who may be interested in developing projects through the Center.

Programs for the Public

Through campus and community outreach programs, the Center is already providing information on a variety of topics. The program schedule includes a Wednesday Noon Series where women and men bring bag lunches to the informal lounge to hear a speaker, watch a film, and hold informal discussions on some basic theme of interest to women. Programs have included an informational talk on "Women's Studies at UC Berkeley;" "Women in Politics," an address and discussion with Berkeley's councilperson Loni Hancock; "Women in the Law," a discussion with Law Professor Herma Hill Kay, and women from the Boalt Women' Association; presentation of a study on "Sexual Orientation and Dream Content in Women," and many others. The diversity and informality of these noon programs help to attract a broad range of interested persons.

The other regular series is "Women in Research," where UC faculty women speak on their original research in progress—papers, lectures, books. This program provides a forum for sharing their findings with campus and community. To date, topics have included: "The Changing Status of Women in Developed Countries," by Professor Judith B. Davis of the Graduate School of Public Policy; "Aesthetics of Black Community Theatre," by Margaret Wilkerson, Lecturer in the English Department; "The Effects of Divorce on the Pre-School Child," by Judith Wallerstein, Lecturer in the School of Social Welfare; and "Primate Behavior" by Professor Phyllis Dolhinow of the Anthropology Department.

In addition to these programs, the Center sponsors visiting individual speakers or timely programs such as Dr. Nawal Sadawy, Egyptian physician, writer and feminist; and Kerstin Aner, member of the Swedish Parliament. "Women in Feminist Research: Workshop and Colloquium" is an ongoing seminar open to those who are interested in or engaged in research studies about women and feminist concerns in all disciplines.

Materials on publishing opportunities are also being produced through this program.

Plans for the Future

The long-range goal of the Center is to develop a sizable and effective research component while retaining a referral and counseling unit. As noted earlier, plans are being made for research development now that the counseling program is established. In addition to compiling the two bibliographies mentioned above, the next step is formation of an advisory board of faculty and other resource persons, as the Center strengthens and formalizes academic contacts. This board will assist in formulating policy, suggesting and screening research projects, identifying potential funding sources and working with academic departments and other campus units. A change in name is also being contemplated as the staff seeks a more descriptive title.

Until extramural funding is obtained, the Center will continue to conduct modest projects within its grasp — producing bibliographies, surveys and reports. For example, in the Spring of 1975, Marilyn Jacobson began an extensive follow-up study on women who have used the Center's resources in order to determine the effect of their contact with this program and to plan adequately for future workshops. The counseling staff anticipates a more specialized effort in the areas of (1) re-entry persons, (2) Third World Women, (3) financial aid, and (4) pre-college counseling.

Because 1975 is International Women's Year, research on women is becoming a major focus in institutions around the country. The Center will place a greater emphasis on publications as it shares with a wider public the news of current research developments in this area and examines the effects of its own projects on the declared majors of undergraduate Berkeley women, women's studies, ageism, and the woman student/employee.

The Center's newsletter *Connections*, first published in April 1975, will continue to provide material concerning women in higher education.

The CCEW - Women's Center is unique within the University of California academic community. Because it actively explores ways of making a university more responsive to the problems and concerns of women, it remains one of the most innovative programs on the Berkeley campus.

Notes

[1]Beatrice Bain, "Women and Academia at Berkeley: CCEW — Women's Center," *Public Affairs Report*, Vol. 14 No. 6, December 1973 (Berkeley: Institute of Governmental Studies, University of California).

[2]Frances M. Davis et al., "Report of the Chancellor's Advisory Committee on the Establishment of a Center for Women's Education," March 1972, U.C. Berkeley.

[3]Jean Dickenson, "Counseling at the Women's Center," *Connections* (CCEW — Women's Center Newsletter), Vol. 1, No. 1, Spring 1975.

Urban Communities

Vol. 16   No. 4   August 1975

Reviving the Inner City:
The Lessons of Oakland's Chinatown

By
Willard T. Chow
Assistant Professor, Department of Geography,
and the Pacific Urban Studies and Planning
Program, University of Hawaii at Manoa

Introduction

Misconceptions about the role and value of ethnic communities continue to blur attempts to understand the American city's past and cloud perspectives on its future. Such misconceptions can thwart efforts to cure the ills of the central city, regardless of the nobility of intentions or the size of expenditures.[1] This paper examines some of the major confusions and offers an alternative way of viewing a central city like Oakland, California, by evaluating the significance of Oakland's Chinese quarter, one of the city's oldest areas of ethnic settlement.

Sequestered in the heart of Oakland for nearly a century, the 40-block area generally known as Chinatown dramatizes the plight of many historic inner city communities that await re-awakened perceptions by residents, public officials and private investors. Both Cantonese and English are spoken in the quarter, and about half the area's population is Chinese. Other residents are white, Black and Filipino, predominantly single males.

Sidewalk delicacies, exotic scents, ornate gates, and venerable buildings clustered in a few blocks in the western half of the quarter give the area a flavor distinct from that of the surrounding townscape. The Victorian style of some of the area's dwellings dates back to the days of Jack London, when the Madison Square (eastern) half of the district was an elegant neighborhood.

During the past decade, the city's ambitious revitalization efforts have begun to disturb the quarter's equilibrium. New high rise offices, part of Oakland's City Center Project, have emerged at its northwest corner. Warehouses and factories still dominate to the south, where railroad, freeway, and waterfront facilities converge. Along the eastern edge of Chinatown is Laney College, built during the late 1960's on what was previously an industrial site, and designed by Skidmore, Owings and Merrill in a style reminiscent of a medieval walled city. Oakland's Civic Center, an expanding complex of offices and public institutions, stands on the

northeastern fringe of the Chinese quarter. In the northwest corner is the four-block portion designated as the redevelopment area.

To the Chinese in Oakland, Chinatown is more than geometric space, real estate or a decorative landmark. Like other places, it is also a "construct of experience . . . sustained not only by timber, concrete, and highways, but also by the quality of human awareness."[2] To those Chinese who have had no other home for much of their lives, Chinatown has served as both a refuge and a stepping stone. The Chinese junk on which children play at Lincoln Playground symbolizes the heritage and hopes of four generations of Chinese-Americans.

Rents are lower in Chinatown than elsewhere in the city, and mothers with young children can work in the nearby sewing factories that became numerous after 1965, when many working class immigrant families settled in Oakland. Help for newcomers and older residents is available from churches and social agencies like the Chinese Community Council, the Chinese Community Center, Asian Health Services, East Bay Asians for Community Action, and Lincoln School. For those residents particularly, Chinatown is not simply a place to eat, sleep and work; it is also their principal "connection" with the job market, the public bureaucracy, and the political arena. A place to turn to in time of need, Chinatown continues to offer its residents assistance within the complex urban systems of Oakland and Alameda County.

Ethnic Neighborhoods: Ambiguities and Choices

Much of Chinatown's timeworn exterior is plainly visible, but the causes of its blight, like those of many ethnic districts, are less apparent. The physical condition of ethnic neighborhoods hinges on the expectations and decisions of lenders, property owners, and public officials as well as residents. The location of transit facilities and other public services, zoning and code enforcement, and the presence or absence of local capital improvements have all affected the well-being of inner city neighborhoods. Significantly, many urban conflicts have centered on the issue of who is to control the development of inner city residential communities.[3] The depressing effects of past discrimination in housing, including the use of racially restrictive covenants, have continued to be reinforced by the practice of "redlining," whereby the flow of private financing into certain neighborhoods has been blocked or diverted.

As confinement to ghettos came to be recognized as a social evil, the alternative of ethnic dispersal and residential integration were generally accepted as desirable goals. But the benefits of dispersal included certain ambiguities, since social well-being could not be defined exclusively in terms of space.[4] It became clear that the quality of life also depends on a complex of expectations and aspirations[5] that might or might not be best served by dispersal, and that accordingly some people might not choose dispersal.

Since freedom of choice in housing can be assured only when ethnic groups have a wide range of alternatives, it follows that if members of ethnic communities are to be able to live where they wish, they must have access to housing both within the inner city and outside it. Yet residential opportunities in Oakland's Chinatown have been increasingly restricted during the past two decades. Publicly funded projects, such as the Nimitz Freeway and the Bay Area Rapid Transit District, have reduced the housing stock. It has become more difficult for Chinese newcomers to find a home in Chinatown and for long-time residents to remain there, despite the efforts of the Oakland Redevelopment Agency to build new low and moderate rent housing at the northwestern corner of the quarter in the four-block redevelopment area.

The following discussion examines some historic aspects of Chinese settlement in the San Francisco Bay Area and discusses the impact of inner city development on ethnic neighborhoods, particularly in Oakland's Chinatown. Some developmental side effects are noted, as well as the benefits of ethnic concentration when it is the result of choice. Also presented is the challenge of providing neighborhoods with a stronger voice in land use decisions and insuring that the community leaders who wield political influence actually defend the interests of the residents they claim to serve.[6] Finally, it is suggested that residents, public officials, and private investors should take a new look at Chinatown. Thus it is not so much new legislation but rather better understanding that can save Oakland's Chinatown and other ethnic neighborhoods.

The writer holds these views: (1) the preservation and rehabilitation of stable inner city neighborhoods is a desirable goal; (2) stable communities with responsive institutions, neighborhood ties, and a sense of common destiny, like Oakland's Chinatown, take years to build and much effort to sustain; (3) the dynamic equilibrium these communities have struggled to achieve can be upset by the changing expectations and collective actions of private investors and public officials; but (4) such actions and decisions often go unchallenged because no single planning agency is willing or able to accept overall responsibility for the cumulative impact of development.

Chinese Settlement in the Bay Area: Some Comparisons

For most Chinese living in American cities, ethnic institutions and subcultural ties to Chinatown have persisted despite a growing emphasis on civil rights and occupational mobility. The experience of the Chinese may well apply to other more recent immigrant groups, such as the Chicanos, Puerto Ricans, and Filipinos, who also tend to cluster in certain districts.[7] For newly arrived Vietnamese sponsored by American families, however, community bonds will be more difficult to sustain.

Chinese enclaves developed as immigrants came to the United States during the last half of the 19th Century. Ousted from most of the rural West by racial harassment and violence during the 1870's and 1880's, thousands of Chinese miners, construction laborers, farm workers, fishermen, and factory workers sought refuge in San Francisco, where clan, district, and community organizations had become exceptionally powerful.

The extraordinary resilience of San Francisco's Chinatown stems from the strength of institutions forged during a period of intense racism and discrimination. Restrictive housing practices favored landlords, while discriminatory hiring gave employers the advantage. Poor Chinese immigrants were exploited by unscrupulous Chinese as well as non-Chinese landlords and employers. Responding to external pressures and pressing social needs, San Francisco's Chinatown became the strongest and largest Chinese community in the United States.

In contrast to San Francisco's Chinatown, most typical Chinese communities in the United States functioned simply as housing, employment, and social centers for Chinese laundrymen, peddlers, laborers, and shopkeepers. Chinese communities like Oakland's provided less security against racial violence than did San Francisco's, but life there appeared to be less congested and less competitive, and allowed residents a measure of freedom from the norms, obligations, and economic constraints that had become entrenched in San Francisco's merchant-dominated quarter.

City ordinances restricting (Chinese) steam laundries from certain sections of downtown Oakland and banning (Chinese) peddlers from the streets were passed in 1880 and 1891, to protect the interests of local businessmen. This pattern of restricted occupancy was common to most Chinatown communities in the American West. Modesto's 1885 ordinance prohibiting (Chinese) steam laundries from residential areas has been cited as the first example of zoning in the United States.[8]

In San Francisco the Chinese quarter flourished in a relatively desirable part of the city. But squeezed between the city's burgeoning financial, hotel, high class retail, and Italian districts, it also won the dubious distinction of having the city's highest population density and tuberculosis rate. Repeated attempts to dislodge San Francisco's Chinatown have proven unsuccessful. The most striking attempt occurred after the 1906 earthquake, with efforts to relocate the Chinese at Hunters Point. Other Chinatowns, less well organized and thus less powerful, have not fared nearly as well.[9]

Oakland's loosely knit Chinese community, for example, was far more vulnerable to competing land uses than San Francisco's, which was fortified by its interlocking institutions and large population. Although the Chinese began to settle in Oakland by the 1860's, they were periodically displaced until 1880, when Chinatown's present site was finally established. Chinatown in Oakland, as in many other American cities, was confined to the light industrial and wholesale district. Racial segregation was widely practiced, and the presence of the

Chinese quarter was tolerated as long as it was located in an area that others considered undesirable for residence.

Oakland: The Reemergence of an Inner City

The Chinese in Oakland became concentrated in an area that was neglected by capital improvement programs, overlooked by code enforcement practices, and zoned primarily for commerce and industry until the early 1960's. The community did not develop into an attractive residential district, but it managed to survive and community spirit remained strong. Churches, clans, and fraternal associations responded to the needs of residents. Racial discrimination in hiring continued to hinder Chinese social mobility until World War II, but the community remained responsive and cohesive.

During World War II, however, Oakland's inner city entered a new era. The influx of many Black workers, recruited primarily from the South, raised the demand for low and moderate rent housing. Most were channeled into "unrestricted" areas of the city near the central business district, where the overcrowding and undermaintenance of older housing led to deterioration during the 1950's. Despite such decay in other parts of Oakland's inner city, Chinatown's housing remained in relatively sound condition. Of the 246 Chinatown parcels appraised in 1953, only one was considered to be in "poor" condition. About 12 percent were rated "fair," 70 percent "average," and 17 percent "good," with two properties classified as in "excellent" condition.

By no means blighted, the Chinese quarter was not initially slated for urban renewal. Official attitudes began to shift by the mid-1960's, reflecting growing concern by Chinese businessmen and property owners about the future of the residential district. The "Oakland Chinatown Redevelopment Project," a preliminary plan prepared by consultants and financed mainly by Chinese businessmen, launched the quest for redevelopment in 1965, when community leaders presented it to the city council.

Racially restrictive housing covenants had been ruled unenforceable in 1948, but it was only after passage of California's Rumford Act in 1963 that racial discrimination in housing was outlawed, and fair housing policies began to change residential patterns in Oakland. Ironically, new problems were created as minorities moved to more attractive homes in newly opened neighborhoods. Opportunities for minorities were also increased as new housing in the suburbs helped to accelerate the filtering process.

Property values in the inner city sagged as the supply of housing available to minorities expanded. Furthermore, suburban growth in the East Bay promoted the development of regional shopping centers that cut into retail sales in the central business district of Oakland, as in most central cities. Beset by lower property values and lower sales, many central cities looked to the federal government for help. Like most cities, Oakland embraced slum clearance and transit programs as instruments of civic progress and central business district revitalization. Urban renewal in Oakland, however, was smaller in scale than in most American cities. Aimed at West Oakland, the most deteriorated section of town, urban renewal left Chinatown unscathed.

The Challenge of Inner City Development

Nationwide efforts to redeem the central city began with the Housing Act of 1949, but the problem was not addressed systematically until the early 1960's, when community organizers and academic critics focused attention on the fact that slum clearance had destroyed low-cost housing while ignoring important human values. Community action and comprehensive planning programs were established in order to involve the poor in the redevelopment process. Such changes heightened the expectations of the poor and helped strengthen their voices in discussions with federal agencies, but they did not significantly alter the balance of power in most American cities. Resistance by the poor to the transformation of the inner city mounted during the 1960's, as thousands of low income residents in Oakland were displaced by freeway and mass transit projects.[10]

Oakland's Chinatown exemplifies an historic district that is being displaced in the name of inner city revitalization. The Bay Area Rapid Transit District facilities and the Oakland Museum, while not classified as redevelopment projects, were financially connected with the Laney College redevelopment project. Since both BART and the Museum were supposed to be beneficial to the redevelopment project, part of their costs were credited to Oakland's share of the project's net expenses. The direct impact of these three public investments has been to reduce the housing stock. The indirect effect will depend upon the kinds of changes that follow on nearby property.

Of the city's 12,000 Chinese residents, fewer than 2,000 now live in the quarter. The majority of Chinese in Oakland are foreign-born, whereas most of the Chinese in the East Bay suburbs were born in the United States. Recent immigrants, including many who came to join relatives in Oakland after a partial relaxation of immigration restrictions in 1962, have had little choice but to disperse into East Oakland. Thus even though the city's Chinese population doubled from 1960 to 1970, the Chinese population of the quarter itself declined slightly in the same period.

Consistent efforts by the Oakland Redevelopment Agency to secure redevelopment assistance in low-cost housing from HUD (U. S. Department of Housing and Urban Development) finally bore fruit in July 1972, after four previous applications had been rejected. Those displaced by ambitious public projects found the promise of more low cost housing through redevelopment unfulfilled in many communities across the country. Widespread complaints about the inefficiency and inflexibility of numerous categorical federal programs heightened the struggle for reform.

Under the Housing and Community Development Act of 1974, bloc grants replaced categorical federal programs such as urban renewal, model cities, code enforcement assistance, open space, water and sewer facilities. Although more flexible than the previous categorical approach, the bloc grants unleashed a new wave of legal, administrative, and political uncertainties. Inner city communities, caught in a grueling struggle for inadequate federal grants, will almost certainly suffer. Conflicts have heightened as more players, representing newly eligible, marginal or moderate income neighborhoods and new private investors, have joined the competition.[11]

Pressures on Oakland's Chinatown

Although new high-rise condominium-apartments have been privately built on Chinatown's western front, and more are planned for the four-block Chinatown Neighborhood Development Project, the situation on the eastern flank is more precarious. Construction of mass transit facilities, BART headquarters, and the Lake Merritt Station has begun to generate changes in the Madison Square section of Chinatown. These indirect effects will have lasting impact on much greater areas than the specific housing the facilities themselves have replaced.

Concern about underutilization of BART's Lake Merritt Station, for example, has prompted efforts to turn part of the section into a regional center for government agencies, even though funding is unlikely and the project appears to be about a decade away from realization. Lake Merritt-Coliseum Development Project (LMCDP), a prime mover behind these efforts, has nonetheless held community meetings to involve citizens in the planning and development process. The project was created in 1973 by the City of Oakland, the regional Metropolitan Transportation Commission, and BART. While LMCDP holds that new housing units (at rents similar to those of demolished units) should be built before any housing is torn down, the demolition of older housing in adjacent blocks may be an indirect consequence of development. New office buildings may trigger more demolition on adjacent properties than within the development area itself.

Bringing about change in a neighborhood requires new perceptions and expectations. But once these are widely accepted, the balance of confidence and risk that keeps neighborhoods in equilibrium can be easily disturbed. If an area is expected to change dramatically, property owners may be reluctant to maintain structures, and lenders may be hesitant to finance such investments. The mere prospect of conversion even without loss of existing housing in a development area, may be sufficient to transform the surrounding neighborhood, especially if most owners are investors and not residents. Earmarking certain blocks as being suitable for either development or rehabilitation by an official planning agency, such as LMCDP, may become a self-fulfilling prophecy, unless the evaluation is effectively challenged.

Assigning the credit or blame for the indirect impact of publicly funded planning and development activities is difficult, particularly since agencies are naturally eager to take responsibility for the "good" changes but not the "bad" ones. Assessing the indirect import of such activities depends on judgments as to what would have happened in the market without public intervention. The public and private sectors are, however, integrally related, as are the planning and development activities of local, regional and federal agencies. As suggested before, no single agency is willing or able to take responsibility for the cumulative impact of inner city development.

How Much Community Control?

It may be difficult for Oakland's Chinatown to sustain organized opposition to further development of the Madison Square section; many Chinese would prefer development and an appreciation of land values. Conflict has erupted over selection of the Project Area Committee (PAC), which was appointed and funded by the Redevelopment Agency to advise it concerning redevelopment within the four-block area. Although PAC lost its funds when the agency's funding ended, the committee is still in operation. Even if a community consensus could be reached, however, it is doubtful that residents in neighborhoods like Chinatown would wield much power. Community involvement requires time, patience, commitment, and the ability to communicate well (in both English and Cantonese). Power in Chinatown has traditionally been concentrated in the hands of community "elders." But their leadership has been questioned recently by those who would like to retain the quarter's stock of low cost housing.

The fate of Chinatown and other inner city communities in Oakland may be contingent upon whether federal community development bloc grants ($62 million over six years) will be used to preserve neighborhoods or to stimulate change. Although Chinatown redevelopment is supposed to receive a large portion of bloc funds, apparently little will be used to rehabilitate the quarter's older housing.

Neighborhood control over the way these funds are to be spent is a major issue in Oakland. The city council, for example, has insisted that its seven designated community development district boards be staffed with experienced Oakland Redevelopment Agency personnel. Community groups, supported by the Oakland Citizens' Committee for Urban Renewal, argue that district board staff would remain loyal to the city council in the event of conflict between the neighborhoods and the city. For all participants, the issue is not simply a matter of how much money is spent in each district; it is also a matter of what kinds of changes will be induced.

The future of Oakland's Chinatown as a residential community for the city's disadvantaged Chinese population is now uncertain. The overriding questions are: (1) to what extent will residents be able to exercise control over development? and (2) who should represent the Chinese community? As we have seen, the decision on whether or not Chinatown will be whittled away may soon be made. Meanwhile conflicts within the community undermine its solidarity. If Chinatown is to survive, its wide variety of community organizations must join in stating common needs and strengthening the physical as well as social identity of the quarter.

Chinatown Housing and Neighborhood Preservation

The need for more housing is widely accepted, but controversies continue over where housing investments ought to be located, and what kind of housing should be made available. New single-family and condominium housing in the suburbs have been in great demand, and have thus been relatively profitable for builders and lenders. Moreover, higher rates of residential mobility that follow new construction mean increased commissions on sales.

In contrast, the alternative of "slow growth" in the suburbs and rehabilitation of the inner city involves a narrower and riskier market. It appears that the option of rehabilitation would encourage residential stability, resulting in less turnover of property, and thus lower sales activity in the real estate market. Proponents of slow growth in the suburbs have been branded elitists, racists, or preservationists. Moreover, advocates of inner city rehabilitation have been accused of "ghetto gilding" and encouraging inefficiency. Nevertheless, both strategies could produce a steady expansion in housing stock, with a minimum of demolition and dislocation.

Providing inexpensive housing in Oakland's Chinatown is essential for neighborhood preservation. The destruction of low rent housing in the quarter has multiplied problems for both young and old, and has also created a dilemma for officials responsible for meeting residents' needs within budgetary constraints. Many elderly Chinese learned to rely on the quarter during periods of blatant racism, and still need many of Chinatown's services. They must now travel long distances for the information, health care, bilingual assistance, and social companionship available in Chinatown. Those in Chinatown with limited mobility would be particularly unfortunate if displaced into East Oakland, where most of the Chinese are now dispersed.

For Chinese immigrant families, perhaps the most acute problem is in the schools, where youngsters often have difficulty with the English language. Special educational programs and bilingual assistance have usually been available in Chinatown, but such programs are often lacking in East Oakland schools, where the Chinese constitute a much smaller portion of the total enrollment in each school. Further dispersal would make such special assistance more difficult to provide and expensive to support than in schools with greater concentrations of Chinese students, although it could be done through busing and other devices.

Thus revitalization and relocation in outlying areas have made special education programs more difficult for both school officials and minority students who need help. The problems of Chinese youngsters in school do not stem from lack of motivation, but rather from lack of institutional awareness of their needs and responsiveness to them. The United States Supreme Court, ruling that San Francisco's public schools must give instruction to minority students in the language that they use, has recognized the necessity for special bilingual education. How promptly, efficiently, and effectively can this be accomplished in the face of increasing ethnic dispersal?

Stable neighborhood communities provide much more than housing. They perform services that benefit the city as a whole. Thus for nearly a century Chinatown has offered information, training, welfare assistance, direction, and hope for the unemployed. Buffeted by regional adjustments and technological shifts, the unemployed and underemployed must often be re-trained, re-qualified, and made aware of opportunities before they can be absorbed or reabsorbed into the mainstream of the economy. Minorities, for example, usually need help in overcoming union employment restrictions. Thus employment programs for ethnic minorities have been much more effective where bilingual staff is available and activities can be adapted to particular needs. Erosion of the inner city base that supports such a mobile labor force has consequences extending far beyond the boundaries of Chinatown itself.

A Reappraisal of Costs and Benefits

Advocates of publicly funded inner city development cite the expected benefits of increased tax revenues and receipt of federal or state subsidies. Project costs that spill over or affect areas beyond the designated development, as suggested earlier, may escape careful examination. The costs of disrupting stable communities, although difficult to calculate, will nevertheless be paid in the increased expenses of various public agencies or in the intangible human losses associated with dislocation, isolation, and loneliness.

Examples of such costs may be found in Oakland. Although property values in the inner city have risen, public outlays have also escalated. The increases have not been due to an upsurge in social programs for the city's disadvantaged, but instead reflect higher costs of police and fire protection.[12] Increased demand for these services may be stimulated in part by loss of stability in Oakland's now scattered low-income districts, where neighborhood ties and communal aspirations have weakened during the past decade.

Moreover, even the benefits of development may fall short of expectations. It was hoped that federal subsidies would lure new private investors into Oakland, but so far the results have not been encouraging. Unless functional problems can be resolved, it is doubtful that ambitious plans for reviving the central business district will succeed. Stable working class communities may play a more significant role in maintaining retail activity than has been generally realized.

Making Oakland More Attractive

In terms of convenient access and parking, suburban regional shopping centers are more attractive for most retail needs than Oakland's downtown shops and department stores. In terms of limited appeal (specialty) retailing, San Francisco and Berkeley have much wider selections of goods and services and more distinctive surroundings. Downtown Oakland serves mainly local residents and its own employees. Even with BART and linkage with the Grove-Shafter freeway, its market is not likely to expand dramatically, at least as presently envisioned. If Oakland is to compete, it must achieve some sort of functional distinction.

Oakland presently lacks the pageantry, local color, variety, and identity that make San Francisco such an exciting attraction for visitors and shoppers. Oakland's city fathers have favored the development of Chinese shops and restaurants in order to bolster the city's nighttime activities. But in the writer's view they have shown little enthusiasm for preserving and strengthening the Chinese community by rehabilitating its older housing. Such a policy could foster the residence of stable working-class and middle-class families, whose presence in turn could help make the inner city a much more active and interesting place, probably a good deal safer after dark, and surely a lot less sterile than unrelieved offices or condominium apartments. Shoppers and visitors might be much more attracted to a Chinatown with kids and their grandparents on the streets than one dominated by office buildings with no social character or special activities other than housing a daytime workforce that leaves for the suburbs when the workday is over.

It is becoming clear that intensive, narrowly focused commercial development can have dehumanizing consequences. San Francisco's Dianne Feinstein and George Moscone, for example, have observed the monumental scale of much building in San Francisco and noted that the structures impose social costs on the city residents.[13] High-rise office buildings alone lack the socializing warmth provided by small shops, businesses, eating places, and other establishments that cater to the needs of neighborhood residents as well as people who work downtown.

With respect to Oakland's inner city, planners have recognized the advantages of mixed commercial and residential development for a safe, attractive, and lively community. But what kind of housing should be encouraged? Exclusive focus on new apartment complexes and high-rise condominiums will foster a typically self-contained pattern of activities, marked by electronic gates and sophisticated security systems. In contrast, the rehabilitation of old housing can instill or strengthen a sense of community pride and cooperation among residents, especially in working class neighborhoods.[14] In the writer's view, the benefits of rehabilitation are more likely to spill over than those of brand-new apartment-condominiums. The "balanced approach," combining rehabilitation of old housing and building anew as advocated by many planners in Oakland, is sound provided that it applies to the entire quarter and not just those blocks within the boundaries of the redevelopment project.

Conclusion

Efforts to increase the availability of low cost housing in the inner city are already under way in many cities, and promising neighborhood preservation programs, like Neighborhood Housing Services, have already started.[15] Private attempts to convert obsolete industrial and commercial areas into new luxury apartment housing in Oakland — such as Portobello — have been remarkably effective, despite the difficulties involved. These developments suggest that radical reform may not be necessary, if public support and private capital can be drawn back into the rehabilitation of inner city housing and the construction of new housing on obsolete industrial and commercial property. If this is to occur, the practices of lending institutions and the policies of government agencies will have to be retooled to recognize the functional value of inner city communities like Oakland's Chinatown.

As we have seen, the decisions of key actors — lenders, landlords, realtors, appraisers, city planning staff and commissioners, elected local representatives, state and federal officials, and community leaders — combine to determine the market value, attractiveness, and livability of the neighborhood. Fresh paint, home repairs, and minor renovations may be within the grasp of Chinatown residents. But the final risks and payoffs of such investments are usually determined in the financial and real estate market, not at home by members of the resident household. Just as both neighborhood decline and preservation result from a series of decisions, so the task of neighborhood preservation and rehabilitation involves cooperation, persuasion, and sharing a common vision of the future among lenders, public officials, property owners, and residents.

In short, new legislation and innovative programs may not be needed; they are already available. The crucial element necessary to enhance the vitality of Chinatown is a clearer vision of its role in inner city revitalization. If residents can exert meaningful influence over the development of their own neighborhoods, then they may begin to see the familiar streets and buildings as a means of realizing communal aspirations, rather than as monuments to social injustice. If public officials recognize the value of stable working class communities like Oakland's Chinatown, then they may regard neighborhood preservation as a way to reduce social costs, rather than as roadblocks to the expansion of municipal revenues. If lenders understand that the risks of financing inner city housing can be reduced through the organized efforts of concerned residents, local officials, and their own staff, then they too may cooperate.

Thus the preservation of inner city neighborhoods can serve their own residents and also help to save the city as a whole. The viability of working class ethnic communities, whether in Chinatown or elsewhere, may encourage middle class residents to stay in a city whose districts and streets are occupied by people who are proud to be there. Preserving these communities may keep the human spirit alive in the heart of the American city.

NOTES

This paper is based on Willard T. Chow's unpublished Ph.D. dissertation: "The Re-emergence of an Inner City: The Pivot of Chinese Settlement in the East Bay Region of the San Francisco Bay Area," Department of Geography, University of California, Berkeley, 1974.

[1]See Michael A. Goldberg and Michael Y. Seelig, "Canadian Cities: The Right Deed for the Wrong Reason," *Planning: the aspo Magazine,* 41(3):8-13 (March-April 1975).
[2]Yi-Fu Tuan, "Place: An Experiential Perspective," *Geographical Review,* 65(2):151-165 (April 1975). See p. 165.
[3]I am indebted to Allan Jacobs, Professor of City Planning, U.C.B., for this point.
[4]David M. Smith, *The Geography of Social Well-Being in the United States* (New York: McGraw-Hill, 1973) pp. 139-141.
[5]See Eleanor Bernert Sheldon and Robert Parke, "Social Indicators," *Science,* 188(4189):693-699 (May 16, 1975). See p. 697.
[6]See three monographs on this topic:
(a) Julian Wolpert, Anthony Mumphray and John Seley, *Metropolitan Neighborhoods: Participation and Conflict Over Change* (Washington, D.C.: Association of American Geographers, Resource Paper No. 16, 1972).
(b) Roger Kasperson and Myrna Breitbart, *Participation, Decentralization, and Advocacy Planning* (Washington, D.C.: Association of American Geographers, Resource Paper No. 25, 1974).
(c) Michael P. Brooks, *Social Planning and City Planning* (American Society of Planning Officials, Planning Advisory Service Report No. 261, September 1970).
[7]See Andrew Greeley, "In the Neighborhood," *Human Behavior,* 4(6):40-45 (June 1975).

[8]Mel Scott, *American City Planning Since 1890* (Berkeley: University of California Press, 1969), p. 75.

[9]See Rose Hum Lee, "The Decline of Chinatowns in the U.S.," *American Journal of Sociology,* 54(5):422-432 (March 1949). See also Calvin Lee, *Chinatown, U.S.A.* (Garden City: Doubleday & Co., 1965).

[10]See Judith May, "Struggle for Authority: A Comparison of Four Social Change Programs in Oakland, California," unpublished Ph.D. dissertation, Department of Political Science, University of California, Berkeley, 1973. See also Edward C. Hayes, *Power Structure and Urban Policy: Who Rules in Oakland?* (New York: McGraw-Hill, 1972).

[11]Anthony Downs in a speech at the HUD/RERC (Real Estate Research Corp.) Urban Renewal and Neighborhood Preservation Workshop in San Francisco (June 26, 1975).

[12]See a series of articles by Bill Martin in the Oakland *Tribune* (May 12-15, 1974), which begin with "Oakland is on the Brink of Bankruptcy," May 12, 1974, p. 1.

[13]Speeches at the annual conference of the San Francisco Planning and Urban Renewal Association, March 19, 1975; see the San Francisco *Chronicle,* March 20, 1975, p. 6.

[14]For statements on the importance of working class neighborhoods see: Suzanne Keller, *The Urban Neighborhood: A Sociological Perspective* (New York: Random House, 1968); and Annette Buttimer, "Sociology and Planning," *Town Planning Review,* 42(2):145-180 (April 1971). See especially pp. 154-168.

[15]*Neighborhood Preservation: A Catalog of Local Programs* (Washington, D.C.: February 1975). Prepared for the Office of Policy Development and Research, Department of Housing and Urban Development, by [the] Real Estate Research Corporation, with the assistance of [the] Center for Urban Policy Research, Rutgers University.

Health and Hospitals: Planning, Governance and Finance

Vol. 16   No. 5   October 1975

Hospitals: From Physician Dominance to Public Control

By
David B. Starkweather
Associate Professor and Director of the
Graduate Program in Hospital Administration
School of Public Health

Introduction: Moving Toward Public Control

The hospital is a major community institution: It is a big business, a big employer, and a "health factory" whose daily routine deals with life or death crises. But hospitals are also being subjected to increasing criticism, largely as the result of high costs of care and growing skepticism about the general conduct of the medical profession. The hospital is the corporate giant in medicine: the house of wonders where advanced technology is turned to man's benefit. Yet it can also be an incredibly costly and inhuman bureaucracy.

Who controls hospitals, and who should do so? In the United States hospitals are now in transition from physician dominance to public control. Several dimensions of that shift are explored here and some alternative approaches suggested.

Public control of hospitals can be viewed in terms of ownership and governance, organizational structure, and the extent to which local community clients have opportunities to participate in decisionmaking.

Ownership and Governance

1. Thirty-five percent of all acute care hospitals in the United States are owned and operated by governments: federal veteran and marine and military hospitals, state psychiatric facilities, and local county or municipal hospitals. Nevertheless, these hospitals remain private institutions in many ways, principally through physician domination of most hospital activities. Very few of these government-owned hospitals have governing bodies — either elected or appointed — that represent the public interest or provide an oversight that is appropriate to the size and importance of their operations.

2. A majority of U.S. hospitals, 53 percent, are "voluntary, nonprofit" institutions: They do not make money for stockholders and are sponsored by local communities. While they do have governing boards, close examination reveals that these bodies are essentially private and self-perpetuating. (By common practice, board members act collectively to choose their own successors.) Moreover, the governing boards that make modest efforts to secure representation of the broad community usually succeed only with respect to certain upper economic and social groups.

3. Finally, 12 percent are organized as profit-making institutions. They are privately owned, either by small groups of individuals who have formed local partnerships that constitute boards, or by national companies with boards elected by stockholders. Many of the latter, in turn, are owned by even larger multinational conglomerates. Thus, ownership of the proprietary hospital industry has recently shifted dramatically. A pattern of dispersed ownership by many small syndicates has given way to concentrated ownership by a few larger corporations. Ironically, this shift has been termed "going public," since the stocks of the take-over corporations are traded openly on various exchanges.

In short, some hospitals claim to be public, and some are public in fact by a strict definition of ownership. But most of them nevertheless operate as if they were private institutions. (For an overview, see Table 1 for the

TABLE I
HOSPITALS IN THE U.S.: OWNERSHIP CATEGORY AND PATIENT USE

	Number of hospitals	Percentage of hospitals	Percentage of patient admissions
Government (federal, state, local)	2211	35	29
Community, nonprofit	3320	53	58
For profit	757	12	13
TOTALS	6288	100%	100%

Source: *Hospital Statistics, 1975 Edition* (Chicago: American Hospital Association, 1975), pp. 19-21.

percentage distribution of ownership of all hospitals in the U.S., as well as the proportionate use of these hospitals by the public, as measured by hospital patient days.)

Internal Power Structure

A major reason for such "privateness" is the dual nature of hospital control: Power is shared between a professional quasi-organization called a medical staff, and a non-physician management. In theory, of course, there is a third and ultimate source of authority in the case of those hospitals having a governing body (board of trustees). The latter is supposed to balance and blend the various forces influencing hospital policy. In fact, however, the typical hospital is a medical menage-a-trois, whose balance is tipped in favor of the doctors. This is true for many reasons, including three discussed below.

Staff as Private Practitioners

First, a hospital's medical staff, though officially chartered by its governing body, conducts its affairs through leaders and committees selected by practicing physicians. The source of medical staff power lies not in the hospital as an institution but in its physicians as individual and independent practitioners.

In fact, the medical staff is not really a "staff" in any sense of hospital employment, but rather a group of private practitioners, each of whom has "staff privilege" in at least one hospital and usually at several. This gives the physician the formal right to admit patients to the hospital, treat them while they are there, and to order the use of various facilities and services financed and provided by the hospital. This situation is called by some a "physicians' workshop" and by others a "doctors' playpen." In short, while the medical staff of a hospital is a formal organization with some structure and responsibility, nevertheless it is better likened to an association of individual physicians, most of whom participate minimally.

Significantly, the term — staff privilege — suggests that the hospital is doing the physician a favor by extending privileges to him, but in fact the situation is the reverse. Hospitals live or die economically depending on whether doctors bring patients to them. Consequently physicians influence the selection of hospital equipment and services; what doctors want in a hospital they are likely to get. Competition among hospitals for such patronage causes duplication of expensive gadgetry.

"Interference" in Medical Practice

Another avenue of physician control is provided by legislation prohibiting any corporation, including a hospital, to "interfere" in the practice of medicine. Originally passed to stop both physicians and patients from being exploited — Painless Parker's Dental Corporation was the defendant in a precedent-setting lawsuit — these laws have since been used by organized medicine to insulate the profession from institutional control. For instance, laws prohibiting corporate medical practice (described below) make it possible for hospital-based radiologists and pathologists to practice as monopolists. They are shielded from whatever normal competitive forces of private medical practice exist, and

also set their own rates.

This is so because a hospital normally grants an exclusive franchise to a single individual or small group of specialists to operate its specialized equipment and supervise its technicians. It is, however, prohibited from setting prices for these services because this would constitute potential interference in the freedom of its radiologists and pathologists to practice medicine in a manner they feel to be professional and appropriate. According to an interpretation of the law, the hospital as an impersonal corporation could, by setting inadequate rates, prevent the physician from performing services he considers necessary for his patient's well-being. In effect, this allows the radiologist or pathologist to work both sides of the economic street: to reap the advantages of monopoly without the external price regulation that is usually imposed on businesses that enjoy a monopoly position.

Peer Review

A third form of medical control is "peer review," a complicated system of medical record review and committee work aimed at quality control of medical practice. It is based on the assumption that only physicians can pass judgment on the quality and acceptability of other physicians' professional practice of medicine. This leaves little room for supervision of medical staff by a hospital, particularly when the hospital is represented by a non-physician governing body or management.

Shifting Power From Physicians

But much of this is changing. Some hospitals are appointing their own full-time, permanent chiefs of clinical services, e.g., chief of medicine or chief of surgery, instead of the typical arrangement permitting such chiefs to be elected by members of the medical staff for one or two years of sporadic volunteer effort. The technology of hospital medicine demands institution-based physicians for many activities that previously could be supervised by volunteer members of a medical staff. Further, recent court decisions have given hospitals as institutions clear responsibility for the quality of the medical care provided on their premises. These decisions run counter to the laws prohibiting corporate interference in medical practice. Presumably in time the latter laws will be modified or invalidated.

Finally, even the physicians' exclusive role in quality review is being modified by new federal regulations and accreditation criteria. They state that while the professional judgment in quality review should remain in the hands of physicians, the process used and the statistical results must be known to and approved by the lay trustees of a hospital.

In short, de facto control of hospitals is moving away from the physicians, whose power has been widely shared among many individual practitioners, and exercised primarily through economic influence based on the ability of doctors to determine admission and occupancy rates. The shift in control toward the lay governing bodies, corporate trustees and managers of hospitals stems from increased dependency of many physicians on hospital-based technology and changes in legal responsibilities and obligations.

Community Participation

But other important power shifts are also occurring. Thus hospital control by private lay boards is giving way to major new forms of public accountability. This trend started in the health field with the community representation movement of the 1960's, spurred by federal funding policies that specified "maximum feasible participation" of the poor.[1] As applied to hospitals, this policy requires boards of trustees to be modified in composition and method of selection. It means that the underserved and the poor must be included as well as upper socio-economic business and professional interests. Moreover, there must be direct representation from different community interests, rather than the self-perpetuation of private trustees. Many hospital boards, however, consider "the community" a vague entity that cannot be directly represented, whereas the business and political institutions that make up the fabric of a community can be and are adequately represented.

So far, in fact, the community participation movement has had little impact on hospital decisionmaking structures. This is so primarily because the features of maximum feasible participation contained in federal law apply thus far to only a few hospitals that have received certain federal grants. Practically speaking, it is doubtful that the forms of community control advanced by the anti-establishment advocates of the late 60's can effectively govern an organization as complex as the typical hospital. While such influence has been effective in smaller primary and ambulatory health centers, it looks unworkable in larger, specialized, in-patient facilities. Further, since most U.S. hospitals are private, nonprofit corporations rather than public agencies, there is no public guarantee against new "community controlled" board members soon evolving patterns of private trusteeship similar to those they were supposed to replace.

Proponents of both approaches — "private trusteeship" and "power to the people" — can marshal persuasive arguments. But neither approach in "pure" form is likely to reduce the many and serious problems facing hospital governance. Hospitals have become so complex that volunteer board members lack both time and expertise required for proper control. Further, as noted earlier, the real power in most hospitals has resided in their medical staffs, not their boards. Consequently new forms of public accountability and control are needed and have already begun to evolve.

Public v. Consumer Control

Public control of hospitals should be distinguished from related forms of consumer influence. Consumer influence is exerted primarily through economic power, but the economic power of individuals in hospital affairs has never been substantial and is waning. The health industry lacks the basic ingredients of a market economy. The consumer is ignorant of what he needs and sources of reliable information are not available to him. Instead he must put himself in the hands of a physician, who is supposed to represent his best interests. But *in economic matters* the physician is likely to behave as a member of a professional cartel, rather than as a marketing agent for his patient. The individual

consumer's economic power is further blunted by various forms of collective purchasing: government reimbursement, union trust funds, and private insurance. In short, the individual consumer lacks an informed choice, his consumption is controlled by others, and whatever choosing among markets he might try to do would have infinitesimal financial impact on the hospitals involved.

On the other hand, *collective* economic power can have a substantial influence on hospitals, and is on the ascendancy. As a major purchaser of care, government is keenly interested in hospital cost control; union trust funds attempt to minimize the payout of money obtained on behalf of their members through collective bargaining; and insurance companies try to reduce the amounts they must pay for their clients' care. Moreover all these "third party payers" prefer new forms of public cost controls, rather than returning to private "market" mechanisms.

The Hospital as a Public Utility

The modern hospital fits the model of a public utility. It is cloaked with the public interest and essential to a community's well-being. Public supervision of hospitals is seen as a logical substitute for the public protection that free market competition is alleged to provide, but that is obviously missing from the health field.

Control by a regulatory body can take two principal forms (and there may be more): regulation by a general public utility commission or regulation by a special hospital commission. In either case, such regulation has three fundamental features, relating to (1) standards of safety and quality, (2) entry to and exit from the market, and (3) financial operations. Each of these is partially reflected in a patchwork of regulations that currently affect hospitals.

Licensing and Accreditation, Including Safety

All states have hospital licensing laws. They operate with minimal standards that generally focus on building safety rather than hospital functions and operations. Nor does hospital licensing deal per se with public need or convenience; if the sponsor of a hospital can build a safe structure he may obtain full permission to operate.

One reason licensing has remained a minimal control is the existence of a private accreditation mechanism. The latter provides some public protection in the case of institutions seeking accreditation — now approximately 75 percent of all hospitals in the U.S. Sponsored by several national hospital and medical associations, the Joint Commission on Accreditation of Hospitals (JCAH) applies standards that range beyond physical plant and include important clinical aspects of hospital operations. Although the JCAH has been criticized for laxity in many instances, such accreditation has had substantial leverage in private medical and hospital affairs. For instance, no physician may receive credit for training obtained in a nonaccredited hospital. In recent years, accreditation has also received an additional public sanction. The 1965 Social Security Amendments that established Medicare and Medicaid stipulated that no financial reimbursements would be allowed to nonaccredited hospitals except under unusual extenuating circumstances.

Franchising: Entry to the Market

Control of market entry is also emerging. In 1966 the "Partnership for Health" measure was signed into law, providing funds for local agencies that would be established specifically to perform comprehensive health planning.[2] Linked to this funding was the proviso that at least 50 percent of the boards of comprehensive health planning agencies must be consumers: an expression of mounting sentiment that professional domination of health care organizations had not worked in the public interest. These agencies were established throughout the nation, generally on a metropolitan basis for urban areas and on a regional basis for rural areas.

Many states then passed statutes granting the agencies a hospital-franchising function. Franchising differs from licensing in that the former grants the right to enter a market — in this case, permission for a new hospital to be built or an old hospital to expand or change its mix of services — only if the proposed change is determined to "serve the public need and convenience." If this decision is favorable, after a lengthy process including public hearings, a certificate of need is granted to the hospital applicant.

By mid-1975, certificate-of-need legislation had been enacted in 32 states, and defeated in 11. States without such laws are covered by regulations of the federal Social Security Administration: Interest expense and depreciation are excluded as allowable costs for reimbursement for care of Medicare patients in facilities constructed without the approval of comprehensive health planning agencies. Again, as in the case of accreditation, provisions for federal financial reimbursement have strengthened public regulation.

In addition, at the federal level, Congress in late 1974 passed new legislation providing for a nationwide network of "health services agencies" designed to supersede the comprehensive health planning agencies that had been established by the 1966 legislation noted above.[3] The 1974 law gave both the federal and state governments tighter control over health facility developments.

Problems in Franchising

How effectively hospital franchising serves the public interest has yet to be demonstrated. At least three problems have emerged. First, comprehensive health planning agencies are unprepared for their task; they are understaffed in number and quality of personnel required to determine public need. Further, they are guided by well-intentioned but uninformed board members whose decisionmaking may be capricious, or who are susceptible to artful manipulation by hospital officials acting in self-interest.

Second, the health industry has been characterized as a "non-system" in many communities, with no rational distribution and mix of health facilities and services. Too many small hospitals are operating inefficiently, and larger hospitals provide a needless duplication of services. It appears that this non-system is likely to be perpetuated if the established industry continues to influence the regulators.

The third problem is the lack of any obligation on the part of franchised hospitals to serve designated jurisdictions with some uniform pattern of basic service. In virtually all other regulated industries such an obligation is basic to the granting of a utility franchise. Certificate-of-need legislation for hospitals thus falls short of protections provided by typical franchise legislation whereby protected right to a territory is awarded in return for an obligation to provide that territory with a uniform level of service. In hospital certificate-of-need legislation no specific jurisdictions are designated, despite the obvious fact that in most regions there is a wide variation in the health services available to different populations. Some are overserved and some underserved.

Operational Control: Some Impediments

Operational control, the third function of utility regulation, is the newest to hospitals. In most regulated industries it is expressed through control of rates. Commission control of hospital rates is under active consideration by several state legislatures, and the organized hospital industry has expressed guarded support of the concept.[4] Implementation of this concept has been slowed by several factors, however, including hospitals' accounting systems and the wide range of services. Hospital accounting is generally insufficient for cost reporting and rate determination because definitions lack uniformity that would permit them to be applied across institutions. The wide range of services among hospitals, coupled with inadequate measures of hospital output, prevents meaningful control of rates. There are significant differences among hospitals in mix of patients, acuteness of patient illnesses, and services offered. The rate schedule for a typical hospital could easily contain 2000 or more constantly changing items. Thus rate setting for hospitals is vastly more complicated than for telephone services, air passenger routes, or railroad freight, whose unit measures of activity and of outcome are more readily identified.

Review of Rates by State Commissions

For these and other reasons, the hospital industry is actively supporting a compromise measure: creation of state-level hospital commissions that would mandate uniform accounting practices, require public reporting of costs, and review rates without actually determining them. Some hospital groups support actual rate setting if such rates are applied uniformly to all buyers, e.g., government, insurance companies, and self-paying patients. These proposals are intended to satisfy the public demand for increased accountability while not, at least initially, creating the problems that would arise if rates were set without an adequate information base. The aim is to establish utility commissions specifically for hospitals, and perhaps eventually for the health field generally, instead of factoring hospitals into state-level "generic" utility commissions. In view of both the complexity of hospital regulation and the fundamental differences between hospitals and other enterprises, this separation seems entirely appropriate.

As of late 1975, rate review regulation had been enacted in 16 states, was pending in 6 and had been defeated in 5. In some states organized medicine is actively opposed to such regulatory bills on the grounds that public control dilutes professional interest. In other states there is cautious support because rate review is seen as a lesser evil than rate setting.

Role of the Federal Government

The federal government exerts substantial indirect public control over the financial operation of hospitals through reimbursement formulae for the payment of Medicare and Medicaid patients. The formulae spell out allowable costs in detail and require annual cost reports. Increasing scrutiny is given to cost factors such as depreciation schedules, medical education expenses incurred by hospitals, "nonprudent" borrowing costs of capital, and business activity not related to hospital services. Further, hospital utilization is placed under increasingly strict control. Government and private insurance payers require detailed reports of operating costs, and extensive scrutiny of hospital financial systems. Quarterly and annual reports are reviewed, and certain incurred expenses are not allowed.

There are two main problems with this method. First, hospitals are continually in danger of having reimbursement denied for expenditures already made. Second, this reimbursement method contains no incentives for efficiency in hospital operation. As primarily nonprofit organizations, hospitals tend to incur increasingly higher expense levels and simply pass the cost along, whereas profitmaking institutions are motivated to contain costs in order to increase profits. In response to this situation, some Medicaid programs are establishing maximum cost reimbursement ceilings whose ultimate effect is widely debated by health economists. They do agree that applying ceilings to hospital costs already incurred is unfair, and further that the method still would provide no positive incentives for efficiency.

Price-Based Controls

As an alternative to cost-based reimbursement, price-based controls offer some advantages. Rates could be established in advance, thus avoiding the problems of retrospective reimbursement. Some incentive for efficiency would be created, since expenses must be reduced if prices cannot be raised.

This method has serious drawbacks, however. The rates would have to apply uniformly to all hospitals or at least to all hospitals in a particular size range or in a certain geographical area. In addition, rates would have to be based on some sort of averaging of cost performance among all hospitals in each rate-setting group; yet this procedure would not recognize the significant differences among hospitals in mix of patients served, relative severity of patient conditions, and scope of services. Also, a "tariff schedule" of hundreds and even thousands of individual hospital services would be extremely cumbersome for a commission to administer, even if qualified personnel were available for the task.

There is also the question of profit-type incentive in an industry composed of nonprofit firms. With rates fixed, why would hospitals act to reduce costs in order to maximize profits, if profits were simply an embarrassment as evidence of "making money on the sick"? Where would the profits be distributed? There are no stockholders, and trustees are prohibited by law from

obtaining any gain from their office. Profits could be ploughed back into new capital developments, but this could operate against the public interest if there are already too many hospitals and too much duplication of expensive equipment.

Some Pitfalls

The evolution of public regulation in the health field has been piecemeal and multiphased, and as a consequence there has been misunderstanding as well as conscious and unconscious noncompliance. Further development of public regulation raises several questions: Would more complete regulation freeze the industry into its present inefficient pattern of sizes and types of hospitals? Would regulation act simply as a protective device for the established forces in the market place?

In other industries regulation has led to restructuring, usually concentration. An obvious flaw of the present hospital system is the existence of too many small institutions that duplicate each others' services. But is extensive concentration a desirable alternative? It may be socially useful for two hospitals to compete in nursing care, i.e., each hospital striving to better the other in this service; but dysfunctional for the same two hospitals to compete in radiologic services, where expensive capital equipment would have to be duplicated and informal controls among radiologists would prohibit open competition.

Definition of geographic jurisdiction remains difficult. The proper "catchment area" for an obstetric service, for example, is clearly different from and smaller than that for heart transplantation. Yet if certain providers are to be franchised to serve the public and in so doing obtain monopoly or oligopoly status, then some geographic basis must be developed for their concomitant obligation to provide services uniformly.

Measures of public service for hospitals are generally inadequate, and the performance of a hospital is difficult to assess. Criteria developed for other regulated industries — counts of power failure, telephone message units, air passenger miles — cannot be paralleled in the health field.

Rate setting in most regulated industries is based on rate-of-return, which in turn is based on calculation of the capital necessary for maintenance and expansion of service. Hospitals are labor-intensive rather than capital-intensive enterprises. The known substitutes for capital-based rate setting are much more complex, and the agencies that administer them could thus become immense red tape bureaucracies staffed by persons attempting to double-guess hospitals' local managements on hundreds of items although they know little about hospital operations.

The Focus of Regulation

Finally, there is the question of the proper focus of regulation. Hospitals are slowly moving from professional to public control. But even if hospitals become truly public institutions there would still be a large unregulated element in health care provision: the practice of medicine. Hospitals are targets of public attention because of their size and corporate impersonality. But simply regulating hospitals without also influencing the business of medical practice would be an inadequate solution, as emphasized by the recent dramatic strikes by anesthesiologists over malpractice insurance.

In the present era of "health care as a right," the real problems of access to medical care are related more to primary and first-encounter care by physicians than to the secondary and specialized activities of typical hospitals. The only way for hospitals to make a crucial difference in this larger realm is for them to increase their control of physicians. While this would be total anathema to the medical profession, it is a beginning trend that many advocates of health care reorganization view as necessary and desirable.

Summary

Professional control of hospitals is giving way to public control, but this trend tends to be obscured by the operation of often conflicting internal forces and external regulations. An important factor is the economics of rising health care costs, medical practice and hospital operations. This complex of forces frustrates those advocates of hospital reform who would like a clear, clean and powerful mechanism of control and change. It is also a useful brake on extremism in a situation where no one can describe the limits of reform or what it would accomplish. Despite the frustrations and inconsistencies of the present pattern of hospital regulation, it does contain checks and balances that should remain until several problems are solved. Until more is known about the effects of increased regulation of hospitals as utilities, the present barriers to complete regulation are indeed socially useful. Thus to place the total regulatory package of safety and quality, market entry, and fiscal operations under the jurisdiction of a single hospital utility commission in each state would invite new forms of stifling bureaucracy, political caprice, and incompetent administration of hospital affairs.

If hospitals were to be regulated as utilities, the greatest potential benefit would probably be the requirement that provides hospitals' specifically defined populations with some uniform standard of service, or "improved access." This is a different public benefit than the cost containment that currently attracts most politicians to the concept. In order to provide uniform service, most hospitals will have to link up with other hospitals and other medical providers in an area to form consortia or federations. This would be a useful phenomenon, since most U.S. hospitals are too small for efficient operation and such federations could increase efficiency. The risk is that the same phenomenon could lead to overconcentrations of power in the oligopolies and monopolies whose effects are beginning to come to light in other regulated industries.

Finally, increased regulation will probably minimize even further the role of economic incentives in promoting hospital efficiency and creativity. In theory and in practice it is possible to have both increased regulation and increased motivation for efficiency. A number of recent experiments and demonstration projects provide economic rewards to hospitals if their actual operations cost less (after some defined period of time, usually a year) than had been expected.[5] Such "incentive reimbursement" methods are in marked contrast to the present methods of retrospective reimbursement based on accumulated costs, a system that rewards nothing but the accumulation of more costs. As desirable and as fundamental as this change to incentive reimbursement seems, the likelihood is great that state legislators will choose utility regulation of hospitals. They may even be pushed into such a move by hospital spokesmen who view regulation as a protective device. But the best means to advance the public interest would be the further selective development of regulation, with new approaches that strongly reward efficient and effective hospital performance.

NOTES

[1] John S. McNamara, "Communities and Control of Health Services," *Inquiry*, September 1972, pp. 64-69.

[2] "Partnership for Health" was the name given to the Comprehensive Health Planning and Services Act of 1966 (PL 89-749).

[3] The 1974 measure was the National Health Planning and Resources Development Act (PL 93-641).

[4] See *Ameriplan*, American Hospital Association Special Committee on the Provision of Health Services (Chicago: 1970).

[5] Bruce A. Goldstrom, *Prospective Payment to Hospitals, Methods of Rate Determination: A Review*, Occasional Papers in Hospital and Health Administration, #2 (School of Public Health, University of California, Berkeley, 1973).

Social Problems and Remedial Policies

Vol. 16   No. 6   December 1975

JUVENILE DELINQUENCY: SEEKING EFFECTIVE PREVENTION

By
Tom Higgins
Public Policy Analyst

Delinquency Prevention: Introduction

Prevention refers to at least two types of strategies aimed at reducing youth crime: the first is youth-centered, while the second focuses on social change and community development. Youth-centered strategies provide counseling, work, education or other services primarily for young people who have committed one or more minor offenses and, rarely, some who have committed major offenses. These efforts also stress diverting the early, minor offender from the criminal justice system before he or she is involved with the juvenile court, probation and rehabilitation institutions. Figure 1 shows how prevention programs using diversion accept young people at various stages in the juvenile justice processing system. Advocates of such a prevention strategy (or diversion strategy as it is sometimes called) believe it reduces the stigma associated with the juvenile justice system. Further, they predict that avoidance of stigma can reduce future crime.

The second type of prevention strategy (also called sociogenic) stresses social change and community development. The focus is on changing the way institutions, especially schools, respond to youth, and increasing the use of resources available to youth in their communities. An example is the encouragement of industry and schools to develop vocational and recreational programs that would benefit many if not all the young people in a community instead of focusing solely on the early, minor offender.

While no community-based delinquency prevention programs rely exclusively on either of these two strategies, programs in California and other states do tend to stress one or the other. Several of the Youth Service Bureaus (YSBs), which developed out of the President's Commission on Law Enforcement, exist in California and provide services to minor offenders diverted from the juvenile justice system. Three Youth Development Programs (YDPs) now operate in California (under the sponsorship of the U.S. Department of Health, Education, and Welfare - HEW) stressing the sociogenic approach. Both the YDP programs and the YSB programs also treat early, minor offenders. Finally, the California Council on Criminal Justice Projects — now under the Office of Criminal Justice Planning — employs a primarily youth-centered approach, with counseling as the most common service. The projects are sponsored under the Omnibus Crime Control Act and number about 140.[1]

Does Prevention Work?

Does delinquency prevention work? Is there sufficient evidence to recommend prevention programs over rehabilitation or other programs and policies designed to reduce delinquency? If prevention efforts appear worthwhile, is there evidence to show which are most effective? Finally, should local and state decisionmakers support the development or expansion of delinquency prevention programs? These are important questions for youth, youth advocacy groups, legislators, city and county officials, and taxpayers and voters as a whole.

Some tentative answers emerge from a review of the probable causes of delinquency and evaluations of prevention programs. The most important conclusions are that many of the important causes of delinquency are difficult to treat by public policies and programs; that treatments underlying most prevention strategies, including diversion, tutoring and youth employment, are not generally effective; and that counseling and adult employment programs may be effective in prevention and therefore certainly deserve more testing in the

Note: Tom Higgins conducted the study on which this paper is based both for the California Department of Finance and in partial fulfillment of the Masters Degree at the Graduate School of Public Policy at UC Berkeley. The study was selected by a faculty committee as one of the best papers written in 1974. Higgins is currently a consultant to the Urban Institute in Washington, D.C. By publishing this study as a *Public Affairs Report*, the Institute of Governmental Studies continues to encourage and give recognition to student writing of high calibre.

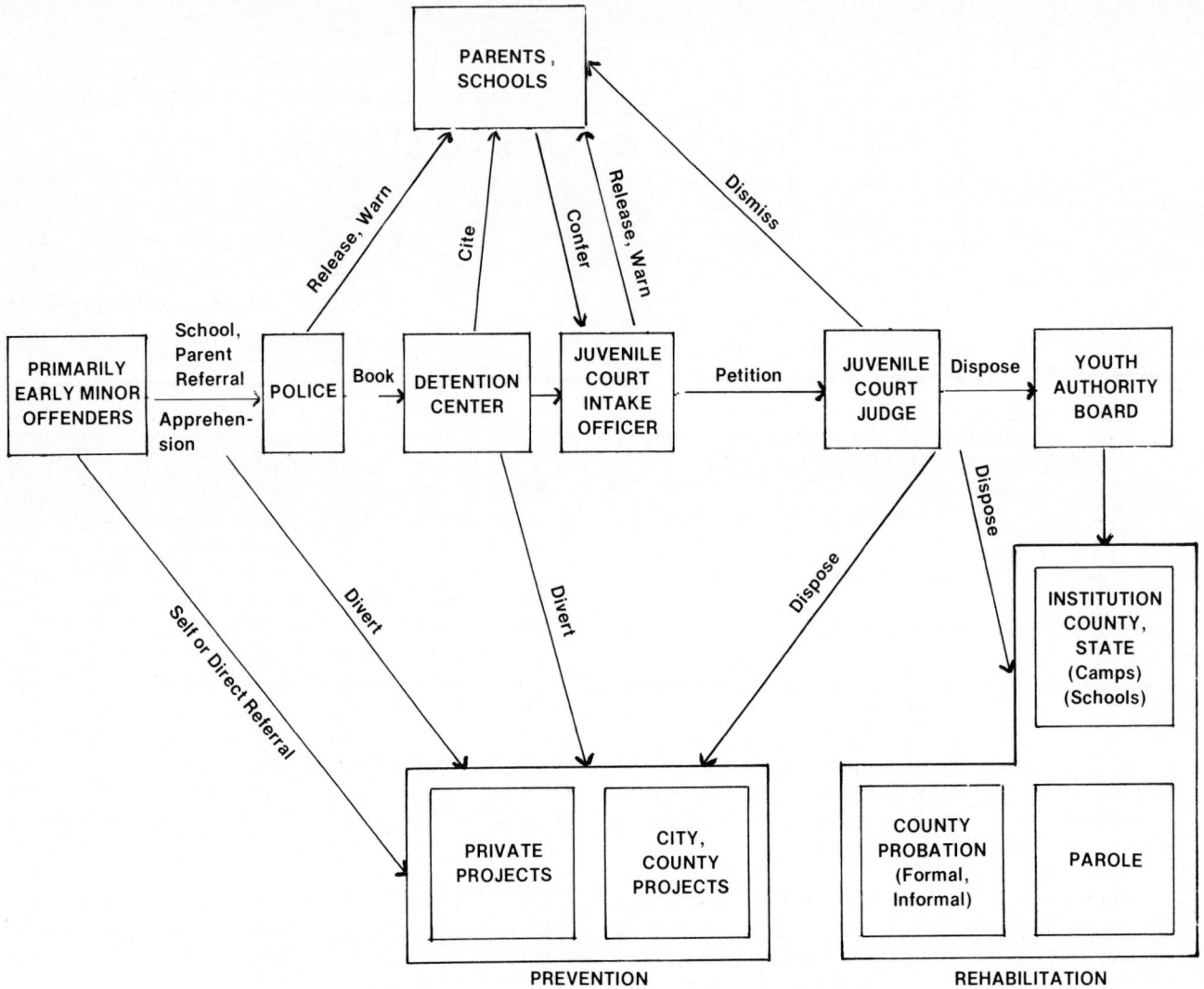

Figure 1
The Flow of Youth Through the Juvenile Justice System

future. Finally, there are some workable experimental designs that should be incorporated into any future delinquency prevention programs sponsored by the state or localities.

Is Prevention Needed?

In California and other states, prevention programs typically expend a major share of their resources in the treatment of early, minor offenders rather than the serious, repeat offenders (or recidivists). It is therefore important to ask whether the early, minor offenders impose large or small costs on society. In short, does it seem necessary or helpful to try to treat these young people?

It is possible to estimate the amount and type of future detected crime that will be committed by youth first apprehended (i.e., caught, but not necessarily arrested) for a minor offense. By using non-index crime as a definition of minor crime,[2] we may make such an estimate through secondary analysis of data provided by a recent study of 10,000 young people born in Philadelphia and followed from ages 10 to 18.[3] According to this analysis, 1,000

youth who are currently apprehended for their first non-index offenses could be expected to bring about a future stream of identifiable direct monetary costs amounting to about $1 million (in 1975 dollars)[4] for *known* offenses. These include only the direct costs of crime against persons and property, not those related to apprehension, prosecution and correction associated with these crimes, nor such costs as the suffering and loss of opportunities that may beset young offenders.

The monetary cost associated with the stream of *known* offenses should be considered a low estimate, because the volume of actual crime is much greater than the volume of apprehended or known crime. We find, in fact, that each 1,000 early, minor offenders who are apprehended represent a stream of monetary costs in actual crime (both known and unknown) that total $11 million (rather than $1 million) in 1975 dollars.[5]

Costs for California

These estimates have significant implications for California. At current rates, there will be about 65,000 juvenile *arrests* for minor offenses in the state in 1975.[6]

Figure 2

Disposition of 1000
Actual Juvenile Offenses

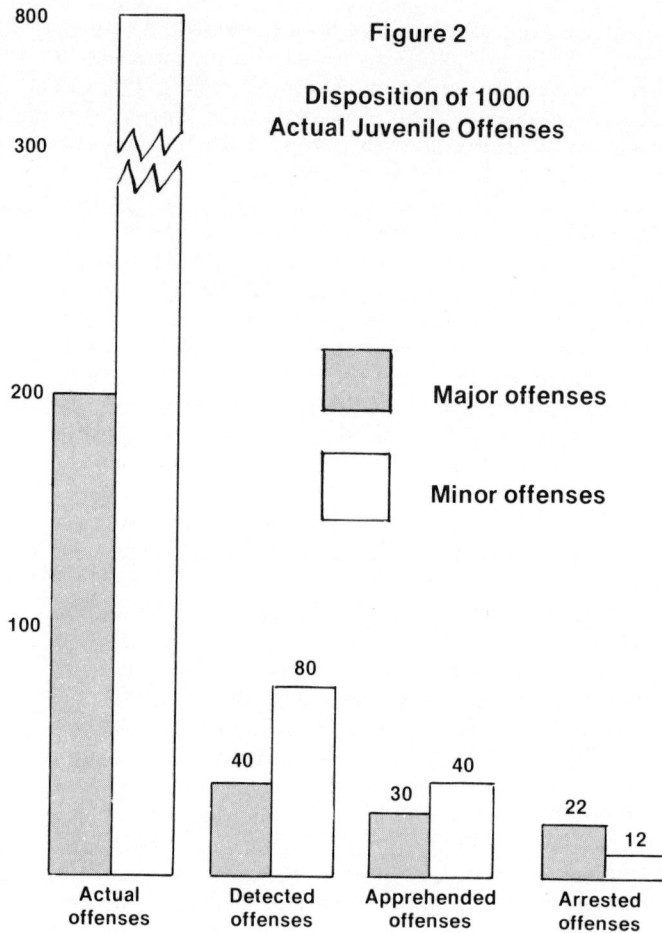

800

300

200

100

80

40

30

40

22

12

Major offenses

Minor offenses

Actual offenses

Detected offenses

Apprehended offenses

Arrested offenses

important to understand that "causes" here means "makes more likely, all other variables taken into account."

Nationwide and international research into the causes of delinquency is voluminous and much of it is contradictory, but there are some consistent findings in the most convincing studies. Three important kinds of causes command substantial evidence and growing certainty, but unfortunately, most of them appear to be difficult to attack by public policy measures. First, there is something about family relationships, about the supervision and affection, the communication and ties between parents and youth that causes delinquency when diminished. Second, diminished attachment and commitment to school causes delinquency. Third, adult unemployment causes delinquency.

In many affluent societies, where family income and employment are stable, research has demonstrated that delinquency can result when supervision, and affection and communication between parents and children, are lacking. In poor societies, even with death and divorce among parents, delinquency is not likely if relatives and friends supervise the youth.[9] Thus, there is evidence for the unique importance to delinquency of family variables. From the simple and often criticized correlational studies of the Gluecks (1950) to the more careful work of Nye (1958), to the extensive longitudinal studies of McCord and McCord (1964), to the recent cross-cultural work of Rosenquist and Megargee (1969), and the causal analysis of Hirschi (1968) — affection and attachment, intimacy and communication and identification between child and parents are found to be important in their effect on delinquency.

Similarly well documented is the unique effect on delinquency of educational commitment, aspiration and attainment. In the 1967 Presidential Commission report on delinquency and youth crime, Jackson Toby indicated that educational variables were thought to be important: "For children unwilling or unable to learn, school is a place where the battle against society is likely to begin."[10] Additional subsequent research has confirmed the importance of the youth's relation to school, either with respect to frustration of legitimate expectation for scholastic success or a simple lack of caring about school and achievement.[11]

Finally, as even a cursory scanning of crime reports during times of high unemployment suggests, delinquency is more likely to occur when family heads are unemployed. Belton Fleisher's study is most convincing in confirming this suspicion. He examined delinquency rates in 101 U.S. cities and concluded, "If 10% of the labor force in a high delinquency area were typically unemployed and if successful labor market policies were to lower the rate to, say 5%... (this) decrease might lower the delinquency rate by 10%."[12] This is not to suggest, however, that income operates wholly independently of familial and educational factors. At least two studies, for example, indicated that youth from affluent families who fail in school show delinquency rates only slightly lower than those of low-income offspring.[13]

This evidence about the causes of delinquency is not

This number of arrests in turn implies apprehensions of 216,000 minor offenses (every 12 of such arrests implies 40 apprehended offenses — see Figure 2). Nonetheless, only about 39 percent of the minor-crime apprehensions are for first-time offenses (the remaining apprehensions relate to minor offenses of recidivists).[7] Consequently, during 1975 in California about 84,500 first-time juvenile offenders will be *apprehended* for minor crimes.[8] (Note that an "apprehension" is a recorded encounter between police and juvenile that may or may not end in arrest.) The dollar figures cited in the preceding paragraph suggest that these juveniles will commit actual future offenses costing $929.5 million (84,500 x $11 million).

Thus it is clear that prevention programs are taking aim at a sizeable problem. The typical target group for prevention programs creates enormous accountable costs and uncertain but undoubtedly burdensome costs in terms of human suffering and anguish. Considering the magnitude of the problems, can they be solved? Can suitable policies be designed to attack the causes of delinquency? For that matter, can the causes themselves be identified?

The Causes of Delinquency

The causes of delinquency are analogous to the causes of pneumonia or skin infections, where a set of variables taken together makes an outcome more likely. It is encouraging for policy makers concerned with designing prevention programs. Can public policies influence parental supervision or affection, or educational commitment and aspiration? Of all the causes, adult employment is perhaps the only variable that is relatively easy to manipulate by government policy. Yet, at present, government policy apparently is encouraging unemployment in an attempt to reduce inflation. Hence, while policy analysts or youth advocacy groups might press for new policies to reduce unemployment, decision-makers are in the awkward position of having to make a trade-off between reduced delinquency through employment strategies and other national goals.

Delinquency Prevention Programs: Some Results

The best evidence to date about the causes of delinquency suggests that it may be difficult to develop programs and policies to alleviate them. Indeed, much of the available evidence on the outcomes of prevention programs confirms this suspicion. For example, five delinquency-prevention projects employing youth-centered strategies, and spanning the years 1937 to 1965, achieved no success. These projects employed control groups; they treated primarily early minor offenders, and offered tutoring, family counseling and job development.[14]

More recently, the Seattle Atlantic Street Center, employing good experimental designs and providing service on a more intensive and longer-term basis than earlier prevention programs, also showed no differences in the offense rates between those treated and the untreated control groups.[15] Here again, services were youth centered, and involved counseling, referral to various community resources and recreation. Also a recent review of about 100 delinquency prevention programs appearing in the literature since 1965 concluded, "Indeed, no (prevention) method has been demonstrated to be consistently effective..."[16]

In California, several youth-centered prevention projects have been evaluated by government agencies and several private consultant firms, with mixed results. Overall, the results lead to the conclusion that prevention strategies generally do not work to reduce delinquency among early, minor offenders.

The Office of Criminal Justice Planning (OCJP), monitoring projects funded under the Omnibus Crime Control Act, has completed several prevention-project evaluations. Few have employed experimental designs or other valid evaluation methods, although three projects have sufficiently approximated good experimental design to be of interest. The latter are the Sacramento Probation Department 601 and 602 Diversion Project, the Santa Clara County Probation Department Prevention Project and the San Diego Probation Department Project. The projects provide a variety of services to youth, including counseling and referral to community services.[17]

The evaluations show that the main method of treatment — counseling at a point before the early, minor offenders are petitioned and appear in court — has not generally reduced delinquent behavior.[18] Moreover, there is another indication that the OCJP

prevention programs have not been successful. Although several California counties with significant numbers of OCJP prevention programs show a leveling off and decrease in juvenile hall admissions over the past few years, several other counties without OCJP programs also show similar leveling off and decreases. Thus, the overall results of the OCJP prevention programs are not positive.

In addition, The California Youth Authority has evaluated several California Youth Service Bureaus.[19] The Youth Authority report concluded that arrests were reduced in a majority of the areas served by the YSBs during the three-year period of evaluation. In some cases the declines in arrest are small and could be due to random fluctuations in arrest rates. Furthermore, an important function of the bureaus was to encourage local police to refer youth to them rather than make arrests. Consequently, police records of community arrests could be declining because of a change in the arrest practices of police, not because of a decline in actual delinquent behavior.

Behavioral Research and Evaluation Corporation (BREC) in Colorado has evaluated several sociogenic Youth Development Programs under HEW sponsorship. Most of the programs evaluated by the firm — many outside of California — show that project youth were generally no less likely to engage in delinquent behavior than the comparison group on probation. This result is particularly significant because the impact of the programs was evaluated by the change in self-reported delinquent behavior of project youth compared to a matched control group on probation. Such an evaluation has considerable merit because of its independence of official or reported delinquency rates, which, as we have seen, can give a false indication of program effectiveness.

Lessons from Orange County and Richmond, California

BREC did find that one, the Community Services Project in California's Orange County, resulted in significant differences in offense rates of well-matched treatment and control groups. What appears to be working here? In terms of content, the Orange County program is not unique. Short-term, individual, group and family counseling are the major treatment strategies. The distinguishing factor in the Orange County project is the large number of community services that cooperated from the outset, a cooperation that characterizes the project's sociogenic approach. Five major county departments, including mental health, probation, welfare, education, and health, agreed on precisely which services would be provided to referrals. It is impossible to say whether this aspect of the program resulted in successful impact, but there is some evidence to support such a conclusion.

No link was demonstrated between delinquent behavior and the sense of stigma associated with processing in the juvenile justice system. In fact, youth in the prevention program came to feel they were negatively labeled, as did the control group on probation. But the important point is that no connection was established between this sense of labeling and the frequency of delinquent behavior. Moreover there is no evidence that diversion from the juvenile justice system reduced either labeling or delinquent behavior.

The Police Department Diversion Project in Richmond, California demonstrated, among other things, that a valid experimental design can be employed without unduly interfering with the normal operations of a police department. The Richmond project created stratified pools of juvenile offenders, allowing serious offenders with no more than two prior felonies to enter a pool randomly assigned to community service agencies, police counseling and probation. Minor offenders, on the other hand, entered a pool randomly assigned to warning and release by the police, or to community services. (Random assignment, of course, helps to insure that youth with a variety of educational experiences, crime histories and family backgrounds receive the same treatment and control, so that any successful results can be attributed to the treatment strategies and not to a unique sample of treated youth.)

An important finding to date is that simply releasing and warning youth — a diversionary tactic in the sense that it minimizes contact with the juvenile justice system — is much less effective than referral to community agencies.[20] Again, the effectiveness of programs involving diversion alone must be called into question.

Finally, a tentative but important conclusion from the Richmond project evaluation is that continuous counseling appears to be effective, and also that it is more effective than immediate or "crisis" counseling. Neither employment nor tutorial services, however, were found to be effective in reducing delinquency.

Weighing Other Sociogenic Approaches

It is possible to imagine other sociogenic approaches in addition to those employed in some of the evaluated projects. For example, youth and adult employment programs serving the whole community, rather than those serving only early, minor offenders, might also be called sociogenic. Also, as noted earlier, there is a good statistical basis for believing that adult employment programs may reduce delinquency. However, the impact of community adult employment programs on delinquency has not yet been evaluated.

On the other hand, it is becoming clear that at least one type of youth employment program — the Neighborhood Youth Corps — has not lowered delinquency. According to a recent study, NYC "did not reduce criminality on the part of enrollees while the youth were working in the program or after they left it."[21] Moreover, as we have seen, several ineffective prevention programs offered youth-employment components.[22]

Turning from employment programs to education and family counseling projects for communities as a whole, the evaluation picture is not much clearer. The best evaluations tell us only whether the projects were successful in specific efforts, such as returning drop-outs to schools, raising the achievement levels of failing students, or improving parents' understanding of childrearing practices. Possible connections between these outcomes and a reduction in any measure of delinquency have not been explored for many of the

programs, such as those sponsored by the Office of Economic Opportunity, or those operating under the Elementary and Secondary Education Act of 1965, the Vocational Education Act of 1963, and the Manpower Development and Training Act of 1962.

Conclusions and Recommendations

This review of some of the costs of delinquency to society, the probable causes of delinquency, and the results of delinquency prevention programs has reached an inescapable conclusion: While the early, minor offender deserves the attention of policy makers, no current prevention strategies can be confidently recommended. The best evidence to date indicates that a major tactic of prevention projects, diverting youth from the criminal justice system, does not reduce delinquency. Counseling has been effective in a few cases, but in many projects it has not. Nor have tutoring or job development for youth shown positive results.

Nevertheless, the review does support a hunch about effective strategies: Continuous counseling of the kind seen in the Richmond project, or the massive cooperation of several community agencies and resources as in Orange County, *may be* effective strategies. Certainly they are worth further evaluation, particularly in light of the relatively low costs of prevention — typically less than $1000 per case per year.

The evidence does not support *increased* state funding of particular prevention projects and instead argues that any new or renewed programs should be small, carefully evaluated and funded for short terms. Funding should be contingent largely upon the merit of the experimental designs. For example, the experimental design procedures of the Richmond project perhaps could be incorporated into ongoing or new prevention projects sponsored by local communities and the state. Such designs, repeated in several settings, might lead to a better understanding of the types of counseling that appear to be effective, at least part of the time.

Further, operators and evaluators of prevention programs should find ways to measure delinquency independently of police action and records. Self-reporting has been used successfully by the Behavioral Research and Evaluation Corporation for this purpose, and also appears in the most rigorous and recent large-scale causal analysis of delinquency.[23] This is not to say, however, that the officially reported rates are never appropriate for an evaluation.

When there are extensive police referrals to a prevention project, it is possible to determine whether declines in official community arrest rates reflect anything more than a simple increase in diversion by examining the numbers and nature of both the referrals and youth arrested. A decline in community petty theft rates, for example, may be much more substantial than random fluctuations or the numbers of petty theft offenders diverted to the project. If so, this would be evidence of a successful project, provided that petty thefts are not also declining in a control area with socioeconomic characteristics similar to those in the project area.

There are significant policy implications in findings that both adult unemployment and lack of school commitment among youth are probably important causes of delinquency. Youth advocacy groups and state analysts should press for experimental designs to be incorporated into any state-sponsored adult employment programs, and into any innovative educational programs intended to increase commitment to and interest in school. Even relatively simple designs, such as the use of roughly comparable groups without random assignment to treatment and control, will probably help show if the experimental programs have any substantial impact on delinquency.

Finally, because there are many advocates of prevention who believe it to be more humane and less costly than rehabilitation, the federal and state governments as well as private, non-profit groups, will probably initiate some new prevention programs in the future. If so, a reasonable approach would be to start with our best hunches about what works. Accordingly, new projects (1) should include efforts to provide job referral and development services for unemployed parents of early, minor offenders; (2) should not employ youth or tutor youth directly; (3) should try a variety of counseling techniques that might facilitate better supervision by parents and communication between parents and youth; (4) should strive to get agreement among a variety of community agencies and schools — before programs are begun — as to precisely what services will be provided; and (5) should incorporate experimental designs that have proved workable in at least some California projects.

NOTES

[1] See Robert Lawson, *An Assessment and Directory of Federally Funded Delinquency Prevention Projects in California*, a report of the California Council on Criminal Justice (November 1973).

[2] Non-index crimes include misdemeanors, petty theft, and other minor offenses that would be considered crimes if committed by an adult; they exclude delinquent tendencies, such as incorrigibility and running away. Index crimes are such major crimes as robbery, burglary, grand theft, auto theft, rape, and homicide, but not drug law violations.

[3] Marvin Wolfgang, Robert Figlio, Thorsten Sellin, *Delinquency in a Birth Cohort* (Chicago: University of Chicago Press, 1972).

[4] A detailed explanation of the cost calculation is presented in *Recommendations for the State of California*, Tom Higgins, for the California Department of Finance, 1975.

[5] Ibid. This estimate holds for a discount rate of either 5% or 10%.

[6] Data from the annual statistics published by the California Bureau of Criminal Statistics. As noted above, delinquent tendencies such as incorrigibility and running away are excluded.

[7] Marvin Wolfgang, et al., op. cit., Matrix 11.1.

[8] This assumes that few young people are first apprehended for multiple offenses.

[9] See Jackson Toby, "Affluence and Adolescent Crime," in *Task Force Report: Juvenile Delinquency and Youth Crime*, The President's Commission on Law Enforcement and Administration of Justice, Vol. 4, Appendix H (Washington, D.C.: 1967), pp. 132-144.

[10] Ibid., p. 143.

[11] See Travis Hirschi, *Causes of Delinquency* (Berkeley: University of California Press, 1969); also Delos H. Kelly and William T. Pink, "School Commitment, Youth Rebellion and Delinquency," *Criminology*, 10 (4): 473-485 (February 1973).

[12] Belton Fleisher, *The Economics of Delinquency* (Chicago: Quadrangle Books, 1966), p. 97.

[13] Erdman B. Palmore and Phillip E. Hammond, "Interacting Factors in Juvenile Delinquency," *American Sociological Review*, 29 (6): 848-854 (December 1964). Also see Albert J. Reiss and Albert L. Rhodes, "The Distribution of Juvenile Delinquency in the Social Class Structure," *American Sociological Review*, 26 (5): 720-732 (October 1961).

[14] William C. Berleman and Thomas W. Steinburn, "The Value and Validity of Delinquency Prevention Experiments," *Crime and Delinquency*, 15 (4): 471-478 (October 1969).

[15] William C. Berleman, James R. Seaburg, Thomas W. Steinburn, "The Delinquency Prevention Experiment of the Seattle Atlantic Street Center: A Final Evaluation," *Social Service Review*, 46 (3): 323-346 (September 1972).

[16] Michael C. Dixon, William E. Wright, *Juvenile Delinquency Prevention Programs, Supplemental Report Containing Abstracts and Rating of Empirical Studies*, Institute on Youth and Social Development, George Peabody College for Teachers, Nashville, Tennessee (October 1974), p. 3.

[17] See *Evaluation of Crime Control Programs in California: A Review*, California Council on Criminal Justice, Sacramento, Calif. (April 1973).

[18] The Sacramento 602 projects shows differences in the recidivism rates for the experimental and control groups of about 10-15% for a period of seven months after treatment. However, it appears that juveniles with cases pending in court and with prior commitment to the Youth Authority may have been excluded from the treatment group but not from the controls. Clearly, this practice biases the results in favor of the treatment. In Santa Clara County the project shows no difference in recidivism between treated and control groups after nine months. In the San Diego project, treated youth did have fewer arrests than the controls in the one year of follow-up.

[19] Elaine Duxbury, *Evaluation of Youth Service Bureaus*, California Department of Youth Authority (November 1973).

[20] Some researchers believe that *any* action minimizing penetration into the juvenile justice system should be considered diversion. See Donald Cressey and Robert McDermott, *Diversion From the Juvenile Justice System*, National Assessment of Juvenile Corrections, Ann Arbor: University of Michigan (June 1973). See p. 8.

[21] Gerald Robin, "Anti-Poverty Programs and Delinquency," *Journal of Criminal Law, Criminology and Police Science*, 60 (3): 323-331 (September 1969). A control group was employed in this study.

[22] The most recent long term evaluation of employment programs for youth involved in prevention programs concludes, "The long term assessment suggests that the work program was related to increased involvement in official delinquency." See James C. Hackler, John L. Hagan, "Work and Teaching Machines as Delinquency Prevention Tools: A Four-Year Follow-Up," *Social Service Review*, 49 (1): 92-106 (March 1975). See p. 92.

[23] Hirschi, op. cit.

Educational Planning and Policy

Vol. 17   No. 1   February 1976

A PRESCRIPTION FOR STUDENT AID: BETTER INFORMATION ON POST-SECONDARY EDUCATION

Report of a Policy Seminar

By
Wellford W. Wilms
Seminar Chairman
Center for Research & Development
in Higher Education

Introduction

Seventy-five years ago, students attending the few existing California colleges and universities were generally assured of well-paying jobs and a privileged place in society. They came from a narrow segment of the population — generally from the middle and upper classes — and needed little more than word-of-mouth information about college choices and the ways those choices were likely to influence their lives. Since then, California has led the nation in developing a postsecondary educational system that opens educational doors to almost anyone who wants to enter.

In 1974, 22 out of every 100 California adults were enrolled in some postsecondary course of study, ranging from dental hygiene and cosmetology to English literature, law, and medicine. This cornucopia of courses is offered by an extensive postsecondary system: 302 adult education programs, nearly 1800 proprietary vocational schools (schools that operate for profit), 103 community colleges, 83 private accredited colleges and universities, 19 state colleges and universities, and nine campuses of the University of California.

But because of a glaring lack of information, students are hard pressed to choose among options in this wealth of educational opportunities. Clearly postsecondary schools should provide more information, but who needs the information, and what topics should it cover? Who should collect the data and how should they be made public? How much will the necessary information cost and who should pay for it? What kinds of materials are already available? What would be the most effective governmental arrangements for collecting useful data,

auditing and publishing it? Would this require new legislation? Are any unintended consequences likely to occur, possibly making some solutions worse than existing problems? What difference does added information make in student choices?

The Seminar and Its Sponsors

These and related questions were discussed at a recent seminar sponsored by the California Postsecondary Education Commission, the Institute of Governmental Studies, and the Center for Research and Development in Higher Education at the University of California, Berkeley. During the session, 47 persons — legislative staff members, researchers, vocational educators, college and school administrators, consumer advocates and students — developed the conclusions and recommendations summarized in this paper. (Seminar participants are listed at the end.) The following discussion treats significant public policy issues in postsecondary education, and suggests specific recommendations for dealing with such problems in California.

Equality or Inequality?

The California postsecondary education system grew out of a desire to provide equal opportunities for all. It developed like an organism, slowly becoming larger and more complex in trying to accommodate large numbers of students from different backgrounds and with different learning styles and goals. Proponents of the existing complicated system maintain that it meets diverse student needs, and provides a broad cross section of the population with educational opportunities on a reasonably equal basis.

But findings by Hansen and Weisbrod, Karabel, Wilms, and others indicate that the way the existing educational system works it may actually do more to maintain and reinforce class inequalities than to overcome them. For example, Hansen and Weisbrod[1] found that students from families with the highest socioeconomic status are likely to attend the University of California. Students of middle status tend toward the state university system; and those from the lowest socioeconomic strata are most likely to go to a community college. They also note that regressive taxation forces the poor to pay proportionately more than the wealthy to support the elite university system.

Vocational Education: The Lowest Rung

Moreover Karabel showed that within the postsecondary system, the least advantaged students tend to occupy the lowest rungs of the ladder — the occupational or vocational programs.[2] A national study of public and proprietary vocational training at the Center for Research and Development in Higher Education at U.C. Berkeley indicated a further distinction.[3] That is, students attending proprietary vocational programs have even fewer resources than their counterparts who attend similar programs in nearby public community colleges. Proprietary school students more often drop out of high school or have come through the low-status vocational or general high school programs, have more trouble with language, and are more often from ethnic minorities than students in the public colleges and universities.

Even more important was the study's finding that, while proprietary school graduates fare as well in the labor market as community college graduates, both groups take relatively low-level and low-paying jobs after graduation. The schools are highly effective in training and placing students in low-status clerical and service worker jobs. But they are not effective in placing graduates in higher-status technical and professional jobs, since these are generally reserved for graduates of four-year colleges. In short, the Berkeley study added more evidence to the growing literature that indicates that simply providing access to a wide range of schools may not do much to equalize opportunities.

The mere existence of a range of types of institutions, which are theoretically open to all, does not equalize effective access or opportunities, because in fact people from different backgrounds and with different opportunity levels tend to go to different institutions, follow different educational programs, and pursue different career lines. For example, if other things were equal, an accounting student at U.C. Berkeley would more likely find a higher-paying, higher-status job than an accounting student at a community college or proprietary school, presumably because years of schooling and the school's prestige are valued more highly than technical ability. Worse still, other things are seldom if ever equal. The U.C. Berkeley student usually already has an edge on the community college or proprietary student because of higher family income, academic high school background (as distinct from a vocational or general high school program), higher verbal and quantitative skills, and the fact that he most likely is white.

Access to What. . .and With What Results?

Most people recognize that a degree from a prestigious university confers more rewards than a diploma or degree from an adult school or community college. But most public policies have not emphasized expanding effective student access to those prestigious programs. Rather, as Salner's study for the California Legislature

pointed out,[4] the least socially potent programs — adult education, community colleges and proprietary schools — are the most readily accessible.[5] In contrast, the most socially potent programs — those in prestigious universities — are the least accessible.

As the postsecondary education enterprise grows and touches more lives, and as the economy's future remains uncertain, prospective students want to know what difference attending a postsecondary school is likely to make in their lives. The answer is important, whether they plan to attend a one-year community college or a proprietary school program, or a long-term graduate program. Also, in the face of shrinking resources and growing demands, legislators and other educational policymakers want to know more about the impact of public revenues spent on education, and seek more information on which to base policy choices.

Consumerism

Three specific developments are pressing schools to divulge more information and on a standardized basis. They are: consumerism, the economic downturn and underemployment. First is the "consumer movement." Consumerism has been powered by two forces: one is the huge federal loan default rate by students at proprietary schools, estimated at 50 percent to 70 percent. The other and more important influence is the desire of students and the public to exert more control over their lives by demanding more from the important institutions supposed to serve them, such as colleges and universities. Recently these desires have encouraged schools to be more accountable to students and taxpayers, and stimulated efforts to protect student rights. Federal legislation has also reflected these new values by shifting financial aid from colleges to students as such, helping to create a market and encouraging student choice.

On the other hand, as college enrollments drop because of lower birthrates, schools' claims about the value of education have increased, but are not always either candid or supportable. For example, as Eric Wentworth reported in the Washington *Post* (April 3, 1975), an advertisement by Montgomery Community College in Maryland suggested that prospective students could go to Harvard for half-price by taking their first two years at Montgomery. The ad failed to note a crucial fact: Harvard accepts few mid-college transfers from anywhere. Thus a prospective student who did not know the student noncompletion rate at Montgomery, or the transfer rates from Montgomery to Harvard, could be grossly misled by the school's advertisement.

Economic Downturn

The second force pressing schools to collect and divulge new information is the continuing stress caused by a faltering economy. Shrinking resources encourage schools to inflate their claims, while reducing graduates' chances to be employed in their chosen fields. Consequently, prospective students want to know more about what they are likely to get for their investment in time and money. Furthermore the education policymaker faced with fewer resources and intensely competing demands, also needs better information to use in developing new options and reallocating resources effectively.

Underemployment

The third element is underemployment. The educational system has kept pace with the economy's effective demand for employees with various educational backgrounds. In order to do this, the postsecondary system has evolved in ways described earlier. But the system is more than keeping pace, and in fact is contributing to what might be called "educational inflation." This new-fangled term is applied to a phenomenon long observed: each new generation needs more education than its predecessor merely to preserve its relative socioeconomic standing and effective opportunity levels. That is, successive generations "have to run faster just to stay in the same place."

The job market has helped enforce this by demanding increasing amounts of education for jobs that remain essentially unchanged. Thus many private and public sector jobs once filled by high school graduates now require four years of college. Similarly, many jobs that once required four years of college now call for graduate degrees.

Meanwhile the higher education experiences have increased people's expectations. But the real nature of the jobs available, and their actual requirements (as distinguished from formal requirements) have changed little. This has caused worker dissatisfaction on a large scale that is now a national problem.

O'Toole calls this "underemployment," meaning that a person works at a job that does not use the skills he acquired in school, and that does not match his expectations.[6] Providing vocationally oriented students with better labor market information, and more accurate and realistic data on the kinds of jobs they are actually likely to get on graduation, should help them select institutions and programs suited to their career objectives.

A Caveat on Educational Data

There are no reliable or valid ways to measure the total effect of education on a person's life. Learning how to think, expanding one's understanding, and enriching one's intellectual and emotional experiences are some of the consequences of education. While such effects are exceedingly important, they are not included in this discussion because it focuses on jobs and occupational mobility.

Even if we agreed on the meaning and interpretation of standard tests like the Scholastic Aptitude Test, we would probably still disagree about what to do. For example, what should be done if students' Scholastic Aptitude Test scores drop year after year? Trow helped pinpoint the dilemma by observing that the centralization of a function from the institutional to the state level leads necessarily to the state's desire for "rational management."[7] State-imposed management procedures depend in turn upon the necessary data being available. But the data available to or supplied by educators may not be helpful in judging educational effectiveness. (What, for example, have instructor-student "contact hours" to do with educational results?)

Data that are unreliable, ambiguous or simply indigestible may lead to clumsy or misguided state intervention. For example, past state efforts to manage education through productivity formulae have rarely produced positive results.

Furthermore the job placement and earnings records of graduates of occupational programs may reflect many things in addition to or instead of the "value added" by schooling — students' sex, ethnic or family backgrounds, a particular job market, or others. What should the state do if some schools' records do not measure up?

Nonquantifiable Aspects and Student Decisions

The central problem is how best to provide adequate, meaningful information to aid public scrutiny, without damaging the delicate and nonquantifiable aspects of education.

Discussants at the seminar felt that the schools' autonomy would be protected if the nonquantifiable aspects of education were pursued but presented on their own merits. The decisions themselves, however, should be made primarily by prospective students rather than by state officials, except when the public good is threatened by fraud or misrepresentation. If prospective students are to make reasoned decisions, they must have reliable and reasonably specific information about school objectives, as well as data from past graduates to demonstrate how well the schools have performed. It would be reasonable for schools that concentrate on the nonquantifiable aspects of education and do not emphasize job placement, to make few if any claims about the occupational benefits of their programs.

Needs for Information

Conference discussants agreed that many audiences need more information about postsecondary education. All schools, colleges, and universities offering career-oriented education should be included in information programs, whether they are public or private. But community colleges and proprietary schools should be the primary focus for informational development, because they enroll the least-advantaged students, who should be given top priority.

Prospective students need and are entitled to have three kinds of information:

1. Information on the current labor market;

2. Information describing the universe of occupationally oriented schools in terms of employment objectives, programs, costs, financial aids, student profiles, admission standards and attrition rates; and

3. Information describing the experiences of past graduates of the particular school or program including placement rates and data on earnings from first jobs after graduation.

Admittedly much information is already available. But because it is buried in technical reports in various state departments, college catalogs, and other varied places, it is of limited use to prospective students. Further, there is little information realistically describing the outcomes of programs.

Discussants generally agreed that while the states have had primary responsibility for providing information and regulating education, their efforts have been relatively unsuccessful. Consequently, the federal government has tried to fulfill these functions. Thirteen federal agencies and 62 recognized accrediting bodies are trying to deal with several splintered aspects of the problem, and the Federal Interagency Committee on Education is attempting to give coherence to the federal effort.

An Information System in California

The Berkeley discussants urged a much stronger state-level role, rather than relying on "the feds." They based this position on their view of education as a basic responsibility of state government. Accordingly they agreed unanimously that the states should take principal responsibility for providing more and better information.

The California Postsecondary Education Commission, already charged with institutional planning, would be the most likely agency to lead the development of an information system in California. There was a strong feeling that the effort should try to standardize the numerous data-collection activities already underway, such as the Higher Education General Information Survey (HEGIS), the Community College Occupation Programs Evaluation System (COPES), The Student Accountability Model (SAM) and others. Discussants also felt that data-collection systems should be developed from the school level up, rather than from the federal level down, making the school the primary unit of information collection. The conferees agreed, however, that the potential for falsification makes it imperative that all school-generated information be audited periodically by a third party. Both school and labor market data should be made available to prospective students on a sub-state regional basis, or county-by-county, perhaps through regional counseling centers, independent of individual schools. The conferees also urged that the state consider using a computerized information facility similar to the Oregon Career Information System (CIS).

Cost

There were no reliable estimates of the cost of such an information system. (Oregon's is the only one in operation, and only limited data were available.) Nevertheless several significant cost-related points were made. Several participants challenged recent testimony before the Federal Trade Commission about the cost of requiring proprietary schools to provide follow-up data on their graduates. There is convincing evidence that the costs of such follow-up data collection are within reason. For example, a 1975 National Opinion Research Center estimate suggests that individual students can readily be followed into the labor market, and that nearly 90 percent of them can be located for less than $5.00 per student. Moreover the Oregon system, developed with support from the Fund for the Improvement of Post-

secondary Education, now operates at a total cost of $5.00 per user.

Despite the reasonable costs, conferees agreed that the student consumers — especially, low-income, career-oriented students — should not have to pay for the service. Instead the developmental costs should be met by the federal and state governments, and the long-term future operational costs borne by participating schools.

Existing Federal Legislation

A variety of laws should be considered to deal with schools' divulging information on the outcome of educational programs. Regulations of the U.S. Department of Health, Education and Welfare for guaranteed student loans require each school to make a good faith effort to give prospective students a complete and accurate statement describing the school and its programs. In cases where students are preparing for careers, the school is required to divulge information about employment opportunities in the specific career, as well as its graduates' placement and earnings in the past. But the regulations are meaningless, because if a school is unable to produce such information on its own, it may use regional or national labor market data.

The same regulations establish standards for schools' student loan default rates, student dropout rates and financial stability. If a school falls below the standards, the U.S. Office of Education can order the school to give evidence that its inability to meet the standard was the fault of the students, not the school.[8] But such a cumbersome system at a centralized level would probably be unenforceable.

The Vietnam Act of 1974 (PL 3508) stipulated that to qualify for GI Bill students, a school must demonstrate that 50 percent of its students who have completed courses over the past two years, and who are available for work, have found employment in the occupations for which they were trained. But the requirement lacks focus, as the words "specific occupation" were dropped from the bill in legislative conference. Thus students seeking training as computer programmers, but obtaining jobs as keypunch operators, would be counted as successfully employed.

Finally, the Federal Trade Commission has completed hearings on a proposed rule that would require proprietary schools to give program and outcome information to prospective students. But even if the rule is adopted, it will only cover proprietary schools, and will be administered federally.

Need for State Legislation

Conferees agreed unanimously that state legislation should be forthcoming, and that it should conform with existing federal legislation. Moreover state legislation should take into account existing state law that empowers a variety of state agencies to oversee portions of the problem, but provides no overall accountability or coordination.

While conferees agreed on the need for regulation, they also felt strongly that safeguards should prevent the regulators from capturing the education industry. Accordingly future legislation should coordinate information generation and dissemination under one agency, but assign auditing and enforcement responsibilities to a different agency.

Unintended Consequences

The possibility of unintended consequences was contemplated, and four principal concerns emerged:

1. If schools' placement records play a major role in attracting students, unless there are some controls or other counter influences, schools will be motivated to recruit only students who are likely to get jobs relatively easily, e. g., white males. But this would leave even fewer options for low-income, minority students and females.

2. Marginal schools serving clienteles that are especially disadvantaged might be forced out of business. For example, the Center's study of public and proprietary vocational training identified a number of proprietary schools in Miami that cater exclusively to Cuban immigrants, offering cosmetology training. The average starting salary for a graduate of one of these schools was considerably less than the federal minimum wage; yet without such training, there is a likelihood the graduates would have remained unemployed and on welfare. If such schools, that have a marginal but positive effect on students' lives, were to be required to provide data showing the earning level of graduates, the schools might be unable to attract students.

3. Regulations might provide no incentives for schools to offer training for labor markets that are specialized and limited but nevertheless important, such as legal aides or horseshoeing specialists.

4. Legislation emphasizing only quantifiable results may have the undesired effect of encouraging schools to undertake only programs that have clearly quantifiable results. Education would then be thought of only as manpower training, ignoring the spiritual, essential but nonquantifiable aspects of education such as its cultural, humanistic, "liberal arts," and spiritual contributions to students' minds and lives.

Recommendations for California

The conference recommended that the Assembly Permanent Subcommittee on Postsecondary Education introduce legislation to designate the California Postsecondary Education Commission as the coordinating body to develop and monitor an appropriate information system that would provide students with the kinds of data described above. The commission should establish a task force of knowledgeable people, and give it sufficient funds to prepare, within one year (by early 1977) a legislative proposal to improve student information. The proposal would have two phases.

The first phase would be experimental, having the following objectives:

1. Defining specific student information needs.
2. Identifying existing information sources and data-collection methods.
3. Coordinating existing information, and perhaps its collection and publication.

4. Identifying new information needs.
5. Recommending standardized information to insure comparability.
6. Reviewing existing state and federal legislation and regulations.
7. Developing a model for information collection and dissemination.
8. Identifying costs and sources of funds to operate an information system.
9. Providing for effective monitoring to insure the accuracy of information, with appropriate enforcement procedures.
10. Providing for periodic system evaluation, including review of costs and benefits to users. Evaluation should specifically consider the extent to which better and more accessible information results in improved choices.
11. Further defining possible unintended consequences and devising safeguards against them.

The second phase would be the establishment of a permanent information system within the state, based on the experiences of the experimental phase.

Summary and Conclusion

Students need more information soon so that they can estimate the likely consequences of their making heavy investments of time, money and hope in postsecondary education. Students often, for example, expect a given amount of schooling to bring them more income and social status than it can provide, partly because the relative value of specific degrees has declined. As the number of degrees earned continues to rise, and each new generation pushes educational levels higher, each succeeding group needs even more education merely to retain its relative standing in society. Prospective postsecondary students need to understand this, if their expectations are to be realistic. As O'Toole has suggested, a severe mismatch between students' expectations and reality may lead to economic and political instability, as well as individual personal tragedies.

Further, when the economy turns down and the job market contracts, students tend to grasp at straws for survival. Often those with the weakest grasp are those at the low end of the economic ladder, who are most likely to enroll in vocational or career programs, and who most need to understand the possibilities and the limitations of the courses offered.

The seminar's recommendations for stepping up the flow of information take into account the fact that schools and their students exist in a delicate social network that could be upset by arbitrary or heavy-handed federal or state intervention. But immediate action is also needed, along with close monitoring to head off undesirable consequences. Government and schools have an obligation to give prospective students the information they need to make the best choices possible for themselves. If complete, standard and comprehensible data can be made available to students, this material will help them minimize ill-informed decisions and aid them in choosing educational programs suitable to their talents, aspirations, opportunities and career goals.

These recommendations also carry long-range implications. As things stand, we lack comparable data about schools' goals and their success in meeting them; consequently, there is no way for the schools or the public to know how well postsecondary education in California is serving the community's needs. With improved collection of standard information, however, the public can more readily evaluate the schools' performance, students can make wiser choices of institutions and programs, and the schools themselves can use that same information to help them do a better job.

NOTES

[1] W. L. Hansen and B. Weisbrod, "The Distribution of Costs and Benefits of Public Higher Education: The Case of California," *Journal of Human Resources,* 4 (2) 176-191 (Spring 1969).
[2] Jerome Karabel, "Community Colleges and Social Stratification," *Harvard Educational Review,* 42 (4) 521-562 (November 1972).
[3] Wellford W. Wilms, *Public and Proprietary Vocational Training: A Study of Effectiveness* (Lexington, Mass.: Lexington Books, D. C. Heath and Co., 1975).
[4] Marcia B. Salner, *Inventory of Existing Postsecondary Alternatives.* Second Technical Report, Postsecondary Alternatives Study, California Legislature (Sacramento: 1975).
[5] Socially potent programs can be defined as programs that improve the individual's social mobility.
[6] James O'Toole, "The Reserve Army of the Underemployed: II — The Role of Education," *Change,* 7 (5) 26-33, 60-63 (June 1975).
[7] Martin Trow, "The Public and Private Lives of Higher Education," *Daedalus,* 104 (1) 113-127 (Winter 1975).
[8] It is not clear how students can be shown to be "at fault." And even if it could be demonstrated, perhaps their "fault" lies in having low incomes or being members of minorities.

Seminar Participants

Wellford W. Wilms, Seminar Chairman
Center for Research & Development in Higher Education
University of California, Berkeley

Kay J. Andersen
Executive Director
Western Association of Schools and Colleges

Kent Bennion, Director
Vocational Education, Region IX
Department of Health, Education and Welfare

Robert Berdahl, Senior Fellow
Carnegie Council on Policy Studies in Higher Education

William C. Bessey
Management Education and Staff Development
Bank of America

Thomas Bogetich
Executive Director
California Advisory Council on Vocational Education

Linda Bond, Consultant
Assembly Committee on Education

Seth Brunner
Experimental College
University of California, Davis

Sherwood Burgess
Director
Heald Business College

Allan Cartter, Professor of Higher Education and Director
Higher Education Institute
University of California, Los Angeles

John Coons, Professor
School of Law
University of California, Berkeley

Gerald Cresci
Dean, Program Planning
California Community Colleges

William Deegan
Higher Education Specialist
California Postsecondary Education Commission

George Ebey
Community College Occupational Programs Evaluation System

Russell Edgerton, Deputy Director
Fund for the Improvement of Postsecondary Education
Department of Health, Education and Welfare

Martha Lee Ericson, Student
Contra Costa College

Paul Franklin
Development Director
Career Information System

Bruce Fuller, Consultant
Assembly Permanent Subcommittee on Postsecondary Education

Russell Y. Garth, Consultant
Assembly Joint Rules Committee

Lyman A. Glenny, Professor of Higher Education and Director
Center for Research & Development in Higher Education
University of California, Berkeley

David Goodwin
Program Officer, Education and Work
National Institute of Education
Department of Health, Education and Welfare

James Goodwin
Assistant to the Vice President
University of California, Berkeley

William R. Haldeman
Higher Education Specialist
California Postsecondary Education Commission

Adelle Hankin, Student
Contra Costa College

J B Lon Hefferlin
Director of Special Projects
Jossey-Bass Publishers

John Iskra
Assistant to State Director of Vocational Education

Marilyn Jacobson, Counselor
Women's Center
University of California, Berkeley

Glen Keffer, Staff Director
State Manpower Planning Office

Dorothy Knoell
Higher Education Specialist
California Postsecondary Education Commission

Eugene C. Lee, Director
Institute of Governmental Studies
University of California, Berkeley

Seela Lewis
Consumer Protection Specialist
Federal Trade Commission

Sally Loyd
Academic Planner, Chancellor's Office
California State Universities and Colleges

Peg McCormack
Office of the Lt. Governor

Bernard Michael, Executive Director
Federal Interagency Committee on Education
Department of Health, Education and Welfare

Kenneth B. O'Brien, Jr.
Associate Director
California Postsecondary Education Commission

Michael O'Keefe
Associate Vice President for Academic Development
University of Illinois

C. Robert Pace, Professor of Education
University of California, Los Angeles

Richard Peterson, Research Psychologist
Educational Testing Service

Tony Pitale
Associate Director
California Advisory Council on Vocational Education

Jaime Soliz
Assistant Director
Education Services Center-LULAC

Herbert M. Stein
Special Administrative Associate to the Chancellor
Peralta Colleges

Herbert E. Summer, Director (Ret.)
Bureau of School Approvals
Department of Education

Harry Summerfield, Professor
The Wright Institute

Zenia Velasquez
Student
Contra Costa College

David White, Associate Specialist
Childhood and Government Project
University of California, Berkeley

Edward Whitfield
Career Guidance Services

Howard Williams
Regional Manpower Coordinator
Department of Health, Education and Welfare, Region IX

John Wish, Professor
Department of Marketing
University of Oregon

Notes to Readers

While reading recent issues of the *Public Affairs Report*, have you thought of questions, suggestions, criticisms or comments that you might like to consider sending in to the editors? Do you have any observations about the choice of topics, or their treatment in the pages of the *Report*? Do you have advice or suggestions regarding future issues?

Letters from readers and requests for copies arrive regularly, but by including this note, we hope to open a "readers' window" that will give us a better sample of what subscribers think about the *Public Affairs Report*, and what directions it might take.

Your comments may also provide substantive observations that could be acknowledged or excerpted in future issues.

—The Editors

Readers' Response

Editors' Note: We wish to thank readers who have responded to the invitation to write. All comments are welcomed, collected and read with care; we find these exchanges valuable and hope for more. Here are excerpts from two recent letters, and a correction in response to a third.

* * *

I enjoyed reading the June 1975 Issue... ("Information, Research and Counseling: The Women's Center in Berkeley," by Margaret B. Wilkerson). It was well done.

I am writing specifically to call attention to just one word that pushed my button, and I feel assured that you will want to give it some thought. On page 3, you refer to a 43 year old woman, a "reformed" alcoholic, who was helped through CCEW workshops.... The word "reformed" has moral implications that perpetuate the myth that alcoholism is some kind of unfortunate character deformation rather than a disease — basically physiological but clearly having complex psychological and behavioral effects. Those who hold to what is called the "medical model" of alcoholism refer to the ones who make it to sobriety and stay there as "recovered alcoholics." I would like those who are persuaded by the psychological model to reflect on why it is that the alcoholic may be accurately described as "dependent, mother-fixated, escapist, self-pitying, egocentric" etc. but that millions of men and women with all of the same psychoneurotic traits are not alcoholic....

Laurel Cook, Editor
Berkeley Health and Medical
Sciences Program
Dec. 18, 1975

* * *

The report ("Juvenile Delinquency: Seeking Effective Prevention" by Tom Higgins, December 1975) is so clear, judicious and enlightening that I want to say, "Hurray for Tom Higgins!" I am enthusiastically using this report in a social welfare class I teach. Having read this report, the students... are now seeking information on the Richmond and Orange County prevention projects.

Mary Jeffress
Field Work Consultant and Lecturer
School of Social Welfare
Jan. 22, 1976

* * *

Correction: With respect to the December 1975 PAR, "Juvenile Delinquency: Seeking Effective Prevention," by Tom Higgins, a correction should be made concerning note 4, which read: "A detailed explanation of the cost calculated is presented in *Recommendations for the State of California*, Tom Higgins, for the California Department of Finance, 1975." In a letter dated January 15, 1976, Jack D. Smith, of the Department of Finance, commented on the present status of the report, which was prepared for the department's use. Since the department has not made a firm decision concerning publication or final format, the "Recommendations..." should not have been referred to as a work published in 1975.

to some indigent persons for whose medical care the counties had previously been responsible (the fourth group described above). At the same time it discontinued reimbursing participating counties for care of patients just above the Medi-Cal cut-off. But the rigid state eligibility standard kept three-fourths of the estimated 800,000 medically indigent persons from eligibility for Medi-Cal services.

Anatomy of the PHPs: The Race for Prepayment

The Legislature gave Medi-Cal directors broad authorization to establish requirements governing contracts for PHPs, but directed that contracts must potentially cost less than the same services under the fee-for-service system.

Acceptable PHP contractors included private insurance companies, nonprofit hospital service plans, medical societies, associations of insurers, county hospital systems and persons or organizations registered under the Knox-Mills Health Plan Act.[4] It is significant that the PHP law required that a contractor *arrange* for services, not necessarily *provide* them.

Physicians participating in a plan could either practice as individuals or organize into groups. Plans using solo practitioners are typically sponsored by a county medical society foundation. The foundation arranges for services with local providers who are paid an agreed-upon fee for each service. The foundation receives a fixed capitation rate and absorbs the financial risk for providing services.[5] Only two foundation plans participated in the PHP program, one in Sacramento County and one in Orange County. The Orange County plan was discontinued after its first year.

PHPs using physicians in group practice may subcontract for additional covered services with independent medical specialists or institutions, local pharmacies, laboratories, and others. Or the group-practice PHPs may be self-contained operations having their own facilities and employing service providers on salary. PHP contractors did not include any insurance company or hospital service plans, and only one county hospital, Contra Costa, was a contractor. Most providers were registered under the Knox-Mills Act.

Under Medi-Cal regulations, PHPs provided the full range of Medi-Cal benefits but were not required to provide major organ transplants, chronic hemodialysis, or long-term care in a county, state, or federal hospital. PHP liability for services was limited to $10,000 a year per enrollee. Beyond that, care continued as fee-for-service. Although the law permitted otherwise, department regulations limited Medi-Cal enrollees to those who received cash welfare grants.

Plans were required to furnish proof of financial security sufficient to pay for service during a month for which the state had made payment. They were also required to seek members within a specified geographic area and not refuse to enroll anyone who was eligible.

The Scramble for Contracts

Convinced that the state could save between $150 million and $300 million a year through this alternative form of health care delivery, Governor Reagan's administration worked assiduously to encourage PHP contractors. Utilization controls that had been imposed on the traditional fee-for-service program were lifted. Great reductions were predicted in administrative costs alone, since PHP contracts would lower the cost of handling prior authorization requests and processing the great number of individual claims.

Response of the health industry was excellent. Many considered the PHP concept to be a good business opportunity, and some saw it as a chance to make a fast buck. The Department of Health Care Services, then in charge of Medi-Cal, was deluged with proposals for contracts.

The department, however, was not ready to handle the pressure of business. Staff assignments changed frequently. Data resulting from four experimental prepaid projects yielded little useful information. Experience of the long-existing nonprofit plans had little relevance, since they served an employed nonwelfare membership. Determining capitation rates was a difficult challenge. The department's Medi-Cal fee-for-service data seemed to be the only basic resource available. Costs were projected by county, and an arbitrary 10 percent reduction was chosen as a negotiation base.

Eager to set a record in reducing costs, the administration rushed to sign up contractors. Each contract allowed the plan to enroll up to a maximum number of Medi-Cal eligibles in a geographic area. To stimulate competition among the plans, frequently more than one contract was assigned in the same area or in overlapping areas, on the theory that competing plans would offer better service. The state contracted with 25 PHPs in the Los Angeles area alone, and in San Diego, contracts were awarded to seven plans covering almost identical territory.

The first prepaid health plan became effective May 1, 1972. By the end of the year, 21 PHP contracts were in effect, with a total enrollment of 147,569 persons or 7.4 percent of the eligible cash-grant recipients in those counties served.

The Showdown: Widespread Criticism

This rapid growth created serious problems that resulted in widespread criticism by a concerned public, ranging from militant welfare rights groups to conservative medical organizations. Critics included some practitioners who opposed comprehensive prepayment plans as a matter of principle. Dissatisfaction in the Los Angeles area led to protests, demonstrations, and disenrollment campaigns. Many friends of the prepayment movement accused the Reagan administration of trying to do too much too soon, thus weakening the whole concept of health maintenance organizations.

Investigations. The department was charged with condoning conflicts of interest, excessive profit making, unethical marketing practices such as misrepresentation in enrolling members, and poor patient care. Legislative committees held hearings, the Legislative Analyst reviewed the role of the department in regulating the PHPs, the audits division of the Department of Finance reviewed the entire Medi-Cal program (in three volumes), and the U.S. Comptroller General reported on the California PHP program to the U.S. Senate Committee on Finance. When the state administration changed hands in January 1975, the new Governor launched still another investigation, and the U.S. Senate Permanent Subcommittee on Investigations held hearings in March 1975.

Conflict of Interest. Recent developments include rapid growth of a relatively new profession of "health care management consultants," i.e., experts concerned principally with the organization and administration of health plans, with the fine art of procuring governmental funds, and not always with the quality of medical care. Many providers seeking PHP contracts employed such consultants, among whom were former high officials of the Reagan administration as well as a number of legislators. Investigative studies revealed that providers using such intermediaries had little difficulty obtaining state contracts. Investigation also showed that some state employees and some members of the Legislature had financial interests in contracting PHPs.

Profit Making. The laws governing prepaid health plans did not expressly prohibit profit making. The Department of Health and its predecessor, the

Department of Health Care Services, contracted with both for-profit and nonprofit plans. About a fifth of the contracts were awarded to *professional* organizations of medical practitioners, which were considered profit making. The remaining contracts were with *nonprofessional* organizations, which had been advised by the department to apply as nonprofit corporations because of a possible conflict with the Business and Professions Code.[6] All complied, but some then set up for-profit subcontractors to provide enrollment, management, medical, laboratory, dental and prescription services. The principal in a PHP could thus earn a salary and profits from several such subsidiaries.

For example, the California Auditor General reported that Consolidated Medical Systems Ltd. (CMS), which had four state contracts in Southern California, was basically a holding company. It bought all its services from affiliates owned by its director and his associates. After studying the audited statements of these affiliates, California Auditor General Harvey Rose estimated that the administrative costs totaled 46 percent and profits 8 percent of the $28 million in capitation premiums paid to CMS between July 1, 1971 and December 31, 1973.[7] (See Chart 1 for a schematic diagram of such arrangements.)

Chart 1

How Funds are Channeled into
Subsidiary Profit-Making Organizations
by Self-Contained PHP Organizations

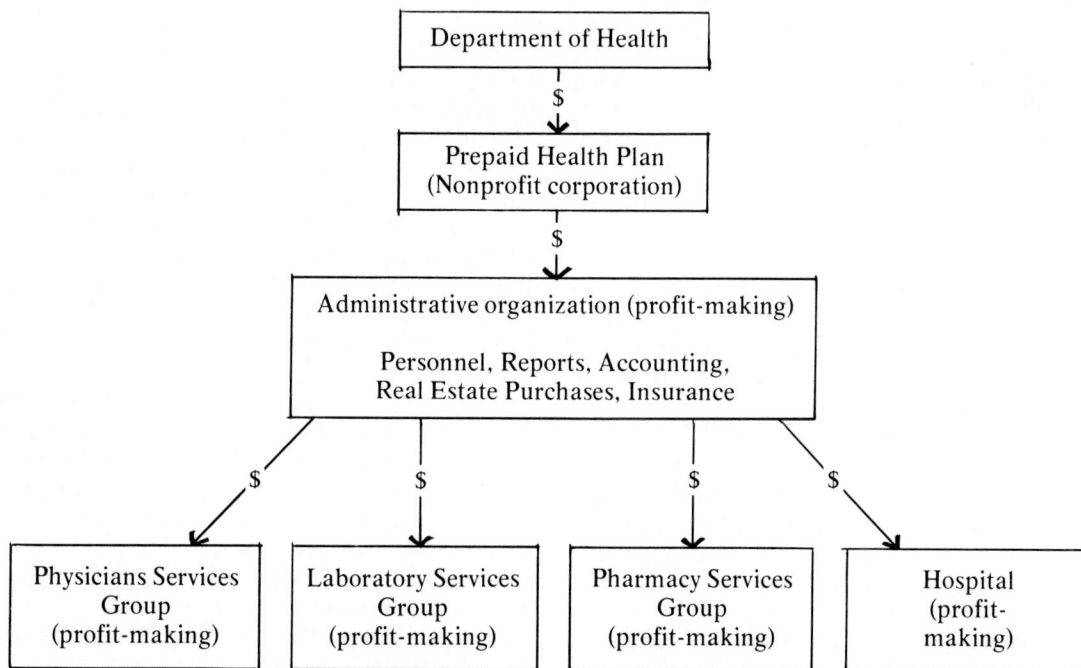

California, Legislative Analyst, *A Review of the Regulation of Prepaid Health Plans by the State Department of Health* (Sacramento: Nov. 15, 1973), page 8.

The Auditor General examined 15 health plans (including CMS) under contract with the state and found that 52 percent of the total $56.5 million paid to them in the three years had been expended for administrative costs and profits combined.

The Department of Health challenged the figures, pointing out that estimates of administrative costs were imprecise, since financial data for some affiliates had not been available, that estimates were based on unaudited reports, and that in any case, they were distorted by start-up costs. The department and the Auditor General also differed on the definition of administrative costs.[8]

Unethical Marketing Practices. Most of the adverse publicity about the PHPs centered around marketing abuses. Competing contractors, especially in Los Angeles areas having high concentrations of welfare recipients, conducted hard-sell door-to-door campaigns leading to charges of misrepresentation and fraud. Since welfare records are confidential, PHP contractors could not be given lists of Medi-Cal eligibles. The Department of Health therefore agreed to mail out health plan brochures to Medi-Cal eligibles within a plan's service area and to bill the PHP for the cost.

Many PHPs, however, chose other methods. For example, PHP salesmen, eager to earn their commissions, sometimes posed as county or state employees, or members of the Medi-Cal staff and told Medi-Cal recipients their benefits would be terminated if they did not join the PHP. Salesmen failed to inform potential enrollees that they would have to get all their care from the plan, and could no longer visit their own doctor or pharmacy. Not until subscribers needed medical service did they find that the new clinic might be miles away, and that promised transportation was often not available.

Widespread indignation over the state's lack of control caused the department to suspend all PHP enrollment in Los Angeles, Orange, and San Diego counties in the fall of 1973, and to oblige enrollers to attend special briefings. Enrollment was resumed after several weeks and all PHPs were required to contact every new subscriber to verify that the plans' services and operation had been clearly explained. In addition, the department began contacting new enrollees to check on the accuracy of the sales talks presented them.

A small percentage of enrollees wanted to get out because of dissatisfaction with service, a desire to return to a personal physician, and difficulty in reaching PHP offices. The department also attempted to facilitate disenrollment of such clients; some were complaining that plans were purposely making it difficult to withdraw. A newly opened state field office in Los Angeles tried to help dissatisfied subscribers. Thereafter, voluntary disenrollments of this type declined steadily from 3.56 per 100 enrollees per month in May 1973 to 2.06 in December; by March 1974 the rate was 1.20 per 100.[9] The department ascribed the decrease to careful verification of all applications for enrollment.[10]

Further Criticism: Inferior Patient Care

The Los Angeles Medical Society, the county comprehensive health planning council, and the health rights organization received hundreds of complaints, not only about fraudulent enrollment practices but also concerning difficulties in obtaining 24-hour emergency care, inaccessibility of clinics, and sometimes impersonal and inadequate treatment.

Henry A. Waxman, Chairman of the Assembly Committee on Health, was not satisfied with PHP audits made by the Department of Health.[11] He maintained that the medical audit teams devoted too little time to the appropriateness and quality of the professional medical practice, and to the overall quality of organizational performance and responsiveness.

Witnesses at the committee hearings pointed out that in many plans PHP physician-to-member ratios were lower than the levels maintained by many well-recognized group practice prepayment plans, that many plans lacked appropriate specialists, and that in some plans physicians had questionable professional qualifications.[12]

The PHPs were also criticized for lack of preventive care. Such care is supposedly a basic advantage that prepayment provides over fee-for-service. Yet the high turnover of PHP enrollees precluded the *continuity* of care that is essential for good preventive service. Besides the voluntary disenrollments, which may have totalled at least 15 percent a year, PHPs were subjected to involuntary disenrollments stemming from members' loss of eligibility. Since the Department of Health limited PHP membership to persons receiving a welfare cash grant, discontinuance of the grant meant disenrollment from the PHP and consequent ineligibility for its services. This particularly affected recipients of Aid to Families with Dependent Children (AFDC) who comprised more than 80 percent of PHP enrollees.

Eligibility of these families for a welfare grant was redetermined every month by the county welfare departments. If an increase in income or resources was reported, or if a family had refused to conform to some procedural requirement, regulations required its removal from the welfare rolls. About 3 percent of PHP members were forced to leave their plans each month because they were no longer eligible for a welfare cash grant — an involuntary disenrollment rate totalling 36 percent a year. Some of these families may have gone on and off a plan several times during the year. At the beginning of 1973, for example, almost half the AFDC families had been receiving aid less than two years, and a third of them less than one year.[13] During the 1973 fiscal year, 240,000 cases were added to the AFDC rolls and 297,000 were discontinued.[14] More than a quarter of the added families had previously been on AFDC.

The president of the California Prepaid Health Plan Council testified before the Assembly Committee on Health that rapid turnover was a major problem.[15] Dr. Lester Breslow, Dean of the School of Public Health, University of California at Los Angeles, testifying at the same hearings strongly recommended that the state establish one-year enrollment in prepaid health plans as an option when people become eligible for Medi-Cal, and periodically thereafter, in order to stabilize the population covered by such plans.[16]

Legislative Action

The Legislature's response to the adverse publicity was to consolidate and strengthen previous statutory provisions governing prepaid health plans in the Waxman-Duffy Prepaid Health Plan Act of 1972 (AB 1496, Ch. 1366, Cal. Stats. 1972). The new provisions, effective July 1, 1973, included a definition of conflict of interest designed to prevent legislators and state employees from influencing the award of contracts; a requirement that PHP financial records be audited annually by an independent certified public accountant; detailed stipulations governing enrollment practices; provider-patient ratios; requirement for public hearings on new contracts and contract renewals; and a provision that prepaid health plans should make "all reasonable efforts" to achieve an enrollment of not more than 50 percent of Medi-Cal beneficiaries by the third contract year,[17] thus increasing the number of non-welfare members.

Legislation passed in 1974 required that public hearings be held whenever specific types of PHP contract amendments were proposed. These would include amendments effecting a reduction of service or availability, an enlargement of the service area, or an increase in the maximum enrollment allowed under the contract (Waxman-Duffy Prepaid Health Plan Act, AB 586, Ch. 983, Cal. Stats. 1974. It became effective January 1, 1975.) The act permitted PHP mergers or reorganizations under specific conditions. Plans contemplating mergers were required to ensure that accessibility to care was maintained and that the new organization was fiscally and administratively sound.

Legislation passed in September 1975 called for further tightening procedures governing PHPs. All books and records of PHPs and their subcontractors were made public records, as were the criteria and procedures used by the Department of Health in conducting onsite reviews of the plans. Summaries of onsite surveys were to be included in the department's annual report. (Ch. 1233, Cal. Stats. 1975.)

Persisting Problems

Despite attempted remedies by the Legislature, many problems rampant in 1972-74 persisted in 1975. Quality of care was an issue, state monitoring was not effective, and charges of misrepresentation in enrollment continued. Hospital care in PHPs was characterized as substandard by physicians representing the hospital surveyors of the California Medical Association in testimony before the U.S. Senate Permanent Investigations Subcommittee in March 1975.[18] A report to the U.S. Department of Health, Education and Welfare in September 1974, identified effective state monitoring and regulation as the principal needs of the PHP program. The report asserted that no effort had been made to improve the statistical system or to force compliance.[19] Misrepresentation in enrollment was charged during 1975 in San Jose, in San Francisco, in Los Angeles, and in Contra Costa County.

New Effort at Reform

An indefinite moratorium on approving new prepaid health plan contracts was announced by Governor Brown in February 1975, (as reported by the San Francisco *Chronicle*, on February 12). Existing contracts coming due would be extended only until June 30, pending a thorough review of the system. As of May 1, 1975, 50 contracts were in effect, compared with a high of 58 in October 1974. Appointment of a high-caliber advisory committee on prepaid health plans was announced, to reconsider the premise of PHPs as an alternative means of providing health care under Medi-Cal. Specifically, the committee was charged with reviewing and evaluating cost and quality control. The committee was also to propose standards and evaluation procedures, and recommend legislative and regulatory changes to carry out proposals. A two-year study was planned.[20]

On June 9, 1975, a committee progress report recommended that the program not be abandoned in spite of the deficiencies and problems associated with PHPs. It urged greatly strengthened regulatory control, higher standards, and experimentation with alternative methods of financing and delivering care.[21]

Two weeks later the state administration dramatically proclaimed a major overhaul of the program as the "termination of Prepaid Health Plan Program," effective July 31, 1975. As noted earlier, the plans would be replaced by institutes for medical services.[22] The new program called for tighter financial and quality controls including a ceiling on administrative costs, greater emphasis on preventive care, and consumer representation on boards of directors. A proposal to limit participation to stable multi-specialty group practices or to community-wide foundations for medical care, was likely to arouse controversy as it would eliminate contractors who arranged services through individual physicians in solo practice (independent practice arrangements). Moreover the requirement for consumer representation would eliminate successful established plans like Kaiser.

Protests by some advisory committee members and threats of suits by PHP contractors led the Department of Health to delay implementation of the new program. They did this to fulfill requirements for public hearings on the proposed regulations, seek necessary legislative amendments to the Medi-Cal laws, and allow time for conversion from the PHP to the IMS system.

Alternatives

It seems doubtful that the state can resolve the PHP predicament without overhauling the entire Medi-Cal system. Perhaps neither prepaid health plans nor traditional fee-for-service is, in the long run, the optimal mode of providing medical care for needy persons. The shortcomings of the PHPs may have arisen from the haste in which they were set up, and the laissez-faire philosophy of the Reagan administration. Nevertheless, even under stricter regulation, PHPs may be unable to provide quality care for a mobile, relatively untutored population with greater-than-average health-care needs.

The successful prepaid plans are mostly those with middle class subscribers, such as the federal employees who comprise the largest single group enrolled in the Kaiser program. In contrast, most of the welfare recipients enrolled by the PHPs live in poverty, an environment known to cause more physical and mental distress than that experienced by higher income groups. Moreover such recipients are generally less educated and often lack skills in using complex systems of medical care.

The effectiveness of the alternative fee-for-service system in furnishing quality care for low-income populations is also debatable. In theory the latter system gives the patient free choice and therefore better care, since he or she can change physicians if dissatisfied. But how much real choice has the Medi-Cal recipient?

Mainstream Care. While 9 out of 10 California physicians treated some Medi-Cal patients in November 1974, almost 4 in 10 said they would not willingly accept a new Medi-Cal patient, according to a survey by the California Medical Association.[23] Moreover, 4 in 10 planned to curtail their Medi-Cal caseloads. One in 5 physicians planned to continue seeing Medi-Cal patients, but to discontinue accepting non-Medi-Cal family members. Medi-Cal patients averaged 10 percent of the caseload of physicians participating in the care of Medi-Cal recipients.

Chief criticisms of the program were low fees, bureaucratic interference in patient care, and excessive paperwork. According to the survey, "the base of physicians available to provide care under the program is narrowing and. . . relatively more care will be provided in the future by those physicians who already have significant involvement in the program." In short, the future of "mainstream" care of the poor does not look good, unless substantial changes are made.

Universal Health Insurance. Universal, compulsory, comprehensive health insurance may be one way to keep the medically indigent in mainstream care. Equal access to the private medical market under present conditions, however, would probably call for an enormous, costly increase in medical manpower, machines, and facilities. In view of the congressional history of Medicaid[24] and the current outcry against high public expenditures for health and welfare despite widespread unemployment and inflationary living costs, the goal of mainstream care for the medically indigent may be somewhat utopian. Thus the likelihood of a truly comprehensive federal health insurance act in the foreseeable future also seems visionary. Unless — or until — public policy embraces a far different allocation of resources than now prevails, it seems reasonable to consider other ways of meeting the medical needs of the less affluent members of our society. Direct health services are a possibility.

Direct Health Services by County Hospitals

California's advisory committee on prepaid health plans recommended that the state "begin a period of intense experimentation in promising methods of financing and delivering care including, but not limited to, development of a special strategy to make better use of county and other publicly owned facilities. . ."[25]

In following this recommendation, a system of *government-provided health care* services might be explored, as being potentially more viable than *state payments to providers* of such services. California already has the skeleton of such a system in the many hospitals for which county governments are now responsible. Although the system has been weakened in recent years by the closure, sale or leasing out of a number of hospitals, they still exist in counties having three-fourths of the state's population.

County institutions in urban areas are able to provide the full range of Medi-Cal benefits, including specialty care. Many counties have begun to consolidate administration of all health services — public health, mental health, hospitals — and to move toward decentralization of ambulatory care into community health centers. If the Legislature were to decide to modify the mainstream concept, and the federal government authorized such a course, the county system could be expanded to meet the needs of all medically needy persons, as well as those eligible for Medi-Cal.[26] Such a system could be integrated with other publicly financed health services — maternal and child health, alcohol and drug abuse, and crippled children's programs, for example — and centralized records could pinpoint the need for social intervention. Moreover the health care system could be coordinated with the counties' other social service programs.

The Medi-Cal Act in 1965 authorized the transformation of county hospitals into community institutions able to serve paying patients as well as medical indigents. At the same time, counties were authorized to bill the state for care of Medi-Cal eligibles who continued to use the county hospital, and to be further reimbursed for uncollected costs of care to medically indigent persons not eligible for Medi-Cal. Many counties admitted patients who paid for care. The additional funds effected significant improvement in hospital staffing and equipment, as well as the upgrading of services.

This experience suggests an experiment in modifying the medical service functions of county health institutions. With sufficient funding, possibly under a prepayment system, they might provide high quality care to a substantial portion of the county population. Such an experiment, moreover, might in the long run be a testing ground for a national health care system, based on regional organization of direct services.

123

NOTES

The writers are indebted to William Mandel, M.D., for his help.

[1] Legislated basic services are: physician's visits, including consultant and referral services; inpatient and outpatient hospital care; medically necessary emergency services; short-term outpatient evaluative and crisis intervention mental health services; medical treatment and referral for abuse of or addiction to alcohol or drugs; diagnostic laboratory and diagnostic and therapeutic radiologic services; home health care; preventive health services including family planning; and preventive dental care and eye examinations for children.

[2] Foline E. Gartside, "Causes of Increase in Medicaid Costs in California," *Health Services Reports* 88:225-235 (U.S. Department of Health, Education and Welfare: March 1973). See especially p. 234.

[3] Not more than two of the following services were allowed in any one month unless permission was first granted by a Medi-Cal consultant: physician's office or home visits; hospital outpatient services; physical, occupational or speech therapy; podiatry services; optometry services; chiropractic services; services of a clinical psychologist; organized outpatient clinic services; and prescribed drugs. All emergency services were exempt from prior authorization.

Most of the following benefits were subject to utilization controls: inpatient hospital services; outpatient laboratory, radiological and radio-isotope; blood and blood derivatives; hemodialysis; nursing home; home health agency services; medical transportation; artificial limbs and braces; hearing aids; assistive devices and durable medical equipment; eyeglasses, artificial eyes, etc.

[4] The Knox-Mills Health Plan Act (California Government Code, Sec. 12530 et seq.), was the basic legislation concerning health care service plans. It imposed limited financial requirements on such plans and required the Attorney General to review their advertising and membership contracts for possible false or misleading statements. The Knox-Keene Health Care Service Plan Act of 1975, which becomes operative July 1, 1976, replaces the Knox-Mills Act, tightens requirements, and transfers responsibility to the commissioner of corporations. (Cal. Stats 1975, Ch. 941).

[5] Providers may share the financial risk by pooling a percentage of their fees. Unexpended pool funds may be distributed to providers via bonuses or increased reimbursement in subsequent years.

[6] California, Department of Health, "Prepaid Health Plans: the California Experience." Unpublished manuscript. (Sacramento: June 1974), p. 10.

[7] California, Office of the Auditor General, Joint Legislative Audit Committee, *Department of Health Prepaid Health Plans* (Sacramento: April 22, 1974), Appendix, pp. 17-20.

[8] Included in Report of Auditor General.

[9] California, Department of Health, *Annual Report to the Governor and Legislature on Prepaid Health Plans* (Sacramento: June 1974), p. 8.

[10] Ibid., p. 9.

[11] California, Legislature, Assembly Committee on Health, Special Meeting on *Prepaid Health Plans, Quality of Care,* Los Angeles, California, December 13, 1973, pp. 2-3.

[12] Ibid. pp. 86-90.

[13] California, Department of Benefit Payments, Aid to Families with Dependent Children, *Social and Economic Characteristics of Families Receiving Aid During January 1973* (Sacramento: April 1974), Table 6.

[14] California, Department of Social Welfare, *Public Welfare in California 1972-73,* Series AR-1-15 (Sacramento), Tables 16-19.

[15] Note 11 above, Appendix 4, p. 4.

[16] Ibid., p. 91.

[17] Health Department regulations required that a PHP "not limit enrollment to Medi-Cal beneficiaries" and to "enroll and maintain" a reasonable ratio of Medi-Cal beneficiaries to other subscribers. (Title 22, Sec. 51845).

[18] *CMA News* 20:5 (March 28, 1975).

[19] Daniel A. Louis and John J. McCord, *Evaluation of California's Prepaid Health Plans* (Santa Barbara, Calif.: General Research Corp., September 1974). Executive summary, p. 4.

[20] California, Department of Health, press release, undated.

[21] California, Prepaid Health Plan Advisory Committee, *Progress Report to the Division of Health Systems Alternatives* (Sacramento: Department of Health, June 9, 1975), p. 1.

[22] San Francisco *Chronicle,* June 27, 1975, p. 1; also *California Health and Welfare Agency, Institute for Medical Services,* pamphlet (Sacramento: July 1975).

[23] California Medical Association, "A Survey of Physician Participation in the Medi-Cal Program," *Socioeconomic Report,* 15:2 (February-March 1975); and "Physician Dissatisfaction with Medi-Cal," *Socioeconomic Report,* 15:3 (April 1975).

[24] The original Medicaid program, enacted as Title XIX of the Social Security Act of 1965, was hailed as a giant step forward in meeting the health needs of the nation's poor. Subsequent amendments to the act greatly narrowed this objective by severely restricting financial eligibility for care and easing requirements on the states that would have broadened eligibility for comprehensive health care.

[25] Note 21 above, p. 2.

[26] A survey in June 1973 showed that on the average 27 percent of the hospitalized patients in county hospitals were ineligible for Medi-Cal but could not afford private care. The same was true of 25 percent of the ambulatory patients. Health Policy Advisory Center, *Closing the Doors on the Poor, The Dismantling of California Hospitals,* Elinor Blake and Thomas Bodenheimer (San Francisco: 1975), p. 75.

Science, Technology and Policy

Vol. 17   No. 3   June 1976

Using Reclaimed Water:
Public Attitudes and Governmental Policy

By
William H. Bruvold
Associate Professor of Behavioral Sciences in Residence,
Department of Social and
Administrative Health Sciences,
School of Public Health

Introduction

California's preoccupation with water has stimulated an on-going search for supplies that can be adapted for a variety of uses throughout the state. Consequently, a source that produces more than 2 billion gallons a day, or *over half* of the state's current daily domestic water requirement, clearly deserves serious attention. Treated or reclaimed wastewater is such a source.[1]

Any program that contemplates the use of water reclaimed from sewage must take into account a number of considerations, including the following six major items. Two leading questions relate to (1) public attitudes toward such reuse, and (2) associated policy questions concerning protection of public health. These two critical issues, the major focus of this paper, are listed in Table 3 along with four other matters that should figure significantly in decisions about reusing water.

One of the four additional points is (3) the cost of reclaiming usable water from municipal wastewater. Technology provides many procedures for refurbishment, but all are expensive.

Another question is (4) the effect of reuse on general environmental quality. Use of reclaimed water has the double environmental benefit of making it unnecessary to discharge degraded water into the environment, while also limiting the need for new dams, reservoirs, and water transport facilities.

A further related factor is (5) the need for new sources of water supply in California. Like desalinized ocean water, reclaimed wastewater represents a new but unconventional source of supply that could benefit the state's water-short areas.

Finally, there is (6) the problem of constructing a separate system to carry reclaimed water to consumers, if it is deemed unsafe to mix reclaimed water with the current domestic supply. Construction of dual water systems, one system for highest quality culinary water, and another for medium quality irrigation and cleaning water, would be expensive in existing communities but less so for new developments.

As noted, this paper focuses primarily upon the first two questions: public attitudes concerning reclaimed water, and issues related to public health. The writer believes that the public should be brought into the technical decision-making process. He also recognizes the public's right to influence early decisions, and not to be restricted to the final implementation stages of proposals. That is, the public should be involved *prior* to bond election campaigns, and at a time when new uses of reclaimed water are initially proposed.[2]

Background and Aim of the Study

This paper deals with the attitudes of Californians concerning the use of reclaimed water and the public policy implications of the findings. Public attitudes toward reclaimed water were assessed in communities where such water had actually been used; at present, public recreational facilities provide the most visible uses. The research therefore focused on five "project communities": California communities whose public recreational facilities were supplied with reclaimed water. They were South Lake Tahoe, Livermore, Thousand Oaks, Mission Viejo and Santee, selected, respectively, in the Lake Tahoe Basin, the San Francisco Bay Area, and in Ventura, Orange and San Diego counties. Five similar "nonproject communities" not using reclaimed water were selected for comparison: Tahoe City, Sunnyvale, Simi, Fountain Valley and Poway, with a parallel north-south geographical distribution.[3] Thus the ten communities surveyed were selected to be representative not only of the geography, but also of the population and water reclamation projects in California.[4]

Specifically, the study sought to measure respondents' attitudes toward 25 general uses of reclaimed water and then to assess policy preferences regarding water treatment and reuse or disposal. The aim was to develop policy recommendations based on the findings, for planning future innovative projects for water reuse.

Twenty-five Possible Uses

Reclaimed water has a wide range of possible uses. As a general test of their attitudes, respondents were asked whether they "would oppose" or "would not oppose" a particular use of reclaimed water in their own community. The questionnaire suggested 25 possible uses, spanning the range from the most intimate personal contact to least intimate personal contact. Many of the lower-contact uses currently exist. The higher-contact uses are presently hypothetical, but possible in the future.

Table 1 shows the percentages of respondents who opposed each of the 25 general uses suggested, ranked in order of total percentage opposed. The use of reclaimed water for drinking and food preparation got the strongest opposition. The lowest level of opposition was directed to irrigation of golf courses

and freeway greenbelts, and road construction. Thus extent of opposition is correlated with the likelihood or extent of close personal contact. As Table 1 indicates, opposition ranged from a low of less than 1 percent to a high of over 56 percent. There were no important differences between respondents in "project communities" and "nonproject communities."

Consistency of Findings

Because the American population is highly mobile, it may be useful to see how closely these California findings coincide with the results of recent attitude surveys conducted elsewhere.

A review located five major studies performed during the early 1970's where representative sampling procedures were used to assess public attitudes toward reclaimed water.[5] The five studies produced remarkably consistent results: more than 50 percent of each sample was opposed to the use of reclaimed water for the highest contact purposes. These results indicate that the public is not yet ready for direct reuse, i.e., it will not yet accept a direct connection between an advanced waste treatment plant and the domestic water distribution system.

TABLE 1

Respondents Opposed to Specified Uses of Reclaimed Water

	Percentage Opposed		
Uses	Project (N=479)	Non-project (N=493)	Total (N=972)
1. Drinking	56.6	56.2	56.4
2. Preparing food in restaurants	56.2	55.8	56.0
3. Preparing food in the home	53.2	55.7	54.5
4. Canning vegetables	54.3	53.9	54.1
5. Bathing in the home	37.6	39.7	38.7
6. Swimming	22.4	25.0	23.7
7. Pumping down special wells*	25.7	20.8	23.2
8. Laundry in the home	21.3	24.2	22.8
9. Laundry, commercial	19.7	24.1	21.9
10. Irrigation of dairy pasture	14.2	14.0	14.1
11. Irrigation of vegetable crops	14.9	13.2	14.0
12. Spreading on sandy areas	14.3	12.2	13.3
13. Irrigation of vineyards	14.5	11.3	12.0
14. Irrigation of orchards	10.9	9.3	10.1
15. Irrigation of hay or alfalfa	8.6	6.5	7.5
16. Pleasure boating	7.9	6.7	7.3
17. Commercial air conditioning	7.5	5.5	6.5
18. Electronic plant processes	6.1	3.7	4.9
19. Toilet flushing, home	5.4	2.2	3.8
20. Golf course hazard lakes	3.1	3.0	3.1
21. Irrigation of lawn, home	3.5	1.8	2.7
22. Irrigation of recreation parks	3.5	1.6	2.6
23. Irrigation of golf courses	2.7	0.6	1.6
24. Irrigation of freeway greenbelts	1.9	0.6	1.2
25. Road construction	1.5	0.2	0.8

*ground water recharge: pushing water into the earth.

TABLE 3

Weighted Factors* in the Use of Reclaimed Water

Policy options**	(a) Public attitudes	(b) Public health	(c) Reclamation costs	(d) Effect on environmental quality	(e) Sources of new supply	(f) Cost of dual systems	Assessment of policy by simple sums
One	-1	-1	-1	+1	+1	0	-1
Two & Three	+1	0	0	+1	+1	-1	+2
Four	-1	-1	+1	-1	-1	0	-3

*A value of plus one (+1) was assigned in the attitude category if public opinion tended to support the policy, and a value of minus one (-1) was assigned if it tended to oppose. A value of plus one (+1) was assigned under all other categories if the policy in question seemed likely to produce desirable results, and a value of minus one (-1) if undesirable. Zero (0) values were used to indicate neutrality.

**See Table 2 for statement of options one through four.

contact. Meanwhile, those who wish to demonstrate that reclaimed water is of high quality should initiate highly visible, well publicized demonstrations using reclaimed water for low-contact purposes not likely to be controversial. Such innovations would give technical experts, health officials, and the lay public experiential and scientific evidence that modern technology can provide water that is reliably of high quality in every respect. If these demonstration efforts are successful we will be a long way ahead in developing public acceptance for reclaimed water that might eventually include intimate personal use and consumption.

Now to combine conclusions reached on the public health effects of and public attitudes toward the use of reclaimed water in concert with the other four policy questions mentioned earlier. It must be emphasized that the overall conclusion provided by Table 3 is an attempt at a summary, built up by assigning a weight of plus one, zero, or minus one, to each of the three groups of policy options outlined in Table 2. The simple weights assigned to the public attitudes category are supported by five of the recent attitude surveys cited here.[15] The weights assigned the public health category are based on the material presented in this paper. Weights were assigned arbitrarily by the writer to reclamation cost, effect on environmental quality, sources of new supply and cost of dual systems categories, and the reader may wish to change some of these. Nevertheless, Table 3 provides an heuristic summary of the six major policy issues involved.

The simple summation of weights across the six categories of Table 3 suggests an assessment of policy on reclaimed water that is in accord with the survey results reported in Table 2: low level treatment and disposal is considered inappropriate, but direct reuse is not yet seen as appropriate. Thus, as noted earlier, the best course of action for the intermediate future is high level treatment and reuse, but with only low to moderate degrees of personal contact. Consequently the cost and feasibility of constructing parallel distribution systems to supply reclaimed water separately from drinking water may determine whether the intermediate solution recommended here becomes a long-term solution. Such dual systems are currently coming into use in certain parts of California and data on how well these work will determine if Okun's[16] recommendation becomes a reality, allowing the recycling of water to become accepted practice.

Summary

Present day technology can, for a price, produce reclaimed water that meets traditional drinking water standards. Nevertheless, much important research remains to be done on the reliability of the technical treatment process, and upon long-term health effects of trace substances not removed during technical treatment, or introduced by it. Public attitudes indicate that consumers will accept the use of reclaimed water for a wide variety of purposes, but *not* including drinking it, or other highly intimate uses. Accordingly, both public health and public opinion data support a policy of beneficial use of reclaimed sewage for those purposes the public will accept—i.e., non-intimate uses—while postponing widespread use of reclaimed sewage for consumption until we have more evidence on treatment plant reliability and on possible effects of trace substances. This policy receives further support from the author's brief analysis of reclamation costs, environmental quality, new supply sources, and dual system requirements.

NOTES

1 Wastewater is the water discharged from sinks, wash basins, toilets and drains in homes, commercial establishments and industries. Reclaimed water is produced when community or municipal wastewater is purified and made suitable for beneficial use.

2 William H. Bruvold, "Human Perception and Evaluation of Water Quality," *Critical Reviews in Environmental Control,* 5(2):153-231 (March 1975).

3 For a detailed account of research methods and results, see Bruvold, *Public Attitudes Toward Reuse of Reclaimed Water* (Contribution No. 137) (Berkeley: University of California, Water Resources Center, August 1972).

4 D. G. Deaner, *Directory of Wastewater Reclamation Operations in California* (Berkeley: California State Department of Public Health, August 1969).

5 The first surveyed ten California communities; the second involved a nationwide poll of the United States; the third surveyed Denver, Colorado; the fourth involved ten Southern California communities; and the fifth covered eight U.S. cities. A detailed critical analysis of each of the five studies can be found in the Bruvold 1975 paper, note 2 above.

6 Pathogens are bacteria, viruses, and other disease-producing organisms. Daniel A. Okun, "Alternatives in Water Supply," *Journal, American Water Works Association,* 61(5):215-221 (May 1969.) Toxins are poisons that lead to impaired bodily functioning including sudden or eventual death. Carcinogens are substances that bring about cancer in mammals, including humans.

7 Perceived quality deals with the taste, odor, and clarity of water.

8 A. A. Rosen, "Health Significance of Taste and Odor Research," *American Water Works Association Seminar Proceedings: Taste and Odor,* 20111:1-6 (June 1975).

9 See note 3 above, Bruvold, 1972.

10 Primary treatment usually involves screening and sedimentation to remove solid matter from wastewater. Secondary treatment usually includes biological action induced to remove dissolved organics from water already given primary treatment. Tertiary treatment often involves removal of biostimulants or nutrients, such as ammonia, from wastewater already given primary and secondary treatment.

Advanced water treatment usually comprises several additional steps such as activated carbon treatment, demineralization, and clarification. These treatments are used in order to meet quality standards for effluents that cannot be attained by ordinary three-step treatment of wastewater. Disinfection by chlorination ordinarily completes treatment of any wastewater and is therefore a part of each mentioned above.

11 William F. Jopling, D. G. Deaner and Henry J. Ongerth, "Fitness Needs for Wastewater Reclamation Plants," *Journal, American Water Works Association,* 63(10):626-629 (October 1971).

12 See note 3 above, Bruvold, 1972.

13 See note 2 above, Bruvold, 1975.

14 See note 6 above, Okun, 1969.

15 See note 2 above, Bruvold, 1975.

16 See note 6 above, Okun, 1969.

Science, Technology and Policy

Vol. 17   No. 4   August 1976

NEW ISSUES FOR CALIFORNIA,
THE WORLD'S MOST ADVANCED INDUSTRIAL SOCIETY

by
Ted K. Bradshaw
Research Sociologist
Institute of Governmental Studies

Introduction

California is a unique society, geographically separated from other states by mountains and deserts, and culturally different in achievement, resources and customs. Thus, observers frequently agree with Carey McWilliams that California is a "great exception"[1] but rarely consider the ways new issues often seem to demand attention in California long before they emerge in other places. This paper builds on the premise that California is exceptional as the world's first, indeed prototypical, advanced industrial society,[2] that its place is on the frontier of social and economic change, and that because of this exceptional character the state must give serious consideration to a new set of policy issues.

California's characteristics include leadership among states and nations in several indices of industrial development. First, the state has the world's greatest concentration of high-technology industry, depending heavily on advanced scientific theory, and involving major research and development projects. The technology is not concentrated solely in aerospace and electronics firms, but is dispersed throughout the entire economic and social system. Second, California has more workers in service-sector industries—such as communications, transportation, finance, sales, and the professions—than any other industrial state in the nation. Third, the growth of new specialized technologies has led to increased interdependence within the society; relations between firms, groups, political bodies, and individuals have become more intense. Fourth, the state is characterized by rapid change and innovation. California is often one of the nation's first states to experience new social problems and to develop new responses. Finally, advanced industrial development has expanded the need for information and knowledge,

so that California leads the nation in education and in the creation of knowledge. In short, these five characteristics form a pattern identified as advanced industrialism, and they signal the emergence of a new kind of society confronting new issues.

It is tempting to call California a "post-industrial society," following Daniel Bell's use of the term,[3] but that concept can lead to misinterpretations. There is no evidence that California's economy has changed so much that industrialism has become peripheral rather than central, the way agriculture became peripheral after the industrial revolution. Admittedly there is an increase in the proportion of the labor force working in service industries—which Bell suggests will replace manufacturing as the central type of work in the post-industrial society—but many of these workers provide support services such as communications, transportation, finance, and marketing for the modern industrial system.

Furthermore, Bell suggests that the post-industrial society gives a central emphasis to knowledge, whereas the major thrust of knowledge development in California seems to be to devise new ways for the industrial system to advance. In short, even though recreation and tourism have increased and professional services have grown, these developments do not justify the conclusion that California is *post*-industrial. Instead, California is strongly committed to one of the world's *most advanced forms of industrial development*, and has created a society to support it.

California as an Advanced Industrial Society

An advanced industrial society represents the latest stage of an ongoing process of development in industrial countries. The characteristics of such a society principally comprise differences in degree rather than differences in kind. Their major emphasis has shifted from machinery and inanimate power to highly sophisticated technologies, scientific knowledge, and more tightly interwoven patterns of relationships. Nevertheless, all parts of the society are not equally advanced; some surviving patterns characteristic of earlier developmental phases survive alongside the new. For example, California's rural logging and marginal farming communities, central city ghettos, and thriving ethnic communities embody ways of life that were characteristic of a past era. Moreover, many major but less advanced parts of the economy are as important to the state's overall life as the most advanced, but the relative *prevalence* of the highly advanced gives California its dominant tone.

This paper first examines each of the five characteristics of advanced industrialism noted above, and then considers the consequences with respect to several policy issues. It is proposed that (1) raising productivity in advanced industrial societies requires new types of public cooperation, (2) new opportunities exist for the wise use of scarce resources, and (3) growth patterns can be redirected to emphasize new directions and transformation rather than simple addition to what already exists. In each of these areas the examination of California's accomplishments and prospects should provide guidelines for well-considered policy responses to future demands. While answers are neither precise nor definitive, the purpose of the discussion is to suggest a new framework for dealing with a new society's novel problems.

Sophisticated technology. The leading characteristic of an *advanced industrial society* is its reliance on new technological developments, especially in industry. The use of sophisticated technologies means that an increasing proportion of the value of a product is a consequence of investment in scientific and engineering knowledge. (In contrast, the value of a product in industrial society comes mostly from physical labor, mechanical energy, or raw materials.) In addition, production processes and the knowledge behind them become increasingly complex. As Nathan Rosenberg points out, as industrial society becomes more advanced, "we may be moving up the scale of increasing complexity in the knowledge base underlying economic activity—from the mechanical to the electrical and electronic, chemical, biological, etc."[4]

Advanced technologies have produced items not known 50 or even 25 years ago, such as tomato picking machines, nuclear power generators, jet aircraft, missiles, communications satellites, laser beams, electronic computers, or pocket calculators. Data provided by the National Science Foundation show that industries producing such new items spend the highest percentages for developing new technologies. For example, in 1972 aircraft and electronics and communications equipment industries spent the highest proportion of net sales on research and development. Aircraft spent 16 percent and electronics and communications spent slightly over 8 percent. In addition, California as a national leader in developing and using advanced technologies, has about 30 percent of the nation's aeronautical engineers. Further, engineers comprise a higher proportion of its labor force than that of any other state.[6]

In addition to creating new industries, California's advanced technology has helped transform the way older industries do their work. All industries have a gap between those plants that lead in the use of sophisticated technologies and those that lag behind. In California a greater proportion uses new technologies, partly because many firms responded to rapid growth by building plants relatively recently and thus were able to take advantage of newer developments. Moreover in some sectors such as agriculture, California has led the nation in expenditures for research and development. The resulting combination of technical skill and advantageous climate produces a higher value of crops per acre than any other state,[7] including such difficult to grow but rewarding specialty crops as artichokes, apricots, lettuce, citrus fruits, and wine grapes.

Furthermore, California has led the nation in adopting technologies to the organization of work. For example, California is recognized as a leader in planning and local government innovation, and the California Legislature is ranked as the nation's most professional, with staffs of well trained consultants working on policy analysis.[8]

The service society. A second characteristic of the advanced industrial society is the proportion of the labor force that provides services rather than manufactures goods. California currently has 70 percent of its labor force in services, the largest proportion of any industrial state in the nation.[9] As La Porte and Abrams point out, the United States is often considered the first "post-industrial" society, having exceeded 50 percent service employment by about 1940, but California passed that mark even earlier, about 1920.[10]

Moreover, while gross figures are important, they may not reflect major changes in California's service industries. For example, personal service workers (e.g., maids and servants) have declined; specialized service workers (e.g., new professionals in education, welfare, medicine, and law) have increased along with the proportion of workers in communications and transportation. Furthermore, in many services—especially communications and transportation—the style of work has become similar to that of industry, where employees deal not with people but with machines that require heavy capital investments.

Intensified interdependence. Sophisticated technology and changing occupational patterns lead to a vastly more complex society marked by increasing interdependence. Such increase reflects a growth in the number of specialties carried out by particular groups or organizations that in turn depend on each other with greater intensity. As technological development increases, a larger variety of specialties are needed by each firm or organization, and to gain access to these skills each group must deal with a greater number of other groups.

For example, a traditional toaster factory has low interdependencies, needs a relatively small number of supplies such as metal, heating elements, plastics, tools and cardboard boxes. The company markets the toaster through a network of distributors and warehouses that deal with similar items. But an advanced industrial firm manufacturing computers or aircraft needs many more kinds of materials and tools, each with fewer substitutes. In turn, these materials and components are more complex, have more parts and originate from more suppliers. The output of the advanced industrial plant is then distributed by a more complicated network, whose installation services and special adaptations increase the number of interdependent links.

In addition, California's interdependence extends to all the society's institutions. One measure of the interdependence and linkage is the availability of telephones: California has about 698 telephones per thousand persons, a higher ratio than any other state.[11]

The government becomes increasingly involved as more regulations are needed to govern relations between firms. Also, there is more interdependence among the various components of government itself, e.g., more links among governmental agencies and between state and local levels. For example, Jones, Magleby and Scott report 386 references to local governments in the Governor's Budget for 1975-76.[12] Furthermore, local governments must deal with regional governments, such as areawide planning agencies and independent water districts. Such interdependence becomes a major source of both strength and confusion for advanced industrial societies.

Rapid change and innovation. The fourth characteristic is rapid change. Alvin Toffler's *Future Shock*[13] noted the acceleration of change in modern industrial societies. Perhaps more than other places, California has felt the impact of change, both in the speed and the multiplicity of innovations. In politics, knowledgeable experts have ranked California as the leading state in policy innovation.[14]

Much of the evidence of the state's rapid change is impressionistic, but has been well stated by Carey McWilliams, who notes that "The scale is so much larger; the tempo of events so much faster; and, in California, everything seems to be reversed, to occur out of the natural state of events, to be upside down or lopsided."[15]

Population growth in California has also contributed to the rapidity of change. As Kingsley Davis and Frederick Styles point out, California "has had the fastest long run population growth of any advanced society in the world, not excepting Japan or Israel."[16] It is of course possible to have rapid social change without rapid population growth, but when the two forces join as they have done in California, the impact is greatly reinforced.

Knowledge and training. The advanced industrial society demands that its citizens acquire the knowledge and expertise to cope with elaborate structures and social issues, and California leads the nation in the generation and transfer of new knowledge. As one indication, California in 1973 received about 23 percent of all federal funds allocated for research and development; the next highest state, Maryland, received only 9 percent.[17] In addition, California's government spends more than that of any other state for research and development.[18] Data showing that almost all sorts of industry in the state employ more professional and technical workers (e.g., scientists, engineers and accountants) than the national average, further demonstrate the significance of knowledge and research for California.[19]

With respect to higher education, California is an acknowledged leader. A greater proportion of its young persons receive college training than elsewhere in the country: nearly 80 percent of California's high school graduates enroll at some time in an institution of higher education.[20] In addition, California students stay in colleges and universities longer than elsewhere; the census reports that the state has a higher proportion of 22-34-year-olds in school than any other except Utah. In short, as an advanced industrial society, California allocates a large proportion of its work force to the generation, as well as the transmittal and use, of new knowledge.

The cumulative effect. California is not highest or first with respect to any *single* indicator, but it is virtually unique in its *combination* of the characteristics indicative of an advanced industrial society. For example, the area around Boston has a high concentration of electronics firms, but high technology has not influenced Massachusetts as much as it has California. Similarly, some areas have a greater concentration of service industries than California—e.g., the greater Washington, D.C. area, Nevada, or Hawaii—yet they lack California's industrial base.

General Policy Considerations

The use of sophisticated technology as the basis for an economy alters some fundamental premises of theories devised for manufacturing economics. For example, when government becomes heavily involved in promotion of research, funding education, regulating markets, and facilitating communication and transportation, then the older concepts of market forces lose much of their presumed ability to explain economic phenomena.

Furthermore, reliance on sophisticated technologies may give rise to unfounded optimism, e.g., that the many problems produced by advanced technology may be solved by even more advanced technology. But dependence on a "technological fix" is risky, as exemplified by problems of nuclear waste disposal, cancer-causing chemicals, and unsatisfactory BART (Bay Area Rapid Transit) performance. Moreover the technologies generate rapid change and produce obsolescence. Finally, the spectre of a large and complicated technology dwarfing the citizenry helps motivate the search for alternatives like those suggested by Schumacher's book, *Small is Beautiful.*[21] Thus, increased use of sophisticated technology seems likely to bring new issues to the front: How can limitations of the technology be overcome? Should limits be placed on the use of advanced technologies? When should old technologies be exchanged for new?

Anticipation and the unknowable. As interdependence increases, it becomes more essential that the complex relationships be understood well enough to permit anticipation of consequences. As with a spider web, a pull on one strand affects all the others. Similarly, in a highly interdependent society one change can cause many others, which themselves may lead to highly surprising results. Although the ability to anticipate consequences may be limited by lack of knowledge or imagination, we can try to guard against unanticipated developments by building a capacity for flexibility and a readiness to change policy quickly as it needs to be changed.

In addition, with rapid change, apparent solutions may no longer be appropriate by the time they are implemented because of time lags between problem-identification and solution-implementation. Thus, in an advanced industrial society, policies that anticipate problems and are adaptable to changing circumstances, are increasingly necessary.

Finally, as knowledge becomes more essential to the operation of industry and government, it becomes vital that the free flow of information be assured and encouraged. California's extensive system of higher education is an important facilitative force, although critics counter with claims that California is overeducating young members of society, and that college degree holders are finding it hard to obtain good first jobs. But as David S. Saxon, President of the University of California, points out, education provides *more than mere entry requirements* for a first job. It provides tools for a full and satisfying life, a lifetime of changing careers in a rapidly changing world, and skills for active participation in the affairs of a modern democratic government.[22] In short, the challenge of education in advanced industrial societies is to help persons of all ages develop the skills to cope at work and leisure with the complexity of modern life.

While all of these policy considerations are important, this paper now focuses on three: the opportunities to increase productivity, the wise use of scarce resources, and the control of growth.

Rising Expectations for Increased Productivity

In advanced industrial societies, achieving higher productivity is an important concern of public officials and agencies. Often the goal is sought through research and development, which implies more output per unit input of labor, raw materials, and capital. But the methods of productivity improvement call for increased regulation of the relations between firms and agencies, as well as increased cooperation.

Thus, improving productivity becomes a matter of prime public concern. For example, the development of the tomato picking machine was a collaborative effort of the University of California, other universities, and private manufacturing companies. The contribution from universities amounted to almost half of the development costs, and included the services of plant breeders, agronomists, and irrigation specialists to develop the new types of plants and farming processes required by machine picking. Furthermore, university scientists, administrators and other officials coordinated with manufacturers, processors and growers in achieving notable success for the machine. One estimate suggests that it brought a 1000 percent return on investment, largely through saved labor costs.[23] (Some other consequences are discussed below.) Additional examples include the new efforts of the State Energy Resources Conservation and Development Commission to stimulate solar-energy production and to explore methods of energy conservation. In these efforts, however, private industry has not been greatly involved because of the lack of sufficient short-term profits.

Another role for government is the sponsorship of prototype projects, or the provision of facilities such as roads and water connections, that are needed to improve productivity. Productivity can also be promoted by governmental actions in the form of regulations that provide for standardized specifications.

The increasing linkages among firms and groups and the growth in interdependency also enlarge the public's stake in improving relations between groups who need each other. In this area, governmental agencies can help by serving as intermediaries. For example, through the establishment of the California Agricultural Labor Relations Board the state sought to help reduce conflict between growers and farm workers, and thus to increase stability in their relationships. Similarly, current efforts to help communities standardize data collection and planning services are intended to facilitate cooperation among governmental units.

Finally, public agencies can minimize exploitation and resentment between groups. This is especially important when certain groups—consumers, workers, owners of small businesses, or minorities—are particularly weak or vulnerable. The disclosure of information such as environmental impact statements, contents of processed food, and industrial accident reports, is often used as a protective device to guard the interests of those who would otherwise be uninformed. These reactions to interdependence are all unique capacities of the public sector and can be used effectively in the advanced industrial society.

Nevertheless, expanding the public role in productivity improvement raises questions concerning public interest. For example, how should the advantages of something like the tomato picking machine be evaluated when many farm workers lose jobs and the specially bred new tomatoes are often criticized as tough and flavorless? As another example, regulations that encourage a firm's productivity may bring harm to a community's environment. On the other hand, effective environmental protection may increase the cost of doing business.

New Opportunities for Maximizing the Use of Scarce Resources

The energy crisis and decline in conventional energy sources is by far the most serious current manifestation of the problem of dwindling scarce resources, but many others are also in potentially short supply. In California, in addition to a natural gas and oil shortage, the production of timber, minerals, and some agricultural products is likely to decline.

While resources have always been limited, the current problem lies in the number under simultaneous threat and the costs of substitutes that require greater investment of energy and capital. The situation poses huge problems for advanced industrial societies, but also offers unique opportunities for those societies to react creatively and sensibly.

Advanced industrial societies have certain advantages with respect to resource scarcity. In general, high technology industries do not use great quantities of natural resources, although they do use much of the

ners in addressing both the pre- and post-earthquake periods, and promoting better integration of post-earthquake recovery efforts into community planning processes.

Responding to Earthquake Predictions: First Steps

Geologists, seismologists, engineers and other experts, should cooperate in describing likely alternative earthquake events—"scenarios"—as a framework for possible responses. For example, the report cited in note 7 (*Earthquake Prediction and Public Policy*), discusses a number of measures that might be taken immediately, or with less than a year of advance warning, or with one or more years of warning (see especially Chapter 9). Similarly Charles C. Thiel's presentation (at the San Francisco earthquake prediction conference of November 7, 1975) suggested response measures scheduled according to available leadtimes, in multiples of 10: (1) 3 days, (2) 30 days, (3) 300 days, and (4) 3,000 days.[9]

Panels of experts and community leaders should think through the implications of possible responses, attempting to anticipate problems, and specifying conditions and requirements for reasonable effectiveness.

Conferences and organized study groups should examine research findings derived from investigations suggested earlier—concerning risk, hazard-mitigation, casualties, losses and economic and fiscal impacts. The conferences should evaluate remedial measures with regard to their equity, acceptability and feasibility. In addition, when the California Seismic Safety Commission completes elements of a draft state policy framework, conferences and public discussion should consider these as well as other contributions to policy formulation. Both expert analysis and general public understanding are essential for policy development and acceptance.

Putting the Pieces Together: The Role of Strategic Planning

The range of policies and research suggested in the interest of earthquake safety emphasizes the complexity of the problems. Putting the pieces together will require strategic statewide "overview" planning of a kind not yet achieved. In sum, the four main planning components are: (1) seismic or earthquake hazard analysis and risk-zoning, (2) earthquake engineering, (3) emergency preparedness, and (4) disaster relief and recovery, including insurance. Informed critics have commented that "the four disaster-related programs. . .are evolving along separate paths rather than in an integrated, interactive manner."[10]

Accordingly, they urge strategic planning that can relate new knowledge about earthquakes and earthquake prediction to society's other protective processes. Continuing efforts should therefore attempt to anticipate future situations, devise appropriate responses, evaluate available trade-offs, assess alternatives, and integrate short-term actions into a long-term program.

A Future Goal

When the principal objectives of seismic safety policy have been achieved, Californians can enjoy acceptably low levels of earthquake risk. Life loss can be reduced to a minimum, property damage restricted to reasonable amounts, critical services sustained, and recovery expedited. Moreover the knowledge gained from each successive earthquake can be put to work in reducing risk even further. In short, we can dramatically diminish the scope of future earthquake disasters—regardless of our ability to forecast precise times and locations—by studying the hazard methodically and applying what we learn.

Notes

[1] See two publications of the U.S. Department of Commerce, National Oceanic & Atmospheric Administration: *A Study of Earthquake Losses in the Los Angeles, California Area*, A Report Prepared for the Federal Disaster Assistance Administration, Department of Housing & Urban Development (1973); and *A Study of Earthquake Losses in the San Francisco Bay Area: Data and Analysis*, A Report Prepared for the Office of Emergency Preparedness (1972).

[2] Remarks on September 17, 1976, at dedication of the John A. Blume Earthquake Engineering Center, Stanford University.

[3] National Academy of Sciences, *Predicting Earthquakes: A Scientific and Technical Evaluation—with Implications for Society* (Washington, D.C., 1976), p. 3.

[4] Ibid, p. 2.

[5] California, Legislature, Joint Committee on Seismic Safety, *Meet-ing the Earthquake Challenge: Final Report to the Legislature. . .* (January 1974), p. 6.

[6] National Academy of Sciences, note 3 above, p. 30.

[7] National Academy of Sciences, *Earthquake Prediction and Public Policy* (Washington, D.C., 1975) p. 119.

[8] The final report of the Legislature's Joint Committee on Seismic Safety suggested appropriate safety measures for critical and high-exposure facilities based on the concept of acceptable risk. (Table 1, p. 9). See note 5 above.

[9] U.S. Geological Survey, *Earthquake Prediction—Opportunity to Avert Disaster* (Geological Survey Circular 729, 1976), pp. 13-16.

[10] Stanford Research Institute, *Basic Concept and Outline of Final Study Report: Technology Assessment of Earthquake Prediction* (Working Paper, July 29, 1975), pp. 25-26.

Women's Opportunities in Education

Vol. 17   No. 6   December 1976

FURTHERING THE MATHEMATICAL COMPETENCE OF WOMEN

Nancy Kreinberg

Project Coordinator
Math and Science Education for Women
Lawrence Hall of Science

Introduction

The educational and occupational opportunities of most women are severely restricted by inadequate preparation in mathematics, and in order to change that pattern, young women need to study math throughout the full range of their schooling. Recognition of this fact has prompted efforts throughout the country—especially in California—to develop the motivation and improve the mathematical skills of females. The movement toward equal education is particularly active in the greater San Francisco Bay Area, where a network of people from government, industry and educational institutions at all levels are working to increase women's participation in studies and occupations where mathematics is the base, and higher income one of the payoffs.

This article analyzes obstacles to young women's mathematics education, describes action programs that can help, and suggests ways for the public to promote improved education of and opportunities for female citizens. Lessons about effective ways to increase math competence and confidence among girls and women can be adapted for the larger population, comprising both males and females, who need help in breaking a pattern of math avoidance that limits educational accomplishment and wastes human potential.

The Pattern of Math Avoidance

While this paper focuses on the mathematical needs of females, it is acknowledged that mathematical competence is essential for full participation by all members of society. It takes more than simple arithmetic to make decisions about jobs, taxes, education, and investments, as well as to evaluate the policy aspects of technological and scientific issues that confront the electorate. All citizens need a degree of mathematical capability to be effective members of a society in which information is often presented quantitatively. Unfortunately, many adults and young people lack mathematical confidence —the willingness to tackle an area of study requiring mathematical computation, to reason mathematically, and to enjoy doing it.

Large numbers of people avoid math, especially those with limited educational opportunities and attainments. But in our society, young women appear especially to lack motivation or encouragement to succeed or excel in mathematics, an area usually considered a male domain.

How Expectations Are Shaped: The Causes of Math Avoidance

Sex-role expectations, and their effects on students' career aspirations and educational progress, have been studied extensively, particularly in the seventies.[1] Findings show that stereotyping on the basis of sex begins early in the nursery and the home, and is later reinforced in the classroom, where textbooks, activities, and teachers' attitudes tend to convey a message regarding comparative competence and originality in math-related areas, i.e., that "boys invent things, whereas girls only use what boys invent."

In particular, the stereotypic assumption that girls are neither good in math nor interested in the subject is especially harmful, since it creates an atmosphere in which young women fulfill this low-performance expectation. Recent studies[2] confirm that many young women do indeed have a variety of negative attitudes toward mathematics, including general lack of interest in the subject and lack of confidence in their ability to do well. Many are unable to see the relevance of math to their present or future interests. Finally, some women believe that math is an inappropriate pursuit for females, or that others will consider it unsuitable for them.

Such negative attitudes might be expected to result in poor math achievement for females. However, Hilton and Berglund's longitudinal study found that small differences in math achievement among boys and girls do not appear until the 7th grade.[3] Before that time, boys and girls are equal in ability and interest in mathematics. In fact, even as far as high school is concerned, a recent National Science Foundation study by Fennema and Sherman[4] found that the differences between males and females in mathematics achievement were very small, and were "not more pronounced with increasing grade level and more difficult material."

Fennema and Sherman concluded:

> Existing evidence suggests that the sex-related differences in studying and learning math cannot be explained fully by any difference in cognitive abilities between the sexes. Even the small differences in performance on spatial visualization tasks cannot account for the very large [numerical] discrepancy between males and females who study math. Therefore *attention must be given to that wide range of variables identified as socio-culture or affective factors.* [emphasis supplied][5]

Children's attitudes toward math and science may be influenced very early by the kinds of toys and games parents provide. Among a small sample of parents of gifted children, Astin[6] found boys were more likely than girls to be given science kits, microscopes, or telescopes. Kirk[7] found that young women who were "science-bound" were significantly more interested in puzzles, in problem solving and taking things apart to see how they work, than those who were not planning to pursue science. Failure to engage girls in such activities, which stimulate inquiry and investigation, may restrict the early practice in problem solving that appears essential for cultivating mathematical and scientific interests and abilities. Matthews noted that

> By the time elementary school days begin girls may be locked into behavior and reaction patterns that are so restrictive of the expansion of the mind that special types of education are needed to thaw out potentiality and encourage the exercise of competence.[8]

Parents may also influence students' mathematical abilities in more subtle ways. Ernest[9] and Kirk note that students turn to their fathers, not their mothers, for help in mathematics, particularly in high school. This preference helps confirm and perpetuate the "math is for men" image.

Teachers, counselors, and other peers often perpetuate stereotyped beliefs that women do not need to study math, that boys are better than girls in the subject, and that women could not or should not become scientists or technicians. Ernest found nearly half of the elementary and secondary school teachers he questioned were convinced that boys are better at math than girls. Many of the talented high school women studied by Casserly[10] reported that their guidance counselors tended to discourage them from enrolling in advanced science and math courses. Some counselors considered advanced math unnecessary for college.

Others thought it superfluous for girls, perhaps even damaging. Thus one counselor in her twenties remarked:

> I just hate to see a girl get in over her head. I always try to place students at a level where I know they'll be successful. I mean, wouldn't it be frightful to spoil a beautiful record by doing poorly in the course your senior year?

Further, because young women rarely consider the possibility of entering a scientific or technical field, or even competing for openings as apprentices in skilled trades, most stop taking math as soon as it becomes optional in high school.[11] Among those going on to college, Lucy Sells in "High School Mathematics as the Critical Filter in the Job Market," identified poor math preparation as the major obstacle to women's entrance into "every major in the undergraduate field except the traditionally female and hence lower paying fields."[12] Sells found that among entering freshmen at U.C. Berkeley in 1972, 57 percent of the males had taken four years of high school mathematics, contrasted with only 8 percent of the females.

In short, a collection of socially determined attitudes and behaviors deters young women from mathematics. Ultimately this bars them from a vast range of career and job opportunities that could otherwise furnish good sources of employment and income.

Female Patterns of Education and Employment

A consequence of girls' being discouraged from pursuing math in school or seeking math-related careers is evident in their response to the job market, for example, in engineering. Because of Affirmative Action pressures, women engineers are now in high demand. Yet despite the fact that in 1975 teacher graduates outnumbered available jobs 2.5 to 1, one-third of all females graduating from college are still earning degrees in education. On the other hand, for the next few years three potential jobs will be awaiting every student with a bachelor's degree in ceramic engineering.[13]

Clearly, opportunities are more plentiful in fields that require a math background, and salaries are much better. Other fields that require high school mathematics beyond algebra include jobs as surveyors, auto mechanics, machinists, carpenters, roofers, electronics workers, and technicians in scientific and industrial laboratories. All of these fields are traditionally male-dominated and higher paying than the conventional female jobs of clerk, salesperson, nurse's aide or typist. For example, students graduating with bachelor's degrees in petroleum engineering in 1975-76 averaged monthly salary offers of $1,398, nearly double that of humanities graduates, who averaged only $775.[14]

Breaking the Pattern

But whether or not they are college-educated, women continue to work in an extremely narrow range of occupations, predominantly in lower-paying, dead-end jobs.[15] Strenuous effort, both by individual women and organizations, will be required to break this pattern and bring about significant change. According to a recent study of the Conference Board's Division of Economic Research, "If the trends of the past 15 years continue, the nation's commitment to equal employment opportunity will be accompanied by only modest changes in the occupational distribution for women."[16]

To ensure that this pattern will not continue, it is essential to eliminate conditions curtailing women's options as students and adults—at home, in school, and on the job. It is particularly appropriate that such an effort take place in California, where employment opportunities for workers with quantitative and technical skills are increasing, and tolerance for innovation has always been high.

Action Programs

What can be done to eliminate the effects of sexism from mathematics education and related professions? What can be done to foster girls' and women's awareness of and interest in math-based careers? Kirk stresses the need to provide early and continuing opportunities for girls' exposure to and participation in mathematics, relating the content of learning to the student's life, both present and future. Casserly sees the need to sensitize counselors, teachers, and parents to the necessity of desexing career expectations. Thus all girls and boys in early junior high school should be encouraged to continue in mathematics, even if their interests in math and science are still vague and undefined.

Both of these researchers would encourage younger girls to discuss possibilities with older ones who have succeeded in high school math and science, and with women professionals in math-based fields. Such female role models can give the support and encouragement often lacking in young women's educational environments.

Several of these factors have been combined in one program for elementary school girls, given at the Lawrence Hall of Science since 1974.

Math for Girls

The Lawrence Hall of Science (LHS) has a dual role as a public science center and a research unit in science education at the University of California, Berkeley. For many years it has developed curricula and programs to increase public understanding of and interest in science. It provides after-school classes in the physical and life sciences, mathematics, and computer science, for children from first grade through high school.

A 1974 survey revealed that only one-quarter of the students enrolling in these classes were females. The Hall's response was to establish "Math for Girls" classes in addition to its regular math classes, in order to provide a non-threatening environment where girls from 6 to 14 could explore fundamental mathematical concepts and applications. Enrollment includes girls with varying backgrounds and interests, who come once a week to the 8-week, 12-hour class. In 2½ years, more than 350 girls have taken the class, and the total number of girls enrolled in other LHS math and science classes has doubled.

"Math for Girls" aims to make it enjoyable to learn mathematics. The classes begin with problems that make immediate success possible, and move along to those the students recognize as difficult but solvable. To insure eventual success, each girl needs to increase her ability to recognize problem-solving strategies, and practice using them. The "recurring theme" curriculum, pioneered by the Madison Project,[17] brings this about. The "theme" concepts include coordinate systems and graphing, recognizing functions and other numerical and geometric patterns, estimating, and techniques of logical problem solving.

The classes are taught by women students at the University of California, Berkeley, who are majoring in mathematics, mathematics education, or computer science. They are selected on the basis of interest and ability in mathematics and their desire to provide role-models for their students. Throughout the eight weeks, there are discussions of girls' competence and interest in mathematics, and the sorts of attitudes that can limit career expectations for women. The importance of taking science and mathematics courses in high school is stressed.

While the all-female environment is useful initially, it is not always possible or even desirable. Therefore, the program is developing ways to help teachers use these strategies in regular school classrooms. Other programs throughout the country are experimenting with teaching strategies in an all-female environment. Fox provided evidence that teaching accelerated math classes to bright adolescent girls is more effective in an all-female environment than in a coed setting.[18] MacDonald has also found that teaching is more effective in an all-female environment in a program on basic math skills.[19]

At Mills College (for women) Lenore Blum's projects to increase the mathematical and technical expertise of women have met with great success.[20] Her pre-calculus course quickly prepares a student for the calculus sequence, regardless of previous background. Ten percent of the Mills students now enroll, a threefold increase in three years. In Fall 1975, enrollment in the Math and Computer Science Department at Mills was the highest of any department on campus. Such an increase in the math and science interests of young women is extremely encouraging.

Conferences for 7th-12th Grade Women

The Lawrence Hall of Science co-sponsors bi-annual conferences for young women from 12 to 18 years old, to encourage girls to pursue math through high school and to increase awareness among students, teachers, counselors, and parents about scientific and technical career opportunities for women. In cooperation with Mills College and the Alameda/Contra Costa Counties Math Educators, and the volunteer efforts of 65 women educators, scientists, and engineers throughout the San Francisco Bay Area, this effort reached 900 students, parents, and teachers in 1976.

The conferences include a general session in which women representing several scientific and engineering professions discuss the challenges and problems of their work. Students then attend mathematics or science workshops that emphasize active participation and experimentation. Mathematical topics include topology, probability, estimating and statistics. Science workshops include investigations in chemistry, biology, physics, geology, computers and marine science. Advanced students attend a seminar in mathematics or science, where women researchers discuss their current work. After lunch, students attend career workshops, where they meet in small groups with women in particular scientific and technical fields, and ask them about their daily work activities.

Meanwhile the parents and teachers participate in sessions on admission requirements and scholarship opportunities, where representatives from state colleges, community colleges and universities lead discussions on ways to reduce sex stereotyping and increase career options for young women. Parents and teachers thus get practical information to use in assisting their daughters and students.

Evaluations of the first two conferences indicated that the girls gained new information about careers in math and science, and that being able to talk to women in these fields was extremely important to many. The following comments are illustrative:

The conference has made me aware of how exciting the chemical industry is and how important it is for me to take more math classes.

. . .

The women had a lot of good, positive, go-out-and-do-it energy. It gave me ideas about environmental biology, something I hadn't known existed.

. . .

It has made me more determined to go to college and reach an important goal. Each lady that I heard speak today gained my respect immediately and someday I wish to be respected as much.

. . .

I realize now that engineering is a *broad* area in which one can interact with other people and be creative.

. . .

I liked the honesty. The speakers really said something. They didn't talk in circles as I had expected.

. . .

I found that I had questions I didn't know I would have. My interests in medicine and research have been deepened and this encouraged me to look further into my interests instead of just skimming the surface. I'm really looking forward to being important in medicine now!

. . .

I feel more confident about starting different kinds of careers, and not so put off because of complicated school courses.

. . .

They answered questions I've wanted to know about for years. Math now seems like it's worth it.

. . .

It made me realize that these opportunities are real and reachable.

. . .

I liked how the women tried and did not give up when they were in school. It showed me that women are very important, just like men.

. . .

It was very good for me to see so many professional women in what I usually think of as careers that are totally male. It changes my opinion of those careers at a much deeper level than if someone had just said to me, 'Yes, it is possible for women to go into that field.' To see is to believe.

What's Ahead: A Network of Women, and Role Models

The lack of career materials portraying women working in science and engineering prompted the Lawrence Hall to develop its own forthcoming guide, *"I'm Madly in Love with Electricity" and Other Comments About Their Work by Women in Science and Engineering.* [21] The booklet evolved from a network of women who began to work together in early 1976 when several hundred science and mathematics educators, counselors and administrators from Bay Area schools, colleges and universities, along with scientists and engineers from industry met at Mills College for a conference on "Educating women for science: a continuous spectrum." [22] Results of the conference included consolidation of the network of people interested in such education for women, and the compilation of a Bay Area directory including their names and addresses.

From over 700 names in this directory, LHS in Fall 1976 mailed 450 questionnaires to women scientists, engineers, and technicians, asking their assistance in developing some pointers for scientific and technical careers. Within a month, 160 women had responded. Questions included: "Are the opportunities in your field expanding or are they limited? Would you advise a young woman to enter your field? What are the difficulties and drawbacks, if any, of being a woman in your field? Do you feel that there is room for you to grow and advance in your present job?" They were also asked to describe their work, including a typical day's activities.

The resulting booklet includes contributors who are engineers, physicists, mathematicians, astronomers, chemists, and life scientists. It does not attempt an exhaustive coverage of all possible careers in these math-related fields, but instead quotes the women's own descriptions of individual career experiences to stimulate the reader's interest. The booklet includes the names and addresses of all the women who responded to the questionnaire, so that students and teachers can call on them to speak at workshops or seminars, or arrange small field trips to their places of work. Relevant publications and sources for further information are also included.

Some negative material was omitted with respect to possible future experience of young women who choose to enter fields where they will be in the minority for some time. The purpose of the screening was to provide a realistic but encouraging picture, so that a young woman would be motivated to learn more about a particular field that catches her interest. The effort was to balance the negative evidence of difficulties with positive evidence of opportunities for women in these male-dominated professions. In fact, a majority of respondents did note difficulties related to being women in their fields.

Despite this experience, or perhaps even because of it, the women emphasized the need for such a booklet and affirmed their commitment to helping young women prepare themselves for scientific or engineering careers. As a feminist cartoonist recently remarked, "women need camaraderie when struggling against all the male institutions."

Since it took a good deal of time to fill out the four-page questionnaire, the sample was undoubtedly biased toward the kind of woman who would have a strong commitment to this type of project. Nevertheless, employers and educators may find it useful to review the problems encountered by many:

As is probably true in any field which is predominantly male, a woman must maintain high professional standards since her credibility may be questioned more readily than that of a male colleague.

. . .

Male mathematicians, while polite, are reluctant to take female mathematicians seriously. This makes you doubt your own ability, which is very depressing.

. . .

Advancement is slow. Geographical handicaps exist for women with husbands or other local anchors. They don't get job offers (assumed they won't move), so they stagnate where they are. This is a very difficult problem. Often women follow their husbands and just take whatever's available there. Very difficult pattern to change.

. . .

The drawbacks are personal: the compromises of having a family and a career. I feel that my son benefits greatly from having a mother who understands the world we live in, but I would not have wanted to work when he was tiny. That is a personal choice, and must be faced by any woman who chooses to combine a career with a family. Science is perhaps tougher on career women, because it moves so fast, and does not take kindly to a temporary drop-out or a less-than-full-time commitment.

. . .

The classical difficulties faced by any woman in science are applicable. Primarily, women are bypassed because they are outsiders to the mainstream of professional 'politics.'

In short, women encounter difficulties in being taken seriously, in combining a career and family, and in obtaining professional power and advancement, since they must be more highly qualified than male colleagues. Most of the obstacles are caused by the attitudes of others, but their solution will probably come largely from efforts exerted by women themselves.

Conclusions

Women are starting to enter traditionally male fields in greater numbers, but active intervention by public- and private-sector forces will accelerate the process of attitudinal change.

The National Advisory Committee on Mathematical Education (NACOM) recommends that the legislature and administrative bodies, parents, and teachers "recognize that mathematics is in no way a less appropriate subject for female . . . [than for] male students and that national interests as well as personal justice indicate that everything be done to open mathematical horizons and opportunities equally to both sexes."[23]

Educators, parents, friends, or future employers should emphasize the need for acquiring mathematical competence, and demand that mathematics training in public schools be made more interesting and relevant.[24] For example, teacher-education institutes and in-service training programs can help teachers compensate for their own poor math training. Several new programs are currently in progress but are not yet widely known or used.[25]

As noted earlier, girls need to know about successful women who can serve as role models in traditionally male fields. This knowledge can be gained by personal contact, or through reading material available to all students and parents. Further, women's studies courses in colleges throughout the nation have generated reading lists appropriate for high school students.[26] While fewer books are available for younger students, some do exist and several organizations distribute them.[27] In any event, use of nonsexist textbooks and learning materials should be encouraged, and negative stereotyping identified and counteracted where it does occur.

Recommendations

Further research is needed to identify circumstances and influences that successfully promote math learning and enjoyment by girls and women. Federal and private funding for women's programs remains low when compared with the size of the problem. Moreover recent National Science Foundation grants to help women-in-science programs were restricted to college and re-entry women. These efforts should be supported, but earlier intervention is essential, and if successful would largely eliminate the need for later remedial efforts.

A number of approaches should be used and their results compared. A Math and Science Education Center for Women should be established as an action and research base to increase the number of women entering scientific and technological fields. Such a center might be housed on a college or university campus, and should include an outreach program for students, teachers, parents, and legislators throughout California, as well as nationwide. Objectives would include improvement of females' mathematical skills and attitudes throughout the educational spectrum, provision of peer and role models to encourage women seeking entry into scientific and technical fields, and effective monitoring of the status and progress of women in these fields. The first center could serve as a model for future regional centers, where programs and strategies could be developed to meet special needs in different parts of the nation.

The first model center could undertake activities like these:

1. Development of action programs and support for existing activities at all educational levels;
2. Collection of materials, resources and information, including data on continuing and new programs for women entering or re-entering math and science;
3. Teacher education, providing inservice and pre-service workshops;
4. Research, linking researchers with practitioners and generating ongoing research;
5. Dissemination, sharing ideas, materials and philosophies with other researchers and educators, attracting funding for center activities, and providing a communication network for individuals, groups, local and state educational agencies concerned with the development of equal education for women; and
6. Evaluation, conducting formative and summative evaluation studies of ongoing programs.

The establishment of a model center in California, where significant groundwork has already been laid,

would enable educators, citizens, business people and legislators to coordinate efforts to insure equity in women's education. Support for these objectives has been demonstrated in conferences and workshops throughout the country. Achieving the objectives means encouraging young women's interest and competence in mathematics, thereby expanding educational and employment opportunities. To do this, the prevalent pattern of math avoidance among females must be reversed. Individual and collective attitudes that discourage women from mathematical pursuits must be changed. In a variety of ways, women's mastery of mathematics must be furthered.

This article has presented some pilot programs that work. The time is right for further concerted efforts, as the public is now realizing that

Mathematics is more than just a school subject. It is a national resource, a national concern and, at times, a national issue.[28]

The nation's interest calls for all its members to participate in a fully productive and rewarding life. For this, women must gain equal access to the resource of mathematical competence.

Notes

[1] See the following: Helen S. Astin, Nancy Suniewick, and Susan Dweck, *Women: A Bibliography on their Education and Careers* (New York: Behavioral Publications, Inc., 1974).

Nancy Frazier and Myra Sadker, *Sexism in School and Society* (New York: Harper and Row, 1973).

Gloria Golden and Lisa Hunter, *In All Fairness: A Handbook on Sex Role Bias in Schools* (San Francisco: Far West Laboratory for Educational Research and Development, 1974).

Vivian Gornick and Barbara K. Moran, eds., *Women in Sexist Society: Studies in Power and Powerlessness* (New York: Basic Books, 1971).

Elizabeth Janeway, *Man's World, Woman's Place: A Study in Social Mythology* (New York: William Morrow and Co., Inc., 1971).

Eleanor Emmons Maccoby and Carol Nagy Jacklin, *The Psychology of Sex Differences* (Stanford, CA: Stanford University Press, 1974).

U.S., Congress, Senate, Committee on Labor and Public Welfare, Subcommittee on Education, *Hearing on S. 2518,* "Sex-Role Stereotyping in the Public Schools," Terry N. Saario, Carol Nagy Jacklin, and Carol Kehr Tittle; 93d. Cong., 1st Sess. (October 17 and November 9, 1973), pp. 397-414.

Pennsylvania, Department of Education, *Sexism in Education,* Joint Task Force Report (1972).

Lenore J. Weitzman, Deborah Eifler, Elizabeth Hokada and Catherine Ross, "Sex-Role Socialization in Picture Books for Preschool Children," *American Journal of Sociology,* 77(6): 1125-1148 (May 1972).

[2] See for example, Patricia Lund Casserly, *An Assessment of Factors Affecting Female Participation in Advanced Placement Programs in Mathematics, Chemistry and Physics,* report to the National Science Foundation, Grant No. GY-11325 (July 1975). Available from the NSF, 1800 G Street N.W., Washington, D.C. 20550.

See also: Elizabeth W. Havens, *Factors Associated with the Selection of Advanced Mathematics Courses by Girls in High School* (Princeton, N.J.: Educational Testing Service, March 1972).

Barbara A. Kirk, *Factors Affecting Young Women's Direction Toward Science-Technology-Mathematics* (Berkeley: Management Technology Career Projects, September 1975).

Maita Levine, *Identification of Reasons Why Qualified Women Do Not Pursue Mathematical Careers,* report to the National Science Foundation, Grant No. GY-11411 (August 1976).

[3] Thomas L. Hilton and Gosta W. Berglund, "Sex Differences in Mathematics Achievement: A Longitudinal Study," *Journal of Educational Research,* 67(5): 231-237 (January 1974). See p. 234.

[4] Elizabeth Fennema and Julia Sherman, *Sex-Related Differences in Mathematics Learning: Myths, Realities and Related Factors,* paper presented to the American Association for the Advancement of Science (Boston: 1976), Symposium on "Women and Mathematics," p. 3.

[5] Fennema and Sherman, p. 7.

[6] Helen S. Astin, "Sex Differences in Mathematical and Scientific Precocity," in Julian C. Stanley, Daniel P. Keating, and Lynn H. Fox, eds., *Mathematical Talent: Discovery, Description, and Development,* Proceedings of the Third Annual Hyman Blumberg Symposium on Research in Early Childhood Education (Baltimore: Johns Hopkins University Press, 1974), p. 82.

[7] Kirk, p. 103, see note 2 above.

[8] Esther Matthews, *Recognizing and Nurturing Scientific Potentiality in Female Children and Adolescents,* paper presented to the Committee on the Status of Women in Physics, at the Joint Annual Meeting of the American Physical Society and the American Association of Physics Teachers, Anaheim, Calif., Jan. 29, 1975. See p. 8.

[9] John Ernest, *Mathematics and Sex* (Santa Barbara: Mathematics Department, University of California, Santa Barbara, 1976), p. 4.

[10] Casserly, pp. 30-32, see note 2 above.

[11] College Entrance Examination Board, Admissions Testing Program, *College Bound Seniors 1974-1975* (Princeton, N.J.: College Board Publications, 1975), table 4, p. 21.

[12] Lucy W. Sells, in *Developing Opportunities for Minorities in Graduate Education,* Proceedings of the Conference on Minority Graduate Education, May 11-12, 1973 at the University of California, Berkeley. See pp. 37-39.

[13] *Scientific Engineering Technical Manpower Comments,* 13(6): 7-8 (July-August 1976), a publication of the Scientific Manpower Commission, a participating organization of the American Association for the Advancement of Science.

[14] *Scientific Engineering Technical Manpower Comments,* 13(7):13 (September 1976).

[15] White women with four *or more* years of college have a median income of $7,176, while for white men with the same years of education, the median is $15,419. For Black women, the median is $8,957 compared to Black men's $10,954. The median for white women with four years of high school is $4,178, for Black women $4,412. The comparable figures for males are $11,507 (white) and $8,779 (Black). *Chronicle of Higher Education,* 12(21):6 (August 2, 1976).

16 Leonard A. Lecht, with Marc Matland and Richard Rosen, *Changes in Occupational Characteristics: Planning Ahead for the 1980's* (New York: The Conference Board, Inc., 1976), p. 2.

17 For a good introduction to the Madison Project and other math programs, see Kathleen Devaney and Lorraine Thorn, *Curriculum Development in Elementary Mathematics: 9 Programs* (San Francisco: Far West Laboratory for Educational Research and Development, August 1974).

18 Lynn H. Fox, "Women and the Career Relevance of Mathematics and Science," *School Science and Mathematics,* 76(4): 347-353 (April 1976).

19 Carolyn MacDonald, *Increasing Women in the Sciences Through an Experimental Mathematics Project*, report to the National Science Foundation, Grant No. GY-11326 (October 1975), pp. 18-19.

20 Lenore Blum, "An Action Program in Progress," speech at the January 24, 1975 meeting of the Association for Women in Mathematics, Washington, D.C. See *Association of Women in Mathematics Newsletter* (May-June 1975).

21 Single copies available from the writer at the Lawrence Hall of Science, U.C. Berkeley, CA 94720.

22 Dr. Jean Fetter, Associate Director of the Center for Teaching and Learning at Stanford University, coordinated the conference. The keynote was by Dr. Estelle Ramey, Professor of Physiology and Biophysics, Georgetown University School of Medicine, and Vice-President of the Association of Women in Science; and a panel of women professionals provided career profiles in various science fields. Fourteen small discussion groups covered topics including pre-college and college preparation in math and science, admission and attrition of women in the sciences, jobs for women in science, problems of the female pre-med and medical student, and a counselor's perspective.

23 Conference Board of the Mathematical Sciences, National Advisory Committee on Mathematical Education, *Overview and Analysis of School Mathematics Grades K-12* (Washington, D.C.: 1975), pp. 148-149. Prepared with the support of the National Science Foundation. Address of the Conference Board is 2100 Pennsylvania Avenue, N.W., Washington, D.C. 20037.

24 U.S., Department of Health, Education, and Welfare, National Institute of Education, *The NIE Conference on Basic Mathematical Skills and Learning*, Vol. 1, *Contributed Position Papers*, October 4-6, 1975, Euclid, Ohio (Washington, D.C.). See Robert B. Davis, "Basic Skills and Learning in Mathematics," pp. 42-50.

25 The Oregon Mathematics Education Council conducts a variety of programs to help "math anxious" teachers become confident and competent math educators. Write to Barry Mitzman, Oregon Mathematics Education Council, 325 13th Street N.E., Salem, Oregon 94301.

26 See Suzanne Howard, *Liberating Our Children, Ourselves: A Handbook of Women's Studies Course Material for Teacher Educators* (Washington, D.C.: American Association of University Women, 1975).

27 See Booklegger Press, 555 29th Street, San Francisco, CA 94131; Change for Children, 2588 Mission Street, Room 226, San Francisco, CA 94110; Council on Interracial Books for Children, 1841 Broadway, New York, New York 10023; Feminist Book Mart, Box 149, Whitestone, New York 11357; The Feminist Press, Box 334, Old Westbury, New York 11568; KNOW Inc., Box 86031, Pittsburgh, PA 15221; Learn Me, Inc., 642 Grand Avenue, St. Paul, Minnesota 55105; Liberty CAP, 1050 Newhall Road, Palo Alto, CA 94303; Lollipop Power, Inc., Box 1171, Chapel Hill, North Carolina 27514; National Foundation for the Improvement of Education, Resource Center on Sex Roles in Education, 1201 16th Street N.W., Washington, D.C. 20036; Schocken Books (Women's Studies), 200 Madison Avenue, New York, New York 10016; Sex-Role Stereotyping Edupak, National Education Association, Washington, D.C. 20036; Women's Action Alliance, 370 Lexington Avenue, New York, New York 10017; Women in Distribution, Box 8858, Washington, D.C. 20003; Women on Words and Images, Box 2163, Princeton, New Jersey 08540.

28 *Overview and Analysis* p. 146, see note 23 above.

Politics: Campaign Finance; Congressional Power

Vol. 17   No. 7   December 1976   Special Issue

UPDATE FROM CAPITOL HILL: POWER AND SENIORITY IN THE HOUSE OF REPRESENTATIVES*

Hon. Norman Y. Mineta
Member of Congress

Introduction

I will admit to basing my discussion on a rather short historical perspective. I was first elected to the House of Representatives just two years ago. During these past two years, I have been very much involved in the activities of the 1974 Freshman Class in Congress. Since I became a Sophomore a little less than 24 hours ago, I am not yet accustomed to this new seniority. Nevertheless, I cannot resist the temptation to look back on being a Freshman, as if these few hours have provided me with great historical perspective.

Our Freshman Class received a great deal of attention, most of it in the breathlessly urgent style of the news media. It is now time to start looking more seriously and dispassionately at the phenomenon of the class of 1974: We should try to assess what it was all about, and what it has meant, as well as what it is likely to continue to mean for the forces of change in the Congress, and for the way this nation conducts its legislative business.

As an active participant in the New Members Caucus, I obviously cannot claim strict objectivity in my analysis. Moreover, since this is November 3, the day after the election, I can hardly claim a thorough analysis of the latest data, i.e., yesterday's voting. However, I would like to outline for you the changes in Congress that I have observed, and the part that the Class of 1974 played in those changes. I hope that some of you will subsequently give more scholarly attention to these observations, and to the political data as they become available.

*This paper is based on Congressman Mineta's lecture of November 3, 1976, the first of five in the 1976-77 annual California Lectures. The series is sponsored by the Institute of Governmental Studies and is presented at Alumni House on the Berkeley Campus. It provides an opportunity for faculty members, students and the public to hear political leaders, scholars and other knowledgeable critics discuss policy issues of concern to Californians.

Shifts of Party Strength in the Congress

For many years, the national media have had one criterion for measuring change in the Congress, and that criterion has been political party strength. Media coverage of the Congressional elections has therefore focused on the net gains achieved in the Congress by one of the political parties. In some elections, such as the six shown in Table 1, there has been considerable change in party strength.

The nine *other* national elections since 1946 produced far smaller shifts in Congressional party strength. As a result, the general consensus was that Congress was not changed much by those elections. Similarly, yesterday's Congressional elections are already being consigned to that category, i.e., there was very little change in party strength. The Democrats gained only two or three seats, thus seeming to support the conclusion that the November 2, 1976 election will provide very little change in the Congress.

I believe that this is an erroneous conclusion, and that the Congress is going through several years of significant change—change which cannot be measured by party affiliation, and which has already forced, and will continue to force, Congress to alter its procedures and its structures. In fact, the tide of change continued right through the 1976 election at nearly the same strength as it had in the 1974 election, *despite* the fact that 1974 saw many party changes, whereas there were few in 1976.

Table 1

Change in Party Strength in Congress

| Year | Net Party Gain | |
	Democrats	Republicans
1946		56
1948	75	
1958	49	
1964	38	
1966		47
1974	43	

Trends in Percentages of New Members

The principal force behind these changes is the consistently greater influx of new Members into the Congress with each election: 1972, 1974, and now, in 1976. This is principally a phenomenon of the 1970's, although it had its precursor in 1964 and 1966, when a relatively large number of new Members were brought in by two consecutive elections. With those exceptions, however, the 1950's and the 1960's were a low ebb for new membership in the House of Representatives. This was particularly true of the 14 years between the 1950 and 1964 elections.

After the 1974 election, much attention was focused on the new Congressmen, who made up the largest Freshman Class since the 1948 elections. The 1974 story was really told as a sub-narrative to the Watergate story: The voters responded to Watergate revelations with reduced confidence in incumbents, particularly Republican incumbents. The large size of the 1974 first-term class was therefore billed as a one-shot occurrence, a footnote to the Watergate year.

On the contrary, 1974 was *not* an isolated event. Both the 1972 and 1976 elections also produced influxes of new Members at rates well above the averages for the previous two decades. The numerical strength of the new Members in the House of Representatives had been in decline during the first half of the 20th Century —gradual decline at first, then the decline became more dramatic. In the first quarter of this century, an average Congress had a House with about 25% new Members. In the 1940's, the figure dropped to about 20%, and in the 1950's, fell to less than 15%. There was a slight increase in the 1960's—as a result of the 1964 and 1966 elections—to just over 15% new Members. Now, with four out of five elections of the 1970's completed, the average for this decade is 16½% new Members.

While this increase in new Members is hardly major, and does not significantly reverse the trends of the 1930's through the 1950's, nevertheless, it *has stopped* an earlier dramatic trend over several decades toward *fewer* new Members in the House. Even more important, it has provided the first steps toward reversing it.

Who is Being Displaced?

Obviously, it takes more than increasing numbers of new Members to affect the pattern of seniority in the House. Both the size of the incoming class *and* the seniority of those Members being displaced are significant.

We find that the rise in new Member influx in the 70's has been paralleled by the voluntary departures of sitting Members. Voluntary departures have been steadily increasing during the 1970's, and 1976 saw a 30-year high of 47 departures. This followed 44 departures in 1974. The recent influx of new Members has largely been filling the seats of these retiring Members.

The exception to this pattern was 1974, when new Members displaced incumbents seeking re-election, as well as voluntary retirees. This is the only aspect of the 1974 election that appears to have been unusual, and

Re-election Rate for Incumbents

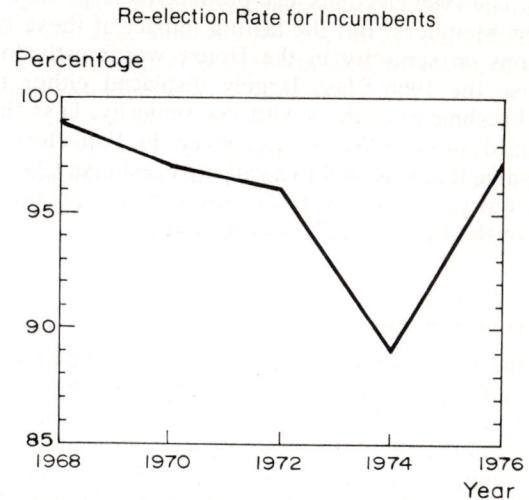

the only part of my message here tonight that can be attributed to Watergate. (See Figure 1 for re-election rates from 1968 through 1976).

One reason for the increase in voluntary departures is the growing attractiveness of retirement for Congressional Representatives. Two explanations are most commonly given:

First, the workload of a Member of Congress has increased greatly and senior Members often complain that being a Representative is just not as much fun as it used to be. Summer recesses, once guaranteed, have become the exception. In the mid-1950's, a Congress was in session an average of about 1000 hours. This past Congress nearly doubled that figure. The average number of recorded votes—on which all Members must commit themselves and be prepared to defend their votes—has increased from an average of 150 in the mid-50's to nearly 1,300 votes in the 1975-76 Congress.

Second, the job seems to hold less and less financial attraction for more and more Members. *Real* salaries have declined markedly in the past six years, due to inflation and a 1969 salary freeze. On the other hand, retirement benefits have been made more attractive. The improved trade-off has undoubtedly acted as a retirement incentive. Moreover, most Members can retire and take jobs in private industry—often as Washington lobbyists—for salaries several times those they received in Congress. These opportunities, together with ambitions for other public offices, induce Members to retire from Congress while they still have productive years before them. In fact, a disproportionate share of this year's retirees are from the middle-seniority levels, rather than from the topmost levels, suggesting a trend away from careerism in the House.

This description of *how* first-termers came to displace senior Members, helps explain *whom* they displaced. In the past, "safe" districts produced seniority, while "marginal" districts were hotly contested, and changed hands fairly often. Consequently new Members tended to displace low-seniority Members, rather than middle- or high-seniority Members. But new Members are now tending to replace the retirees, who are high- and middle-seniority Members. For example, the 1964 elecit tends to give the debate over spending proposals a different tone. It becomes less a matter of "Do we spend or not spend?" and more a matter of trade-offs: "Is there something we could get rid of that would make room for this?" As those questions arise, the less senior Members, who have no past association with the creation of existing programs, are most likely to take the attitude that there are no sacred cows among the agencies and programs, and that all should be scrutinized. This scrutiny asks:

(1) whether each program has contributed toward meeting the goals for which it was created;

(2) whether the goals have been met, or could be better met by other programs; and

(3) whether the program is still needed.

In short, it is the low-seniority Members who have no prior commitments and nothing to lose by throwing out an ineffective program and trying something else.

If one wished to phrase all this in a less friendly way, one could say that new Members are learning that it will be increasingly difficult to act on their own ideas by adding new programs to the top of the heap. They are increasingly aware that the first step in taking new legislative initiatives will hinge on clearing out some existing deadwood.

Emphasis on Legislative Oversight

These factors have made the new Members adamant advocates of a new emphasis on legislative oversight: that Congress should not just create programs, but also consistently review them to make sure they do the job for which they were created. This realization has also led to broad support for further changes in legislative spending procedures, facilitating this kind of review and scrutiny and making it a regular, mandatory function. Two Freshmen, Congressman Jim Blanchard of Michigan and myself, authored the (proposed) Government Economy and Spending Reform Act, which would automatically terminate the authorization of every federal program and agency at regular intervals—in this case, every four years—unless Congress reviews the program and then specifically votes a reauthorization. Of course the primary objectives of this bill relate to matters other than seniority:

1. The bill would restore accountability in those programs or agencies that now have open-ended authorizations, and consequently never have to seek Congressional reauthorization;

2. It would introduce zero-based budgeting as a management tool in the review of each program. However this legislation would also have the secondary effect of further eroding the prerogatives of seniority. Our bill would bring the oversight function and the power to scrutinize program performance directly to the floor of the House, where every Member can participate. A senior Committee Chairman or woman would no longer be the only effective watchdog over an agency.

Our bill has attracted broad bi-partisan support, with over 100 co-sponsors in the House, many of them new Members. In the Senate, the bill was championed by Senator Edmund Muskie, and had cleared the committee hurdles before Congress adjourned. This legislative effort will definitely be continued next year.

Issues and Generations

I turn now to a related aspect of seniority that is often observed but difficult to quantify. The differences between senior and junior Members are often not due to seniority *per se*, but rather reflect the differences in the issues that were important *when a Member was first elected*. The interests of new Members tend to reflect new or emerging issues, while veterans echo the issues and styles of problem-solving that prevailed when they first came to Congress. In Presidential politics, it has been fashionable of late to talk of rebuilding the New Deal coalition. But Congress is only now coming out of the New Deal. Let me illustrate the influence of the past. When I began my service in the House last year, there were 12 Congressmen who had begun their service under Franklin Roosevelt. There was one Member who had entered the House under Herbert Hoover, and had served 46 consecutive years as a Congressman! These 13 Congressmen were not just *any* 13 Members. They were among the most powerful figures in the House.

A decade ago, commentary on American life began to use the phrase, "generation gap." This term could be applied to the pronounced change in the public issues recognized by our society. Thus we had one "issue-generation" from the New Deal through the Great Society. It was characterized by such issues as: the creation of alphabet agencies to solve virtually any and all domestic problems; the acceptance of government responsibility for economic growth and security; and the pursuit of hot and cold wars. Since then, we have had a very distinct new generation of issues: disillusionment with the Vietnam War; distrust of government resulting from Vietnam, Watergate, and the intelligence agency abuses; and emerging environmental issues and questions about the adverse effects of growth.

Tilt to the New Generation

The generation gap just mentioned is only now reaching its peak in the Congress. That is, only now are the number of post-Great Society Members equal that of the more senior Members. In 1975, at the beginning of the 94th Congress, 41% of the Members had won their first Congressional election during the 1970's. At the beginning of the forthcoming Congress, these "new generation" Members will for the first time constitute a majority. The 94th and 95th Congresses are thus the tilting point where numerical power in the House shifts from one generation to the next.

Consequently the urge to scrutinize past policies and programs will increase in the 95th Congress. Moreover the senior Committee Chairmen and women will find the gap between themselves and the majority of House Members widening still further.

The generation gap has also created an ambivalent relationship between the junior Members and the House leadership. On one hand, the least senior Members and the leadership are natural allies: the leadership has a long history of being selected by the membership and of being their agent. The Chairmen and women have only recently been made elective, and therefore accountable to the Caucus; and in fact, that accountability has rarely and only recently been exercised. The redistribution of power away from Committee Chairs and seniority—often forced by newer Members—has enhanced the power of House leaders, as well as the power of the Caucus. That continuing trend, combined with the personality of Tip O'Neill, will give us a strong Speakership in the next Congress. On the other hand, Members of Congress who fill the leadership posts will be on the "older" side of the generation gap, accustomed to the thinking and the allegiance of their peer groups in Congress.

Changes at the Top

In particular, it remains to be seen whether leadership policies are to be determined by *when* the Member came to Congress, or *when and by whom* he or she was elevated to a position of leadership. In 1972 and 1974, great numbers of new people were introduced into the lower seniority ranks of the House. Now, in 1976, we have that trend continuing; but suddenly, we also have this century's most dramatic changes at the top of the power structure. Three of the four top leaders in the House and Senate are retiring. With the retirement of Carl Albert, and with O'Neill's rise to the Speakership, a chain reaction of new elections for other leadership posts has ensued.

As a result, next month (December, 1976) virtually all of the leaders of the House will owe their authority to the vote of the Majority Membership of the 95th Congress—a majority of whom will be junior Members. Even the Committee Chairmanships are being extensively reshuffled. Just under half of the Chairmen in the House either were replaced by the Caucus in 1974; or were replaced during the 94th Congress; or departed at the end of the 94th Congress. Throughout the House power structure, there should be a new sense of accountability to less senior Members. There should also be a more equitable distribution of power than at

any time during the last two decades.

Conclusion

We will all know soon enough whether all this will come about as smoothly as I seem to have suggested here. The Majority Caucus meets in one month. In any event I hope my remarks will renew your interest in the questions of power and seniority in the House. I also hope your interest will lead to new investigations on the subject, that are more thoroughly documented and more scholarly than my own. I would certainly appreciate having the benefit of your observations and findings.

A major question remains: Will these trends—higher retirement rates, larger first-term classes, and lower seniority among Members—be continued in 1978 and beyond? In short, were the last three elections a short-term reversal of the 20th Century trend toward higher seniority in the House, or are they part of a counter-trend and a new reality that will be with us for a long time?

Regardless of future events, however, the recent past has already provided enough of a shift toward new membership, and away from seniority and careerism, to halt the trend of the first six decades of this century, and partially reverse it. Seniority became increasingly entrenched during those six decades, and it has subsequently been forced to recede.

I am not now trying to demonstrate that these changes will necessarily produce either a better Congress or better legislation. That would be a different statement, for a different audience. The point is that Congress has changed significantly. Regardless of whether future elections bolster these changes, the House of Representatives is already a *different* body:

1. in the numerical strength of new Members,
2. in length of service,
3. in seniority, and
4. in the prevailing "generational" philosophy.

These fundamental changes in the composition of Congress have, in turn, forced fundamental changes in the Congressional power structure and in the process by which legislative decisions are made.

Author Index

Anderson, Stanley V.
Developing the Ombudsman's Role
In Health Care Services, 72–76

Ardell, Donald B. and Richard P.
Hafner, Jr.
Comprehensive Health Planning in
the San Francisco Bay Area: Problems and Prospects for the "Federation Experiment," 38–43

Bain, Beatrice
Women and Academia at Berkeley:
CCEW–Women's Center, 32–37

Bradshaw, Ted K.
New Issues for California, the
World's Most Advanced Industrial
Society, 136–141

Bruvold, William H.
Using Reclaimed Water: Public
Attitudes and Governmental Poli-
cy, 130–135

Cahalan, Don
Drinking Practices and Problems:
Research Perspectives on Remedial
Measures, 6–11

Childs, Alfred W., and Margaret
Greenfield
See Greenfield and Childs

Chow, Willard T.
Reviving the Inner City: The Lessons of Oakland's Chinatown, 96–
102

Fay, James
Changing Regulations: Campaign
Finance in the Golden State, 44–
52

Fay, James and Thomas
Leatherwood
Public Funding of Political Cam-
paigns: Attitudes and Issues in
California, 77–83

Glenny, Lyman A.
Comprehensive Planning for Higher
Education: Focus on New Priori-
ties, 1–5

Greenfield, Margaret and Alfred W.
Childs, M.D.
Prepaid Health Plans: California's
Experiment in Changing the Medi-
cal Care System, 122–129

Guthrie, James W.
Public Control of Public Schools:
Can We Get It Back? 53–57

Hafner, Richard P., Jr. and Donald B.
Ardell
See Ardell and Hafner

Higgins, Tom
Juvenile Delinquency: Seeking Effective Prevention, 109–114

Kreinberg, Nancy
Furthering the Mathematical Competence of Women, 147–153

162

Leatherwood, Thomas and James Fay
   See Fay and Leatherwood

Lee, K. N.
   The Utility of Public Utilities: Desalination and Local Government
   in Coastal California, 18—24

Merewitz, Leonard and Stephen H.
Sosnick
   Public Expenditure Analysis: Some
   Current Issues, 25—31

Mineta, Hon. Norman Y.
   Update from Capitol Hill: Power
   and Seniority in the House of Representatives, 154—159

Nathan, Harriet and Stanley Scott
   Fluoridation in California: A New
   Look at a Persistent Issue, 63—71

Scott, Stanley
   Learning to Live with Earthquakes:
   Research and Policy for Seismic
   Safety in California, 142—146

Scott, Stanley and Harriet Nathan
   See Nathan and Scott

Seiden, Richard H.
   Suicide: Preventable Death, 58—
   62

Sherman, Patricia A.
   Corrections: A Critical Analysis Of
   The Prison System in California,
   84—89

Sosnick, Stephen H. and Leonard
Merewitz
   See Merewitz and Sosnick

Starkweather, David B.
   Hospitals: From Physician Dominance to Public Control, 103—
   108

Wilkerson, Margaret B.
   Information, Research and Coun-
   seling: The Women's Center at
   Berkeley, 90—95

Wilms, Wellford W.
   A Prescription for Student Aid:
   Better Information on Post-Secon-
   dary Education, 115—121

Zwerling, Stephen
   The Politics of Technological
   Choice: Some Lessons from the
   San Francisco Bay Area Rapid
   Transit District (BART), 12—17

Subject Index

EDUCATIONAL PLANNING AND POLICY

Comprehensive Planning for Higher Education: Focus on New Priorities, 1–5
Public Control of Public Schools: Can We Get It Back? 53–57
A Prescription for Student Aid: Better Information on Post-Secondary Education, 115–121

HEALTH AND HOSPITALS: PLANNING, GOVERNANCE AND FINANCE

Comprehensive Health Planning in the San Francisco Bay Area: Problems and Prospects for the "Federation Experiment," 38–43
Developing the Ombudsman's Role In Health Care Services, 72–76
Hospitals: From Physician Dominance to Public Control, 103–108
Prepaid Health Plans: California's Experiment in Changing the Medical Care System, 122–129

POLITICS: CAMPAIGN FINANCE; CONGRESSIONAL POWER

Changing Regulations: Campaign Finance in the Golden State, 44–52
Public Funding of Political Campaigns: Attitudes and Issues in California, 77–83
Update From Capitol Hill: Power and Seniority in the House of Representatives, 154–159

PUBLIC FINANCE

Public Expenditure Analysis: Some Current Issues, 25–31

SCIENCE, TECHNOLOGY AND POLICY

The Politics of Technological Choice: Some Lessons from the San Francisco Bay Area Rapid Transit District (BART), 12–17
The Utility of Public Utilities: Desalination and Local Government in Coastal California, 18–24

163

Fluoridation in California: A New Look at a Persistent Issue, 63–71
Using Reclaimed Water: Public Attitudes and Governmental Policy, 130–135
New Issues for California, the World's Most Advanced Industrial Society, 136–141
Learning to Live with Earthquakes: Research and Policy for Seismic Safety in California, 142–146

SOCIAL PROBLEMS AND REMEDIAL POLICIES

Drinking Practices and Problems: Research Perspectives on Remedial Measures, 6–11
Suicide: Preventable Death, 58–62
Corrections: A Critical Analysis Of The Prison System in California, 84–89
Juvenile Delinquency: Seeking Effective Prevention, 109–114

URBAN COMMUNITIES

Reviving the Inner City: The Lessons of Oakland's Chinatown, 96–102

WOMEN'S OPPORTUNITIES IN EDUCATION

Women and Academia at Berkeley: CCEW–Women's Center, 32–37
Information, Research and Counseling: The Women's Center at Berkeley, 90–95
Furthering the Mathematical Competence of Women, 147–153

INSTITUTE OF GOVERNMENTAL STUDIES

RECENT PUBLICATIONS

(to May 1977)

Monographs and Bibliographies

1977

Costonis, John J., Curtis J. Berger and Stanley Scott
Regulation v. Compensation in Land Use Control: A Recommended Accommodation, a Critique, and an Interpretation. 91pp $3.50
Waldo, Dwight
Democracy, Bureaucracy and Hypocrisy. 23pp $2.50

1976

Jonsen, Albert R. and Michael J. Garland, eds.
Ethics of Newborn Intensive Care. 193pp $4.00
Pers, Jessica S.
Government as Parent: Administering Foster Care in California. 124pp $5.50
Wengert, Norman
The Political Allocation of Benefits and Burdens: Economic Externalities and Due Process in Environmental Protection. 43pp $2.50

1975

Field Research Corporation
Public Opinion of Criminal Justice in California: A Survey Conducted by Field Research Corporation. 156pp $7.00
Scott, Stanley
Governing California's Coast. 454pp $9.75
Pressman, Hope Hughes
A New Resource for Welfare Reform: The Poor Themselves. 122pp $4.50
Lee, Eugene C. and Bruce E. Keith
1974 Supplement, California Votes, 1960-1972: A Review and Analysis of Registration and Voting. 4pp $1.50

1974

Lee, Eugene C. and Bruce E. Keith
   California Votes, 1960-1972: A Review and Analysis of Registration and Voting.   172pp $7.50
Gwyn, William B.
   Barriers to Establishing Urban Ombudsmen: The Case of Newark.   93pp $4.50
Tompkins, Dorothy C.
   Furlough From Prison. Public Policy Bibliographies: 5.   61pp $5.00
Tompkins, Dorothy C.
   Selection of the Vice President. Public Policy Bibliographies: 6.   26pp $3.75
Wyner, Alan J.
   The Nebraska Ombudsman: Innovation in State Government.   160pp $6.75

1973

Fitzharris, Timothy L.
   The Desirability of a Correctional Ombudsman.   114pp $3.00
Hidén, Mikael
   The Ombudsman in Finland: The First Fifty Years.   198pp $8.00
Niskanen, William A., George F. Break, Charles S. Benson (with Paul M. Goldfinger, E. Gareth Hoach-lander and Jessica S. Pers) and Arnold J. Meltsner
   Tax and Expenditure Limitation by Constitutional Amendment: Four Perspectives on the California Initiative.   70pp $2.50
Telfer, Judie
   Training Minority Journalists: A Case Study of the San Francisco Examiner Intern Program.   124pp $4.00
Tompkins, Dorothy C.
   Strip Mining for Coal. Public Policy Bibliographies: 4.   86pp $5.00
Tompkins, Dorothy C.
   Court Organization and Administration—A Bibliography.   200pp $8.00
Weeks, Kent M.
   Ombudsmen Around the World: A Comparative Chart.   101pp $3.00
Wyner, Alan J., ed.
   Executive Ombudsmen in the United States.   315pp $5.50

Monographs and Bibliographies are available from the Institute of Governmental Studies, 109 Moses Hall, University of California, Berkeley, California 94720. Checks should be made payable to the Regents of the University of California. Prepay all orders under $10.00. California residents add 6% sales tax; residents of Alameda, Contra Costa and San Francisco counties add 6½% sales tax.